SEX ROLES AND PERSONAL AWARENESS

Barbara Lusk Forisha
University of Michigan, Dearborn

Sex Roles and Personal Awareness

GENERAL LEARNING PRESS
SCOTT, FORESMAN AND COMPANY

Manufactured in the United States of America

Published simultaneously in Canada

Library of Congress Catalog Card Number 77-93120

ISBN 0-382-18030-5

For information write to: General Learning Press, 250 James St., Morristown, N.J. 07960

Since this page cannot accommodate all of the credits, the following page constitutes an extension of the copyright page.

To Bill

Credits

PREFACE

Taking a quick glance through history, we note that sex roles have been with us all along. The cave man braved the elements to bring home the bacon while his wife waited at home to cook it. Our New World explorers traveled thousands of miles in search of spices while their wives spiced up dinner. Colonial men killed and dressed game while their wives dressed the children. It is only recently, though, that we have begun to examine such roles.

Sex Roles and Personal Awareness examines the impact that sex roles have on our lives and explores alternative patterns of development. If this book causes the reader to question his or her attitudes, behavior, or beliefs concerning sex roles, we may be taking a step in the right direction. We may indeed move a little bit closer to a society where both men and women will be free to bring home the bacon and to cook it.

This book is intended to be used as the main text in a variety of courses, including Psychology of Sex Roles, Sociology of Sex Roles, Psychology of Women, and Sociology of Women. It may also be used as a supplementary text in such courses as Personal Adjustment, Marriage and Family, or Social Psychology. In addition, because the subject of sex roles is becoming increasingly popular, this book may prove attractive to the general public.

The text is divided into four parts. Part I studies the differences between men and women (Chapter 1) and examines the origin of sex roles (Chapter 2). Part II examines the visionary possibility of men and women assuming traits of both sexes (Chapter 3) and shows the impact that this may have on love and marriage (Chapter 4). Part III studies sex roles as they presently exist. We see how most men and women are molded into sex roles (Chapter 5) and follow the scripts for these roles throughout their lives (Chapter 6). Then we examine love and marriage as they exist within traditional roles (Chapter 7), and we study the impact that social class and ethnic group have on love and marriage (Chapter 8). This part concludes with a look at the barriers to becoming fully human that are present in our current world of work (Chapter 9). We then step into parenthood (Part IV) and show how children are socialized into roles (Chapter 10). We also note the influence that parents have on these roles (Chapter 11). The book then concludes with a look at the future—whether we can move beyond our sex roles and become fully human (Epilogue).

Many helpful features will assist students in studying the topic of sex roles. This book covers both the male and female points of view, so that students will not get a one-sided picture. Rather, they will see both the benefits and disadvantages of each role. Illustrative case studies taken from journals my classes kept over a three-year period will enable students to see portraits of themselves through others. They will be able to relate to the experiences of others since these experiences may be similar to their own. An exercise at the end of each chapter will assist students in applying what they have learned in the chapter to their unique, individual situations. Other helpful tools include a list of references at the end of each chapter, and a glossary and name and subject indexes at the end of the book.

The individuals who helped to shape the ideas contained in this book are too numerous to mention. My first thought is of the students in my initial class in Sex Roles whose openness, thoughtfulness, and clear-sightedness caused me to reevaluate my own position vis-à-vis sex roles. As they examined their own behavior in terms of masculinity and femininity, they challenged me to reexamine my own. In working through their processes of change, I was led into my own. The dialogue begun in that class has continued over the semesters with succeeding classes of students. Their story has contributed greatly to this book.

Secondly, I would like to thank another group of individuals, primarily students, who gave of their time to work on the book itself: those students who helped in collecting research material and those who read and reviewed the emerging manuscript. In particular I thank Jeff Pilkington, Sandy Stevens, Joe Otrhalek, and Debbie Bush. Most especially, however, I thank Toni Cyll for her precision in checking reference materials and her skill in editing—in the process of which innumerable commas were added to the text and many ambiguities clarified. In addition, I am indebted to the skill of Chris O'Brien, who typed the first draft, and Carol Crawford, who sped her way through at least three drafts, always meeting every deadline.

Third, the editorial help given by General Learning Press has been continuous and invaluable. My thanks to Walter Kossmann and Judy Green for their support of this endeavor; to Bob Cunningham for his careful and sensitive editing; and most especially to Janice Lemmo, who has spent unending hours in careful perusal of the book, who questioned ambiguities, who challenged inconsistencies, and who shepherded this work through the publishing process from unedited manuscript to a completed book. Janice has, as one of my students would say, a low tolerance for "normal human errors," a quality to be prized in an editor.

Fourth, the academic reviewers who read the manuscript provided both support and constructive criticism throughout the process of writing and revising. I very much appreciate the assistance of Leonard Benson, North Texas State University, whose critiques were accompanied by humor; Helen M. Hacker, Adelphi University, whose review raised many important issues; Barbara Matthews, Palm Beach Junior College, whose comments were very helpful; Lenore Seltzer, San José State University, whose penchant for detail aided me significantly; and Jacqueline P. Wiseman, University of California, San Diego, whose helpful criticisms were always balanced by appreciated support.

Finally, I wish to thank my family: my children Debbie and Mark for their tolerance of my preoccupation with the typewriter during long periods of time when they might have wished otherwise; and my husband Bill for never allowing me to avoid, in our academic or personal lives, the issues that I have raised in this book. Consequently, this book has been part of an evolving process of growth in my life, a process that continues beyond the completion of this book.

Barbara Lusk Forisha
University of Michigan, Dearborn

CONTENTS

f.11- 1, 2, 5&6
7, 9, part of 10 & 11
(or all?)

III ANDROGYNY AND SEX ROLES: THE REALITY 140

xiv

SEX ROLES AND PERSONAL AWARENESS

Introduction

A child is born. With all the strength it can muster, it tenses its vocal cords and makes its presence known to the world. We recognize the infant as a small, vulnerable, dependent, and very rudimentary human being. Yet we also recognize, and perhaps dream of, the untold potential inherent in a new life. Will this infant shake our world views with intellectual theories or scientific inventions? Will the adult-to-be command fleets of ships, rule nations, and write international agreements? Will this small person excel in sports, write a prize-winning play, or devise a musical production? Or will this infant grow up to clean, cook, and sew for those who aspire to such heights? Will this infant find its identity in the shadow of those who explore their potential in the outer world or will this infant be one of the explorers?

Many of us assume that the answer rests in part on the anatomical sex of the child. If the child is a boy, *he* may indeed

We are perceivers. The world that we perceive, though, is an illusion. It was created by a description that was told to us since the moment we were born . . .

Carlos Castaneda, *Tales of Power*

. . . dogs are bound by biology, but humans can soar on the wings of conventionalized misrepresentation.

Jules Henry, *Culture Against Man*

We live in a web of ideas, a fabric of our own making . . .

Susanne Langer, "The Growing Center of Knowledge," in *Philosophical Sketches*

---

someday be President of the United States. If the child is a girl, however, *she* may wait on him, tending to his social and interpersonal needs. It is true, of course, that most of us, whether male or female, never run governments nor lead scientific revolutions. But it is also true that there is power in having a dream of far-flung possibilities. Such a dream opens doors and broadens horizons. The child that is born male enters a world of broad horizons; theoretically he is faced with a number of possibilities in life, possibilities available to him because he is male. But what dreams do we have for the child that is born female? What doors are open to her? With the announcement that the infant is a girl, almost all of the doors slowly close. Yet a few doors are also closed to boys. For boys, a closed door conceals the nurturant, sensitive, vulnerable side of their personalities.

The previous paragraphs illustrate the impact on our lives of familiar assumptions about masculinity and femininity. We assume that boys will achieve and that girls will nurture others. We also assume that boys will be assertive and that girls will be receptive. Such assumptions about masculinity and femininity are part of a larger set of expectations about how men and women ought to behave. This set of expectations is called *sex roles*. We expect men and women to play roles that are appropriate to their sex. Often, too, we assume that they should take on these roles because it is in accord with the nature of the universe or a divine plan. In other words, our assumptions about boys and girls are part of our larger belief systems. Boys must not cry, because that is not masculine . . . boys must be masculine and girls must be feminine . . . that is the way it has always been . . . that is a universal truth and the way Nature or God intended for it to be.

In the preceding sentence we have outlined the train of thought that usually supports the assumption that it is bad or wrong for boys to cry. Such a train of thought is often not clarified or verbalized but remains hidden in a web of unconscious assumptions about the nature of men and women and the nature of the universe. We assume that it is true and rarely question it. As the statements that open this chapter suggest, however, many thinkers challenge this easy acceptance of "truth." They point out that much of our world is an illusion, that we misrepresent the world to ourselves and indeed live in "a fabric of our own making." If our perceptions and assumptions are not equivalent to "truth," then piece by piece we can examine each of them. And in doing this, we might very well conclude that there is no reason why boys can't cry and girls can't dream of great adventure. Have we misled ourselves for so many hundreds of years?

Yes, this appears to be the case. We have taken for granted the historical forms of masculinity and femininity, and we have shaped the inner potential of men and women to fit these preconceived *forms*. In so doing we have possibly restricted and suppressed the potential inherent in the *process* of their own experience. For example, the feelings of a young girl who out of her *own experience* finds sports central in her life, or the inclinations of a young boy who prefers ballet to hockey sticks and footballs, are in accord with their experience of their own inner *processes*. But the aspirations stemming from these processes—to be a sports star or a ballet dancer— are not totally acceptable within the traditional forms of masculinity and femininity. In the past, many boys and girls, men and women, have yielded their inner dreams to adapt to the outer forms, assuming that this is the way it must be.

However, we no longer have to forfeit our inner dreams. We can go beyond the traditional forms of masculinity and femininity to become total human beings. In other words, the female athlete and male dancer are indeed possibilities.

WHY WE STUDY SEX ROLES

This leads us to our reasons for studying sex roles. By studying the impact on our lives of masculine and feminine forms, we can learn more about ourselves. We can learn about how we have come to be where we are and consequently what the future holds in store for us. But our knowledge can extend even further. With our knowledge we can exercise some control over our lives; hence we can direct our future. Thus, it is not only knowing what our future holds in store for us that is important, but how we can get the most out of it.

In addition, the topic of sex roles is particularly important because of our position in time. We are at a time of great cultural change, perhaps of the greatest cultural change in the last several hundred years (see Leonard, 1972). We have come to the end of the industrial age, we have in certain areas reached the limits of our technological resources, and we are moving into a postindustrial era (Rapoport & Rapoport, 1972). Many of the forms and structures that were suited to the last century may no longer suffice for the coming century. Young people and minorities have already questioned many of these structures; in particular, the Women's Movement has been instrumental in causing the forms of masculinity and femininity to be reevaluated. Today, moreover, more and more people are joining in the challenge to traditional structures. Hopefully such challenges and evaluation will lead to a new synthesis in which the best of the traditional is merged with the most promising of the new. It is possible that in the future we will all be able to enjoy the best of both masculine and feminine worlds.

SOME BASIC ASSUMPTIONS

Before we begin our exploration of sex roles, it is important to be aware of certain preconceptions about the nature of human beings on which this book is based. As with many issues in the social sciences, ideas concerning the nature of humanity and the topic of sex roles are subject to much controversy. Opinions and interpretations vary depending on who is examining the theories and the data and drawing the conclusions. But for any study we must have some basic assumptions. The assumptions for this study are based on the humanistic school of thought.* They are as follows:

1. Human beings have the choice of creating their own alternatives; in other words people have some measure of freedom and are not wholly determined by external or internal forces. In addition, people are responsible for the ways in which they choose to utilize this freedom. Furthermore, we increase our freedom by increasing our awareness. As we become more aware of *how* we have come to be where we are, we enlarge our capacity to change where we are. Increasing awareness leads to increasing options. With more options we have greater choice and hence greater freedom.

2. Human beings do not necessarily benefit by adjusting themselves to society as it now stands. They will be truer to themselves and thus to others if they listen to their inner promptings and seek out a path that best suits their own individuality. Such an enhancement of individual potential will ultimately benefit society at large.

3. Human beings who have developed their potential to a high degree are worthy of study as examples to the rest of us. Most of the research in the social sciences is aimed at determining what is normal human behavior. Through the use of statistics, social scientists arrive at a standard, or norm, by which other patterns of behavior are measured. Although this type of study tells us a great deal about how most people actually behave and thus is very valuable, it tells us little about how people *can* behave. If we want to explore the full heights of human growth, we must look not only at what is normal but also at what is exceptional. The exceptional tells us that we all can use our potential more fully.

*The humanists include psychologists like Carl Rogers and Abraham Maslow. They believe that although we are motivated by our inner impulses and shaped by our outer environment, we are essentially free to choose our own direction. Moreover, that direction, if well chosen, will not lead us into conflict with others nor will it bring us rewards only at the expense of others. Rather, the humanists argue that humans who choose well benefit both themselves and society.

Since each of us has our own world view, not everyone will agree with these assumptions. Individuals will come to their own evaluation of the topic of sex roles, the forms of masculinity and femininity, and the nature of being human. With the assumptions of this book in mind, however, we can now proceed to the study at hand: sex roles and their impact on our lives.

REFERENCES

Leonard, G., *The Transformation*, New York: Delacorte Press, 1972.

Rapoport, R., and Rapoport, R., "The Dual-Career Family: A Variant Pattern and Social Change," in C. Safilios-Rothschild, ed., *Toward a Sociology of Women,* Greenwich, Conn.: Xerox College Publishing, 1972.

1

CULTURE AND BIOLOGY: WHY ARE MEN MASCULINE AND WOMEN FEMININE?

He is playing masculine. She is playing feminine.

He is playing masculine because she is playing feminine. She is playing feminine because he is playing masculine.

He is playing the kind of man that she thinks the kind of woman she is playing ought to admire. She is playing the kind of woman that he thinks the kind of man he is playing ought to desire. . . .

So he plays harder. And she plays . . . softer. . . .

How do we call off the game?

Betty and Theodore Roszak, **Masculine/Feminine**

1

Masculine and Feminine: Are Men and Women Really Different?

Many of us believe that we are freely choosing the direction our lives will take. Although it is my contention that we are indeed free, many of us forfeit this freedom and accept instead the illusion of choice. In many areas of our lives we may believe still that we **have** made a choice: We "choose" to be strong and independent, to solve our own problems, and to work most of the days of our lives. We may also "choose" to be understanding, considerate, receptive, and to spend most of our lives helping and pleasing others. Most of these behaviors, however, as well as many others, have been shaped and molded by what our society today thinks is "masculine" and what it thinks is "feminine." Such societal expectations are called *sex roles*.

The major theme of this book suggests that some of the ways in which we conform to sex-role expectations obstruct our development as full human beings. If we recognize that we have not indeed

When man is intimately related to life, he neither ties himself to restricted goals that he must pursue; nor is he confined by directions and instructions and rules, or restrained by patterned or conditioned responses and techniques. He is free; he is open; he is direct; he encounters life with all of his resources; and he lives in accordance with the unique requirements of each situation as it unfolds before him.

Clark Moustakas, **Creativity and Conformity**

"chosen" many of our behaviors, attitudes, and emotions but rather are playing out a script with either a masculine or a feminine role already written out for us, *then* we have the opportunity to search further within ourselves, to uncover our own unique desires and talents, and to make choices that are more creatively appropriate for our own individual development.

THREE CASE HISTORIES

Three case histories in this chapter illustrate the process of discovering which of our behaviors are determined by sex-role expectations. Once individuals discover this, they can then evaluate these behaviors in the light of their own awareness of themselves as unique individuals operating in a particular environment. The humanist school of thought holds that knowledge of our identity comes *ultimately* from within, not from without. To truly discover this identity, we must first shed the expectations of others, including the expectations called sex roles. Let us examine how the behaviors of Marlene, Edward, and Annette were influenced by sex-role expectations.

MARLENE

Marlene was the third and last daughter in a lower-middle-class family. She was regarded as the "most intelligent, gifted daughter." She excelled in her studies, the arts, and sports. Her parents were very proud of her and expected her to *do better* than her female friends in whatever she did.

Although urged to become independent, she was protected, in fact, by her parents and seldom allowed away from the supervision of her mother or another adult. Usually she thought of herself as independent and believed she made her own decisions, but in fact she generally did as her parents expected. Because her wishes as a rule coincided with those of her parents, she remembers little need for them to punish or restrict her as a child.

Competition with others was a major factor in her life. Her mother constantly pointed out how so-and-so was doing and wasn't it nice that Marlene had done better or wasn't it too bad that she had done worse. In junior high she recalls crying a lot because she was nervous and frightened that she would not match up to the efforts of her best friend, Lynda.

Marlene learned to win her parents' approval by meeting their expectations. In addition, she states:

> *I was also taught some absolutes. Generally they were in the form of: Nice girls do not ——— . And you can fill in the blank with a number of words such as drink, smoke, take drugs, swear, win when competing with boys, etc. The former four made sense to me and do now; the latter never has. One could also rephrase this negative sentence in a positive manner, retaining its negative connotation, by stating: Nice girls do ———. This could also be filled in with such things as remain virgins until they are married, watch out for other girls who might take your boyfriend away, etc. Needless to say, I have a*

very strong concept of what nice girls are and have generally been thought of and treated as one. A lot of this I appreciate but deep down I have conflicts and question such absolutes. No one is that "nice"!

In high school Marlene's interests began to revolve around boys. Although she was still competitive, she realized that it was important not to do better than a male. Moreover, it was important to be going out on dates, no matter who the boy was.

One went out with an image! Somewhere along the line it was probably nice if you liked the guy. I dated just to date. From my senior year in high school to the middle of my senior year in college I was always dating someone.

The logical extension of this preoccupation with boys, men, and dates was the assumption that her meaning of life would be found in marriage. Marlene was strongly aware of this expectation but has held it in the back of her mind until recently, since it was strongly in conflict with her own need for achievement. This is a common dilemma for capable young women: They are urged to excel as young adults, though not to outdo men; then they are supposed to give up this aspect of their lives in order to turn their talents to interpersonal relations. Marlene summed up this dilemma in the following poem, which suggests the frustrations of the sex role prescribed for young women:

I was taught to be competitive,
    Yet I must never win.
I was taught to go to college and to be intelligent,
    Yet what would I do with it? Marry?
I was taught to be aggressive and achieve,
    Yet I must be submissive.
I was taught to be independent,
    Yet I was dependent on everyone and his *brother!*
I was taught to make my own decisions,
    Yet I never knew what I wanted or what to do.
I was taught that nice girls do not drink or smoke or
    swear or . . . the latter generally not discussed.
I was taught to be feminine
    And I do not know who I am.

Before commenting on Marlene's development we should consider the parallel case of a young man who was brought up to accept a similarly rigid role in life—the one prescribed for males.

EDWARD

Edward was the only boy and the middle child in a family of three children. His father was a construction worker, and his mother stayed home to raise the children. Edward learned to read at an early age and was fascinated by books. His parents, particularly his father, however, were concerned that Edward was too quiet and seemed at first not to have any inclination toward sports. Consequently, they continually urged him to become more active and to explore his world. When he did so, Edward recalls today, he had to get used to the many cuts and lacerations he received. But his parents accepted them calmly since they were pleased that at last he was becoming a "real boy."

Edward's entrance into the school world left mostly remembrances of a terrifying nun whom he recalls as "a Marine sergeant in a penguin suit." Daily encounters with this symbol of the school system reduced him to tears.

My father was furious! His son was a crybaby. Lecture after lecture on being a man was drilled into my head but it did no good. I was terrified and all my father could think of was to call me a sissy.

Soon, however, Edward turned to sports and began to excel. By the fourth grade he had become a "sports freak" who played baseball on two little-league teams each summer and basketball all winter.

I found I liked to play and I was good at it. You should have seen my father eat it up. At last he had that son to play catch with! I don't think anything was so strongly reinforced as my enthusiasm for sports. My coaches and my father worshipped victory. To win was the only acceptable outcome of competition. To lose was to be damned, to be weak, to be less of a man. My grade-school football coach was the biggest blowhard of this crap I have ever met; his quest for victory was an obsession and his fear of defeat was neurotic. He kicked and ranted, he raved and all but killed us, but we won. Thank God!

The competitive ethic learned in sports was carried into the academic and the social spheres in high school. We were taught to thrive on competition and achievement. Failure was not to be tolerated. I was taught the school's conception of what it is to be a man. I was to be intelligent and extremely logical in all circumstances, I was to be a leader who helped

*those less fortunate. I was to be strong and support the weak. I
was to strive continually for mental, physical, and spiritual
greatness. In short, I was to be godlike.*

*A man also was supposed to be a great lover and to have
good-looking girlfriends. He was also supposed to be able to
kick the shit out of anyone who crossed him. Great respect was
given to the victor of a fight.*

*A lot of emphasis was placed on the future acquisition of
status symbols such as Eldorados, mansions, and of course a
harem of the world's most desirable women.*

In addition to such messages from his school and peer group,
Edward was strongly encouraged to be self-reliant. For example, by
age 15, he was required by his father to pay his school tuition and
other expenses. His father felt "a man should be self-supporting,
independent, strong, and self-confident."

Edward is currently reevaluating much of this training:

*I was sucked into this achievement vacuum of my own volition.
I could feel its pull, which received extensive positive reinforcement from my family, my girlfriend, her parents, and my
peer group. I am now slowly fighting the suction power of this
vacuum and beginning to surface with a clearer, more autonomous outlook on life. . . . Right now I feel light, almost high, as
if weight has been taken off my mind and body. I don't feel
pressured anymore to be "masculine," to be a Rock of Gibraltar, a pillar of strength, aggressive, logical, analytic, argumentative, competitive. . . . I feel like a baby discovering himself for
the first time.*

IMPLICATIONS

Currently both Marlene and Edward are becoming aware of
the possibilities of greater choice outside the traditional expectations of masculinity and femininity. For Marlene, as for most young
women, this means coming to grips with the fact that she does not
know who she is, that she has incorporated into her own self-image
the expectations of her parents and gladly met these expectations.
She has not been encouraged to explore, to test her own limitations,
to make her own decisions. Yet she has been encouraged to excel as
long as this did not risk making her seem less desirable to potential

husbands. Now at 22 she is realizing a conflict between the goal of achieving success on her own and the underlying, more subtle, but more forceful expectation that her satisfaction in life will be found in marriage. In other words, her identity would not be achieved on her own but would be derived from her future husband. She is struggling to find out what she really wants and who she is.

Edward, on the other hand, was encouraged to achieve, and to be independent and self-reliant from babyhood. He was to be best in school, in sports, and in competition for attractive women. The message was clear and unidirectional: Be strong, be self-supporting, achieve, never fail. In large part he accepted this mandate and met its expectations. Nonetheless the burden of such demands is reflected in Edward's final evaluation of himself: The ethic stressing achievement at all costs by which his life was guided was not his own but one shaped for him by others. Now at last he, too, is beginning to determine his own needs and to discover who he is.

These two case histories illustrate the awakening many young people are experiencing today as they reevaluate their past, examine their present, and reconsider their future goals. Both Marlene and Edward accepted and to a large extent fulfilled the expectations concerning sex roles of both their parents and their culture. As they reexamine their past, however, they discover that many of their attitudes, beliefs, and behaviors were not the result of their own choice but rather the choice of others. They are now in the process of sifting out their beliefs and expectations, rejecting those that do not fit. This is not an easy process. On the other hand, Marlene and Edward are young and have not yet invested much time and energy in developing an adult life-style. For people in their 30s, 40s, and 50s, the process of reevaluation is much more wrenching, for they have invested much of themselves in developing their pattern of life. Still, today many older people are also coming to a new awareness of themselves as persons in their own right. The case study of Annette illustrates this new enlightenment many adults are experiencing.

ANNETTE

Annette, now 45, has come to her "awakening" after many years of adopting and accepting the traditional sex roles. She married early because "girls are supposed to marry," and she assumed that she would find happiness in this marriage. Her early lack of fulfillment was attributed to her lack of children, so as soon as possible she had her first and only child. Neither wifehood nor motherhood were particularly rewarding for Annette. She questions, now, whether she would have had a child if she had recognized that she had a choice. Nonetheless, for twenty years she remained a dutiful wife and mother, ignoring the inner rumblings of discontent. Finally, with her child entering college, she heeded her own inner processes and sought therapy for herself. This led to her decision to return to school.

Annette now talks about her awakening and reveals how firmly entrenched at the unconscious level are the concepts of masculinity and femininity first taught in our childhood.

> *There was a time when I was the picture of the female stereotype and I believed in this stereotype, too. Men were adventurous, competitive, aggressive. Women were passive, docile, loyal. Men went out into the world, women stayed home to keep house and rear children. Girls were not supposed to go to college. I believed it all and did it all that way. My husband was the center of my world and he was the boss in the family (luckily he was not too bossy). I felt myself subordinate to him because he was a more important person than I. . . . I was also quite satisfied with this state of affairs because this is the way I thought it was supposed to be. It never occurred to me that things might be different—this was the way society was structured. Several years passed and I eventually began to question my identity. Thank goodness! All was not lost. I was no longer submerged in my husband's person. But I was not much of a feminist. The first rumblings of the most recent feminist movement left me untouched. It was very slowly that I began to understand just what they were talking about. . . . I don't know where I stand now but it is no longer in the "Dark Ages."*

IMPLICATIONS

Although Annette still feels bound by the attitudes, expectations, and behaviors that guided most of her adult life (and is not yet ready to change these patterns), she has undergone much questioning of her beliefs. This questioning has allowed her to reevaluate the traditional roles assigned to men and women and to seek alternatives. Many of us do not even reach this beginning stage of awakening. In order to evaluate our positions we will now examine more fully the traditional definitions of roles and statuses, particularly those called masculine and feminine.

ROLES AND STATUSES

Roles and statuses have often been compared to the scripts and parts played out in a dramatic production.* In performing on the stage each actor and actress is assigned a certain part and given a certain script. The part determines his or her position in the play; the role provides the script for acting out this part. Similarly, on the stage of life, we are given or achieve certain positions (Linton, 1936). These positions, which we hold in society, are called *statuses*. And just as in a play where other performers are needed in order for each part to have meaning, a status can only have meaning when it is compared with another status. For example, the status of husband is defined only in relation to the status of wife, the status of boss only in relation to the status of employee, and the status of professor only in relation to the status of student.

The statuses listed above are said to be *achieved statuses*. These statuses have to be earned and depend to some extent on the abilities of the individual. For example, a husband achieves his position only after he marries, and an employee is recognized as such only after he or she is hired. Some statuses, however, are "assigned to individuals without reference to their innate differences or abilities" (Linton, 1936, p. 115). These statuses are called *ascribed statuses* and are usually more encompassing than achieved statuses. Examples of ascribed statuses are age and sex. These can be assigned at birth (masculinity and femininity) or can be assigned later in life (teen-ager, adult). We can see from these examples that many statuses are overlapping. A person can be both male and a husband, or female and a professor.

Like parts in a play, each status also implies a set of expected attitudes and behaviors appropriate for that status. These rights, obligations, and expected behavior patterns are defined as *social*

---

*Some sociologists have recently criticized this view of roles and statuses as being static. They argue that the process of shaping our roles is dynamic; we constantly shape our roles as we interact with the environment. However, since we tend to follow the generalized guidelines for behavior that are accepted and expected by society, we shall, for the moment, hold to the more static view.

roles. Let us examine the social role of a person holding the status of mother: She is expected to care for her children, see that they are properly clothed and fed, and even prepare cookies for PTA meetings. A mother who lets her children "run loose" or appear in ragged attire in public, or who fails to show up for PTA meetings, is thought *not* to be demonstrating appropriate *role behavior.* Some would even assume that her attitudes are inappropriate and result from a lack of proper regard for the welfare of her children. These expectations about role behavior are generally shared by both the person who assumes the role and other persons with whom he or she interacts.

Most individuals maintain several statuses at once and are expected to display behaviors appropriate for each. Often these role behaviors are compatible, as are those of worker and father. However, sometimes these role behaviors are generally incompatible, as are those of mother and worker. In these cases, dissonance between two sets of expected behaviors or what sociologists term *role conflict* results. The role conflict women experience between their domestic and work worlds will be explored in Chapter 9.

Another type of conflict often occurs in the process of growing up. Young people such as Marlene and Edward who come to see themselves as independent individuals may experience dissonance between the roles of son and daughter (as defined by their parents and society) and the business and social roles that they "try on" in the search for their own identity. For example, the newly achieved statuses of "single career woman" or "bachelor lawyer" involve expectations that one is relatively available for after-five business and social engagements. This often conflicts with expectations attached to the statuses of son and daughter by the parents. They may think that the young person should be available for family activities and celebrations. Such role dissonance produces conflict both within the young people themselves, and in their parents who have been accustomed to playing out certain role expectations over a period of years.

SEX ROLES, GENDER IDENTITY, AND MASCULINE/FEMININE STEREOTYPES

Certain roles, such as son, mother, and career woman, are molded by a more encompassing set of expectations. These expectations pertain to our anatomical *gender*—whether we are male or female. As we have noted, each gender has a set of expected roles assigned to it. Thus, masculine and feminine, as they are used here and in much of the current literature, are terms that refer to sex roles. On this basis, a boy is supposed to act "masculine" and a girl is expected to act "feminine." The impact of sex roles on our behavior influences all that we do and is more significant than any other role in influencing our beliefs, attitudes, and behaviors (Moss, 1967). Yet, we take these roles for granted and do not analyze them or see them as separate from ourselves. We do not see that perhaps we can act differently. We wonder, how have sex roles become so entrenched in our lives?

The Institutionalization of Sex Roles The formation of sex roles has occurred over centuries. The expectations of what it means to be masculine and what it means to be feminine have been molded, changed, and redefined, as men and women have dealt with new settings, new environments, and new cultures. Although sex roles are dynamic, they have become institutionalized in each culture and are thus difficult to change.

The vested interest of business and government is one reason that sex roles have remained institutionalized. Until recently, for example, children's textbooks included dozens of stories about "adventurous" boys and "domestic" girls but never stories of domestic boys and adventurous girls. Mothers were shown with short hair neatly curled, wearing modest dresses and aprons, generally smiling with plates of cookies in their hands. Fathers, however, were depicted at work or doing other *important* things. Because of the revision of sex roles today, publishers have been required to withdraw such books and to produce new ones with less stereotyped characters.

Yet, even as books are changing, the attitudes they have produced remain within us. It is at least fifteen years since I have seen the neatly groomed mother *cum* apron in her kitchen with a plate of cookies. But I *know* that mothers wear aprons and make cookies because I unconsciously absorbed this from all the books I read as a child. Even at this moment my daughter is in the kitchen, decked out in an apron, and asking that I join her in such a venture. Obviously, I have other things to do but at the same time I feel guilty that I am not there with her, hands coated with flour, and smiling at the delight of it all! So much for the impact of institutionalized sex roles.

It is apparent from the previous discussion that sex roles, as well as all other roles we play, are closely interwoven with the fabric of society. The adoption of certain roles, all of which are reciprocal, allows humans to be somewhat predictable in the ways in which they interact with each other. This predictability is rewarded by society because it is no longer necessary for people to invest time or energy to understand and respond to unexpected behavior. For example, in many university classrooms, professors deliver lectures from the podium, assign readings, and require that both lecture and reading material be returned to them on examinations. Students, in the reciprocal status, also play predictable parts: Some pay conscientious attention, some think of other things, a few sleep, and most forget about the class upon adjournment. Both students and professors are content: Such behavior on both sides is predictable. If, however, professors come to class wearing casual clothes, remove their shoes and sit Buddhalike on the desk, talk without formal notes, give no exams, and expect the students to think for themselves, students are generally confused. The role-breaking behavior of such professors demands a different behavior on the part of the students. They, too, must deviate from their usual roles in response to this unexpected behavior. This requires time and energy.

Clearly, society as a whole, and individuals in particular, have an investment in seeing that people conform to expected sex-role behavior. Yet, some people choose to become role-breakers—to move away from traditional sex roles. The move away from traditional sex roles has provoked in many people a variety of responses. Adults often incur the surprise, humor, and hostility of others when they stray from appropriate sex-role behavior. Although tolerance for the working mother has increased in recent years, school officials and youth-group leaders still portray astonishment and disapproval that such a woman cannot be found at home when activities of the school or other groups expect her assistance. Men who express their feelings openly are still regarded with some dismay. As one student remarked about a colleague of hers in a counseling office, "He is so open, I really admire him, but part of me still wonders if he is homosexual."

Such questioning and concern remind us that we may have deviated from the path of appropriate behavior. A large part of our population, for example, still regards homosexual men and women as "sick," reflecting extreme reactions to what is "deviant" or does not meet the norm. In a lesser light assertive women and expressive men are regarded with suspicion—they too do not meet the norm. Many individuals react to such subtle (or nonsubtle) disapproval by keeping at least their surface behavior in line with usual social expectations. They avoid the discomfort of conflict by acceding to social norms.

On the other hand, some people welcome the move away from traditional sex roles. One man in his 30s, in a discussion about career women, said of his wife who had just reentered the professional world, "Yes, it has unsettled our lives. But, you know, I find her just a little bit more fascinating than she was before." His face lit up and he smiled as he made this admission. Other marriages have broken up over the same issue.

We can see from these examples the importance that sex roles play in our lives. They cause us to lead our lives according to certain patterns, and often to pass up some favorable opportunities. How do we learn these generalized expectations of sex-differentiated behavior?

Learning Sex-Differentiated Behavior Several instances of such learning situations have already been suggested. We learn expectations for our gender from the time we are wrapped in the respective blue and pink blankets in the hospital nursery (some hospitals are now using yellow) and begin to receive differential treatment from the adults in our environment. We learn from the pictures on the cartons of toys (if we have not already heard this from our parents) that some toys are for girls and some are for boys. We meet differential treatment in the schoolroom, the girls being rewarded for good behavior, the boys being allowed a wider spectrum of behavior since "boys will be boys." The media blares at us in newspapers, magazines, radio, television, and motion pictures how men and women should look, talk, or behave. The vocational counselor realistically (in terms of our current world) advises girls to lower their aspirations and boys to shoot for the top. From all corners, appropriate conceptions of sex-role behavior are reinforced throughout the life cycle.

Some people justify our learning to be specifically masculine or feminine, because they fear that a homogenization of the human race will result if we do not properly learn these roles. They fear, in other words, that all of us will look and act as if we have come from the same mold. Such fears are ill founded.

There is no possibility that all men and women would ever

merge into one sex, for we are born either male or female from an anatomical viewpoint. Sex is biologically determined, and all humans possess either a penis or vagina.* Thus on the basis of anatomical differences, 95 percent of the population develop unequivocal gender identity (Oakley, 1973). Between 18 months and 3 years nearly all of us become sure that we are either boys or girls (Kagan, 1964; Kohlberg, 1966). Basic maleness or femaleness is established. And although some researchers have shown that there are large components of cultural conditioning in the development of gender identity, we usually assume such identity in accordance with our biological sex or our anatomy. We will now examine what is expected of people because of their gender and how well people conform to these expectations.

Sex Roles and Masculine/Feminine Stereotypes In American society, our concepts of masculinity and femininity traditionally assume that the range of human characteristics is divided into two stacks, and that one stack is ascribed to men and the other to women. Although some traits, such as sincerity, are shared by the two sexes, many traits are assigned only to one sex. This division of behaviors and attitudes into two separate categories—masculine and feminine—often exists more in belief than in actuality. Nonetheless, such concepts have an enormous influence on the lives of human beings. We often experience the influence of such a generalized system of concepts more in our failure to meet expectations than in our fulfillment of them. Thus, we feel inadequate when we do not measure up to our expectations about "what a man does" or "what a woman does."

According to the traditional stereotype, being masculine means being assertive, being interested in things rather than people, being analytical and manipulative, and being able to "get things done." Men are thought to be able to see themselves as separate from their environment. They are supposed to be able to stand back and analyze any problem—whether it has to do with people or things—and from this analysis to be able to come up with a solution. Men are traditionally skilled in leadership. Violence is tolerated if men have to use it to defend their own rights or territory. According to this stereotype, men's sense of self-worth depends

---

*In a few babies the penis may be so small that it looks like an enlarged clitoris, or the clitoris may be so large that it looks like a small penis. And in even fewer instances, babies have the genitals of both sexes. They are called hermaphrodites. All of these exceptions, however, are rare.

on meeting these expectations: being strong, analytical, and dominant.

On the debit side, being masculine means being unexpressive, and unemotional. Men are not expected to cry, to be sad, or to be vulnerable. It is true that such stereotypes are slowly changing today (Tavris, 1977). However, the *macho* male who, like a John Wayne character in the movies, can face any situation at any time without trembling or quivering is still very much with us. Even though cultural overtones vary, the strutting stance of the Mediterranean male and the characteristic stiff upper lip of his Anglo-Saxon counterpart are both designed to show an unflinching strength in the face of any adversity. Also on the debit side, men as a rule are not expected to be adept in managing their interpersonal affairs. They are often shown as having some difficulty taking care of the small details of life involving unimportant social or domestic concerns. That sphere of life belongs to women, and is described as "women's work."

According to the contrasting traditional stereotype for women, being feminine implies interdependence, interest in others, and a skill in interpersonal relationships. In all functions revolving around the biological and social spheres of life women are supposed to be supreme. They are thought of as nurturing, tender, receptive, empathetic, and submissive. They smooth the way for others, namely men, who do not have such capabilities. The self-esteem of women is viewed as being derived from serving well and pleasing others, particularly men.

On the debit side, being feminine means being inferior to men in all the affairs of the world. Supposedly, women do not achieve in the world, cannot do mathematical problems, and are useless in an argument based on rational grounds. Women are said to be too emotional for the larger world and thus better suited for the home. One study describes woman as nurturer, temptress, and knower (intuitive, not logical), and adds that the focus for women is a "close identification with organic life and its perpetuation" (Lifton, 1964, p. 31).

The clusters of traits associated with masculinity have often been called *instrumental;* those associated with femininity, *expressive* (Parsons & Bales, 1955). What is clear from these traditional definitions of masculine and feminine traits is that men are supposed to more easily find their place out in the world while women are more suited for domesticity. According to these concepts men, who are unskilled in managing the intimate details of their lives, require the services of women, who excel in this area. Conversely, women, who are inept in the affairs of the outside world, require the financial support and protection of men.

Many research studies (for example, see Maccoby & Jacklin, 1974; Stewart, 1976) have documented the collection of traits specifically associated with men and women. In reviewing such evidence, however, we should remember that the researchers are interested in showing that the average for men in their sample is different from the average for women with respect to any particular trait measured. But in nearly all cases such traits overlap for both sexes so that, for the most part, individual men and women may not differ much from each other. For example, a recent study (Forisha, 1976) shows that among a particular sample of students, men are more "open to experience" than women. This means that on the average men scored higher than women on Fitzgerald's (1966) Openness to Experience Scale. Yet a number of men and women have the same scores and many women scored higher than many men (see Figure 1). Another example is taken from the work of Anastasi (1958), who reports that on a test of arithmetical reasoning boys did better than girls. However, it is clear that although the average of the boys' scores is higher than that of the girls', many girls did as well or

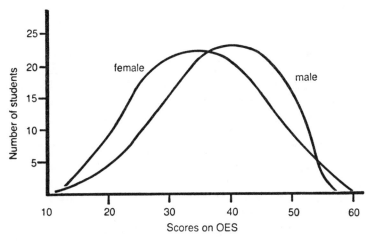

Figure 1 Distribution of 325 university students tested on Fitzgerald's (1966) Openness to Experience Scale (OES)

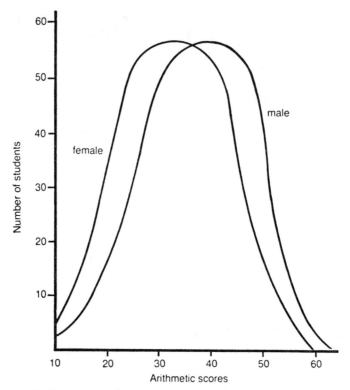

Figure 2 Distribution of boys and girls on a test of arithmetic reasoning (modified from Anastasi 3rd ed.. 1958. p. 455)

better on this test than many boys (see Figure 2). So, although this type of research tells us that differences exist between groups of individuals, it tells us little about particular individuals. In such cases differences within each group are likely to be greater than differences between the groups.

A research study by Bennett and Cohen (1959) documents differences between groups of men and women and supports the stereotypical views we just mentioned. According to Bennett and Cohen, for example, women typically have greater social concern and social skills than men; paradoxically women also have both greater controlled rage and greater personal happiness. Men, on the other hand, demonstrate more competence, intelligence, creativity, and mastery over their environment. In addition, women's thinking tends to be guided by factors related to their interpersonal environment and to be geared toward seeking approval from others. On the other hand, men's thinking is judged more in terms of self-formed standards and is geared toward competing in what many men see as a mildly hostile, competitive society.

The impact of masculine and feminine stereotyping was shown in the case histories of Marlene and Edward (pp. 12–16). Both are in touch with the expressive side of their nature. Both are skilled in the academic and business worlds. Yet how do they evaluate themselves in relation to their different experiences of being human? For Marlene it is fine to write poetry, to feel, to put others first. Her conflicts revolve around her need for achievement. She should achieve something in the world—but not too much. And if she doesn't make it, she can drop out of that world and become a wife and mother. Pressures in that direction are strong. For Edward, on the other hand, it is not all right to write poetry, to express sadness, or to develop the more sensitive side of his character. He is supposed to put all his efforts into achieving something in the world despite the fact that he might not want to achieve. His measure as a man will come from the status of his job, the size of his bank account, and a high level of sexual potency. Edward, therefore, has been taught to found his self-image on external accomplishments while Marlene tends to regard herself as others do. Like many women who are limited by the traditional sex role, she may eventually evaluate herself as she is evaluated in the eyes of men.

The foregoing discussion about the concepts of masculinity and femininity, which has illustrated how "we think we are," has often been translated into how "we ought to be." The move from *de*scription to *pre*scription is easily made. Yet do the above characteristics really describe us, let alone prescribe us?

Existence of Sex Differences All of the traditional stereotypes for men and women previously listed have been documented in various research studies. A recent landmark report by Maccoby and Jacklin (1974), however, asserts that most of these differences exist more in myth than in fact. After an exhaustive review of over two thousand studies, Maccoby and Jacklin claim that only four differences have been clearly shown to exist. Although other differences have been found in individual pieces of research, Maccoby and Jacklin argue that these studies are not yet conclusive because of either lack of proven research methods or lack of confirmation in other studies. Three of the four differences that they believe have been conclusively proven are within the realm of cognitive ability. Females excel over males in tests of verbal ability, while males

CULTURE AND BIOLOGY

excel in tests of mathematical ability. It should be noted, however, that such differences are noted only after adolescence. In addition, adolescent boys and adult men excel in tests of visual-spatial ability whereas girls and women do not. Only one difference was found in personality characteristics: Maccoby and Jacklin confirm the popular assumption that males are more aggressive than females. It has been agreed for some time that males are more aggressive physically than females, but some researchers (Oakley, 1973) argue that women use more verbal aggression than men. Even in this form of aggression, however, Maccoby and Jacklin claim that men are more aggressive.

Other studies reviewed by Maccoby and Jacklin claim to report differences in anxiety, compliance, competitiveness, and passivity. However Maccoby and Jacklin do not accept these studies as definitive since the researchers approach the subject from differing theoretical frameworks and thus give differing definitions of the traits measured; still other researchers introduce into their studies methodological flaws that make it impossible to draw generalizations from their findings.

Another review of the literature on sex differences (Stewart, 1976) suggests that the biggest differences between the sexes may be in their interests and values. It is not clear whether such differences are due to some innate causes (that is, differences at birth) or whether they are due to differing experiences during our lives. Nonetheless these differences have been shown to exist. In our society men tend to be more interested in scientific, mechanical, political, computational, and physically strenuous or adventuresome activities while women seem to prefer literary, musical, artistic, social, and sedentary activities. Men as a rule emphasize economic and political values while women pay more attention to social, aesthetic, and religious values.

The suggested differences between men and women may be further confirmed in the future by additional research. On the other hand, the differences that, it is agreed, have been consistently reported may no longer exist if current conceptions of child-rearing and family style change radically.

In the meantime, because of the few verifiable differences between men and women in cognitive and emotional areas, many researchers are now beginning to turn to the concept of androgyny as an alternative to thinking solely in masculine and feminine terms.

THE ANDROGYNOUS ALTERNATIVE

Androgny is derived from two Greek words—*andro* meaning man, and *gyne* meaning woman. It describes persons who are neither strongly feminine nor strongly masculine in behavior but seek to keep open for themselves the full range of human emotions and behaviors. Thus, for any situation that arises, they are able to choose the most appropriate response (Bem, 1974, 1975). In accord with their own inner potential they may select a behavior pattern from the full scale of conventional masculine or feminine sex roles. Such individuals can be either assertive or tender or perhaps a combination of both qualities, depending on which is the appropriate response to their problem and its environment. They have the freedom to be changing rather than fixed human beings—individuals in process rather than finished end products. They are able to respond genuinely, authentically, and openly to their experiences.

At this point, I think I should state that the path toward an androgynous life-style is not an easy one. It may be strewn with difficulties that are different for each status and culture. For example, in America many young people on university campuses are attempting to move toward an androgynous life-style. Many find, however, that they lack the personal strength needed to carry this life-style into the adult world of marriage and work. Many older adults have this strength but are unable to erase patterns of behavior that have influenced their lives for three or four decades. The different social strata in America also face different obstacles. Sociologists tell us that the upper-middle class has more psychological and economic freedom with which to undertake new ventures in life-style. On the other hand, the lower classes often struggle under the weight of necessity and the upper class under the weight of tradition.

Similar inequities may be found in reviewing non-American cultures. Scandinavian people, for example, have as a whole begun to support more androgynous norms. Consequently, Swedish youth are appalled at the "sex-role hangups" of their American counterparts. On the other hand, individuals of Latin and Middle Eastern backgrounds believe in male superiority and female inferiority. Yet men in these cultures are more expressive (a hangup of American men). All of these examples show that people in each culture face difficulties in becoming fully human. Still in all cultures, at all times, there are individuals who have risen above the pressures of social norms and who have moved away from stereotyped masculinity and femininity toward an androgynous life-style.

Process-Oriented Versus Role-Oriented Behavior Such unstereotyped behavior is *process oriented* in that behavior springs spontaneously from the ongoing content of experience. In the process-oriented mode of being, we allow our own experience (our sense of who we are at that moment) to shape the forms that we create and the roles that we play. We trust ourselves and our own inner judgments rather than the evaluations of others. We are open to both our inner and outer experiences, and continually learn more about ourselves and our world. This experience enables us to correct past errors of judgment. In process orientation we may make mistakes, but we are willing to admit that we have done so. We accept the reality that we and our environment are constantly changing and we allow ourselves to be part of that change. Modern sociologists would say that process orientation allows and fosters a constant negotiation with ourselves and with our environment in a never-ending chain of mutual adaptations. However, the final evaluation and decision-making processes (as the humanistic psychologists and sociologists have stated) come from within and not from the expectations of others.

Specifically, process-oriented individuals are always in *process*. This requires courage, strength, and the willingness to sacrifice the security of the familiar for total uncertainty. To shape our lives in a process-oriented fashion—to be all that we are and to remove masculine and feminine restrictions—is not an easy choice. Yet the rewards are a deeper satisfaction with ourselves and with others and a greater excitement about the adventure of living (see Maslow, 1970).

On the other end of the continuum from process-oriented behavior lies the role-oriented pattern of behavior. *Role-oriented* behavior takes its shape from external norms and the expectations of others. When behaving in a role-oriented fashion, we tend to distrust our own inner experiences and rely on the judgments of others—whether they are intimates with whom we are closely associated or "experts" on one subject or another. We confuse what *we* want for ourselves with what others want for us; this confusion causes us to unconsciously adopt the wishes of others as our own. Often we are unaware that we have suppressed our own viewpoint and used that of others to shape our lives to fit the external form. In

TABLE 1. Process- and Role-Oriented Individuals

Process-Oriented Individuals	Role-Oriented Individuals
1. **Power found within self**	1. **Power found in relationship** to other people, institutions, ideologies
2. **Characteristics** Courage Responsibility Awareness Self-disclosure Present-centered Self-directing Empathetic	2. **Characteristics** Seek stability and see. self as controlled by environment Limited awareness Limited self-disclosure Past- and/or future-centered Antagonistic
3. **In relation to others** Let others be themselves Nonpossessive Relate to unique world of other by transcending own	3. **In relation to others** Want others to change Clinging Dominating "What I win, you lose"
4. **Tolerance of ambiguity** Integration of dichotomies such as masculine/feminine	4. **Need for categories** Right/wrong Black/white Masculine/feminine

role-oriented behavior, we fear change and seek stability; we look for clear-cut divisions and avoid uncertainty. Also, we are too fearful and too uncertain to admit our mistakes. On the other hand, we often find the illusion of security and safety in role-oriented behavior. In this security lies the appeal of role orientation.

Later chapters (especially Chapters 3, 4, 5, and 7) will more fully explain the process-oriented and role-oriented alternatives. Table 1, however, summarizes the major characteristic of process-oriented and role-oriented living. This table (and the theory behind it) does not seek to establish a new dichotomy to replace the old masculine/feminine mold. Instead, it seeks to provide end points for a continuum of behavior. We are all somewhat process oriented and somewhat role oriented. It is my contention, however, that the degree to which we increase our process orientation determines the degree to which we increasingly utilize our freedom.

Characteristics of Process Orientation There are two aspects of process orientation that have particular relevance here.

The first involves the degree of freedom and choice we utilize in selecting our roles. The second concerns the transcendence of dichotomies or the ability to go beyond divisions into two halves. Each of these topics will be dealt with at some length below.

Choosing and Creating Our Own Roles In process orientation we do not totally escape our roles. Instead, we *choose* to play certain roles that we have previously recognized and selected as appropriate channels for our present interaction with others and with the environment. Process-oriented people consider how each role available to them meets their needs and then decide which one to choose. They are not dependent on their roles nor unconsciously molded by them. They do not unwittingly accept definitions of what it means to be masculine or feminine, husband or wife, professor or student. Moreover, they are willing to change and/or modify roles to better suit their perception of their own uniqueness in interaction with the environment. Because of their willingness to change and modify roles to suit themselves, process-oriented individuals in fact create and shape their own roles. They are the creators of their own lives, not the unknowing actors of a script imposed on them by the society or culture in which they live. In short, process orientation is distinguished from role orientation primarily along the dimension of choice. It acknowledges the fact that by *choice* we may decide to play the roles traditionally assigned us by society or disregard them.

The question of role reversal often comes up in discussions about our options either to choose our own new roles or to accept the traditional roles imposed by society. If we abandon the old roles expected by society, we may often feel ourselves alone and threatened. As a result, we may be led to seek the security of a new role—even one just the opposite of the script we formerly followed. Author Elizabeth Janeway remarks that "it is possible to move away from one stereotype with impunity if there is shelter near another" (1971, p. 123). Yet the acceptance of *another role* is not entirely satisfactory. We have changed the script and bought new costumes. But the script has still been written by others, the costumes designed by others. Eventually the new role will be found restricting. We have not moved away from role orientation until we *create* our *own* script and design our *own* lives.

Many students have reported their attempts at adopting "liberated" or "process-oriented" roles. As one man recalled:

I simply began playing the role of the process-oriented individual who treats both males and females as equals. This sounds great, except that it was only a front—the process-oriented feeling wasn't there. Only a hypocritical emptiness existed and this wasn't the answer. After some initial thought it came to me that process-oriented individuals aren't that way because of behavior but because these attitudes are an integrated part of their being.

The androgynous, process-oriented approach to life is *not* merely another role. It is rather a creation of our own, a creation springing from the interaction of our aware self and our environment. Along the way to process orientation, however, many of us need to try on new roles and wear new costumes in order to broaden our repertoire and increase our experience. Experiments in role reversals can show us more about what the grass is like on the other side of the fence and eventually give us the empathy, courage, and understanding to help take down the fences. Nevertheless journalist Ellen Goodman (1974) speaks disparagingly of the hope for ultimate change through role reversals. She concludes, though, that maybe these "flip-flops" may be the necessary Act I of a play before the more exciting and authentic Act II.

Several role reversals experienced by my students have brought predictable and not-so-predictable responses. One young man who takes care of the house for a working wife while he goes to school was preparing a surprise dinner one evening, complete with flowers and wine. His relatives, who dropped in without notice, found him in the kitchen, wearing a T-shirt that had been stained pink in the wash and his wife's ruffled apron. His shocked parents and siblings called repeatedly in the following days, offering to help him out so that he could attend a football game or some other masculine event. The fear provoked by his role reversal was shown by the repeated phone calls. Janeway (1971) reports on how difficult it is to accept a person who does not conform to his or her accepted role:

> To those around him, a role-breaker is a deviant, whose behavior is incomprehensible. It awakens hostility because no one knows where he will stop, or what he may be capable of doing. His behavior provides no clue to what can be predicted about his actions (p. 116).

Another student reports her experiences in this area. On one occasion she had a male friend type a paper in a university business office while she hung over his typewriter and offered advice. This drew joking remarks from many who passed by. On two other occasions male friends cooked dinner for her. After one of these meals, she says, she happily volunteered to do the dishes. She comments on these experiences:

> *These were all minor events. But the point is that if there is a mutual exchange of give and take, the outcome is nice. If the roles of what you give and what you take are also exchanged, your experiences are enriched. It prevents the dullness of taking things for granted. In the man/woman type relationship I think there is a tendency for the fun to go flat through becoming routine.*

Role reversals can be fun and a novel way to increase our awareness. But in this sense they are perhaps only a beginning of the process-oriented journey. As Goodman states, role reversals may be part of Act I; let's not treat them as if they are the Finale.

Transcendence of Polarities The second aspect of process orientation is the fact that process-oriented individuals *transcend* or go beyond the ordinary dichotomies supposed by many to exist in masculine and feminine sex roles. Western thinking has a long history of dualism in which complex phenomena are reduced to polar opposites and thus to categories that are more readily understood (Watson, 1976). The human being, for example, is a complex creature, capable of being both active and passive, assertive and receptive, independent and dependent. Such variability introduces a large degree of unpredictability in assessing possible behaviors, attitudes, and emotions. But if we view all the above behaviors as pairs of polar opposites and ascribe one half of each pair to one sex, we reduce the complexity of human beings by half. In so doing, we also increase their predictability. The role-oriented individual is lured by such predictability and resulting security to believe in such dichotomies. The process-oriented person, on the other hand, recognizes—sometimes only intuitively—that such polarities are probably mere human inventions upheld by centuries of habit. The process-oriented person believes that individuals can be both active and passive, assertive and receptive, taking and giving—alternately and at the same time.

Block (1973) speaks of the integration of sex-role characteristics that occurs at the higher levels of development.

TABLE 2. The Development of Androgyny

Developmental Stage	Sex-Role Orientation	Characteristics
Stage A: Infants	Human	Lack of differentiation between sex-role expectations
Stage B: Children and most adults	Masculine or feminine	Differentiation between sex-role expectations; reliance on either/or alternatives
Stage C: Some adults	Androgynous	Integration and differentiation including transcendence of masculine and feminine dichotomy

With the articulation of notions about the self, awareness develops of values, predispositions, and behaviors that depart from traditional sex role definitions, and these more complex, sometimes conflicting, aspects of self must be integrated.

At the integrated, or highest, level of ego functioning, . . . the individual has evolved for himself-herself an identity consonant with history and aspiration. With respect to sex role identity, the definition given by the individual represents an integration of traits and values, both masculine and feminine. Such sex role definitions, integrating both aspects conventionally considered feminine and those traditionally defined as masculine, I refer to here as "androgynous" to emphasize their nonparochial nature (p. 66).

The theme of transcendence in regard to sex roles is also emphasized by another team of researchers (Rebecca, Hefner, & Oleshansky, 1976) who argue that there are three stages of sex-role development: the first undifferentiated, the second polarized, and the third transcending these polarities (see Table 2). The undifferentiated stage occurs in infancy and very early childhood before we have become consciously aware of sex-role expectations, before we know that boys and girls are different. The polarized stage begins in early childhood and, for many, continues throughout adult life. In this stage we maintain either a masculine or feminine sex-role orientation. The final stage is achieved when we allow ourselves to be "in process" and without regard to gender choose the best alternative for ourselves at any particular time. According to Rebecca,

Hefner, and Oleshansky, "To a transcendent person, assigned gender is irrelevant to decision making" (p. 96).

These researchers argue that the transition from A to B, from the undifferentiated stage to the polarized stage, is generally smooth because of support by our socialization procedures. On the other hand, the transition from B to C, at least in our current culture, is stormy and conflict-laden because society does not support an androgynous orientation. This transition is often provoked by personal crisis which propels the individual to seek a personal integration of what were formerly viewed as polarities. Another theory, developed by Block (1973), also suggests that the prelude to androgyny is one of conflict resolution. This theory agrees with the thinking of many other theorists about what I am calling the process-oriented journey. The resulting rewards are great but the way is hard. And we have the choice to set out on the journey or to remain at home.

SUMMARY

The stories of Marlene, Edward, and Annette illustrate our awareness of changes that are occurring in relation to sex roles today. Individuals, young and old, are beginning to reassess traditional conceptions of masculinity and femininity and are beginning to reevaluate the roles that have shaped their lives. Roles are the clusters of behavior associated with certain statuses or positions in society. The most significant roles affecting our lives are those ascribed because of our anatomical sex—the sex roles of masculine and feminine. Masculine and feminine roles prescribe how we should think, feel, and act depending on whether we are men or women. Moreover, these roles have been confirmed on the descriptive level by many studies showing the existence of numerous differences between men and women. However, more recent research confirms that only a few of these sex differences actually exist.

We are perhaps more alike as men and women than we have been led to believe by the traditional stereotypes. The similarities of men and women appear to overreach their differences, thus giving theoretical substance to the supposition that we might all better live our lives as androgynous human beings who are free to choose from the best of masculine and feminine worlds rather than limit ourselves to a single world. Androgyny is part of a process-oriented approach whereby we choose the behaviors, emotions, and attitudes most appropriate for our unique situations regardless of traditional dichotomies that hem in role-oriented people.

EXERCISE: SEX-ROLE REVERSAL

Read this to yourself silently or have someone read it to you. Sit back quietly and close your eyes. Imagine for a moment that you are all alone. No external distractions can enter your world. No external circumstances can limit your freedom to experience any possibility with your unlimited imagination.

Now imagine that you are a person of the other sex. If you are a man, imagine that you are a woman. If you are a woman, imagine that you are a man. Notice any changes in your physical self. How do you feel in this new body? Stronger, weaker, softer, more forceful? What restrictions do you notice? What freedoms?

Now take yourself through a typical day as your new self. How do you feel when you get up in the morning? When you go to work? When you go to school? Or suppose that you stay home. What do you do differently? How do you feel about yourself now? Take as much time as you need to assess your feelings.

Return to your own body now and become yourself again. Is the return pleasant or unpleasant? What do you like most about being yourself?

Now discuss with others what you learned in this experience about the differences between masculinity and femininity. How did your experiences compare with those of others?

REFERENCES

Bem, S. L., "The Measurement of Psychological Androgyny," *Journal of Consulting and Clinical Psychology*, vol. 2 (1974):153–62.

Bem, S. L., "Sex-Role Adaptability: One Consequence of Psychological Androgyny," *Journal of Personality and Social Psychology*, vol. 4 (1975):634–43.

Bennett, E. M., and Cohen, L. R., "Men and Women: Personality Patterns and Contrasts," *Genetic Psychology Monographs,* vol. 59 (1959):101–55.

Block, J. H., "Conceptions of Sex Role: Some Cross-Cultural and Longitudinal Perspectives," *American Psychologist,* vol. 28 (1973):512–26.

Brenton, M., *The American Male,* New York: Fawcett World, 1970.

Goodman, E., "Flip-Flops: New Disease of the Sexes," *San Francisco Examiner,* October 6, 1974.

Janeway, E., *Man's World, Woman's Place,* New York: William Morrow, 1971.

Kagan, J., "Acquisition and Significance of Sex-Typing and Sex-Role Identity," in M. L. Hoffman and L. S. Hoffman, eds., *Review of Child Development Research,* vol. 1, Russell Sage Foundation, 1964.

Kohlberg, L., "A Cognitive Developmental Analysis of Children's Sex-Role Concepts and Attitudes," in E. E. Maccoby, ed., *The Development of Sex Differences,* Stanford, Calif.: Stanford University Press, 1966.

Lifton, R. J., "The Woman as Knower," in R. J. Lifton, ed., *The Woman in America: Some Psychohistorical Perspectives,* Boston: Beacon Press, 1964.

Linton, R., *The Study of Man* (1936), Englewood Cliffs, N.J.: Appleton-Century-Crofts (Prentice-Hall), 1964.

Maccoby, E. E., and Jacklin, C. N., *The Psychology of Sex Differences,* Stanford, Calif.: Stanford University Press, 1974.

Maslow, A. H., *Motivation and Personality,* 2nd ed., New York: Harper & Row, 1970.

Moss, H. A., "Sex, Age and State as Determinants of Mother-Infant Interaction," *Merrill-Palmer Quarterly,* vol. 13 (1967):19–36.

Moustakas, C., *Creativity and Conformity,* New York: D. Van Nostrand, 1967.

Oakley, A., *Sex, Gender and Society,* New York: Harper & Row, 1973.

Parsons, T., and Bales, R. F., *Family, Socialization and Interaction Process,* Glencoe, Ill.: Free Press, 1955.

Rebecca, M., Hefner, R., and Oleshansky, B., "A Model of Sex-Role Transcendence," in A. Kaplan and J. Bean, eds., *Beyond Sex-Role Stereotypes: Readings Toward a Psychology of Androgyny,* Boston: Little, Brown, 1976.

Stewart, V., "Social Influences on Sex Differences in Behavior," in M. S. Teitelbaum, ed., *Sex Differences,* New York: Anchor Books, 1976.

Tavris, C., "Men and Women Report Their Views on Masculinity," *Psychology Today,* vol. 10 (January, 1977):34–38.

Watson, B. B., ed., *Women's Studies,* New York: Harper & Row, 1976.

2

The Origins of Sex Roles: Is Anatomy Destiny?

A review of the literature on the origins and bases of sex roles leads almost inevitably to the conclusion that theorists have often selected their data and drawn their implications from this data in order to suit their own preconceived ideas. To state this more simply: If a researcher believes that men are superior in most worldly functions, he (in the past it has generally been *he*) will select a specific group for study and also individuals or traits from within that group for specific investigation so that he will prove exactly that—that men are superior. Yet, these procedures and deductive processes are quite acceptable to established science. Underlying the questions asked by scientists, the particular sample selected, and the emphasis placed on certain findings lies the value orientation of the scientist.

Let me state at the outset that in the case of sex-role research the value orientation has been predominantly masculine. This is

. . . it is doubtless impossible to approach any human problem with a mind free from bias. The way in which questions are put, the points of view assumed, presuppose a relativity of interest; all characteristics imply values, and every objective description, so called, implies an ethical background.

Simone de Beauvoir, *The Second Sex*

---

because the research has been carried out largely by men for a largely male audience. Thus, research results have been interpreted in a framework that *assumes* the predominance of the male. (After all, who for the most part is doing the research, and with whom are the results being shared?) Bernard states this succinctly:

> Whatever the objectives of research on sex differences may have been, its latent function has been, in effect, to rationalize and hence to legitimate the status quo, including of course its role structure, especially the inferior position of women (1976, p. 11).

Bernard affirms here that underlying value judgments, rarely examined, often run too deep to be noticed; nonetheless they slant our selective perception and our emphasis on particular trends within the data we survey. The *assumption* that men are suited to govern the world and women to tend the hearth, even if not raised to the conscious level, may influence in fact the data we select and the conclusions we draw from them. And if with French philosopher and sociologist Simone de Beauvoir we concede that "the representation of the world like the world itself is the work of men" (1953, p. 133), then any study of women is likely to result in a reassertion of the superiority of men.

Thus, one of the difficulties in assessing the results of research on the origin of sex roles is the inherent, unavoidable bias of the researchers. As Watson (1976) points out, one of the major issues raised by the "new" researchers, many of whom are women, concerns the study of knowledge. How is it that we know what we know? A review of sex-roles literature sometimes leaves us with the feeling that we know very little about the basis of sex roles.

A second reason for varied and often contradictory conclusions stems from the insufficient evidence that is available. Evidence on earlier cultures (prehistoric humans and later hunting and gathering societies) has been gathered from scattered fragments of their culture; and the theories scientists construct around such fragmentary evidence may lean in almost any direction. Moreover, even in later periods we have little direct evidence on women. As Bullough points out, "only a handful of women have managed to break into the pages of history" (1974, p. 3). It is men who have been generals, kings, writers, composers, thinkers, and doers. The historical past, like the present, reveals a world made by men. Records and reports from previous centuries have, by and large, been written from a man's point of view. Therefore, a history of women or of sex roles will be primarily a history of men's attitudes toward women and sex roles. Men's attitudes, like women's, are subject to the political and social outlook current of the day. And the political and social outlook of most historical periods regarded women as the inferior sex.

One final point should be made. Most of the literature on the origins of sex roles is concerned with the question of nature versus nurture: Are sex roles biologically defined by the anatomy of males and females, or have they been determined by the culture in which we live? As Rohrlich-Leavitt (1976) points out, this question is itself a reflection of the dualistic thinking that dominates the Western world. Again we find a tradition of classifying material into either/or categories. And we also find two schools of thought, each tending toward one end of the spectrum—either sex roles are innate or they are created by the culture. A more balanced view would probably suggest that sex roles are a product of both the human organism—

psychological *and* biological—and its environment, not of only one of these two factors. This latter view represents a process-oriented approach (see pp. 30–36), and it sees some justification in arguments from both nature and nurture theorists.

HISTORICAL ORIGINS

Most anthropologists have concluded that males have always and everywhere been dominant (Hays, 1972). Even in matrilineal societies (societies in which the line of descent is through the mother) political and economic power usually rests with the male. For example, in the matrilineal societies of the Arizona Hopis and the Ashanti of Ghana, husbands exert little influence over their wives; yet, women are still under the authority of their male kinfolk. An explanation suggested by many social scientists is that this development has been caused by the superior physical strength of the male and the reproductive functions of the woman.

> During the prime of their lives, women were usually pregnant, probably at least once every other year. . . . Even though there was a high proportion of miscarriages and a high infant mortality in the past, still the continued pregnancies and the slow development of the child from infancy to puberty curtailed the scope of feminine activities. Men, on the other hand, were free to leave the home, to roam at will in the forest, to hunt, to fight, even to contemplate (Bullough, 1974, p. 5).

In addition, man's greater physical strength found him better prepared for defense and protection. In return for such protection woman offered her obedience (Bullough, 1974, p. 335). As Ashley Montagu phrases this: "Woman is the cricket on the hearth; man is the eagle on the wing" (1970, p. 12).

De Beauvoir expands on the psychological implications of such physical differences: With his greater freedom and greater strength man developed pride in transcending his environment, whereas woman was a "plaything of nature," acted on by mysterious, obscure forces that caused her to become pregnant and to lactate seemingly at the whim of the gods (1953, p. 57). Whereas man transcended life and animal nature, woman was assured only of the repetition of the animal cycle. According to this view, man was obviously the superior creature.

Other theorists argue that man's superiority was *not* so

obvious. At a time in history when women's reproductive functions were regarded as mysterious, men could claim no credit for the creation of children. Women appeared to have control over life and death. In defense against this awesome power and in order to confirm their superiority, men took over all other power-conferring functions for themselves by asserting their superior physical strength and subjecting women to their will.

Hunting and Gathering Societies Despite men's professed superiority, women achieved a measure of economic power in hunting and gathering societies, which have existed throughout most of human history. They accomplished this by gathering roots and berries, thus contributing substantially to the sustenance of the larger group. Unfortunately, however, not all research on hunting and gathering societies acknowledges the contribution of women. Research has resulted in two main points of view, each of which reflects the assumptions the researchers bring to their work.

One view of hunting and gathering societies by anthropologists—the traditional viewpoint—centers around the activities of the hunters rather than the gatherers. Such societies are seen as territorial groups in which men bonded together and exercised control over their women. They are assumed to be patrilocal because the male determined the place of residence. These societies also are perceived as encouraging warfare to solve intergroup disputes, thus promoting the development of male aggression and the superiority of men over women (Watson, 1976, pp. 182–189).

However, not all early societies were patrilocal (Gough, 1975), nor were all early societies focused around hunting (Watson, 1976). Yet, until recently most anthropologists who studied patrilocal societies that were organized around hunting assumed that their conclusions applied to all hunting and gathering societies (see Gough, 1975). Thus, in the recent past, male anthropologists have made such sweeping statements as:

> Hunting is the master behavior pattern of the human species (Laughlin, 1968, p. 304).

> Our intellect, interests, emotions and basic social life—all are evolutionary products of the success of the hunting adaptation (Washburn & Lancaster, 1968, p. 293).

The emphasis on hunting in patrilocal society puts the male (men were usually but not always the hunters) front and center as the dominant sex in human evolution.

From these basic assumptions, emphasizing patrilocality and the central role of hunting, other anthropologists have argued that men have always been aggressive and, in fact, natural killers.

> ... *organized predatory violence* has always been a male monopoly, whether practiced against game animals or those enemy humans defined as "not-men" (and hence also a kind of prey animal). This is the important step in the move toward human warfare. It is not that man (or rather *men*) in the course of his evolution either learned to be a killer or lost his capacity to ritualize. He always was a killer—he still ritualizes. What he learned was the use of weapons, the predatory skill, and above all the organization of predation in male bands (Tiger & Fox, 1971, p. 213).

From this argument it is a small jump to the argument that as men learned to organize themselves, they also acquired (for men only!) the capacity to rule (see discussion of Tiger, pp. 57–58).

A second viewpoint—that of recent researchers—has begun to take more into account the social organization as a whole. The new research indicates that hunting was just one of many activities of interest in a given society. In fact, the subsistence provided by gathering, which was primarily the work of women, often outweighed that provided by hunting. According to these researchers such societies appeared to be nonterritorial and bilocal, that is, focused around both men and women. They rejected aggression and warfare and valued egalitarianism and personal autonomy (Watson, 1976, pp. 182–189).

Sex-role differentiations in hunting and gathering societies were, according to this view, minimal. The sexes cooperated with each other in almost all activities. The principal joys of these people lay in shared companionship, lovemaking, and rituals expressed in song and dance. Women in these societies are seen as strong, active, and economically independent. Moreover, their men—whether hunters or not—are seen as "gentle people" (Turnbull, 1968; Leacock, 1972).

One example of this type of society is found among the !Kung people in Africa who have retained their hunting and gathering patterns into the current century. The !Kung camps are not patrilocal in that they consist of "a core of siblings—both brothers *and* sisters—and their offspring of both sexes, who share a claim to the ownership of their waterhole" (Lee, 1972, p. 350). The !Kung are not territorial but migrate to a new setting when conflict occurs. Moreover, food is not possessed nor fought over by individuals but shared with all members of the group. In this society, the heroes, who are also the great curers and healers, are the older people who hold the rights to the waterholes. Fighters are regarded as deviant individuals, for the !Kung have no fondness for aggression and violence. "The violent-tempered man and the proud man are sorry misfits among the !Kung" (Lee, 1972, p. 360).

New Stone Age If our ancestors were "gentle people" rather than "killers," as they have often been portrayed (Tiger & Fox, 1971), we have come a long way from our primitive origins. Most anthropologists and other theorists agree on an important change that took place between ten and twelve thousand years ago at the start of the New Stone Age. Human beings in the valleys of the Tigris-Euphrates, the Nile, and the Indus rivers learned to increase their food supplies by growing grains and other plants and domesticating certain animals. This discovery drastically affected human society, which took on forms more familiar to us than were those of earlier periods. During this time men came to lay claim to the lands they occupied and to the women who bore their children.

Most cultures from this time forward have been patriarchal, that is, measuring descent through the father's line. Once the importance of parentage was recognized, men began to enforce customs that would certify that a child born of a woman was theirs. Women were to remain chaste and virginal until marriage, remain absolutely faithful in marriage, and bear only the children of their husband. The necessity of a more cloistered life for women was ordained by men's need to be sure of the legitimacy of their children.

The Spread of Christianity The patriarchal system was greatly strengthened by the spread of monotheistic religions like Judaism, Christianity, and Islam. Christianity, which has had a powerful shaping influence on Western society, is described by Bullough (1974) as antifeminist. To the Christian theologian of the Middle Ages women were temptresses who lured men from more profitable work. At worst, women were seen as dangerous, unclean, vicious, and depraved; they were slightly tricky at best. This view was transmitted to the Protestant Reformation. Martin Luther, for example, strongly believed in the inferiority of women and affirmed that, "with tricks and cunning women deceive men . . ." (in Bullough, 1974, p. 198).

Despite the partriarchal system and its reinforcement by Christianity, some women in Europe during the Middle Ages wielded a measure of real power. The prioresses and abbesses in charge of convents often had both spiritual and material power. Noblewomen on large estates often assumed positions of authority when their husbands went off to feudal wars or crusades to the Holy Land. Such women were left at home with the responsibility of running the estate—a job comparable to that of managing a business enterprise today. Most women in the Middle Ages and early modern times, however, lived in humble surroundings, usually working side by side with their husbands in the fields or shops. Yet, these women, too, in those days and throughout much of history were essential to the economic maintenance of the family. Thus, although people believed in the inferiority of women, women were able to attain a measure of effective power and, in some instances, real equality with men.

The Industrial Revolution With the arrival of the Industrial Revolution (1700s and 1800s) the way of life of everyone in the industrialized countries—including women—supposedly improved. Theorists of modernization believe that, as society develops, ascription—for example, the assignment of roles because of sex differences—declines. Moreover, it is a common assumption that as the overall achievement of the society rises, the position of women improves too (see Hochschild, 1973). However, this belief is challenged by numerous current studies which show that the position of women declined after the start of the Industrial Revolution, and in fact continued to decline as industrialization gained in momentum (Boserup, 1970; Smith, 1970).

As industrialization in the 1700s progressed, men took over jobs formerly held by women and transferred these jobs from the home to the factory. "Home," as we know it today, that is, divorced from work, began to come into being at that time. Although poor women took advantage of the opportunity to earn small amounts of money by toiling long hours in the factories (as Sayers states, "No one has ever complained that poor women should toil alongside their men; the objection is only to work that is pleasant, exciting, or profitable" [in Roszak & Roszak, 1969, p. 119]), middle-class women remained at home. Having a well-dressed woman in a well-kept house became a mark of self-esteem to men who worked away from home. Kate Millett, the contemporary feminist, remarks, summarizing Friedrich Engels, the nineteenth-century socialist, that when a woman serves no economic purpose, men "convert her into a decorative or aesthetic object with only limited uses" (1970, p. 121). Sayers also elaborates on the advantages of this system to men:

> The middle class found that keeping an idle woman at home was a badge of superior status; man must work and woman must exploit his labor. If woman submits she can be cursed for her exploitation, if she rebels she can be cursed for competing. Whatever she does will be wrong and that is a great satisfaction (in Roszak & Roszak, 1969, p. 120).

The idle status of women was also reinforced by a revamped view of Christianity that drew on the ethical part of the Biblical tradition emphasizing the dignity of women. This view, however, stressed woman's angelic and unworldly nature, which was easily perverted into weakness and inability to do "real" work (Hiller, 1947, p. 428).

The Victorian Era With the advent of the Victorian era in the 1800s, woman was further removed from the workaday world, enshrined on a pedestal, and kept as a prisoner of her sex. The Victorian woman was to be chaste, genteel, and occupied with womanly accomplishments, such as needlework and embroidery, in order to fend off idleness. Motherhood gained in importance as children, who were previously treated like little adults, were now allowed to be children. Although the new mystique of motherhood further elevated woman, it still guaranteed her inferiority to men. As in all periods of history, social status was derived from association with the world of work and tangible accomplishments. On a pedestal, idle, alone, except for the tending of children, the Victorian woman had no outlets for her need to achieve things in life. She often had to escape from life by retreating to bed with undiagnosed "female" frailties, a victim of psychosomatic illnesses resulting from her blocked emotions.

This was the culture in which Sigmund Freud came into his own and decreed that women were the inferior sex. (Freud will be discussed in more detail on pages 58–59.) Other scientific thinkers of the day, such as Fernseed, argued that the higher stages of evolution were marked by the preeminence of the male as compared to the female (1881, p. 74). Bagehot stated that the inferiority of woman was in the natural order of things:

> ... the male is the defender and provider, wherever such defense and provision are necessary; the female is the nurse. ... The attempt to alter the present relationship of the sexes is not a rebellion against some arbitrary law instituted by a despot or a majority—not an attempt to break the yoke of a mere convention; it is a struggle against Nature; a war undertaken to reverse the very conditions under which not man alone, but all mammalian species have reached their present development (1879, p. 207).

On the other hand, men like John Stuart Mill and Friedrich Engels spoke against this position. Mill (1869) considered the subjugation of women to be the result of the savagery of men—a savagery born of cultural values, not of biological differences between the sexes. Engels (1884) attributed the subjugation of women to early historical and economic conditions. In many ways this was an important breakthrough in nineteenth-century thinking. Regardless of the validity of Engels' historical theory, his argument for the human-created nature of the relationship between the sexes opened the door to the possibilities of change. Millet comments on Engels' contribution:

> If patriarchal marriage and the family, though prehistoric, have their origins in the human past, they cease to be immutable, and become subject to alteration. In treating them as historical institutions, subject to the same processes of evolution as other social phenomena, Engels had laid the sacred open to serious criticism, analysis, even to drastic reorganization (1970, p. 120).

Modern Times While an increasing number of thinkers today agree with Engels, there has not been a complete revolution in thinking about women. We are still strongly influenced by remnants of the Victorian era. Although more women are in universities and the work force than ever before, and although women have more legal privileges than in the past, many men and women continue to believe that women belong in the home. Bettleheim, a prominent psychologist, stated not long ago:

> We must start with the realization that as much as women want to be good scientists or engineers, they want first and foremost to be womanly companions of men and to be mothers (1965, p. 15).

In addition, various studies show that the status of women has declined in modern times. In just the last twenty-five years, women's status relative to men's in terms of earnings, job status, and privileges has deteriorated (Knudsen, 1969).

However, there are signs of change. Arafat and Yorburg (1976) note the emergence of a new woman in their recent study of young, educated, urban American women. She is not fatalistic but rational and secular, not family-centered but individualistic. In a recent review Stewart (1976) also notes that changes are occurring, but primarily in the younger generation of women. Despite these changes, however, she finds that the conceptions of adult-role possibilities for males and females have not altered significantly. Although young women today are more liberated in their beliefs, they are still influenced by the strong emotional undertow left over from a more traditional upbringing. In addition, they are realistic about the difficulties nontraditional women encounter in what is still a traditional society.

How far are we then from English novelist and poet Robert Graves' soliloquy on the real woman, which was first published in 1964? He states:

> Man's biological function is to do; woman's is to be.... A real woman is content to dress with a difference, to make her home unmistakably her own, to illuminate any company she enters, to cook by instinct, not by the cookery book. This is her evidence of being, the proof of which lies in her sense of certitude (in Roszak & Roszak, 1969, pp. 36–37).

Graves refers to the biological functions of men and women. Let us now ask ourselves to what extent recent research supports his claim.

THE BIOLOGICAL ARGUMENT

The biological argument is based on selected research on animals and neonates (newborns) as well as on experiments with hormones (Rosenberg & Sutton-Smith, 1972). It is considerably more subtle, and also less emphatic in its results, than Martin Luther's early statement:

> Men have broad and large chests, and small narrow hips, and are more understanding than women, who have but small and narrow

chests, and broad hips, to the end they should remain at home, sit still, keep house, and bring up the children (in Deaux, 1975, p. 13).

Physical Differences in Humans There are, of course, some physical differences between male and female adults as well as neonates, aside from the obvious differences in the genitals and reproductive systems. Hormonal secretion in the adult male is continuous rather than cyclic as in the female. It consists primarily of *androgens* (male sex hormones) such as the very powerful substance, *testosterone.* Adult females have two sex hormones, *estrogen* and *progesterone,* which vary in their relationship at different times. Moreover, adult males and females differ in shape, size, muscularity, and endurance during physical exertion. There is possibly a difference also in the rate of metabolism (chemical changes within our body cells) between men and women. In addition, females as a rule mature physically faster than males. This trait is characteristic of females in all social groups. It is important to point out, however, that as in all other measures of human characteristics, these physiological differences are differences between *means* (averages), not absolute differences between two groups of people. Even in the distribution of hormones, there is great overlap between men and women. There is a greater difference in hormone distribution within one sex than there is between the sexes.

Other physical differences in males and females have been reported in regard to newborns. Males tend to be larger, to weigh more, and to have more muscular tissues. They are more active and irritable than females. Moreover, newborn boys show a lower sensitivity to the sense of touch, and possibly to other stimuli as well. Again, there is no known cause for such differences, but some investigators hypothesize that they may be caused by a greater amount of testosterone (Bardwick, 1973). Others simply attribute them to the greater vulnerability and lower degree of maturity in the male organism as opposed to the female organism (Oakley, 1972).

There is also evidence that males are susceptible to a higher rate of physical disorders, many of which are degenerative in nature. Montagu (1970) was one of the earliest writers to point out that males are susceptible to sixty-two sex-linked disorders that are carried on the X chromosome. Since males carry (and maleness is determined by) an X and a Y chromosome, disorders carried on their only X chromosome are not counteracted by normal genes which would be carried on a second X chromosome. On the other hand women have two X chromosomes. Therefore they are less likely to have sex-linked disorders because their second X chromosome would counteract genes carried on the first. Unless the one chromosome carrying the genes for the disorders is matched by similar genes in the other chromosome, the disorders do not appear. In addition Money (1973) points out that males are more prone to psychosexual and sex-behavioral diseases. The reason, he states, is not known.

One possible reason for the greater vulnerability of the male has been suggested (Oakley, 1972): Each human fetus is initially female. In some fetuses, male physical development is initiated by a genetically programmed release of androgens between seven and twelve weeks before birth. Theorists such as Oakley and others have hypothesized that this dose of androgens, which is released in male fetuses only, represents a critical period in male development; for unknown reasons it appears to widen the range for error in the developing organism. As Money suggests, this is but one example of "a broadly applicable principle of female precedence" (1973, p. 16). It has been suggested that the greater vulnerability of the male has been compensated for by some mechanism that increases the number of male babies conceived as compared to female babies.

For example, there are 106 male births to every 100 female births. This is an already diminished proportion from that at conception, since early abortions amount to from 120 to 160 males per 100 females in one study, and 122 males per 100 females in another (Money, 1973). In addition, throughout their lives men have a higher mortality rate than females, even though female vulnerability increases during the child-bearing period. Although there are still slightly more males than females during the marrying ages, males and females are in equal proportions by age 50. Thereafter males die off more rapidly (Money, 1973, p. 17).

Research on Animals Still unanswered is the question of what these differences have to do with sex-role behavior. Seeking an answer, some researchers have turned to studies of animals. Goy (1968) demonstrates that within a month after birth male rhesus monkeys like to wrestle, push, bite, tug, and engage in rough-and-tumble play. On the other hand, female monkeys begin to act shy and to turn away from fights. Jensen and Bobbitt (1968) show that male monkeys achieve independence earlier than female monkeys.

In the first few weeks of life these male monkeys also demonstrate higher activity levels and a tendency to engage in biting, hitting, pushing, and shoving. Harlow's (1962) studies of macaque monkeys also show similar results. Young males, for example, are likely to make a threatening gesture if attacked, whereas females tend to withdraw. He also finds that females develop passivity early. They don't initiate play and seem to avoid rough kinds of behavior. Harlow concludes:

> These secondary sex-behavior differences probably exist throughout the primate order, and moreover, they are innately determined biological differences regardless of any cultural overlap. . . . We believe that our data offer convincing evidence that sex behaviors differ in larger part because of genetic factors (1962, p. 5).

His conclusions, however, are not generally accepted by all researchers. Money comments on Harlow's studies:

> It would be going too far on the basis of this kind of evidence, to equate masculinity with aggressiveness and femininity with passivity, as has sometimes been fashionable. . . . Harlow's own studies do show, however, that proper exercise of patterns of energy expenditure in childhood play are essential to the final emergence of adult sexual patterns. . . . Monkeys, male and female, raised in individual cages and deprived of play with their agemates failed to develop normal sexual behavior and were hopelessly unable to master the art of copulation even under the tutelage of a cooperative, experienced mate (1973, p. 24).

In addition, Money points out that almost all of Harlow's female monkeys raised in isolation from their real mothers failed to become pregnant. A few of them that did become pregnant failed to mother their newborn infants properly. Often they treated the infants quite roughly and sometimes crushed them to death. The proverbial "maternal instinct," which supposedly guarantees that a mother is biologically attuned to her children, appears to be only another prop for traditional mythology.

Thus, we see that the evidence on animals is open to differing interpretation. Are early differences in sex-role behavior due to hormones or to very early patterns of interaction between males and females?

Experiments on animals by other researchers seem to indicate the dominance of testosterone, the male hormone, over estrogen, the female hormone. Goy (1968) injected pregnant rhesus monkeys with androgen and found that newborn female infants tended to become either masculinized or hermaphroditic, that is, of indeterminate sex. They displayed typically "masculine" characteristics, such as aggression, roughness, chasing, and mounting. Levine and Mullins (1966) injected 4-day-old female rats with testosterone and found that they failed to develop normal female physical characteristics. Pfeiffer (in Valenstein, 1968) substituted testes for ovaries in young female rats and found that they became masculinized. When he implanted testes, while still allowing the ovaries to remain in place, the rats were again masculinized. Although castrated rats with implanted ovaries became feminized, noncastrated rats to whom ovaries were given developed in a normal masculine fashion. Such studies seem to show that testosterone is more dominant than estrogen. However, these studies, although instructive on the relative weight of the sex hormones, say little about animal behavior, let alone human behavior.

Evidence on Humans The evidence on humans can be interpreted in two ways. Money (1973) conducted research on hermaphrodites, most of whom were males according to their chromosomal makeup but female or indeterminate in their anatomy. His research indicates that the sex of rearing takes precedence over the chromosomal sex—that hermaphrodites brought up to think of themselves as females took on female behavior in spite of their chromosomal makeup. An interesting case involves boy twins. As the result of a surgical accident shortly after birth, the penis of one of the boys was mutilated. After consultations between the physician and the parents, it was decided that the best solution to the problem was a sex reassignment. Through surgery, the genitals were given a feminine appearance. The child has since grown up as a "normal" girl (Money & Ehrhardt, 1972). Hampson states:

> Psychologic sex or gender role appears to be learned—that is to say, it is differentiated through learning during the course of the many experiences of growing up. In place of a theory of innate constitutional psychologic bisexuality we can substitute a concept of psychosexual neutrality in humans at birth. Such neutrality permits the development and perpetuation of many patterns of psychosexual orientation and functioning in accordance with the life experiences each individual may encounter and transact (1965, p. 125).

Money concludes from the same evidence:

One is confronted with the conclusion, perhaps surprising to some, that there is no primary genetic or other innate mechanism to preordain the masculinity or femininity of psychosexual differentiation. ... Psychosexually, also, genetics and innate determinants ordain only that a gender role and identity shall differentiate, without directly dictating whether the direction shall be male or female (1973, pp. 18–19).

At the same time, studies of transsexuals—individuals who psychologically believe themselves to be members of the sex opposite to the one of their chromosomal and anatomical heritage—do not point in the same direction. Transsexuals, unlike hermaphrodites, do not want to belong to the sex in which they have been reared and which accords with the pattern of their chromosomes and sex organs.

How do we explain such unusual sexual developments? Some researchers believe that a fault may occur in the socialization process as the individual is growing up, which they say accounts for the anomaly. However, researchers in this field have not been able to demonstrate this thesis in a majority of cases (Benjamin, 1966). Contrary to Hampson and Money, who look toward the sex of an individual's rearing as basically definitive, Stoller (1964) hypothesizes the intrusion of an unknown "biological force" that determines sexual identity. Bardwick (1973) carries Stoller's biological force further by hypothesizing a second critical stage of masculine development. In the first, well-documented stage, testosterone causes the development of male gonads and genitalia. Bardwick suggests that there may be a second critical stage during which a second dose of testosterone causes the development of a "male" brain, whereas the absence of testosterone during this period causes the absence of a male brain. As a result the individual develops a "female" brain. She suggests that, in this second stage as in the first stage, "masculinization of the central nervous system at the critical stage is more liable to error than feminization" (1973, p. 38).

What can we conclude from these contradictory research studies? It is possible, of course, that Bardwick's thesis is true. However, to state that fetal or neonate brains are masculine or feminine may be stretching a point beyond reasonable justification, if this leads to the assumption that having a "male" brain causes one to be agressive, assertive, and analytic as suggested by "masculine" stereotypes. Such behaviors exist, as we know, on a continuum and are not split into two neat sets—one masculine, the other feminine. It seems unlikely that two differentiated "brains" could produce the wide array of behaviors found among members of both sexes. The question of "male" and "female" brains nevertheless remains a live issue in some sectors of the behavioral sciences.

Thus we see that the biological evidence is inconclusive. Obviously, there are physiological differences between males and females. But these differences are very subtle, and we have seen that in some cases they are overridden by the sex in which an individual is reared. It is difficult to conclude that such differences provide evidence for differential behaviors between the sexes. Most particularly, they do not provide evidence for male dominance and male superiority over females.

After a thorough review of the biological research, Barfield states:

> In summary, while it need not and cannot be argued that the individual human being is a biological *tabula rasa* at birth, the slate of *a priori* assumptions concerning social-biological characteristics should be blank (1976, p. 110).

Or, in more simple terms, we do not have enough evidence to conclude that our biology determines our social characteristics.

THE SOCIOCULTURAL ECHO

Barry, Bacon, and Child Various researchers and theorists in the social and behavioral sciences have come to conclusions that support the basic hypothesis that sex roles are more determined by biology than by culture. The work of Barry, Bacon, and Child (1957), for example, lends tentative support to the biological argument. In examining various societies, these researchers found certain consistencies: Girls are usually trained to be obedient, responsible, and nurturing whereas boys are encouraged to be obedient, achieving, and self-reliant. Yet, they also found certain variations. Societies that place a premium on physical strength tend to make stronger distinctions between the sexes than do those in which physical strength is less highly valued. In addition, the researchers report data from some societies in which men have the main child-care duties because of a shortage of women. Despite these variations these researchers emphasize the consistency they find across different cultures. From this data they conclude that the universality of sex-role behavior and task division implies a biological basis for behavior. Moreover, they argue that it is advisable to condition children into sex roles early, since biological differences occurring after puberty will always cause individuals to act according to their biological sex. Early conditioning will counteract this biological force. These authors further suggest that many of the problems of American women may be due to the fact that they were inadequately prepared during childhood for adulthood as women.

This is a good example of how data can be interpreted in various ways depending upon the value orientation of the theorists. Although the data could be used to show that social patterns are learned because of the variability of behavior across cultures, Barry, Bacon, and Child chose to emphasize the universality of some patterns of social behavior and conclude from this that there are innate biological predispositions underlying this universality. Their conclusions, though not necessarily their data, speak strongly for the biological basis of sex roles.

Mead, Ardrey, and Lorenz Other researchers make the same point. Margaret Mead, in *Male and Female* (1950), reviews various primitive cultures and speaks of "the different gifts of each sex" as well as the "special superiorities" of each. Her argument rests on the fact that women must mother children, and implies that they have "special gifts" to do so. Since women have sole rights to child care, men have absorbed other functions and powers for themselves. If women were to threaten men, the men might become anxious and impotent, which would obviously be unhealthy for a society. It is surprising to note that Mead argues in a diffuse way for the biological origins of sex roles in complete disregard, it would appear, of her earlier work which will be reviewed later in this chapter.

Mead's most recent position is reinforced by other anthropologists who have studied groups of animals and humans. The works of Robert Ardrey (1966a, 1966b), Konrad Lorenz (1966), and others has popularized the notion of the territorial animal (primarily male) and of the bonding and pecking order occurring among males in the primate world.

Lionel Tiger Some researchers find that this view of the animal world is easily translated into terms of human behavior. In addition to viewing hunting and gathering societies as male-dominated and seedbeds for the killer instinct, the anthropologist Lionel Tiger and his colleagues find similar patterns among civilized humans. In *Men in Groups* (1969) Tiger asserts that sex differences are biologically based, since men have a natural bonding instinct that leads them to form groups and thus to create cohesive political organizations. Thus the power within any society is naturally given to men, who have the group training and group support they need to rule. Tiger states: "Women leaders do not inspire 'followership' chiefly because they are women . . . and women cannot become political leaders because males are strongly predisposed to form and maintain all-male groups. . . ." Tiger concludes: "It may be a species-characteristic of *Homo sapiens* that the 'spinal column' of *Homo sapiens'* community must be very predominantly male" (1969, p. 101).

In a more recent book, *Women in the Kibbutz* (1975), Tiger and Shepher chronicle the increasing division of labor by sex over three generations of living on Israeli collective community farms (kibbutzim). They assert that there is no sociological need for such a division to exist. Women are choosing to return to the home, they claim, and this choice is reflective of, and in accord with, what may be the species-specific, mother-child connection. In this work Tiger completes his biological interlocking of the societal system: Just as men have an innate instinct to bond with other men, women reportedly have the same propensity to bond with children. Tiger and Shepher's conclusions are based on the fact that the women are *choosing* to return to service- and child-oriented tasks. But it would be interesting to examine, in psychological terms, whether this is a matter of choice or rather the illusion of choice.

Such a question would probably not occur to other psychologists and sociologists who have helped institutionalize the belief that anatomy is destiny, and that differences between men and women spring from differences in their physiology. Sigmund Freud, Erik Erikson, and Talcott Parsons have been notable in lending legitimacy to this point of view.

Sigmund Freud Sigmund Freud (1856–1939), a Viennese psychoanalyst, has had an immeasurable impact on modern psychological thinking. His impact on both psychological theory and everyday life has been greater than that of any other psychologist. Freud was the first to fully explore and popularize the concept of the unconscious—that inner and largely unknown reservoir of impulses and drives motivating the majority of our behavior. Through this exploration, he systematized various approaches for uncovering unconscious material, such as irregularities in language (the "Freudian slip") and the analysis of dreams. His theories led to a revision of child-rearing practices as he convinced much of the world that the first six years of a child's life were most important in shaping his or her adult personality.

Two strains of thought run throughout Freud's work: The first is the emphasis on biological drives—primarily sexual in nature—as the underlying basis of healthy and unhealthy development; the second is the emphasis on the superiority of the male as opposed to the female. His belief in the superiority of men stems from his reliance on biological interpretations of drives and motivations. This interpretation is summarized in his contention that "anatomy is destiny." He argues that since women are anatomically inferior to men (a woman is an incomplete man), they are psychologically inferior as well. He comments that although a "man of about thirty strikes us as a youthful, somewhat unformed individual whom we expect to make powerful use of the possibilities for development," a woman of the same age

> frightens us by her psychical rigidity and unchangeability.... There are no paths open to further development; it is as though the whole process had already run its course and remains thenceforward insusceptible to influence—as though, indeed, the difficult development to femininity had exhausted the possibilities of the person concerned ... (1933, p. 135).

Freud admits, however, to a basic lack of understanding of the nature of women. In a letter he says: "The great question that has never been answered and which I have not been able to answer, despite my thirty years of research into the feminine soul, is 'what does a woman want?'" (Jones, 1953, p. 421). Moreover, many critics attack Freud for his tendency to universalize into general laws of human nature those neuroses and incapacities he discovered among upper-class Viennese women during the Victorian era. Thus, although Freud's statements have had great weight in aligning sex-role behavior with biology, they are highly suspect, even to many Freudians. One such psychologist comments: "Anatomy may be destiny ... but it must be remembered that these circumstances of anatomy or destiny loom as large or small as the social rules of society make them" (Seidenberg, 1973, p. 149).

Erik Erikson Erikson, a psychoanalyst in the tradition of Freud and one of the most prominent developmental psychologists of the twentieth century, has also done much to maintain the myth that masculinity and femininity are related to the reproductive system. In his famous block-building experiment (1968), he found that when given a set of blocks with which to play, girls tended to build circular structures and boys to build vertical ones. He ascribes such patterns to a rather mystical tendency in humans to reproduce externally their own genital physiology. However, the work of other scholars, such as Maccoby (1966), shows that the tendencies for girls to provide contextual arrangements, and boys more penetrating, aggressive ones, in any area of life (including play with blocks) is easily explained by the strong cultural conditioning process which instills passivity—even on the intellectual level—in women, and assertiveness in men.

Talcott Parsons Parsons, a sociologist associated with the structural-functionalist school, draws back somewhat from direct support of the biological point of view. Yet he reaches conclusions that rest ultimately on biology. Parsons tends to accept society *as it is*. He assumes that conflict will be minimized and happiness maximized if we adjust ourselves to societal norms, which are described as shared beliefs about appropriate or inappropriate patterns of behavior in social groups. His view also assumes that conflict is necessarily negative (Parsons & Bales, 1955).

Parsons has been attacked by critics for implying that *what is* is what ought to be and that men and women are most functional (that is, most in tune with the needs of society as a whole) when they adapt themselves to the institutionalized structures of society. In regard to sex roles, for example, Parsons and Bales (1955) argue that there are two roles that need to be filled within a family, one instrumental—the capacity to do things—and one expressive—the capacity to feel things. For man to adopt the instrumental role and woman the expressive role is most *functional* for the children, the family, and society. Implicit in this position is a further assumption that the husband who chooses to stay home, or the wife who chooses to pursue a career, are by this very fact *dysfunctional*. (By *dysfunctional* is meant a practice that, according to the structural-functionalist school, hinders the achievement of group goals or upsets the equilibrium of the group.)

This point of view has been adopted by a number of psychologists who also argue that both instrumental and expressive functions are valuable, and that men and women have special talents that suit members of each sex for their respective functions. Erikson, who was discussed above, defends this position. Another psychologist, David McClelland (1964), agrees that both men and women have special talents, but he claims that each role is of equal importance.

Whatever one may think of the above theoretical position, there can be no doubt that in the world as it exists today, masculine and feminine roles are *not* equally valued. Therefore we must suspect the position of psychologists, sociologists, and anthropologists who argue that sex roles should not be changed—that the important but undervalued feminine role should be maintained and given a higher value. Two objections can be made to such a position. First, how can the evaluation of women be changed for the better without a change in the feminine role itself after so many years of devaluation? Second, is it likely that men would really *want* to give equal status to women, even if women remain in their traditional role? It appears very unlikely that the feminine role *as it is* will ever be valued to the extent of the masculine role (as it is), and this is what makes this position of "separate but equal" so attractive to many men—and to some women.

THE SOCIOCULTURAL COUNTERARGUMENT

Researchers who argue that biological differences are less important than social and cultural factors in developing sex-role behavior base their argument on several major issues. First, they cite cases of animal behavior that show variations from those cited earlier, and they question further the relevance of animal behavior to human behavior. Second, they cite evidence of cross-cultural variation in sex-role behavior, arguing that such variation means that sex-role differentiation is not biologically determined. Third, they question the "functionalism" of current sex-role expectations, pointing out that for many individuals, and for society as a whole, traditional sex roles are not functional at all but instead cause strain, psychological and physical disease, and generally lowered use of human potential.

Sociocultural proponents argue that biological researchers have overlooked evidence that does not fit their case. Weisstein

(1971), for example, points out that there is a large variety of behaviors in the animal kingdom covering the entire continuum of behavioral patterns. Differing behavioral patterns range from those of the Tamarins, where females are more aggressive and competitive than males, to those of the Titi monkeys, night monkeys, and marmosets, where males are nurturant and "mothering." She also points out that most primate research has studied baboons and rhesus monkeys, which are among the most irritable and aggressive breeds of primates; they are not exemplary of primate behavior, let alone human behavior. Moreover, even Harlow's male monkeys have recently demonstrated their ability to mother infants in the absence of females (Mitchell, Redican, & Gomber, 1974).

Jane Lancaster Jane Lancaster (1973) also argues that researchers have substantiated their male biases by focusing on short-term observation of adult male primates. Long-term observation, including studies of female and nonadult primates, has revealed that most animal groups are not centered around males. She argues instead that *most* primate groups are held together by a matrilocal or mother-centered core that provides the group with stability and continuity. Since in most monkey and ape societies the promiscuity of the mating system makes paternity unknowable, the mother and dependent child form the central core of society. Young males may temporarily attach themselves to the group, but they usually wander off at puberty. Lancaster reports on other studies of troops of rhesus and langur monkeys in India that were observed to be entirely organized around adult females. In one troop, after many months, when a male was allowed to join them, his presence made no impact on the daily routine (p. 34).

Other researchers (Burton, 1972; Mitchell & Brandt, 1972) also report on groups of monkeys in which fathers took over the main care of the young, thus refuting the notion by analogy of an inherent "maternal instinct" in female animals and humans. For example, the father in some species of New World monkeys assumes the total burden of care for an infant. In a group of macaque monkeys studied in Gibraltar, "it is the leader male who is the preeminent influence in socialization of the infant" (p. 173) from its birth through the first weeks of life. Such findings have led to the conclusion, stated by Lancaster (1973) and others, that in such groups of primates and other animals as well, the major division of labor is not male/female but rather child-rearing/nonchild-rearing.

It is the function of caring for a child that limits the extent of other functions, not the sex of the animal doing the caring.

Thus we see that there are at least some exceptions to the evidence cited previously in support of male-organized societies. It may indeed be the case that male-organized societies will be found to be in the minority when the total range of primate behavior has been studied. This new information—together with recent interpretations of gatherer-hunters as "gentle" and egalitarian people—provides a potentially strong attack upon the biological argument that favors inequality of sex roles in humans. In addition, many social and behavioral scientists are skeptical of the relationship between primate and human lives. Can we argue that the complexity of human life has a direct parallel to the relative simplicity of the animal world? Weisstein thinks not and retorts to those who draw such parallels: "It would be reasonable to conclude [from such work] that it is quite useless to teach human infants to speak since it has been tried with chimpanzees and it does not work" (1971, p. 218).

Margaret Mead's Early Work Some theorists find Margaret Mead's earlier work supportive of the sociocultural position, as opposed to the biological. In *Sex and Temperament in Three Primitive Societies,* written in 1935, Mead discusses three cultures of New Guinea and their "sex roles": She describes in detail the Arapesh, among whom both sexes appear to have developed feminine traits; the Mundugamor, among whom both sexes approximate our "masculine" stereotypes; and the Tchambuli, among whom the females are "masculine," and the males "feminine." From these findings Mead concludes:

> Many, if not all, of the personality traits which we have called masculine or feminine are as lightly linked to sex as are the clothing, the manners, and the form of headdress that a society at a given period assigns to either sex ... the evidence is overwhelmingly in favor of the strength of social conditioning (1969, p. 260).

Whiting and Edwards Other researchers agree with Mead's statement that sex roles are a product of social conditioning. Whiting and Edwards (1973) state that the typical division of functions between men and women—arranged so that women, who were the primary caretakers of children, could remain at home—led to the differing socialization for men and women. The fact that women worked near home and men farther away led to varying interaction with children of both sexes and accounts for the differences in sex-role behavior. They conclude that, although there may be a biological base for task assignments, there is none for resulting behaviors.

> All of the behaviors that are characteristic of males and females seem remarkably malleable under the impact of socialization pressures, which seem to be remarkably consistent from one society to another (1973, p. 187).

It is possible, however, to argue that the conduct of the research just described was guided by the presuppositions of the researchers. The research conducted by Barry, Bacon, and Child (see pp. 56–57) was similar to that of Whiting and Edwards. However, both groups reached different conclusions. Whereas Barry, Bacon, and Child conclude that the consistency found in sex-role behavior supports the argument for biologically based sex roles, Whiting and Edwards argue that the variability found among cultures emphasizes social conditioning. As Fee states:

> It may turn out in the end that neither biology nor culture are intrinsically apologies for the oppression of women, but that the unexamined political and cultural assumptions that are hidden in any given theory account for the nature of the conclusions (1976, p. 220).

Jeanne Block Other researchers studying groups of nonprimitive peoples in varying cultures are also discovering variability—and consistency—in sex-role definitions. Jeanne Block (1973), in her study of six industrialized cultures, finds that Americans are more rigidly sex-typed than other cultures, while Swedes and Danes are less so. In her opinion these results are indicative of the fact that it is possible to move away from sex differences reflecting "narrow definitions of sex roles held over from harsher and less civilized times" (p. 72).

Helen Hacker Hacker (1975) reexamines the same data that cause Tiger and Shepher (1975) to conclude that mothers have a biological predisposition to stay with their children and that they "choose" to retain their feminine role. She argues that the initial equality between men and women in the Israeli kibbutzim was only superficial, and that "there was never any wholesale commitment to the concept of role interchangeability" (p. 189). Instead, as she points out, "The emphasis was on changing women's roles without any corresponding change in men's roles" (p. 189). Men, she states, were not expected to participate in feminine service functions but women were encouraged to share in masculine productive functions. Thus sex equality was envisioned as a masculinization of the females' role rather than as a more androgynous alternative.

In addition, some women who had attained positions of authority, which were traditionally held by men, were subtly induced to yield these positions to talented new male immigrants. The women then went back to work in the kibbutz kitchen, says Hacker, encouraged by rationalizations about men's greater physical strength and capacity to bear arms. There was, therefore, no true ideological commitment in the kibbutz to sex-role equality nor any change in the unconscious imagery about the functions of the sexes. Women were encouraged to work alongside men as long as there was a great need for labor. They were no longer encouraged to do so when economic requirements became less stringent. Since the early implementation of sex equality was therefore superficial, the "third generation of the kibbutz sees no point in pretending to an equality that it does not have, that is not very rewarding, while losing the advantages of traditional femininity" (p. 191).

Hacker's argument, it seems to me, reaches a more subtle layer of significance than Tiger's. Sex-role equality, according to her, is not a superficial, easily achieved ideal; it requires the shifting of many unconscious and unstudied premises about the nature of men and women. Easy or quick changes, if successful, often leave scars, and it is not surprising that some women may "choose," as Tiger says, to forfeit the scars and superficial rewards of their new functions for the traditional "delights" of femininity. Again, we may raise the question: Is this really a choice?

One Final Argument There is a final argument against the views that insist on a biological explanation of traditional sex roles. This argument is raised by researchers who claim that our existing sex roles for man—regarded as the provider—and for woman— regarded as the nurturer—are dysfunctional. That is, these roles hinder the development of fully functioning individuals within our society. One would expect that if men and women were fulfilling their natural functions, this would bring harmony and internal peace into their lives. Parsons, McClelland, Erikson, and others who share this view argue that this would be so. However, Rossi (1968), Komarovsky

(1950), and other researchers have conducted extensive studies that seem to show that the traditional roles are indeed dysfunctional for many individuals.

Chesler's (1971) work and a survey conducted by the Department of Health, Education, and Welfare (1970) show that women do not benefit from marriage. Instead, their findings indicate that marriage as an institution creates' ill health in many women. As Bernard states, "We incorporate into our standards of mental health for women the defects necessary for successful adjustment in marriage" (1972, p. 57).

In addition, Jourard (1964) shows that the traditional masculine role for men may lead to more frequent illnesses, a lowered capacity to love, and an earlier rate of death. All these writers use the functionalists' own bases to argue that some changes in masculine and feminine roles in our society would be more functional and beneficial for many individuals. Such changes in our sex roles may indeed lead to a society composed of healthy, fully functioning human beings.

BIOLOGY VERSUS CULTURE: A SUMMATION?

Reviewing the conflicting evidence about the biological or cultural origins and bases of sex roles is a little like listening to a series of eyewitnesses to an accident as they recount opposing views of what they saw and—if pressured—do not hesitate to contradict their own stories. One set of witnesses, viewing the evidence on the biological versus the cultural origin of sex roles, concludes that there is evidence of hormones or "biograms" (Tiger's word) relating to human behavior. The next set of witnesses asserts that all evidence points to the social origins of such behavior. What adds to the confusion is the tendency of the first set of witnesses to do an about-face at any time and begin shouting out their agreement with the other side. Simultaneously, members of the second party may rush to join the first set of witnesses. We can be certain of only one thing: No definitive answer about the origins and bases of sex roles has been provided by any research done up to this time.

We can draw, however, the following tentative conclusions:

1. We are influenced to some extent by our biological heritage, probably as a result of differing amounts of hormones in our

physiological system. However, many hormonal differences are as great for members of a single sex as they are between the sexes.

2. Cultural influences have been known to override what may be biological predispositions toward certain behavior patterns for men and women. Evidence is provided by the examples of some primitive societies and some cases of sex reassignment. Such cases demonstrate that, at least in some instances, the biological predisposition can be completely overridden by the impact of socialization, which is the complex process by which people come to accept their cultural and social patterns.

3. All studies cited provide evidence of the variability of human behavior and its ability to adjust in the face of social and cultural determinants. Therefore, it appears almost irrelevant to draw conclusions about humans from tentative biological findings about the behavior of animals.

4. For many individuals in our society traditional sex roles are dysfunctional, producing strain, disease, and sometimes death. The fulfillment of "what is natural" could hardly bring so much discomfort in its wake. This then suggests that traditional sex roles are neither harmonious nor "natural" for many individuals.

5. It is impossible to sort out definitely all the biological and cultural influences on human behavior unless all people of both sexes were to be raised in the same manner. Since this could scarcely happen—at least not under any foreseeable conditions at this time—the biological versus cultural controversy appears to have reached an impasse.

My overall conclusion from this review accords with that of Chafetz (1974), Duberman (1975), Janeway (1971), Money (1973), Oakley (1972), and Stewart (1976). In view of contrary evidence and of the variability of human behavior as a result of cultural factors, I believe that almost all—if not quite all—human behavior is learned, including masculine and feminine roles. Like a judge deciding among contradictory witnesses, I realize the inescapable subjectivity of this choice. I am reassured, however, by the fact that so many other researchers are coming to the same conclusion.

Rosenberg and Sutton-Smith in a recent review state:

> ... although there are biological differences between the sexes at birth, the overlap in behavior is so extensive and human malleability so great that both sexes are capable of exhibiting most forms of human behavior. At this time there are few behaviors that may be viewed as solely within the province of one sex. The fact that human cultures throughout history have made use of sex differences need not imply that they will continue to do so (1972, p. 88).

If we assume that masculinity and femininity have in large part been created by humankind and are not written into our biological heritage, then the forms we call sex roles may be changed by ourselves and generations to come. If these forms are malleable and changeable and humanmade, there is no biological or natural reason why they have endured over the centuries. What then leads to the tenacity with which men—and women—cling to them as prescriptions by which to lead their lives?

POWER AND MYTHOLOGY

The myths or systems of belief supporting the traditional differences between the sexes are closely allied to perceptions of power. In our discussion of role behavior (pp. 18–19), we learned that roles are the attitudes and patterns of behavior attached to particular statuses. Each status also carries a certain amount of power and prestige. Therefore the person with higher status—in terms of power—has more influence and is more dominant within any given interaction.

Many theorists argue that role distinctions are maintained by those who believe they do *not* have enough intrinsic or personal power; they therefore need the power derived from their superior status. Chafetz (1974), Duberman (1975), Horney (1969), and others believe that all men fear the power of women, a power that originates in infants' images of their mothers. Consequently, men must keep for themselves all other sources of power and defend their high-powered status in order to compensate for this fear. One method of defense has been to acknowledge their superiority over women. This gives men the upper hand, no matter how inadequate or powerless they may find themselves to be in any given situation (Janeway, 1971). It is no wonder that men refuse to acknowledge that their position is neither natural nor divinely ordained. If they

were to concede that their position is just the result of social circumstances, their superior position would become open to question and
vulnerable.

I must state, however, that the belief system of male superiority has been accepted by many women. Although women as a result
must relinquish power, they do gain the security afforded by the
protection of the privileged class—men. Power for men and protection for women are strong incentives for maintaining the myth of
traditional sex roles.

The process by which sex-role differences became rigidly established as social myths is not unique. The same or similar process
occurs in a number of other areas of life. Stevens (1973) provides an
amusing story of a man and a woman marooned on a desert island.
Each at first adopts the tasks closest to hand. For example, the
woman catches the fish, while the man makes the fire. Through
force of habit each continues the tasks. Later, they generalize their
behavior to others by creating stereotypes, which are frozen as a
result of the creation of social institutions. Eventually these institutions are divinely legitimized:

> A philosophy or a theology is born to "justify" why women *must* catch
> fish and men *must* build fires. Say, for example, that the first woman
> was sprung from the goddess of the sea, and the first man from the fire
> god of the mountains. Fish-catching is built into the nature of women
> in the image of the primaeval sea goddess. And fire-building is the
> command issued to men by the father god of the mountains. . . . The
> social institutions of the island are *legitimated*. Men and women not
> only know how to behave. They feel that they *must* behave the way
> they do (pp. 63–64).

And so it is with our beliefs about the nature of men and women,
including the superiority of men over women.

Beliefs that may have begun by observation of behavior have
been rigidly fixed as if in concrete. Thus they shape the lives of
succeeding generations. Many writers on the subject of sex roles find
that the roles of men and women have been shaped largely by the
power differential between the sexes. Men adopt the position of the
powerful, the "One," according to de Beauvoir. As a result they are
certain in their stance and proud in their bearing, insensitive to
underlying innuendos, and prone to confuse their beliefs with absolute truth. Women, on the other hand, are the "Other." They are
more sensitive to the interpersonal undertow, more responsive,

more flexible, and more desirous of pleasing others. If some characteristics of women are worthy of emulation, others are not. Though
women may cultivate patience and endurance, their lack of power
may lead to mediocrity, laziness, frivolity, and contrariness (de
Beauvoir, 1953, p. 562).

In such a power relation, moreover, there is a tendency for the
powerful to choose for themselves the most valued traits, and assign
to the "Other" those which, though least desirable, are still necessary. Traits leading to vulnerability, such as softness, tenderness,
and emotionalism are often valued by men but denied in themselves. Such traits are assigned by men to women. As Slater (1970)
comments, men put their "rejected and denied impulses off on
women." They assign the care of emotions to them and thus maintain an "affective neutrality" by "keeping women's emotional lives
in a 'psychological zoo' where the animal can be appreciated from a
safe distance" (in Millman, 1970).

In view of the fact that the sexes are seen as separate and
distinct, a latent hostility between them seems inevitable. Horney
postulates that it is "contrary to human nature to appreciate without resentment beneficial qualities in another which one does not
possess in himself" (1969, p. 113). This statement requires some
clarification. Horney is not suggesting that all people must be the
same in order that they not resent each other. Instead she is suggesting that undeveloped qualities within a person will respond
antagonistically to those same well-developed qualities in another
person. For example, if men repress the feminine within, they will
harbor a resentment against the feminine outside themselves. If
women fight against the masculine inside themselves, they will
project this fight onto the men they encounter in the outer world.
This principle, as briefly touched on by Horney above, is strongly
developed in the theories of the psychoanalyst Carl Jung (1971) and
specified in relation to masculinity and femininity by the humanist
Abraham Maslow (1971). In short, those traits that we have suppressed or allowed to be undeveloped within ourselves will cause us
to resent those traits in others.

A logical extension of this theoretical position is that qualities
that we have suppressed within ourselves must somehow be made to
seem less valuable and less threatening when they are embodied in
another. In regard to sex-ascribed traits, both men and women tend
to depreciate the characteristics of the other. Men do this with the

qualities they have assigned to women in two ways.* First, they may elevate women and put them on a pedestal where the virtues of their emotional and virtuous nature do not need to be contaminated by worldly work. This effectively removes them from men's sphere. Second, they may devalue them so that their weakness, ineffectiveness, and love of sensual pleasures determine that they will be incompetent in any task men wish to undertake themselves.

Women, too, may bear a latent hostility to men if they perceive them as having traits they themselves cannot possess. Women fear and often are angered by the rational and physical power of men. They assure their own inner and emotional superiority by viewing men as creatures of "fragile egos" or "small boys in men's clothing." Thus they talk away the power difference and assert their emotional and moral superiority over members of the more powerful sex. Such assumptions about the weakness of the other sex further perpetuate the distinctions between men and women. Fear of the other sex in its otherness is thus counteracted by myths of superiority and/or weakness. These myths, in turn, remove the possibility of equality and are assumed to have the weight of unchanging, eternal truth.

Despite these myths, Janeway (1971), de Beauvoir (1953), and others argue that the allotment of masculine and feminine role behaviors is not a universal given of each sex. Instead, it is a social conditioning process that emerges from the need of each sex to maintain its power in relation to the other. Indeed, the current reaction to the women's liberation movement comes from this same source. There is security for both men and women in knowing what they must do with their lives, what sort of tasks are appropriate, what behaviors to expect of themselves and of others. The imposition of sex roles assures a predictability and consistency in our behavior in work and love. In times of change and uncertainty, sex roles offer security by providing familiar interpersonal structures. The traditional forms of power are familiar and grant a certain security. Yet, if the freedom to be fully human is to be gained, this security found in outer forms must be relinquished. The next chap-

---

*The use of the terms "men" here and "women" below does not imply that this is a rule which holds without exception. Rather, it outlines a general tendency in the psychology of human beings. Many men and women have (by fortunate circumstances and/or by choice) transcended the latent hostility which lies between the sexes. It is one of the beliefs of this author that many more can do so by reclaiming the suppressed parts of ourselves so that in our own wholeness we can honor the wholeness of others.

ters will explore the question of how we can find security within ourselves rather than in the structures of masculinity and femininity.

SUMMARY

Historically men have been considered the superior sex. They traditionally have viewed women either as elevated above worldly concerns or as too weak or too incompetent for such matters. Social scientists of every persuasion have argued either in favor of these traditional sex roles or for equality between the sexes. Anthropologists have found troops of monkeys and other primates that demonstrate behavior focused alternately around males or around females. (Apparently the focus depends on who's doing the finding!) In addition, primitive societies have been described as either male-centered or egalitarian. Biologically inclined researchers have demonstrated the effect of chromosomes on animals and occasionally on people. Some conclude that hormones determine sex-role behavior, others conclude that they do not. Sociologists have argued that society as it is now requires men and women to fill sex-appropriate roles. They have also demonstrated that many of these roles are dysfunctional both for individuals and for a postindustrial society. Finally, anthropologists, sociologists, and psychologists have all demonstrated the variability of human behavior and its adaptability under the impact of cultural conditioning.

The latter findings appear to numerous observers, including myself, to be very hard to dispute. Human behavior, in most cases, adapts to its circumstances. The variety found in human behavior is a response to the variety of human circumstances. Such variety and adaptability leads to the conclusion that resulting behavior patterns are, to a large degree, the result of interaction between the individual organism and its environment. Such adaptability and variety does not support the idea that masculine and feminine roles are predetermined solely, or in large part, by our biological heritage.

Masculinity and femininity are structures that have for centuries guided the lives of men and women and shaped the decisions which they made. Yet, these structures have been shaped by people, and can be changed by people. We are in the process of such a change today, a time when more individuals are taking the risk of being more fully human, exploring more of their potentials, and choosing a more androgynous life-course. Such individual changes will have an impact on the forms by which many live, and though the forms change more slowly, they too are beginning to change. We may someday have a society in which human potential is indeed *human* potential without respect to male or female gender.

EXERCISE: YOUR INNER SELF AND THE "OPPOSITE SEX"

Make a list of all the qualities you associate with the sex other than your own. Make as long a list as you can, even if you think some of the qualities are trivial. Include both the qualities you view negatively and those you view positively.

Now put a plus before the qualities you evaluate positively, and a minus before those you evaluate negatively.

Focus on the negative qualities. Why do you see them as negative? Are you afraid that people with these qualities might in some way hurt you? Reject you? Trap you into doing something you don't want to do? What qualities in you allow you to be hurt or trapped? What can you do about it? Are you afraid of finding any of these qualities in yourself?

Discuss your findings with other members of the class. How were your results similar? In what ways did they differ?

Now focus on the positive qualities you listed. How many of these qualities do you see in yourself? Look now at the ones you don't have, even though you see them as positive. Sit back, close your eyes, and imagine that you possess these qualities. How would your life be different? Would you behave differently? Feel differently? Take a moment to consider this.

Now think about what you can do to bring these qualities into being in yourself. Once again, see how your results compare with those of others in your class. How would their lives differ from yours? How would they bring these qualities into being in themselves?

REFERENCES

Arafat, I., and Yorburg, B., *The New Women: Attitudes, Behavior, and Self-Image,* Columbus, Ohio: Charles E. Merrill, 1976.

Ardrey, R., *African Genesis,* New York: Atheneum, 1966a.

Ardrey, R., *The Territorial Imperative*, New York: Atheneum, 1966b.

Bagehot, W., "Biology and Women's Rights," *Popular Science Monthly*, vol. 14 (1879): 207.

Bardwick, J., "Infant Sex Differences," in C. Stoll, ed., *Sexism: Scientific Debates*, Reading, Mass.: Addison-Wesley, 1973.

Barfield, A., "Biological Influences on Sex Differences in Behavior," in M. Teitelbaum, ed., *Sex Differences*, New York: Anchor, 1976.

Barry, H., III, Bacon, M. K., and Child, I. L., "A Cross-Cultural Survey of Some Sex Differences in Socialization," *Journal of Abnormal and Social Psychology*, vol. 55 (1957): 327–32.

Benjamin, H., ed., *The Transsexual Phenomenon*, New York: Julian Press, 1966.

Bernard, J., *The Future of Marriage*, New York: Macmillan, 1972.

Bernard, J., "Sex Differences: An Overview," in A. Kaplan and J. Bean, eds., *Beyond Sex-Role Stereotypes: Readings Toward a Psychology of Androgyny*, Boston: Little, Brown, 1976.

Bettleheim, B., "The Commitment Required of a Woman Entering a Scientific Profession in Present-Day American Society," in *Women and the Scientific Professions*, an MIT Symposium of American Women in Science and Engineering, Cambridge, Mass.: MIT Press, 1965.

Block, J. H., "Conception of Sex Role: Some Cross-Cultural and Longitudinal Perspectives," *American Psychologist*, vol. 28 (1973): 512–26.

Boserup, E., *Woman's Role in Economic Development*, London: George Allen & Unsin, 1970.

Bullough, V., *The Subordinate Sex: A History of Attitudes Toward Women*, New York: Penguin, 1974.

Burton, F., "The Integration of Biology and Behavior in the Socialization of *Macaca Sylvana* of Gibraltar,"in F. E. Poirier, ed., *Primate Socialization*, New York: Random House, 1972.

Chafetz, J. S., *Masculine/Feminine or Human?: An Overview of the Sociology of Sex Roles*, Itasca, Ill.: F. E. Peacock, 1974.

Chesler, P., "Patient and Patriarch: Women and the Psychotherapeutic Relationship," in V. Gornick and B. Moran, eds., *Woman in Sexist Society: Studies in Power and Powerlessness*, New York: Signet, 1971.

Deaux, K., *The Behavior of Men and Women*, Monterey, Calif.: Brooks/Cole, 1975.

de Beauvoir, S., *The Second Sex,* New York: Alfred A. Knopf, 1953.

Duberman, L., *Gender and Sex in Society,* New York: Praeger, 1975.

Engels, F., *The Origins of the Family, Private Property and the State* (1884), New York: Charles Kerr, 1902.

Erikson, E., *Youth: Identity and Crisis,* New York: W. W. Norton, 1968.

Fee, E., "Science and the Woman Problem: Historical Perspectives," in M. Teitelbaum, ed., *Sex Differences,* New York: Anchor, 1976.

Fernseed, F., "Sexual Distinctions and Resemblances," *Quarterly Journal of Science,* vol. 3 (1881): 741.

Freud, S., "Femininity," in *New Introductory Lectures of Psychoanalysis* (1933), New York: W. W. Norton, 1964.

Gough, K., "The Origin of the Family," in J. Freeman, ed., *Women: A Feminist Perspective,* Palo Alto, Calif.: Mayfield, 1975.

Goy, R. W., "Organizing Effects of Androgen on the Behavior of Rhesus Monkeys," in R. P. Michael, ed., *Endocrinology and Human Behavior,* New York: Oxford University Press, 1968.

Graves, R., "Real Women," in B. Roszak and T. Roszak, eds., *Masculine/ Feminine: Readings in Sexual Mythology and the Liberation of Women,* New York: Harper & Row, 1969.

Hacker, H., "Class and Race Differences in Gender Roles," and "Gender Roles from a Cross-Cultural Perspective," in L. Duberman, *Gender and Sex in Society,* New York: Praeger, 1975.

Hampson, J. L., "Determinants of Psychosexual Orientation," in F. A. Beach, ed., *Sex and Behavior,* New York: John Wiley & Sons, 1965.

Harlow, H., "The Heterosexual Affectional Response System in Monkeys," *American Psychologist,* vol. 17 (1962): 1–9.

Hays, H. R., *The Dangerous Sex,* New York: Pocket Books, 1972.

Health, Education and Welfare (Department of), "Selected Symptoms of Psychological Distress," Public Health Services, Health Services, and Mental Health Administration, 1970.

Hiller, E. T., *Social Relations and Structures,* New York: Harper & Row, 1947.

Hochschild, A. R., "A Review of Sex Role Research," *American Journal of Sociology,* vol. 78 (1973): 1011–29.

Horney, K., "Distrust Between the Sexes," in B. Roszak and T. Roszak, eds.,

Masculine/Feminine: Readings in Sexual Mythology and the Liberation of Women, New York: Harper & Row, 1969.

Janeway, E., *Man's World, Woman's Place,* New York: William Morrow, 1971.

Jensen, G. D., and Bobbitt, R. S., "Monkeying with the Mother Myth," *Psychology Today,* vol. 1 (June 1968): 41.

Jones, E., *The Life and Work of Sigmund Freud,* vol. 2, New York: Basic Books, 1953.

Jourard, S., *The Transparent Self,* New York: Van Nostrand Reinhold, 1964.

Jung, C. J., *The Portable Jung,* ed. by J. Campbell, New York: Viking, 1971.

Knudsen, D., "The Declining Status of Women: Popular Myths and the Failure of Functionalist Thought," *Social Forces,* vol. 48 (1969): 183–92.

Komarovsky, M., "Functional Analysis of Sex Roles," *American Sociological Review,* vol. 15 (1950): 508–16.

Lancaster, J. G., "In Praise of the Achieving Female Monkey," *Psychology Today,* vol. 7 (September 1973): 30–39.

Laughlin, W. S., "Hunting: An Integrating Biobehavior System and Its Evolutionary Importance, in R. B. Lee and I. de Vore, eds., *Man the Hunter,* Chicago: Aldine, 1968.

Leacock, E., "Introduction," to Frederick Engles, *The Origin of the Family,* Chicago: International Publishers, 1972.

Lee, R. B., "The !Kung Bushmen of Botswana," in M. G. Bicchieri, ed., *Hunters and Gatherers Today,* New York: Holt, Rinehart & Winston, 1972.

Levine, S. N., and Mullins, R. F., Jr., "Hormonal Influences on Brain Organization in Infant Rats," *Science,* vol. 152 (1966): 1585–92.

Lorenz, K., *On Aggression,* New York: Harcourt Brace Jovanovich, 1966.

Maccoby, E. E., "Sex Differences in Intellectual Functioning," in E. E. Maccoby, ed., *The Development of Sex Differences,* Stanford, Calif.: Stanford University Press, 1966.

Maslow, A. H., *The Farther Reaches of Human Nature,* New York: Viking, 1971.

McClelland, D., "Wanted: A New Self-Image for Women," in R. Lifton, ed., *The Woman in America,* Boston: Beacon Press, 1964.

Mead, M., *Male and Female,* New York: William Morrow, 1950.

Mead, M., *Sex and Temperament in Three Primitive Societies* (1935), New York: Dell, 1969.

Mill, J. S., *The Subjection of Women* (1869), New York: Oxford University Press, 1966.

Millett, K., *Sexual Politics,* New York: Avon Books, 1970.

Millman, M., "Some Remarks on Sex-Role Research," paper delivered at the meeting of the American Sociological Association, Washington, D.C., August 31–September 3, 1970.

Mitchell, G., and Brandt, E., "Paternal Behavior in Primates," in F. E. Poirier, ed., *Primate Socialization,* New York: Random House, 1972.

Mitchell, G., Redican, W. K., and Gomber, J., "Males Can Raise Babies," *Psychology Today,* vol. 7 (April 1974): 63.

Money, J., "Developmental Differentiation on Femininity and Masculinity Compared," in C. Stoll, ed., *Sexism: Scientific Debates,* Reading, Mass.: Addison-Wesley, 1973.

Money, J., and Ehrhardt, A. A., *Man and Woman, Boy and Girl,* Baltimore: The Johns Hopkins University Press, 1972.

Montagu, A., *The Natural Superiority of Women,* New York: Collier, 1970.

Oakley, A., *Sex, Gender and Society,* London: Maurice Temple Smith, 1972.

Parsons, T., and Bales, R. R., *Family, Socialization and Interaction Process,* Glencoe, Ill.: Free Press, 1955.

Pfeiffer cited in E. S. Valenstein, "Steroid Hormones and the Neuropsychology of Development," in R. L. Isaacson, ed., *The Neuropsychology of Development: A Symposium,* New York: John Wiley & Sons, 1968.

Rosenberg, C. G., and Sutton-Smith, B., *Sex and Identity,* New York: Holt, Rinehart & Winston, 1972.

Rossi, A., "Transition to Parenthood," *Journal of Marriage and the Family,* vol. 30 (1968): 26–39.

Sayers, D., "The Human-Not-Quite-Human," in B. Roszak and T. Roszak, eds., *Masculine/Feminine: Readings in Sexual Mythology and the Liberation of Women,* New York: Harper & Row, 1969.

Seidenberg, R., *Marriage Between Equals,* New York: Anchor Press/Doubleday, 1973.

Smith, P., *Daughters of the Promised Land,* Boston: Little, Brown, 1970.

Stevens, E., *Oriental Mysticism,* New York: Paulist Press, 1973.

Stewart, V., "Social Influences on Sex Differences in Behavior," in M. S. Teitelbaum, ed., *Sex Differences,* New York: Anchor, 1976.

Stoller, R. J., "A Contribution to the Study of Gender Identity," *International Journal of Psychoanalysis,* vol. 45 (1964): 220–26.

Tiger, L., *Men in Groups,* New York: Random House, 1969.

Tiger, L., and Fox, R., *The Imperial Animal,* New York: Holt, Rinehart & Winston, 1971.

Tiger, L., and Shepher, J., *Women in the Kibbutz,* New York: Harcourt Brace Jovanovich, 1975.

Turnbull, C., *The Forest People,* New York: Clarion Books, 1968.

Washburn, S. L., and Lancaster, C. S., "The Evolution of Hunting," in R. B. Lee and I. de Vore, eds., *Man the Hunter,* Chicago: Aldine, 1968.

Watson, B., *Women's Studies: The Social Realities,* New York: Harper & Row, 1976.

Weisstein, N.,"Psychology Constructs the Female," in V. Gornick and B. Moran, eds., *Woman in Sexist Society: Studies in Power and Powerlessness,* New York: Signet, 1971.

Whiting, B., and Edwards, C. P., "A Cross-Cultural Analysis of Sex Differences in Behavior of Children Aged Three through Eleven," *The Journal of Social Psychology,* vol. 91 (1973): 171–88.

II

ANDROGYNY AND SEX ROLES: THE VISION

At every moment you choose yourself. But do you choose yourself? Body and soul contain a thousand possibilities out of which you can build many I's. But in only one of them is there a congruence of the elector and the elected. Only one—which you will never find until you have excluded all those superficial and fleeting possibilities of being and doing with which you toy out of curiosity or wonder or greed, and which hinder you from casting anchor in the experience of the mystery of life, and the consciousness of the talent entrusted to you which is your I.

Dag Hammarskjold, **Markings**

---

*if i listen
very closely to me*

*i can hear
that i am
afraid to listen*

*yet each time
i override that fear
i make a new friend
of my being.*

Connie, a student

3

The Vision of Androgyny: The Individual in Process

Against the backdrop of the socially created forms of masculinity and femininity, all of us play out our lives. If the forms indeed determine our behavior, have we no choice in guiding our own destinies? Must we succumb to that which is already predetermined? Numerous social scientists answer with a resounding "No!" Evidence in support of this answer comes from many spheres. On the pages of history we find the names of individuals—for example, Abraham Lincoln, Albert Schweitzer, and Eleanor Roosevelt—who have transcended the cultural forms and shaped their own destiny. Similarly, in the world of the arts we find individuals such as Leonardo da Vinci, William Blake, and Charlotte Brontë who also have drawn on their own inner experiences to create the shape of their own world.

Let me cite other examples to further show that it is possible for human beings to transcend the forms imposed by the external

They tell me, "If you find a slave asleep, don't wake him up; he may be dreaming of freedom." And I reply, "If you find a slave asleep, wake him and talk to him about freedom."

Kahlil Gibran, **Spiritual Sayings of Kahlil Gibran**

No one is a greater slave than he who imagines himself free when he is not free.

Johann Wolfgang von Goethe, in R. Seidenberg, **Marriage Between Equals**

---

society. In psychological studies of college students a sizable percentage score well above the norm on tests of ethical development (Kohlberg & Kramer, 1969). In studies on conformity, there is a small but significant number of college students who remain autonomous in experimental situations designed to induce conformity (Crutchfield, 1955). In fact, in almost any experimental situation, nearly one third of the tested population does not meet the expected norm. Half of this "deviant" population tends to fall below the norm, and half above. If we focus on the latter group—those above the norm—we still find a sizable population whose behavior is not entirely explainable in terms of their cultural environment or their biological heritage. I believe that these individuals demonstrate the capacity we all (or almost all of us) have to increase our choices and base our decisions on the process of our inner experience rather than succumbing to the strictures of socially created forms.

Those of us who wish to widen our options and utilize our freedom must not confuse form and process. If we do, we find that we are not in touch with reality, but rather with what we think is reality. This is a fragile world that crumbles when confronted with contrary inner impulses and visible outer circumstances. It is a world—a form—that proves insubstantial when we have to deal with the realities of life and its problems.

The confusion of form and process is one that develops in most children while they are growing up. For example, in some families when children feel angry, parents respond, "You are just tired," and children learn that they are tired and not angry. In so doing, they learn to distrust their inner experience. Or, other children may experience sadness and genuine grief at the loss of a beloved toy or pet animal. The parents, who are afraid of their children's hurt, may cuddle and hold them until they giggle and laugh. The result is that many adults smile when they are sad and feel tired when they are angry, with no clear recognition of their inner process. They have adopted the outer form—the smile and the fatigue—as a substitute for their own feelings. Erich Fromm, a prominent psychologist, states that Americans learn to be "happy" regardless of what they feel inside: "Friendliness, cheerfulness, and everything that a smile is supposed to express, becomes automatic responses which one turns on and off like an electric switch" (1971, pp. 268–269).

In adolescence and adulthood, however, many individuals choose to shake off the impact of social forms that have taught them not to recognize their own feelings. Joanna Fields, a pseudonym for a British psychologist, notes such a moment in the diary she was keeping in her mid-twenties. She recognizes here an inner self that has previously been hidden or ignored:

> It seemed to me that perhaps my previous ignorance of the ways of this self might be sufficient reason why I had felt my life to be of a dull dead-level mediocrity, with the sense of real and vital things going on round the corner, out in the streets, in other people's lives. For I had taken the surface ripples for all there was, when actually happenings of vital importance to me had been going on, not somewhere away from me, but just underneath the calm surface of my own mind. . . .
>
> I began to have an idea of my life, *not as the shaping of achievement to fit my preconceived purposes, but as the gradual discovery and growth of a purpose which I do not know* (1975, p. 357).

Here, Joanna Fields has described precisely our definition of living *in process* as opposed to living with the forms created by preconceived purposes or social injunctions.

The confusion of form and process occurs frequently in regard to masculinity and femininity. Very often we assume that "what is appropriate for a woman (or man)" is necessarily "what I feel is appropriate for me." Most women, for example, want to get married and have children. This desire overrides a desire for productive work outside the home. But do they really want to get married, or do they just think they do because that is what they have been taught? Similarly, do men really want to work all the days of their lives or do they believe they do because that is what they have learned?

As we come to question ourselves and the traditional sex-role expectations, we may indeed find that the traditional roles of masculinity and femininity are insufficient for our purposes. For example, men may find that they need to express emotions, or women may be required to take assertive action in order to provide for their home and family. At such times we may feel trapped by the ideological "shoulds" and "should nots" connected with the traditional roles of masculinity and femininity. We then may seek a new framework, more in accord with the particular demands and desires of our life.

PROCESS ORIENTATION AND ANDROGYNY

For those who experience dissatisfaction in fitting themselves to the norms of masculinity and femininity, the vision of the process-oriented, androgynous life has great appeal. Let me refer you back to our previous discussion about the androgynous alternative (pp. 29–36). Please keep in mind that androgynous individuals are neither exclusively feminine nor masculine in behavior. They are free to choose unstereotyped solutions to problems that arise in life. Such unstereotyped behavior is a process-oriented solution rather than a role-oriented solution, which is limited by the traditional view of sex roles.

If we accept the concepts of androgyny and the process-oriented solution on an intellectual level, we shall certainly perceive the benefits of freedom and the removal of restrictions. However, as we grow in awareness we also tend to realize the emotional security found in the familiar reality of learned patterns of behavior—in the familiar roles of masculinity and femininity. At this point considerable conflict may arise between our desire to hold on to familiar forms and our desire to experiment with the new forms which may be more suited to our inner process.

Yet we must separate ourselves from the past and move toward the unknown in order to grow. Helen Lynd (1972), a social philosopher, illustrates this point with a reference to the story of *Doctor Zhivago,* who moved between his home village and the city as he came "to spin at last out of his own renewed substance, filaments binding him to life" (p. 169). "The true prophet," she states, "is he who goes into the unexplored wilderness and who returns to be a leader and life-giver to his people" (p. 169).

As in all separations, however, there is conflict and grief. We experience loss at letting go of our pasts. Most of us, struggling at this level of awareness, do not let go easily but rather feel pulled between two opposing alternatives: We can stay where-we-are or we can move toward the vision of where-we-can-be. In the grip of such conflict there is a tendency for most of us to view the alternatives in absolute terms, and to see what-is and what-might-be as two irreconcilable conditions. From this newly created dichotomy we create a measure of familiar certainty in our world. We can then retreat to the past or fling ourselves at the future; we believe we cannot reconcile the new and the old. In fact, this is not so; but in the anxiety produced by conflict we often make our choices seem so clear-cut. Though we may rebel at the limitations of such a black-and-white view, we feel security once again in knowing that there is a black-and-white view, that the world has regained some recognizable form. Even when the choices appear less than satisfactory, we find security in having, or seeming to have, once again, only two alternatives.

Nevertheless, some individuals forsake this security and arrive at the realization that a process-oriented approach to living meets their needs better without providing alternatives that seem cast in stone. The reality and the vision are not static and separate but changing and interwoven through the ongoing present. These individuals come to accept themselves as they are, in both their limitations and their freedom, allowing themselves to grow and in time to transcend the dichotomies of masculinity and femininity.

The concept of androgyny has been criticized by some (Secor, 1974) as a static concept, a visionary state, that does not encompass or acknowledge the difficulties of historical process. This is not true in regard to the process-oriented concept of androgyny. It is *not* a distant destination but a *process* evidenced by a willingness to be most completely wherever it is that we are right now. In this process we let go to our existence. "Letting go" does not mean that we *change* nor that we *give up* the struggle but that we allow ourselves to *be* most fully exactly what we are. We allow ourselves to do whatever seems appropriate at the moment. Thus, we must sometimes let go of antiquated forms and create new ones that arise out of the flow of our own experience. I am reminded of a quotation from T. S. Eliot's poem "Little Gidding":

> We shall not cease from exploration
> And the end of all our exploring
> Will be to arrive where we started
> And know the place for the first time.

When we are most fully *where we are,* we move toward a process orientation that I believe must be an androgynous orientation as well. I shall support this point through the discussions in this chapter. I will also explore the characteristics of process orientation as seen by many humanistic psychologists and the relationship between process-oriented living and androgyny.

CHARACTERISTICS OF PROCESS-ORIENTED INDIVIDUALS

There is a certain difficulty in describing the characteristics of the process-oriented individual. The term "characteristics" seems to have a static quality about it. Therefore, in using that term we tend to create a new static form rather than treating the individual as being in process. Part of this difficulty lies in the fact that, as process runs through our language, it almost always appears static. Also, these characteristics do describe a *static form*. But this form is seen commonly in individuals who are living in process in the present. With this in mind we will now describe process-oriented individuals.

Process-oriented individuals are less bound by roles, in general, than other people. They are less bound by their personal and cultural past. Less energy is tied up in maintaining the self that has been or in constructing the self that might be. Such individuals live more completely, honestly, and authentically in the present.

In order to do so, they must be able to risk losing outer security and find their security within. If they cannot rely on external structures, shaped by the past, nor give the illusion of certainty to an uncertain future, they must be able to rely on the inner strength that allows them to stand alone. Abraham Maslow, a leading humanistic psychologist, refers to this inner strength as "secure high dominance" (1971, p. 164), whereas Erich Fromm, another humanistic psychologist, calls it the "power-to-be" (1971, p. 184).

Such inner power leads to a feeling of unity with the world rather than antagonism toward it. In touch with their own humanity, process-oriented individuals recognize the humanity of others, and know that we are all related in the world in which we live. Moreover, they realize that we are related also to our environment, and as the ecologists are currently warning, destruction of that environment leads ultimately to self-destruction. Such a feeling of relationship is quite different from the more common feeling of antagonism in which we feel as if we are "one, alone, against the world." This antagonistic feeling comes psychologically from the insecurity bred from lack of strength. If we are strong and sure of our strength, we need not defend ourselves against the world, but can join with it in a sense of identification, trust, and responsibility. If we know ourselves, in our full humanity we touch also the humanity common to all. Consequently, in our treatment of others there is compassion, understanding, and empathy. There exists among people who feel related to others a common ground upon which we may acknowledge our humanness.

The sense of unity with others allows process-oriented individuals to join with one another while retaining their individuality. They do not need to exercise control and domination over others, for they exercise their power in the expansion of their own potential. They can stand alone or can stand with others. They have the strength to be themselves and consequently can accept others as they are. They move easily between the mountain and the city, solitude and solidarity.

Moreover, process-oriented individuals can run the risks of expanded awareness. They are willing to look honestly at themselves and their world. They allow incoming information to be fully heard even if they must revise their preconceptions. In addition, they are more aware of their inner feelings and they allow themselves to experience these feelings. Moving beyond increased awareness, process-oriented individuals are willing to share themselves with others, to communicate openly their inner and outer experience in an ongoing dialogue with the world. Such self-disclosure requires strength, but it is risky only if we are overly dependent on the approval of others. If we are strong enough to live with or without outside approval, we can afford to be transparent.

Finally, process-oriented individuals can risk themselves in other arenas. They are less afraid of failure and can therefore choose to participate more fully, to be more concerned, to be more committed and involved in all activities and relationships.

In summary, process-oriented individuals, resting on the basis of their inner security, are open, direct, committed, involved, fully willing to engage themselves with life, to risk and not be overcome. They respond authentically and spontaneously to their environment. They have met the requirement of moving beyond the confines of our society and culture and, in the process, have come in contact with the reality they have been searching for.

Let us now consider some case histories that illustrate concretely the points I've been discussing so far in this chapter.

ANGELA

Angela is an intelligent and attractive 20-year-old woman who has recently reached a moment in time in which the masculine and feminine dichotomies, so clearly outlined in her background, have come together for her into a synthesis that is wholly her own. As the eldest of five girls, she was led into "masculine" pursuits by a father who would rather have had boys. By the age of 13 she could play a good game of football and basketball and fix almost any mechanical breakdown. Although she enjoyed sports and mechanics, as she grew into adolescence, she found that these inclinations conflicted with her own desires (shaped by social norms) to be "feminine." A period of being feminine followed, in which she dressed and behaved in suitable boy-chasing adolescent ways. This new departure brought mixed reactions of disappointment and pride from her father. At this time in her life she saw the "masculine" and "feminine" ways as being completely opposed and she chose the latter.

This self-imposed and socially reinforced dichotomy that Angela experienced was further reinforced by her feelings of ambivalence toward her mother, who presented a similar set of dichotomies. Angela's mother was a construction engineer who supervised large groups of men in the building of apartment complexes. She was assertive, competent, and direct in the accomplishment of her work, a traditionally "masculine" pursuit. When she returned home in the evening, however, she became meek and subservient, catering to Angela's father, and adopting the traditional feminine role. In Angela's mother, the dichotomies of masculine and feminine were stark and clear-cut rather than integrated. It was apparent also that the "feminine" side of Angela's mother was the "socially approved" side but the less fulfilling and less satisfactory.

The difficulties experienced by Angela's mother as a woman professional are seen in Angela's own personal struggle. She had no model of how to be strong and competent and yet, at the same time, feminine. She oscillated between her own masculine and feminine sides, seeing them as mutually exclusive. One side of herself found fulfillment in competing well on a women's basketball team. The other side of herself took over when she worked as a cocktail waitress in the evening. Again, there was little meeting of the two halves.

In the year or two preceding the following self-description, however, Angela's moment of insight suddenly occurred. She realized that it was possible, indeed, to be both masculine and feminine. Exposed to the university world, developing new academic talents in herself, she struggled to transcend her own dichotomy of masculine and feminine and created a new integration for herself. The following is Angela's account of where she is presently.

I am me. I am a woman. I am feminine, I am masculine. I am emotional, I am logical. I am domineering, I am submissive. I am me.

I imagine everyone who plunges into the depths of the self is struck by the complexity of feelings and emotions and how they are entwined with our actions. And I imagine I am not alone when I wonder if there is ever a point reached when we can fully understand ourselves; when our whole being is expressed in every movement, every decision. That is what I am striving for: the understanding needed to "know myself" and the courage to admit it.

Where am I now? How many steps have I taken on this uphill journey? I don't know for the steps seem to be getting shorter and the hill is turning into a mountain. But, here I am, plodding along, feeling immense pleasure every time I look back over the distance I've already traveled.

I feel that the first and hardest step I had to make was to be perfectly secure in my femininity. That would give me the assurance I needed to display the other facets of my personality—to act on my feelings, to act without the fear that other people would not accept those actions. For once I accepted myself others need not accept me. I was no longer vulnerable to them.

An excerpt follows from my diary—two years ago—referring to my job, and how I must always look and act happy in front of the customers:

"I'm caught in a role, and I can't get out. I'm trapped into being charming and pleasant, while the more serious side of me—the major side of me—is locked away.

"But isn't it safer that way? Now, all of my dreams and goals are protected. Those fragile parts of me cannot be broken—because I don't trust anyone enough to let them get too near. If something slips out, what do I do? Laugh—make it casual. Then, if anyone else laughs, they're laughing at the joke, not the dream. And I'm protected forever from the person because the joke serves as a wall—a wall others can never get through. All laughter must stop there. . . .

"I know now that my private thoughts are really me. My dreams and goals and ambitions are what I'll eventually become, but the dreaming of them is what I am.

"I'd sooner put my life in other people's hands than entrust my hopes to them. Is that selfish? I sometimes think I'm untrusting—maybe I am. But I have to be certain the me of the future is safe. I can't risk my life so callously. If it shuts other people out, I'm sorry. But it's that important to me—it's my life."

Almost two years ago. How much I've changed in those two years. Was that closed, scared person really me? It must be for I can remember my feelings of insecurity. How much better I feel now that I've thrown away those stifling chains. . . . My God, is that what "liberated" means—no longer vulnerable to those fears?

Yes, I can look back now and say I've grown. I can look at the path I trod—blurry at times, but nonetheless there. And I can look at the future, one of hope. . . . Trust is a requirement for happiness—trust in others and most importantly, in yourself: the knowledge that you really can do anything you set your mind to. And the realization that you are not alone—that there are people to help you, people you can help.

I'd always thought that liberation meant throwing away your femininity and assuming a masculine role. But it doesn't *mean that at all. It means throwing away all false roles—being yourself, however many of those selves there may be. And it means to choose how you want to spend your life—not to follow gropingly in someone else's footsteps.*

IMPLICATIONS

Angela has incorporated many of the process-oriented characteristics into her own life. She is willing to increase her awareness, to be open with others, and to tolerate the uncertainty of not knowing exactly where she is going. Angela recognizes that growth is an ongoing process, and the important point is not where we are along the road but that we are on the road and willing to make the journey. The qualities that she has brought together in her own story are those commonly called "masculine" and "feminine," and it is with a definite sense of euphoria that she realizes that she can be both.

The excitement that Angela experiences is typical of the heightened energy achieved by an individual when old obstacles are overcome. Yet this is not a "final solution" but one step along the way. Life is a journey, and the gains we make along the way often have to be made again. Someone once said that each accomplishment is only the beginning of a new obstacle. This is hard to accept in the moment of accomplishment, but those who are open to themselves are usually willing to continue the fight when the next roadblock comes into view. Angela will no doubt realize this in time, and most likely make new commitments to her journey.

OTHER PERSONAL ACCOUNTS

At some point in their lives other people also have experienced the joy that comes with the release from old inhibitions and restraints. Such joy crosses both sex and age lines, for process orientation and the experience of freedom have little to do with either. (However, many psychologists believe that the heights of attainment in personal growth are reached only in the later years of life [Erikson, 1950; Maslow, 1970].) Each individual experiences this new-found freedom differently. For Angela, it means becoming more fully herself in the company of others. Other people become more fully in touch with their emotions and experience more control over their own choices. Indeed even the realization of how very little they know of themselves indicates that their own journey toward process orientation has begun.

Ellen, a woman of 20, realizes that she is at the beginning of her journey:

I cannot lie to myself and say that I am aware or in touch with myself; I know that I am not. But this understanding is the first step in actually becoming aware of other people and their feelings and thoughts, as well as becoming aware of myself.

Mary Beth, divorced in her 30s, realizes a new acceptance of self:

I am a female person. I am unique and yet similar to other people. Like everyone else, I am a product of my socialization, and yet, as an adult, I can control my life. I am responsible for my own decisions. Life sometimes is confusing, but I am finally deciding what I want out of it. Sometimes the process is disappointing. It is hard to find out things about yourself which you don't like. I change what I can and accept myself too.

Antonio, a 22-year-old man, echoes Mary Beth's sentiments:

I decided that to be a strong man is nothing more than being a strong human being. To be strong is to be in touch with myself and to learn how to deal with the environment in an authentic way. To be strong is to be able to forgive the past and to challenge the future. To be strong is to accept my ignorance and do something about it.

Finally, Jane, now 56, comments on her experience of self:

I now feel free to experience a complete range of emotions, for emotions are neither male or female. They are human and I am human. I am free to laugh, cry, express pleasure and love, and to express the anger I sometimes feel.

There are difficulties, however, in being more open with others. Sylvia, in her mid-20s, recognizes the difficulties and the fear many experience in allowing themselves to be vulnerable, as her statement shows:

Pouting, the cold shoulder, sarcastic remarks, etc., were techniques I used to convey ideas in my mind. I still find myself doing these things but I am conscious of the fact that they are devious tactics. I could express my feelings much more clearly by verbalizing them but I hesitate to do so. Telling someone how you feel about them is frightening. I become vulnerable if my feelings are unreciprocated. Also, open expression of emotions is like being naked in an auditorium. I am embarrassed to expose my inner self.... However, accumulating feelings inside of me has produced tensions resulting in illness in the past. Perhaps my recent changes in attitudes will even improve my health.

It is only fair to point out to readers that, in my opinion, the process-oriented journey is never easy. But the awareness of freedom we experience is exhilarating. And it will provide the momentum that will be necessary when the temporary plateau is left behind and the upward climb begins once more.

RESEARCH ON ANDROGYNY

As we can see, in being fully human and living a process-oriented life, we transcend the familiar masculine-feminine dichotomy. Process-oriented individuals, therefore, are most often androgynous, for they must choose from the full range of human qualities—both masculine and feminine—unlimited by culturally imposed restrictions. On the other hand, androgynous individuals are not necessarily process oriented. In Angela's case her adolescent years reflected both the masculine and feminine components of herself, due to the early influence of her father and her mother. She had not, however, until recently, been able to integrate these components, which is a part of process orientation. With the integration of herself she is now comfortable with both masculine and feminine behaviors and experiences the choice, the freedom, and the actualization of potential that occur in process-oriented individuals.

It is well documented by Maslow (1970, 1971) and others (Bugental, 1965; Rogers, 1961) that the self-actualizing, fully functioning, or in our terms process-oriented individual is not bound by cultural restrictions, including the concepts of masculinity and femininity. The traditional sex-typed dichotomies of active-passive, reason-feeling, assertive-receptive, instrumental-expressive disappear in process-oriented individuals. They are therefore free to fully develop both the masculine and feminine sides of their natures. It is only, Maslow points out, in less healthy people that such characteristics are considered polarities or opposites (1970, pp. 178–179).

Maslow goes on to state that self-actualizing or process-oriented people tend not to bear hostility toward the opposite sex, and do not even think in terms of "the opposite sex" (p. 189). Self-actualizing men in fact "tend to treat women as partners, as equals, and as full human beings rather than as partial members of the species" (p. 196). Maslow explains that this easy acceptance of the other sex rests on inner security. By accepting the feminine and masculine parts of ourselves, existent in both sexes, we have little need to project the disowned parts of ourselves onto the world. Thus men who accept their feminine selves—the tender, nurturant, receptive aspects of themselves—will not experience the inner conflict that accompanies personal repression of these traits. Similarly, they will not project their own conflict upon the women in their world. If we are at peace with ourselves, we can be at peace with others. As Theodore Roszak aptly comments: "The woman that most needs liberating is the 'woman' that every man has locked up in the dungeons of his own psyche" (1969, p. 101).

Bem's Studies on Androgyny Support for the contention that androgyny leads to a more fully human life comes from recent research on sex roles. Sandra Bem (1974, 1975) tested students on her androgyny scale and found that the more androgynous students could be both independent if they were pressured to conform, and expressive if other more analytic choices were available. These androgynous students did not lose one side of themselves while gaining another. On the other hand, it was noted that the highly masculine students were independent but not expressive, while highly feminine students were expressive but not independent. There are, therefore, indications that the androgynous students had the best of both worlds.

Sandra Bem's scale for measuring androgyny is distinct from earlier tests in that it allows a person to be both feminine and masculine. (Previous tests were constructed so that masculinity and femininity were mutually exclusive—a person would be rated masculine or feminine but not both.) Individuals taking the test rate themselves on such feminine characteristics as "affectionate," "cheerful," "childlike," and "compassionate" and on such masculine characteristics as "acts as a leader," "aggressive," "ambitious," and "analytical." The androgyny score is then computed by subtracting the masculine score from the feminine score—the nearer to zero one is, the more androgynous.*

Bem's results have received some tentative support from other researchers. Rebecca, Hefner, and Oleshansky (1976) postulate that the androgynous individual is morally mature and is engaged in a "process orientation allowing and fostering adaptation to varied occupations, life styles, and expressive roles" (p. 95). Block (1973) offers some preliminary evidence that "greater maturity ... is accompanied by more androgynous, less sex-typed definitions of self" (p. 521). In her sample, however, she finds this more true of males than females.

Studies on Masculinity and Femininity We may well ask why such information in support of androgyny has only recently been discovered. In fact, some earlier studies did give an indication that androgynous people tend to develop more culturally valued traits in later life. But these researchers did not study androgyny as such. Because they believed that masculinity and femininity would be mutually exclusive, subjects were classified as either masculine or feminine. Yet we can infer from the results reported about boys who scored higher on femininity and girls who scored higher on masculinity than their peers that androgyny leads to a more fully human life. Let us now examine some of these early studies on masculinity and femininity.

Evidence for Females All these studies point rather consistently to the conclusion that women high in femininity tend to be more anxious than their peers (Webb, 1963; Gray, 1957; Cosentino & Heilbrun, 1964). In addition, girls high in femininity demonstrate poorer social adjustment than less feminine girls (Heilbrun, 1968). On the other hand, there is evidence that some girls high in masculinity are extremely well-adjusted. In a study by Williams (1973), high-school girls who saw themselves possessing the typically masculine traits of confidence, self-reliance, competitiveness, and assertiveness were the healthiest with respect to current personality functioning. Deutsch and Gilbert (1976) found that the

---

*Recent work with the Bem Sex-Role Inventory has made a further distinction in determining androgyny. In order to be androgynous a person must be high on both masculinity and femininity as opposed to low on both clusters of traits (Bem, 1977).

"masculine" women in their sample had a more positive self-concept in contrast to the more feminine women. Similar results were obtained in a large study of high-school students (Forisha & Farber, 1976).* Heilbrun (1968) also found that girls high in masculinity were very well-adjusted; they were both instrumental and expressive (terms indicating clusters of masculine and feminine traits respectively), whereas feminine girls were expressive but not instrumental. Therefore these girls high in masculinity were, in the new definition, androgynous since they possessed both masculine and feminine traits.

In Heilbrun's study, however, there was evidence that a second group of girls high in masculinity were poorly adjusted and socially alienated. There was overall greater maladjustment in fact among girls high in masculinity than among other groupings, just as the better-adjusted girls were also found in this category. Thus, in a group that might be termed androgynous we find both well-adjusted and maladjusted individuals. This supports the contention stated earlier that androgyny is necessary for fully human living but is not sufficient in itself.

Evidence for Males Upon examining the evidence for males we find that it is much more ambiguous. For some age groups Webb (1963) found that boys high in femininity were high in anxiety, while for other age groups the reverse was the case. Gray (1957) also had mixed results, which indicated that boys high in masculinity had greater social acceptance and yet were also higher in anxiety. Forisha and Farber (1976) found that self-concept correlated highly with masculinity for boys as well as for girls. These results are similar to those reported earlier by Cosentino and Heilbrun (1964), who stated that high femininity in either sex led to high anxiety. All these results suggest that, at least in adolescence, boys and girls are more attracted to masculine traits regardless of their own gender. This suggestion concurs with Block's (1973) findings that both American men and women value masculine qualities more than men and women in five European countries.

Another study (Harford, Willis, & Deabler, 1967) found personality traits that differentiated between high- and low-masculine men. High-masculine men were aloof, tough, practical, unpreten-

---

*Studies by Deutsch and Gilbert and Forisha and Farber are not earlier studies and the researchers were aware of the concept of androgyny. However, because the researchers found the measure of masculinity and femininity individually more important in their results than the measure of androgyny, their studies are cited here.

tious, and suspicious. They tended to be emotionally dissatisfied, prone to guilt and anxiety, and apt to manifest neurotic tendencies. Low-masculine men, on the other hand, were warm, sensitive, sophisticated, accepting, and responsive. In addition they were brighter than the first sample. Thus, from the point of view of process-oriented values, the low-masculine men appear to do rather well.

A series of more complex studies by Mussen (1961, 1962) also found some attributes favoring the low-masculine male over the high-masculine male. Mussen studied a group of 17- and 18-year-old males and then twenty years later observed the same group. While the low- and high-masculine males did not differ during adolescence on measures of instrumental behavior (although low-masculine boys were rated as more expressive and high-masculine boys rated higher on measures of social adjustment), the results of the later study were somewhat different.

At this time those who had been previously described as low-masculine were more dominant, more self-accepting, more introspective, more sociable, and more likely to be leaders. Moreover, they demonstrated more self-assurance and more positive self-concepts. At the same time the high-masculine men rated higher in ego-control, self-sufficiency, and the ability to adapt to stress. Although the picture is not entirely clear, it is apparent that many dimensions of a healthy life-style are found among men low in masculinity. And this is despite pressures they probably received from their early peer groups and society, which must have weighed more heavily on them than on men rated high in masculinity.

From our definition of androgyny we can see that men rated low in masculinity and high in femininity fit the definition more closely than high-masculine men. They have retained the instrumental capacities associated with masculinity, while gaining expressive traits associated with femininity. It is perhaps not surprising then to find that in certain respects, such as leadership, self-acceptance, and self-assurance, they rated so well.

CREATIVITY AND SEX ROLES

The evidence reviewed above has suggested that the androgynous individual may be mature (Block, 1973), self-confident and self-reliant (Williams, 1973), warm and sensitive (Harford, Willis &

Deabler, 1967), and self-accepting and self-assured (Mussen, 1961, 1962). In addition there is considerable theoretical speculation, backed by research, that androgynous individuals are more creative than their peers. Or, if we were to phrase this more conservatively (and possibly more accurately), there is evidence that the creative person is androgynous. Bardwick states this point very strongly:

> ... the stereotyped male, like the stereotyped female, is not creative. While independence and autonomy are perceived as masculine characteristics, a high degree of sensitivity is feminine. Many studies now conclude that the really creative individual combines "masculine" and "feminine" personality qualities. That is, a high degree of bisexuality exists in those who are truly creative. Alternately we may say that the creative individual is open and can know wide-ranging experiences. The creative person resists pressure to be limited and conform to the sex-role stereotype (1971, p. 203).

Bardwick's "bisexuality," used in the psychological sense, is equivalent to the newer concept of androgyny. She states clearly that both feminine and masculine traits are required in order to lay the groundwork for creative expression. Stereotyped masculine men lack the sensitivity and stereotyped feminine women lack the autonomy to be truly creative.

This contention is supported by considerable research. In numerous studies of creative men, Barron (1963) has found that all these men scored higher on measures of femininity than their peers. Getzels and Csikszentmihalyi (1964) in a study of university-level art students found that the males were more timid and sensitive than college men in general, and the women were more dominant than college women in general. Each sex thus possessed a higher degree of traits associated with the other sex than its peers. These findings are similar to those of Fitzgerald (1966) who studied men and women who were "open to experience" (generally acknowledged to be a component of creativity). Fitzgerald observed that men high in this factor were more feminine than their peers, whereas women who scored high on "openness to experience" were dominant, outgoing, and strong in masculine traits.

In short, we can state that creative individuals tend to be both masculine and feminine in combining independence and autonomy of thought with sensitivity and inspiration. In this manner they provide the ingredients for creative production. "It is in the fusion of the feminine and the masculine that part of the gift of creative individuals lies" (Hammer, 1966). If this is so, why then are men reputed to be more creative than women (Maccoby, 1966; Bardwick, 1971)?

A recent study (Forisha, 1976) suggests a possible answer. In this study young college men and women were measured on tests of creativity and then assessed in terms of their creative production. It was found that there were no differences between men and women in creative ability. However, when creative ability was related to creative production there was a distinct difference between the sexes. Men who scored high on creative ability also scored high on creative production. In other words, men who were creative did creative things. They carried their creative ideas out into the real world. On the other hand, women with the same capacities tended to let them lie fallow and were no more creatively productive than their less gifted peers. This seems to imply that women have difficulty translating their creative inspiration into creative doing, whereas men do not suffer from this disability. Here again, as earlier, the evidence suggests that women have learned to "be" whereas men have learned to "do."

To summarize, in theory and in research the androgynous individual appears to have a greater capacity for creation. This is a reasonable finding that agrees with the theoretical view that androgynous individuals (who are also process oriented) live life more fully than do those who are confined by sex-role stereotypes. In all areas of their lives they allow the ongoing process of their experience to determine the path that they will take rather than molding their lives to socially imposed forms and structures. In their lives as in their work, such nonstereotyped individuals would be more creative than their peers. We must add that historically men have more often demonstrated the creative combination of masculine and feminine traits than have women.

THE UNDERSIDE OF ANDROGYNY

In the preceding sections, evidence has been presented that gives empirical support for the view of the process-oriented, androgynous person as confident, competent, and creative. However, our knowledge of androgynous individuals is not so simple and clear-cut. Although it appears that women who possess masculine (as well as feminine) traits are self-confident and "well-adjusted" individuals, they do not produce creatively as frequently as men—at least among high-school and university populations. Moreover, women who are creative (and by earlier implication most likely androgynous) may be prey to heightened anxiety and conflict. Helson (1967) in her study of creative college women finds that although these women are imaginative and achievement oriented, they experience overwhelming feelings of emptiness, desolation, and loneliness more than their less creative peers.

Androgynous men also face fears and conflicts. Men are subject to more sex-role pressures in adolescence and early adulthood than women. And there are strict psychological penalties, at that time, for males who deviate from sex-role norms. Therefore, men who deviate may in fact be more anxious, moody, and occasionally withdrawn than other men. Fitzgerald (1966) points out that men who are "open to experience" are more anxious than their peers, suffer more role conflicts, and in fact are under more pressures from society because of their lack of conforming behavior.

This evidence suggests that at least some, if not most, androgynous individuals may at times experience greater anxiety and stress than more traditionally sex-typed individuals. There are at least two possible explanations for this. First, such individuals are confronting—and sometimes disregarding—social norms. Society does not always look fondly on those who choose their own way. Undoubtedly there is greater external stress in choosing a process-oriented—and in this case, androgynous—path. Moreover, it is not surprising then that the evidence suggests that men, at least in their youth, pay a heavier price than women. Societal norms are generally applied more harshly to those in a more powerful position than to those in a less powerful one. In our society men hold that position, and thus societal pressures to be typically masculine are stronger than the complementary pressures for women.

Second, it is also possible that androgynous, process-oriented individuals experience their inner conflicts more deeply than other individuals. They are more aware of themselves and others and know what is going on both inside and outside themselves. They respond, perhaps more authentically, to the pain of the human condition, although at the same time they also experience a more profound satisfaction and delight in living than others.

Angela, whose story was told earlier in this chapter, is witness

to the emotional peaks and valleys accompanying increased awareness. In her struggle with two sides of herself, she was often despair-
ing and wondered if she could ever come to terms with who she was.
However, in her integration of her two sides, she has experienced a
deep satisfaction and energizing excitement, as she has allowed the
full complexity of herself to be in harmony.

Psychologist Carl Rogers outlines clearly the advantages, as
well as disadvantages, of such heightened awareness and fuller
living as he speaks of the progress his clients have made in therapy
and beyond:

> ... an undistorted awareness, an openness to experience, leads to a
> more sensitive living, with greater range, greater variety, greater
> richness. Though such openness to experience may frequently be
> frightening because it demands changes in the way we perceive the
> world, it is also basically more satisfying in its open confrontation of
> the complexities of living. It seems to me that clients who have moved
> significantly in this direction in therapy live more intimately with
> their feelings of pain, but also more vividly with their feelings of
> ecstasy; that anger is more clearly felt, but so also is love; that fear is
> an experience they know more deeply, but so is courage (1972, p. 26).

This may also be the experience of the process-oriented, androgynous individual.

INTERPERSONAL IMPLICATIONS

We have considered the advantages and disadvantages of the
androgynous, process-oriented life-style as presented in the theoretical and empirical literature. What implications can be drawn from
this literature about how these complex, androgynous individuals
fare in the social and interpersonal world? This is a subject that will
be explored more fully in the next chapter but a few research
studies, presented here, will set the stage for later discussion. Most
of the research pertaining to androgyny and interpersonal relations
(except for that focusing on couples and marriage) pertains primarily to women rather than men. This is not too surprising when we
remember that for women, pleasing men has traditionally been of
prime importance. Thus, researchers have usually assessed the

impact of woman's strength and dominance (masculine characteristics) on her interpersonal relations.

In general, the woman who scores high on tests of masculinity appears to be well-received in the interpersonal world. Early studies found, for example, that college women with high masculinity scores were likely to be more attractive to men and more interested in men than were other women. By contrast, college women with high femininity scores were less attractive to men and more interested in the companionship of women. Moreover, Maslow's (1939) studies of dominance in women found that more dominant women were more sexually active and enjoyed sex more. If we draw upon Masters and Johnson's research, we may assume that their male partners also enjoyed sex with them more than sex with other women (1974). Thus, on some counts at least, androgynous women appear to surpass their more feminine sisters.

This conclusion is further supported by the research of Spence and Helmreich (1972), who found that both men and women generally preferred masculine competent women holding masculine positions to feminine women—either competent or incompetent—holding feminine positions. There are at least two possible explanations for this finding: (1) both men and women may concede that anyone who can do a good job in a masculine occupation or pursuit is worthy of regard; or (2) since the women in this study did not openly contradict any typical feminine values, such as respect for the family and motherhood, they were perhaps not viewed as *un*feminine but simply as more masculine than usual. There is evidence that if women express opinions that oppose traditional feminine role values, they are less liked than traditional women, but that did not appear to be the case here (Shaffer & Wagley, 1974; Seyfried & Hendrick, 1973).

A third possible explanation is provided by the latest research of Spence's colleagues (Patterson, Helmreich, & Stapp, 1975). When the subjects of the research were asked to write out their subjective impressions of stimulus persons (those who were evaluated by the subjects) before completing the questionnaire (which had been used in the previous study), they no longer favored the women high in masculinity. The opportunity to clarify their thoughts before being cued by a questionnaire resulted in a lower evaluation of the women seen as high in masculinity. Only women favorably disposed to the Women's Movement continued to highly evaluate these women. Other females and all males under these conditions now approved most highly of the competent women high in femininity. This study strongly suggests that many changes in people's attitudes about sex roles may still be somewhat superficial. We should not take people's professed liberation from sex roles too seriously unless there is evidence that belief has been integrated into action.

Therefore, while on some counts androgynous women or women high in masculinity fare well, on others they are behind their more traditional peers. It may well be that both men and women admire and are attracted to the "strong woman," but are wary of the threat she may pose to persons engaged in more traditional life-styles.

If androgynous women are both attractive and threatening to most men, what of the androgynous men in relation to women? There is still an emphasis on the strong, highly masculine male as the real winner of women's hearts. This is the stereotype that Woody Allen (himself a highly creative and androgynous character) both envies and—in his deliberately bumbling way—emulates in his films. He illustrates in his own life the difficulties of achieving a successful romantic alliance because he himself is so far from the masculine ideal. In a recent television interview he was asked about his love life and if his stardom had diminished his trouble "getting girls." He replied that stardom had helped some because he was known and he met more people, but that the end result was that he was "still not making it, but with a higher class of women."

His answer, as usual, in a quietly humorous way, illustrates the difficulty of not fitting the stereotypes. But his answer, in another way, is illustrative of another stereotypical image: the bumbling, inept, but endearing male who doesn't quite fit in the world as it has been handed to him. Yet, recent evidence suggests that both stereotypes—the strong, invincible male and the inept, hapless one—may be on their way out. As we move toward seeing people as people, all such sex-role stereotypes will be slowly dismantled. Recent evidence (Tavris, 1977) indeed shows that this is the case. She states, from an extensive survey, that women no longer desire the strong masculine male but are looking for sensitivity and responsiveness in the men to whom they relate.

This is another indication that maybe, at last, we are coming to see that sensitivity does not imply weakness, nor does strength necessarily imply invulnerability. These two opposites, like all others, are part of a larger whole. As women become more assertive, and men allow themselves to be sensitive, we will all be more fully human, and each of us, whether male or female, can carry that strength and that sensitivity into our relationships with others.

SUMMARY

Process-oriented individuals are less bound by their past and less concerned about their future. They live fully in the present, which in effect encompasses both past effects and future hopes. Based on a strong sense of inner security, process-oriented persons can choose to be alone or with others. They experience without distortion or denial their inner feelings and input from their environment. They communicate honestly both with themselves and with others. They are ready to risk themselves in active commitment in their relationships and their life.

The process-oriented life is the androgynous life, although the opposite is not necessarily the case. It is clear that process-oriented individuals transcend masculine-feminine stereotypes and thus are free to live more fully without restraints. The joy accompanying such experiences of freedom is illustrated by the personal accounts included in this chapter. There is an experience of lightheadedness and release; there is the knowledge that we have the right of choice that accompanies each new obstacle we overcome on our individual journeys. Such freedom is often experienced by those who have committed themselves to living in process and becoming more fully human. In doing so, they have made the choice to be who they are rather than as society would have them be.

Despite theoretical and subjective accounts relating the benefits of androgyny, the research in the sex-role literature still does not fully substantiate the viability of the androgynous alternative as opposed to the masculine and feminine molds. One explanation for the inconclusive research findings may be that there are both benefits and liabilities to an androgynous orientation in our current society. While androgynous individuals benefit from their lack of role orientation, at the same time they may suffer—occasionally or often—from living in a society still oriented to traditional roles. Similarly, at the same time as process-oriented individuals are laying a foundation for a new integration of self, they are experiencing their pain, as well as their joy, more fully.

EXERCISE: INSTRUMENTAL AND EXPRESSIVE SUBPERSONALITIES

Read this exercise silently to yourself. Then sit back, close your eyes, and allow yourself to take a fantasy trip.

What qualities do you have that are expressive? Soft, tender, and nurturing? Allow the expressive side of yourself to be symbolized as a "subpersonality," and choose a name for this expressive part of yourself.

What qualities do you have that are instrumental? Assertive, strong, and logical? Allow this side of yourself also to be symbolized as a "subpersonality." Give this part of yourself a different name.

Let the two subpersonalities have a dialogue with each other. What does each of them do for the total self? Have them tell each other of their respective strengths and weaknesses.

Do you feel more comfortable being the expressive or the instrumental self? Does one side dominate the conversation? Does one side usually give in? Do the two sides work harmoniously or antagonistically with each other?

If they are antagonistic, is it possible for them to work out an agreement to share equally in a peaceful coexistence?

End the dialogue of the two subpersonalities and return to your usual self. Now discuss your "fantasy" with members of your class. Were your instrumental and expressive qualities and their strengths and weaknesses similar to those of your classmates? How did your dialogue compare with those of others?

REFERENCES

Bardwick, J., *The Psychology of Women: A Study of Biosocial Conflict,* New York: Harper & Row, 1971.

Barron, F., *Creativity and Psychological Health,* New York: D. Van Nostrand, 1963.

Bem, S., "Bem Sex-Role Inventory (BSRI)", in C. G. Carney and S. L. McMahon, eds., *Exploring Contemporary Male/Female Relationships,* La Jolla, Calif.: University Associates, 1977.

Bem, S., "The Measurement of Psychological Androgyny," *Journal of Consulting and Clinical Psychology,* vol. 2 (1974): 153–62.

Bem, S., "Sex-Role Adaptability: One Consequence of Psychological Androgyny," *Journal of Personality and Social Psychology,* vol. 4 (1975): 634–43.

Block, J. H., "Conceptions of Sex Role: Some Cross-Cultural and Longitudinal Perspectives," *American Psychologist,* vol. 28 (1973): 512–26.

Bugental, J., *The Search for Authenticity,* New York: Holt, Rinehart & Winston, 1965.

Cosentino, F., and Heilbrun, A. B., "Anxiety Correlates of Sex-Role Identity in College Students, *Psychological Reports,* vol. 14 (1964): 729–30.

Crutchfield, R. S., "Conformity and Character," *American Psychologist,* vol. 10 (1955): 191–98.

Deutsch, C. J., and Gilbert, L. A., "Sex Role Stereotypes: Effects on Perceptions of Self and Others and on Personal Adjustment," *Journal of Counseling Psychology,* vol. 4 (1976): 373–79.

Erikson, E., *Childhood and Society,* New York: W. W. Norton, 1950.

Fields, J., in M. J. Moffat and C. Painter, eds., *Revelations: Diaries of Women,* New York: Vintage, 1975.

Fitzgerald, E., "The Measurement of Openness to Experience: A Study of Regression in the Service of the Ego," unpublished dissertation, University of California, Berkeley, Calif.,1966.

Forisha, B., "Creativity and Mental Imagery in Men and Women," unpublished paper, 1976.

Forisha, B., and Farber, R., "Sex-Role Orientation and Self-Esteem: The Value of Masculinity," unpublished paper, 1976.

Fromm, E., *Escape from Freedom* (1941), New York: Avon Books, 1971.

Getzels, J., and Csikszentmihalyi, M., *Creative Thinking in Art Students,* Chicago: University of Chicago Press, 1964.

Gray, S. W., "Masculinity-Femininity in Relation to Anxiety and Social Acceptance," *Child Development,* vol. 28 (1957): 203–14.

Hammer, E., "Creativity and Feminine Ingredients in Young Male Artists," *Perceptual and Motor Skills,* vol. 19 (1966): 414.

Harford, T. C., Willis, C. H., and Deabler, H. L., "Personality Correlates of Masculinity-Femininity," *Psychological Reports,* vol. 21 (1967): 881–84.

Heilbrun, A. B., Jr., "Sex Role, Instrumental-Expressive Behavior, and Psychopathology in Females," *Journal of Abnormal Psychology,* vol. 73 (1968): 131–36.

Helson, R., "Personality Characteristics and Developmental History of Creative College Women," *Genetic Psychology Monographs,* vol. 76 (1967): 205–56.

Kohlberg, L., and Kramer, R., "Continuities and Discontinuities in Childhood and Adult Moral Development," *Human Development,* vol. 12 (1969): 93–120.

Lynd, H., "Alienation: Man's Fate and Man's Hope," in J. Glass and J. Staude, eds., *Humanistic Society: Today's Challenge to Sociology,* Santa Monica, Calif.: Goodyear, 1972.

Maccoby, E. E., "Sex Differences in Intellectual Functioning," in E. E. Maccoby, ed., *The Development of Sex Differences,* Stanford, Calif.: Stanford University Press, 1966.

Maslow, A. H., "Dominance, Personality and Social Behavior in Women," *Journal of Social Psychology,* vol. 10 (1939): 3–39.

Maslow, A. H., *The Farther Reaches of Human Nature,* New York: Viking, 1971.

Maslow, A. H., *Motivation and Personality* (1954), New York: Harper & Row, 1970.

Masters, W. H., and Johnson, V. E., *The Pleasure Bond: A New Look at Sexuality and Contentment,* Boston: Little, Brown, 1974.

Mussen, P. H., "Long-Term Consequents of Masculinity of Interests in Adolescence," *Journal of Consulting Psychology,* vol. 26 (1962): 435–40.

Mussen, P. H., "Some Antecedents and Consequences of Masculine Sex-Typing in Adolescent Boys," *Psychological Monographs,* vol. 75 (1961), No. 506.

Patterson, K., Helmreich, R., and Stapp, J., "Likeability, Sex-Role Congruence of Interest, and Competence: It All Depends on How You Ask," *Journal of Applied Psychology,* vol. 2 (1975): 95–109.

Rebecca, M., Hefner, R., and Oleshansky, B., "A Model of Sex-Role Transcendence," in A. Kaplan and J. Bean, eds., *Beyond Sex-Role Stereotypes: Readings Toward a Psychology of Androgyny,* Boston: Little, Brown, 1976.

Rogers, C., *On Becoming a Person,* Boston: Houghton Mifflin, 1961.

Rogers, C. R., "A Humanistic Conception of Man," in J. F. Glass and J. R. Staude, eds., *Humanistic Society: Today's Challenge to Sociology,* Santa Monica, Calif.: Goodyear, 1972.

Roszak, T., "The Hard and the Soft: The Force of Feminism in Modern Times," in B. Roszak and T. Roszak, eds., *Masculine/Feminine: Readings in Sexual Mythology and the Liberation of Women*, New York: Harper & Row, 1969.

Secor, C., "Androgyny: An Early Reappraisal," *Women's Studies*, vol. 2 (1974): 161–69.

Seyfried, B. A., and Hendrick, C., "When Do Opposites Attract: When They Are Opposite in Sex and Sex-Role Attitudes," *Journal of Personality and Social Psychology*, vol. 25 (1973): 15–20.

Shaffer, D. R., and Wagley, C., "Success Orientation and Sex-Role Congruence as Determinants of the Attractiveness of Competent Women," *Journal of Personality*, vol. 42 (1974): 586–600.

Spence, J. T., and Helmreich, R., "Who Likes Competent Women? Competence, Sex-Role Congruence of Interests, and Subjects' Attitudes Toward Women as Determinants of Interpersonal Attraction," *Journal of Applied Social Psychology*, vol. 2 (1972): 197–213.

Tavris, C., "Men and Women Report Their Views on Masculinity," *Psychology Today*, vol. 10 (January 1977): 35.

Webb, A. P., "Sex-Role Preferences and Adjustment in Early Adolescents," *Child Development*, vol. 34 (1963): 609–18.

Williams, J., "Sexual Role Identification and Personality Functioning in Girls: A Theory Revisited," *Journal of Personality*, vol. 1 (1973): 1–8.

4

Person to Person: The Intimate Relationship

Individuality and relatedness are the bases of human existence. Although all of us can actualize our own potential to the full extent of our sensitivity, awareness, and abilities, many of us do not. We do not realize that only by developing our own humanity can we come to understand and identify with the humanity of others. As we explore the full depth of our own existence, we discover the remarkable paradox of human life: the infinite height and depth of human potential contrasted with our own finiteness. It is only with other humans that we share both the excitement of possibilities and the recognition of limits. Thus the full development of our own individuality and awareness leads to a recognition of our underlying relatedness to others. In learning that we have ourselves, we also find that we have each other.

The process-oriented relationship, the spontaneous affirmation of another on the basis of individual security and strength, is possible for those individuals who allow themselves to be fully

Every person born into this world represents something new, something that never existed before, something original and unique.

Martin Buber, *Hasidism and Modern Man*

The fact that we are all human beings is infinitely more important than all the peculiarities that distinguish human beings from one another.

Simone de Beauvoir, *The Second Sex*

---

human. Most of us build our relationships on our own need to escape our aloneness and separateness. Process-oriented individuals, in contrast, build their relationships on the acceptance of their own aloneness. It is in the acceptance of their own aloneness that they find the capacity to move beyond separateness in a process-oriented relationship. Such relationships do not eliminate individuality but in fact strengthen it. Let us examine the characteristics of a process-oriented relationship.

CHARACTERISTICS OF A PROCESS-ORIENTED RELATIONSHIP

A process-oriented relationship is characterized by a growing openness and honesty between partners. They do not have to watch what they say, to be suspicious, to anticipate the other's reaction, to try to make a good impression, or to suppress their thoughts and feelings, whether negative or positive. They can drop their defenses and reveal themselves. By allowing themselves to experience pain, fear, and grief, they can consequently allow others to do the same. They work, play, and enjoy life to their fullest potential and accept this behavior in others. By doing this each partner may "let himself be naked not only physically but psychologically and spiritually as well" (Maslow, 1971, p. 17).

Thus, by letting themselves be, process-oriented individuals let their partners be. As a result they have little desire to change or improve their partners. They accept their vices as well as their virtues. Without possessiveness and jealousy they allow their partners to explore all aspects of themselves and they accept the change and growth that results from this exploration.

It is important to note, however, that this acceptance of themselves and their partners does not preclude conflict in the relationship. Rather, conflict is seen as a positive factor. It is regarded as a potential source of growth rather than as a measure of incompatibility that will cause the relationship to dissolve. Emotions of anger and fear are expressed as honestly as those of love and joy, and the same open communication characterizes both the conflict and harmony in any given relationship. In this manner process-oriented individuals transcend all the dichotomies of human emotions and behaviors normally found in interrelationships. They accept their own individuality but yet go beyond it.

Individuality and a transcendence of that individuality are therefore important aspects of the process-oriented relationship. Let us see how two psychologists view these poles of human existence. Frederick S. Perls (1969), in the formulation of his famous "The Gestalt Prayer," places a strong emphasis on individuality. In this short verse Perls points out that we are all individuals who "do our own thing," and that we are not in this world to live up to each other's expectations. However, he goes a step further by saying that if two individuals should happen to find each other by chance, "it's beautiful" and if this should not be the case, "it can't be helped."

Another psychologist, Walter Tubbs (1972), however, in his amendment to this prayer emphasizes the necessity of going beyond the self. He feels that if we all just "do our own thing" we may lose each other and ourselves. In addition, we find each other by actively reaching out, not by chance. We make things happen rather than letting them happen. Tubbs writes:

"BEYOND PERLS"

If I just do my thing and you do yours,
We stand in danger of losing each other
And ourselves.
I am not in this world to live up to your expectations;
But I am in this world to confirm you
As a unique human being.
And to be confirmed by you.

We are fully ourselves only in relation to each other;
The I detached from a Thou
Disintegrates.
I do not find you by chance;
I find you by an active life
Of reaching out.

Rather than passively letting things happen to me,
I can act intentionally to make them happen.
I must begin with myself, true;
But I must not end with myself:
The truth begins with two.

Walter Tubbs

Some critics have suggested that Perls, in "The Gestalt Prayer," has overemphasized individualism while excluding the ongoing shared relationship (Dublin, 1976, p. 142). Tubbs, on the other hand, has described a relationship in which each person relates to the other as a fully human person. Although the individual begins with himself or herself, he or she must realize, in part, the potential in interaction with others.

The two statements taken together represent the poles of human separateness and human relatedness, both of which have a place in the life of process-oriented, androgynous individuals. Moreover, if we find ourselves, we have the capacity to find each other. As Fromm (1956) reminds us, the capacity to love a person follows upon the capacity to love all people. We do not find a person to love; we *are* loving persons. Let us explore further the meaning of love and its role in the process-oriented relationship.

WHAT IS LOVE?

Love as a concept encompasses many desires, feelings, beliefs, and commitments. The following quotation indicates the many meanings we attach to love:

> I love you. Sometimes it means: I desire you or I want you sexually. It may mean: I hope you love me or I hope that I will be able to love you. Often it means: It may be that a love relationship can develop between us or even I hate you. Often it is a wish for an emotional exchange: I want your admiration in exchange for mine or I give my love in exchange for some passion or I want to feel cozy and at home with you or I admire some of your qualities. A declaration of love is merely a request: I desire you or I want you to gratify me or I want your protection or I want to be intimate with you or I want to exploit your loveliness. Sometimes it is the need for security and tenderness, for parental treatment. It may mean: My self-love goes out to you. But it may also express submissiveness. Please take me as I am or I feel guilty about you, I want through you to correct the mistakes I have made in human relationships. It may be self-sacrifice and a masochistic wish for dependency. However, it may also be a full affirmation of the other, taking the responsibility for mutual exchange of feelings. It may be a weak form of friendliness, it may be the scarcely even whispered expression of ecstasy. "I love you," wish, desire, submission, conquest, it is never the word itself that tells the real meaning. . . (Meerlo, in McCary, 1975, p. 124).

Most of the ways in which love is discussed can be classified as conditional love. We give our love to others on the condition that they in return will meet our own needs. If our needs are not met, the love disappears. Such love and the relationships that result are role oriented and represent the *reality* in which most of us find ourselves. These topics will be discussed in Chapter 7.

We also notice that Meerlo describes love as the "full affirmation of the other," in which one takes the "responsibility for a mutual exchange of feelings." This love is found in process-oriented relationships, which represent the *vision* of how we might better live in a rapidly changing world. Such love will be discussed here.

LOVE IN A PROCESS-ORIENTED RELATIONSHIP

As we have seen, the process-oriented relationship is characterized by an acceptance of individuality and a transcendence of that individuality. Love in a process-oriented relationship also incorporates these characteristics. Thus both partners remain strong and unique individuals, yet are able to join with each other without losing their own sense of self.

> The dynamic quality of love lies in this very polarity: that it springs
> from the need of overcoming separateness, that it leads to oneness—
> and yet that individuality is not eliminated (Fromm, 1971, p. 287).

Love thus affirms the individuality of each partner rather than
consuming it. Love, as Fromm states, is not the possession of
another nor the dissolution of self in the other but rather a celebra-
tion of the individuality of each in such a way that the ensuing "we-
ness" of the two is greater than the sums of the "I-ness" of each (p.
289).

In role-oriented relationships the concepts of aloneness and
togetherness of self and other remain opposites. We act as if there
was a limited fund of energy available; the energy we devote to
ourselves is "taken" from the other partner, and the energy we give
away depletes our own self. Thus in many relationships we see
partners giving up their individuality in order to form what they
hope will be a more encompassing union. The actual result is that
they give up their rights to be fully human; they abandon their
inner strength and become mutually dependent upon each other.
They can no longer stand alone.

There are numerous classic examples in which partners in a
relationship sacrifice their own individuality to meet what they
suppose are the needs of the other. Several years ago, a newly
married friend of mine gave up all outside activities, even reading
books and magazines, because her working husband wanted to
know that she was home all day thinking of him. On the television
show "All in the Family," Mike, married and in his 20s, says to his
friends, "No, I can't go skiing, the wife wouldn't like it." (As it turns
out, he did go skiing and *he* didn't like it, which is quite a different
thing altogether.) The thinking underlying my friend's behavior
and Mike's statement goes something like this: "If I upset my
partner, he or she may be upset, angry, or sad, and will make my life
uncomfortable and may eventually end the relationship and then I
will be alone." The thought of being alone is one that frightens
many individuals. In the words of a bereft young 19-year-old friend
who had just left a steady relationship: "Now what will I do on
Saturday night?"

In process-oriented relationships, on the other hand, such basic
dichotomies are resolved. Moving from a basis of inner strength,
what we give to the other partner enriches our own self, what we do
for ourselves enhances the other partner. Thus affirmation-of-the-
self and affirmation-of-the-other do not oppose each other but com-

bine in a cooperative or joint pattern that increases the vitality of each partner's individuality.

Thus the strength of such love is based on the fact that each partner can stand alone and does not require the other to live a fulfilling life. Each has the strength to live in the present and find meaning in creative enterprise. And yet from this strength comes the ability to reach out to others, to love, to give, to care, and to go beyond the boundaries of one's own self.

Many women returning to school and career after a time at home become aware of renewed feelings of strength and independence. This reflects positively on their relationships with their family, provided the family is willing to grow as well. Anna, a middle-aged woman, writes:

> I started back to school with my husband's blessings—he liked the extroverted me, not the timid, unconfident me that I had become. . . . Now it is full-time school and part-time everything else. And I find I'm more independent and yet freer to be more expressive to my family. I find myself less jealous, less clinging, less possessive. Of course, all these changes are subtle. . . . We as a family still have a long way to go. . . . and I myself am still at times very unsure of my capabilities but I can actually "feel" all of us growing and it's a much nicer feeling than being static.

Thus, love in a process-oriented relationship is based on strength—the strength to stand alone and to accept the ensuing change and growth resulting from reaching out to others. Our growth also leads us to move away from roles, especially those described as masculine and feminine.

ANDROGYNY AND LOVE RELATIONSHIPS

We recall at this point that individuals who are able to move away from sex roles—to partake of both masculine and feminine characteristics—are androgynous. But they are not simply androgynous; they are also well-grounded in themselves and in their own sense of strength.

Rossi (1964a) feels that in order to have an equal partnership in marriage young people must be committed, from childhood forward, to a growing sense of self. In these cases when they get married both partners engage in whatever work best suits their own temperaments, and share the nurturing of whatever children they have. Role assignments and behavior patterns are not sex-linked but are based on the desires and capabilities of each partner. Moreover, with a full acceptance of themselves and their partners, both physically and emotionally, both partners engage in an exciting independent life and share their experiences fully.

Rostow (1964), in observing apparent trends among young educated women, found that they were developing ideals and goals compatible with the above model. Although these young women tended to favor marriage over a career, most chose to combine the two and displayed a willingness to work at overcoming the difficulties that such a life-style might present. These young women tended to see marriage as a cooperative effort in which both partners have a number of goals and fulfill a number of needs. The woman's needs for achievement could be fulfilled within such a relationship, as could the man's nurturing needs.

Such a relationship today requires a greater adjustment on the part of men than of women. In part, this is so because most women in our society receive training for work-oriented achievement, both in their education and in early work experience. Although in the traditional marriage this achievement orientation is rechanneled into domestic pursuits (Stein & Bailey, 1976), it also provides the foundation for continuing achievement in the world of work. In addition, there is some societal support today for women to direct their needs for achievement into the outer world. Men, on the other hand, have generally had no training for caretaking, nurturing, and domestic activities. Moreover, they have always learned that their "work," whatever that might be, is of first importance. Thus, for men to share in the domestic activities as well as share the work world with their wives is a difficult transition to make. This is particularly so since societal support for the domestic husband is almost nil. Rostow (1964) makes clear that the man in an equal marriage will suffer more initial adjustments and that the success of such a venture hinges on the willingness of the male both to share the "man's world" with his wife and to enter as an equal participant into what has traditionally been the "place of woman."

> Success depends to a considerable extent on having a husband who is as willing as his wife to do battle against the inner and outer forces which divide men from women and to join her in seeking the rewards of an extended partnership (p. 224).

THE EGALITARIAN MARRIAGE: MYTH OR FACT?

Although Rossi (1964a) and Rostow (1964) have theorized about the prospects of egalitarian marriages, there is considerable doubt among other researchers that such marriages exist today. Gillespie (1971) states frankly, "The egalitarian marriage as a norm is a myth" (p. 457). It would be too much to expect such marriages to exist "as a norm." But can we even say that they exist at all? Garland (1972) avoids reference to the norm when he agrees with Gillespie that the "egalitarian family" is a "type of family which apparently exists mainly and almost exclusively in the minds of family sociologists, for almost all empirical research indicates that the vast majority of American families are a long, long way from being 'egalitarian' in structure" (p. 200). Yet despite his belief in the myth of the egalitarian marriage, Garland has found one such marriage that exists. In my willingness to study the exception, I am content with a sample of one.

Garland's Sample of One In a sample of fifty-three dual-career professional couples Garland (1972) discovered one that is strictly egalitarian, that is, the couple has a relationship in which tasks are assigned without regard to gender. If the term is more loosely defined so that some tasks are gender-associated but both partners share in career and household responsibilities, Garland reports a sample of ten families that can be called neo-traditional. In both categories the women's as well as the men's careers were of significant importance to the household. Only in the egalitarian marriage, however, were the husband's and wife's careers of equal significance.

Garland reports that the careers of the egalitarian couple were for them "as much a natural part of their lives as eating or breathing." In response to a question about sharing responsibilities for child care the husband of this couple responded:

> *No, we've never distinguished in any way. The kid was even bottle fed. I've probably done more child care than she has, from newborn on. The first night he was home he cried and she woke up. The next day she gave me a long lecture on maternal instinct, and she never woke up when he cried again. So much for that!*

This one instance is sufficient to illustrate the fact that egalitarian marriages (in the strictest sense of the word) are indeed possible, despite claims to the contrary by authorities on marriage and its role in society.

Poloma's Findings on Primary Control and Husbands
However, not all researchers agree. Poloma (1972) studied the same sample, but reports other results. After extensively interviewing the wives, she found that most of the women paced their work to fit their family demands and that, if tension increased, the woman was the one to rearrange her schedule in order to be more flexible. Each of these women asserted that her work had lower priority than her husband's and none desired to be more successful than her husband. This research is supported by recent research in which Bryson, Bryson, Licht, and Licht (1976) studied couples in which both partners were psychologists. They found that the husbands were extremely productive and satisfied with their job situations and family lives, whereas the wives tended to be less productive than their husbands, less satisfied with their jobs and family lives, and more aware of sexist discrimination. Somewhere within the privacy of their family lives it would appear that primary control and attention had been allotted to the husbands rather than the wives. Therefore, even in marriages having the appearance of equality as a result of the duality of commitment to both career and family on the part of both spouses, there is still some measure of traditional sex-role orientation. If the situation gets tough, it is the woman who makes the accommodations.

Rapoport and Rapoport: Dual-Career Marriages in Britain Two studies done in Britain have been landmarks in the research on dual-career families. One major study by Rapoport and Rapoport (1972) outlines the stresses and strains of a dual-career marriage. Unlike Garland, the British researchers prefer a looser definition of egalitarian marriages and assume that their dual-career marriages fit that definition. However, it would appear from their article that most of their couples are instead neo-traditional (in Garland's definition) since again it is the wife who adjusts if the combination of marriage and career becomes stressful.

Nonetheless, the Rapoports' research contributes substantially to our knowledge of life-styles significantly different from the traditional ones. The thirteen couples in the study were themselves well aware of their departure from the traditional and regarded their life-styles as experiments in social innovation. For the most part, almost all these couples claimed to be happy with their arrangements, although they were all subject to situational conflicts: "There is an element of psychic strain involved in allowing two major areas of life, so different in their demands and characteristics, to be so highly important" (p. 222). The strain was felt first in abandoning leisure activities, limiting friendships and kin relationships, and curtailing activities and time spent with the children. All the couples stressed the necessity for good health and physical fitness in all members of the family in order to maintain their life-style. The strains of this pattern, however, were not intrinsic but were due to the stress induced by "experimenting with post-industrial social structures in the contemporary environment, which is for the most part still geared to the values of an industrial society" (p. 219).*

Despite the semblance of equality in these marriages there are also shades of traditional role divisions, just as in the marriages studied by Garland and Poloma. If the overload became too great, it was the woman who took up the slack and rearranged her schedule to meet critical domestic needs. In addition, the women seemed to accept this situation without complaint and to be grateful for what they regarded as small mercies. The Rapoports state:

> The women tended to accept as "inevitable" for the present that they would have to bear the main brunt of child-care and domestic organization, so that there would "naturally" tend to be more strain on the wife's career-family/role-cycling than on the husband's (p. 236).

Even with this concession to traditional sex roles, such marriages are coming closer to the process-oriented, androgynous model of relationships. Unhappily, they do fall short of egalitarianism as derived from the concept of process orientation.

---

*The term postindustrial refers to a society in which increasing the quantity of production is no longer the most important criterion for maintaining the society. This implies that production governs values and behavior in an industrial society. The argument made by the Rapoports, and explored more fully in Chapter 9, is that our current society, a postindustrial one, no longer needs to be governed by the ethic of production which urges individuals (primarily men) to work continually at top efficiency in fierce competition with each other to create economic goods. Competition yields to cooperation, and quantity to quality, and economic values to human and ecological values in a postindustrial world.

Bailyn on "Coordinate" Marriages in Britain The second British study, by Bailyn (1970), included more couples and reviewed the marital happiness of people engaged in a variety of life-styles. She finds that the likelihood of a successful relationship diminishes if either partner places highest priority on career achievement. For example, the chances for marital happiness were least among those couples in which the man placed his career first and the wife was also a career-oriented woman.

Nonetheless, in what Bailyn terms "coordinate" marriages, there is at least the same prospect for a successful relationship as in more conventional marriages. These marriages involve the integration of both career and family within the partnership and within each individual. They do not represent role reversals but rather a combination of both career and family orientations in both partners.

Coordinate marriages, nevertheless, appear to have some shortcomings. In Bailyn's sample they seem to occur most frequently among couples with sufficient income to ease the responsibilities of home maintenance and child care. Moreover, in accordance with Rostow's observations, Bailyn found that the husband's attitude was the most important factor in predicting success of the partnership. In most of these marriages, however, the husbands were willing to make the adjustments necessary to approach a more equal partnership. Thus although they were successful in their work and rated themselves as ambitious, they still gave a higher priority to their families.

INTIMATE RELATIONSHIPS: EMPHASIS ON THE INDIVIDUAL

Up to this point in our discussion of intimate relationships, we have assumed that such relationships involve the institutions of marriage and parenthood. Indeed, this is the approach taken in much of the literature. There is no dictum, however, which states that people who are intimate are also married; or if they are married that their relationship must be either exclusive or heterosexual. Neither is there a dictum which states that marriage must entail children.

One of the assumptions of the structural-functionalist school of sociology is that society is founded upon the *family* unit. What lies behind this assumption? Belief in the family as the basis of society rests on the concepts that 1) men and women need each other and cannot survive alone, and 2) the purpose of legitimate sexual behavior—defined as existing within a legal relationship—is primarily to bear children.

Suppose we wipe out these concepts and assume that men and women can survive alone *and* together, and that sexual behavior is one of the powerful means of communication between human beings. If we accept these alternative assumptions, we have no reason not to accept, as the social scientist James Ramey (1975) does, the *individual,* rather than the *family,* as the building block of a postindustrial society. This basic hypothesis has led Ramey to postulate that people may live in "networks of intimate friendships" rather than primarily in families. He has studied 380 such individuals. Among them there are many variants of intimate friendships, of which marriage is only one. And he found that marriage does not necessarily preclude other forms of relationships.

Ramey's "Primary Relationships" In his recent work, which is of particular relevance to this chapter, Ramey emphasizes "primary relationships." Usually but not always they involve the legal institution of marriage. Of the variety of possible forms of "primary relationships"—relationships which absorb most of the energy of the individuals involved—Ramey speaks most highly of the "peer relationship" or "peer marriage." He defines such a relationship as

> ... a partnership, the purpose of which is to permit and promote the growth of each partner and of the partnership itself, built around an ongoing dialogue to which each partner brings input from all unshared areas of experience (1975, p. 22).

Peer relating requires trust, openness, and a willingness to experiment, as well as ongoing dialogue between partners. Partners in a peer relationship remain individuals in selecting their activities and friends, which may include friends (intimate or not) of the opposite sex. Both members of a peer relationship are likely to be pursuing careers they see as equally significant. Most partners in peer relationships select their friends from a wider age range than the traditional couple. In addition, most peer relationships become sexually open after an initial period in which the mutual relationship is established.

Ramey sees some difficulty in bringing children into such a relationship. He finds that many peer couples choose not to have children simply because the added obligation of children would require much rearrangement of their time. In fact, Ramey finds that a major distinction between people in his study is not the traditional distinction between being single and being married; rather it is between having children and remaining childless. In an age when more young couples are deciding to remain childless, and many people are deciding to remain single, Ramey's formulation of a society based on individuals rather than on families appears realistic. Ramey finds, moreover, that the individuals in his study tended to be satisfied with their life-style and to be leaders in their community. They saw themselves as risk-takers, adaptable to change, growth-oriented, and able to cope with life as it comes. In addition, they seemed to be self-assured, self-reliant, and creative individuals. In our terms as well as Ramey's, the focus in the lives of these individuals is on process, not content.

Sexual relationships outside the peer marriage are common. But, in reality the incidence of such extramarital sexuality may, in fact, be no higher, or only slightly higher, than in traditional marriages: Kinsey (1948, 1953) notes that about thirty years ago, 50 percent of American husbands and 26 percent of American wives were reported as having had extramarital affairs by the age of 45. By 1968 these percentages had risen to 60 percent for males and 40 percent for females (Gebhard, in Hunt, 1973). However, the key difference lies in the attitude toward this extramarital sexuality displayed by traditional couples and Ramey's subjects. Whereas traditional couples try to conceal these relationships and often feel guilty for having them, those in peer relationships discuss and share them with the partner. Thus, a more open attitude toward these "secondary relationships" prevails.

But, we may ask, doesn't jealousy enter the picture and have a detrimental effect on peer relationships? In fact, because one requirement for entry into a peer relationship is nonpossessiveness, jealousy has a very insignificant effect on such relationships. "Jealousy is not a barometer by which the depth of love may be read. It merely records the degree of the lover's insecurity. It is a negative, miserable state of feeling, having its origin in a sense of insecurity and inferiority" (Mead, 1960). It would appear, from Ramey's study, that these individuals can enter into a union in which the major purpose is the enhancement of the growth of each individual as well as the enhancement of the relationship.

In regard to sex roles, there is a strong tendency in peer relationships toward a division of tasks without regard to gender. Both men and women clean and cook, as well as go to work. However, there do appear to be some traces of traditionalism in these relationships. Although tasks are divided, they are not divided equally. Most working wives in the peer relationship, as in other kinds of relationships, continue to do most of the domestic chores. In addition, when children are involved, the woman bears the major responsibility of child care and must deal, Ramey says, with the conflicts that emerge from raising children and maintaining a career. Therefore, the causes of stress, as well as the mechanisms developed to deal with them, are similar to those outlined by the Rapoports (1972). In both cases the woman continues to fulfill most of the domestic functions.

Conflicting Results of Ramey and the Rapoports In studying individuals who graduated from a university in 1960, the Rapoports (1972) found that the majority of married men with children found primary satisfaction in their family (55 percent) and secondary satisfaction in their career (30 percent). An even greater number of married women with children put family first (80 percent), with only a few giving primary emphasis to career (4 percent). In his study of 380 individuals in intimate relationships, Ramey presents statistical figures as well: 87 percent of the males ranked career first and 67 percent ranked family or love second, whereas 95 percent of the women put family or love first and 82 percent put career second. There are some interesting inconsistencies in the two sets of results. First, a majority of the Rapoports' men place family first whereas a large majority of those sampled by Ramey place career first. Second, although women in both studies placed interpersonal relationships above career, the percentage in Ramey's study exceeds that in the Rapoports'. This is especially surprising in view of the fact that many women in Ramey's study did not have children and all of those in the Rapoports' study did. Conclusions from this comparison are naturally tentative but these figures suggest that those entering into "peer relationships" are still strongly motivated by the concept of the man as "breadwinner" and the woman as "nurturer."*

The implication of most of the previously cited analyses of "equal" relationships is that, in a truly integrated marriage or partnership, both partners will have careers and will be strongly involved in interpersonal relationships. As we have seen in Ramey's study, the commitment to interpersonal relationships does not necessarily entail raising children. Just as it is possible for people to fulfill themselves in creative enterprise without actually engaging in what might be termed a career, it is also possible to fulfill our need for love without tending children. However, the combination of career and family interests for each partner is one way—perhaps the most likely way—for many individuals to fulfill both their instrumental and expressive needs.

In addition, for an equal partnership to exist, both partners must have equal personal financial resources. There is some evidence, for example, that the power differential between husbands and wives is strongly influenced by the employment status of each. Although Blood and Wolfe (1960) maintain that the power of husbands and wives is determined by the "personal resources" of each, Gillespie (1971), in attacking this position, states that the power is determined not by nebulous "personal resources" but by the income-producing potential of each partner. She finds that in most homes husbands still earn more money and are dominant. In homes where the wife earns more money she is the dominant partner. But in no case are they equal. This accords with Garland's research (1972) which uncovered only one egalitarian marriage. Garland found that in each case in which the wife had a higher income, she also was psychologically dominant within the home. He termed this marital pattern a "matriarchy" and stated that both partners found the situation unsatisfactory.

Thus it appears that both partners in a relationship must maintain a career in order to equalize the balance of power associated with work and income in our society. However, at the present time, the more satisfactory relationships, as perceived by the partic-

---

*Douvan (1976) suggests that these conclusions may apply only to the age groups studied and not to younger people. All of the above research has been conducted on samples with an average age of approximately 32 to 38, indicating that these individuals grew up in the 1940s and 1950s. A younger age group exposed only to the less traditional norms prevalent after 1960 may indeed manifest less traditional inclinations.

ipants, are those in which the husband has a slight edge in terms of power and, as a result, in psychological dominance. If society gradually drops the importance placed on achievement-oriented accomplishments, or if we are more successful in raising people who can withstand the influence of these values in our culture, we may grow toward a time when such balances of power need not be maintained by status and income, when a more human (and a more humane) estimate of worth is derived from the personal strength and the personal caring of each individual.

The studies cited earlier regarding "coordinate" and "equal" marriages illustrate important ways in which couples are implementing the vision of a partnership transcending sex-role sterotyping. Although evidences of sex-role typing are visible, these studies show that a union based on equality and individuality is possible even in our current world. We may reasonably anticipate that these initial studies and observations in the sex-role literature reveal just the tip of an iceberg, and that the rest of the iceberg will emerge as the waters of fear, inadequacy, and conformity recede.

LOVE AND SEX BEFORE MARRIAGE

Recent studies of sexual behavior among young people indicate that new patterns of relating are developing which *do* give more emphasis to the individual and less to the traditional family unit. Sorensen (1973), in a large national survey, found that young people were emphasizing the importance of good communication and companionship in their relationships. This emphasis supersedes a direct interest in marriage or in sexuality *per se* (although nearly one half the young people surveyed had experienced sexual relations). Many of these young people, aged 13–19, are refusing to play the "dating game" and are seeking new ways of relating to the opposite sex. Sorenson concludes:

> Our data show that some boys and girls are seeking to generate a society that values love and affectionate relationships and that treats men and women as whole people rather than as sexual beings. . . . It is true that adolescents are making some mistakes. . . . But in general they are trying to become whole and feeling people (pp. 374–375).

Moreover, studies of cohabitation (Macklin, 1974) also reveal that young people are more interested in affection and companionship than in a purely sexual relationship or a traditional marriage relationship. Macklin found that among college students about one third chose to live together, or at least to share a bedroom, several nights a week. The majority of these young people are monogamous, have strong affectionate relationships, and yet at the moment do not plan to get married. Most of them have found that in their relationship, verbal and nonverbal communication has the highest priority. They do not see in their own lives strong evidence of sex-role scripting, and they are joined in a search for a meaningful relationship.

It is, no doubt, true that many of these relationships will yield to more traditional ones as the young people grow older. Yet it is also very likely that many of these people will remain more open than their parents and possibly set new and more egalitarian patterns for the mature male/female relationship.

TWO CASE HISTORIES

The following accounts illustrate both the newer concept of a "peer relationship" and the beginnings of process-oriented changes in a more traditional relationship. Both couples are finding ways to create new forms and to revitalize old forms in order to achieve more fully their own individual goals.

EILEEN AND DEREK

Eileen and Derek are examples of individuals seeking and finding satisfaction in relations which break away from the standard sex-role stereotypes. The relationship between them began six years ago when Eileen was 16 and Derek 21. Eileen was experiencing her first taste of adult independence by choosing to live away from her parents' new home in order to finish school with her high-school class. She lived 2500 miles from her parents with a friend of her grandmother's, and worked part-time to pay her out-of-state tuition fee. Derek at the time was just beginning his work in a therapeutic facility for children. The relationship continued over the next four years as the couple lived separately and together, alternating between the state where they had met and the new location of Eileen's parents. After four years they got married and settled in a different part of the country while Eileen finished school and Derek continued in his profession. Currently both are working full-time.

Eileen comes from a home in which traditional sex-role stereotypes were not observed. Her mother loved her teaching career; her father, though committed to his work, enjoyed cooking and caring for children. When Eileen and her brother went to nursery school, they were sometimes cared for by their grandmother during the day; in the evenings they were cared for by both mother and father. Both children were raised to be independent, analytical, nurturing, and caring. Since their mother worked, both children undertook household tasks as preschoolers and experienced a great amount of independence. Despite this independence, Eileen has strong and close ties with her family. She admires her mother greatly and confides in her freely. Moreover, she is close to her brother whom she describes as her best friend.

Eileen examines her early expectations of what women do:

So in my eyes mothers had careers, and grandmothers raised children and did homemaking tasks. I never associated the two together.

When asked at 8 years of age what she wanted to be, Eileen remembers stating: "A lady astronaut or a psychiatrist." She added, "My husband will take care of the children until they are old enough to enter nursery school."

Although tomboyish as a child, Eileen remembers with surprise that she turned quite feminine overnight when she reached adolescence: "It was almost as if I went to bed at night as a tomboy and woke up in the morning as a teen-age girl." She recalls being relatively happy with this state of affairs, and popular and well-liked in school. Shortly thereafter she met Derek, a young man also from a nontraditional home. At the age of 20 Eileen married Derek.

You might wonder what a career-oriented, so-called independent girl like myself is doing getting married. My answer can only be that I found a person with whom I can be a very close friend, lover, and companion, whom I also love very dearly. I have had the best time of my life with him, for he can make me happy and sad, laugh and cry, and feels I am the most important person in the world. He is wonderful, nutty, funny, brilliant, unpredictable, loving, caring, responsible, charming, romantic, honest, and trustworthy. We get along fantastically! He is everything and even more than I wanted in a man.

She describes Derek's nonsex-typed orientation:

He is as much a different male as I am a different female. He loves to cook and do domestic things. He likes to work with children.

She comments, moreover, that Derek tends to be more emotional than she, whereas she is the logical one. Thus emotionally and in role divisions both partners partake in masculine and feminine orientations.

In describing her marriage Eileen emphasizes freedom:

Our marriage is not geared along traditional lines. If I am to succeed in marriage, my husband has to understand and accept without reservation my need for individuality and expression outside the home. Derek understands, accepts, and welcomes this need because he does not want to get trapped into the male syndrome of being the sole supporter of a family.

I feel freedom within a marriage is a very essential aspect. . . . I had gotten into the habit of doing a lot of traveling before we got married and was afraid I would have to give it up. However, I go on more trips now than I had ever done before. . . . Derek has never so much as expressed resentment or hostility or tried to talk me out of going on my numerous trips.

On Eileen's return from trips the couple engage in standard sex-role behavior for about a week:

When I come back from my summer trip, we go through about a week in which our normal sex-role behavior is changed. We behave like Ozzie and Harriet. I cater to his every whim and he caters to mine. We try to be together every hour. . . . But thank goodness this lasts for only about a week. By that time we are both tired of falling over each other's feet and being smothered by each other. We go back to our normal relationship, which lasts until the next year.

In addition to their willingness to allow each other freedom to meet their own needs, Eileen stresses the importance of honesty and finds it crucial in their relationship:

I feel one reason we get along so well is because we are completely honest with each other. We have never gotten into the trap of lying about our actions. I am able to talk to him as a friend or lover and know he listens to what I say.

In recent months, the freedom which they extend to each other, and the honesty with which they share their lives, has been extended to extramarital sexual encounters:

We are both free to develop friendships with members of the opposite sex outside our marriage. Very early in life I was taught that the double standard should not exist for the male or female in any way, shape, or form. If I allow my husband to go out and have relations with other women, I expect the same in return. Miraculously we both have the same feelings. . . . Derek and I have discussed this aspect of a marriage for many years, and decided our marriage was strong enough to give it a try. Since then we have always told each other of the complete experience if the opportunity arose. . . . It may seem strange, but these affairs have made us appreciate each other more. These have been very fruitful experiences because they have helped open up another side of our feelings and personalities. . . . One has to remember that in many marriages a person would be playing with fire if he or she had outside relations and were honest about it. Therefore, each person has to evaluate his or her own situation to determine if something like this would work.

Eileen finishes this discussion of her marriage:

In conclusion, we have what is essentially an "open marriage." I know I am completely satisfied and happy living with Derek. I am married and yet feel single. My freedom, goals, and independence have not been hampered. I am in a relationship in which I know the avenues for attaining my desires are open. I feel I have the best of two worlds and I like it that way.

IMPLICATIONS

Eileen and Derek are engaged in a process-oriented relationship very much like Ramey's description of a "peer marriage." Both have freedom to pursue their many interests in work, recreation, and friendship. Eileen's account reflects her love for Derek and her delight in him. She perceives his feelings as being similar in kind to hers. They each have freedom to be themselves fully. There is no trace of a desire to improve or change each other, though they care deeply for each other and facilitate each other's self-directed growth.

Moreover, there is strong and open communication between the two. At present the relationship appears to be a healthy and fulfilling one.

This relationship may yet be tested as the individuals mature. Their sexual experimentation outside of marriage is very recent. It may indeed be that they can incorporate sexual freedom into the fabric of their marriage. However, some recent case studies (Rogers, 1972; Masters & Johnson, 1974) illustrate that there are usually strains involved in tolerating extramarital affairs for either party. Yet from Ramey's work one might hypothesize that these strains are not caused by the multiplicity of relationships but are due rather, as the Rapoports state, to the conflict between an innovative life-style and a society adhering to traditional values, one of which is the permanence and *exclusivity* of the marriage relationship. There are couples, as Ramey points out, who have developed extremely satisfying life-styles, including both primary and secondary sexual relationhsips. Eileen and Derek may be one of these.

In addition, Derek and Eileen are aware of the added burden that will be placed on their relationship if they choose to have children. (At the moment they anticipate doing so.) From the studies of dual-career families, it has been shown that the additional time and energy required to raise a family often causes at least one of the partners to relinquish some outside activities. Women usually make the greatest sacrifices, even in "equal" relationships.

There is also substantial evidence that young egalitarian marriages become much more traditional in time. Couples who share the management of finances and household responsibilities in their first years of marriage slowly slip into traditional sex-typed divisions of labor after five years of marriage. Joint decision-making policies often become male-dominated policies, and married women begin to define their husbands' role as the "breadwinner" and their own role as the "mother and homemaker"; they no longer view each partner primarily as a companion to the other (Safilios-Rothschild, 1972). In addition, it appears that the wives are the first to demand exclusivity of function by slowly excluding the husband from household responsibilities.

The arrival of children further causes egalitarian marriages to revert to traditional forms. Rossi (1968) speaks of the gut-level feelings—remnants of our early socialization patterns—that surface with the birth of children. Unresolved role conflicts revolving around motherhood most often send women back to the kitchen.

Even if the woman maintains an outside job, the importance of such an activity diminishes. Rossi, in speaking of working women, states, "There is considerable evidence that these wives' preoccupation with being able to maintain the traditional housewife role prevents them from achieving truly egalitarian marriages" (1964b).

Therefore, it is not possible to predict whether the egalitarian union of Eileen and Derek will continue as it is or whether it will succumb to the stresses found in older relationships. However, there are no guarantees in any relationship. We are all, individually and together, subject to the unknown contingencies that may shake our world. Thus it is wise to evaluate this relationship only in the present. From this vantage point it is a healthy union. Both young people are intelligent, loving, caring, and independent individuals from relatively nontraditional backgrounds. They are using their talents and strengths to risk exploring all the growth-potential which, individually and together, they may offer each other.

BETH AND GLEN

Beth's story is quite different. She grew up with a home-loving (or perhaps we should say with a duty-bound) mother, who was overprotective and manipulative and a father who was preoccupied with work and emotionally absent from the home. The mother decided early that Beth was to be the "perfect daughter" and within the framework of an intense mother-daughter relationship set out to make her so. There was little resistance from Beth, who experienced strong dependence upon her mother as well as feelings of guilt over the hatred she sometimes felt toward her. Beth grew up with an overwhelming desire to be feminine, and she believed that "being feminine meant being married, home-bound, and house-oriented."

After finishing college and working a year, Beth married Glen, a gentle, attractive, achievement-oriented man who also came from a traditional background. During the next years Beth had four children and began to experience migraine headaches. Nonetheless, she believed that her role was divinely ordained to remain in the home. She felt guilty for her inability to be content. She prayed each morning, "Please, God, help me just to get through this day."

Beth talks about the period when she began to shape her own life. The catalyst for her own questioning was Betty Friedan's book, *The Feminine Mystique.*

Then Betty Friedan walked into my life. I remember well the tears of relief, just to know that there were others who felt as I felt, who shared even my damnable feelings. Oh, the all-encompassing pleasure of release! I could now allow my feelings and questions to surface, if only for my own scrutiny. The guilt feelings were there, too, like poisonous snakes, weaving in and out of my thoughts, spraying their venom. I believed that my husband wanted me to function according to the prescribed role and because of this I remained quietly domesticated on the exterior. Inside the conflict roared and ravaged. . . .

I was alone and terrified, but I knew that I had to liberate the real me that had been trapped inside for so long, or I would explode. Then, before I realized what was happening, I found myself sharing some of my introspection with my husband. To my surprise and great delight, he fell madly in love with my newly exposed personhood. And the migraines disappeared overnight.

This psychological breakthrough resulted in Beth's return to school and to teaching children. She has been studying and teaching for several years, and she now takes a look at where she is today:

I feel that I am now a complete person, by my own definition. I am a woman with a personal life; I am a giving and a receiving friend to my husband and to others; I am a mother who participates in the instruction and nurturance of children; and I am a homemaker whose primary interests lie in the cultivation of a healthy atmosphere for all of us. No one role receives all of me. Rather I see possibilities for growth and enrichment in the challenge to apply the desirable human attributes to these various spheres of my life. As the children become increasingly independent, I will devote more of my time to my career. I like where I am.

Beth sees that both she and her husband are "living a change." They are preparing for a time when she will support the family so that he will have the opportunity to explore a second career, which he has long wanted to do. Both are ready to give equal weight to Beth's desires and ambitions when her education is complete. Both are loosening the confines of sex-role stereotypes for their children, hoping to enable them to become full human beings like themselves. Beth says that someday she will write a book about how androgynous children grow up. In her book "there will always be the fun and freedom of enjoying shared interests in an atmosphere where love and joy can burst into real and spontaneous happiness."

IMPLICATIONS

Beth and Glen have a strong, fulfilling relationship. There are traces of traditional patterns in their life-style, but they have modified the tradition in which they lived so long in order to meet their newly expressed needs. Love and tenderness are in their story as well as honesty and freedom. Although they come from more traditional homes than Eileen and Derek, and have more demands upon their time because of their large family, Beth and Glen have also found a way to move outside the confines of their roles to become more fully human. They anticipate taking even more risks and growing more as the years go by.

Both of these couples are creating new life-styles to meet the present situation which are not just a carry-over from the past. Yet each couple's life-style is unique, shaped around the individualities of the people involved. Moreover, in both relationships there are uncertainties and ambiguities, which are also accepted at this time. Both couples have taken the less traveled road described in Robert Frost's poem "The Road Not Taken." Around it Beth built her story:

Two roads diverged in a wood, and I—
I took the one less traveled by,
And that has made all the difference.

SUMMARY

The process-oriented relationship is one in which individuals remain strong and yet transcend their own individualities in relating to another person. In such a relationship, each person accepts the other fully, allowing each individual to be his or her own unique self. Individuals in a process-oriented relationship maintain a vital and growing relationship over the years. "Dual-career families" and "peer relationships" are two examples of the way in which individuals are attempting to live in process-oriented relationships. Yet even in these relationships there are evidences of traditional masculine/feminine role scripting and of the strain caused by trying to live a nontraditional life-style in a traditional society.

Despite the strains, most of the people studied in recent research are satisfied with their life-style. Ramey (1975), for example, finds that his subjects are vital, capable, satisfied individuals who often emerge as leaders in their work and in their community.

Young couples like Eileen and Derek and older couples like Beth and Glen are discovering the satisfactions of such a relationship and will establish new orientations that will soon be more prevalent in what the Rapoports (1972) refer to as a "postindustrial society."

In this chapter and the previous one we have examined a growing alternative to traditional role orientation. In the next four chapters we shall examine the reality which to one degree or another guides our lives—the shaping of our lives by roles.

EXERCISE: BEING ALONE AND BEING WITH OTHERS

Sit back and prepare yourself for another fantasy trip.

In your "mind's eye" gather about you all the people who are most important in your life. Now slowly watch them fade away and notice that you are alone.

How do you feel being alone? Are you frightened? Anxious? Serene? Content? Take a few minutes to examine how you feel being totally alone.

Now bring back all the people whom you love. One by one let each of them approach you. Tell each one how you feel about him or her. Let the person answer back. When each of you has said all you want to say, say goodbye to this person and let another one come forward. Continue until you have spoken with each of the people in your fantasy.

When you have finished, consider the following questions:

How much of your feeling for each person is based on your own need? How much on your own strength?

How willing are you to let the other person be himself or herself? How willing is he or she to let you be yourself?

How much of this have you in fact told these other people? How much have you held back? Did you hold back even in a fantasy situation?

If you hold back, in fact or fantasy, what is the reason? Do you fear hurting others? Do you think they can't take it? Do you fear losing their approval and/or acceptance? Are you afraid that they may leave you?

ANDROGYNY AND SEX ROLES: THE VISION

To what degree did you "own" your own feelings? Did you start statements with "I"? Did you speak only for yourself? Or did you use the plural "we," or the general "you"? Did you refrain from evaluating others by saying "you are ... ," or did you focus on yourself by beginning with "I am ... " or "I feel ..."?

Overall did you learn some positive things about yourself? Did you learn some negative things? Now discuss with members of your class what you learned from this fantasy trip. Were your experiences similar? Did they hold back during their trip? How did their reasons compare with yours? Remember that any learning you do about yourself, whether positive or negative, is an achievement, not a liability. As we become more aware of ourselves, both positively and negatively, we enlarge the scope of our freedom and can learn to better accept human imperfections in ourselves as well as in others.

REFERENCES

Bailyn, L., "Career and Family Orientations of Husbands and Wives in Relation to Marital Happiness," *Human Relations,* vol. 2 (1970): 97–114.

Blood, R., and Wolfe, D., *Husbands and Wives,* New York: Free Press, 1960.

Bott, E., *Family and Social Network,* London: Tavistock, 1957.

Bryson, R., Bryson, J., Licht, M., and Licht, B., "The Professional Pair: Husband and Wife Psychologists," *American Psychologist,* vol. 31 (1976): 10–16.

Cuber, J. F., and Harroff, P., *Sex and the Significant Americans,* New York: Penguin, 1965.

Douvan, E., "The Family in the 1970's," speech presented at the University of Michigan-Dearborn, Dearborn, Michigan, December 8, 1976.

Dublin, J. E., "Gestalt Therapy, Existential-Gestalt Therapy and/versus 'Perls-ism,'" in E. Smith, ed., *The Growing Edge of Gestalt Therapy,* New York: Bruner/Mazel, 1976.

Fromm, E., *The Art of Loving,* New York: Harper & Row, 1956.

Fromm, E., *Escape from Freedom* (1941), New York: Avon Books, 1971.

Garland, T. N., "The Better Half? The Male in the Dual Profession Family," in C. Safilios-Rothschild, ed., *Toward a Sociology of Women,* Greenwich, Conn.: Xerox College Publishing, 1972.

Gebhard, P., cited in M. Hunt, *The Affair,* New York: New American Library, 1973.

Gillespie, D., "Who Has the Power? The Marital Struggle," *Journal of Marriage and the Family,* vol. 33 (1971): 445–58.

Kinsey, A. C., Pomeroy, W., and Martin, C., *Sexual Behavior in the Human Male,* Philadelphia: W. B. Saunders, 1948.

Kinsey, A. C., Pomeroy, W., Martin, C., and Gebhard, P. H., *Sexual Behavior in the Human Female,* Philadelphia: W. B. Saunders, 1953.

Macklin, E. D., "Cohabitation in College: Going Very Steady," *Psychology Today,* vol. 8 (June 1974): 53.

Maslow, A. H., *The Farther Reaches of Human Nature,* New York: Viking, 1971.

Masters, W. H., and Johnson, V. E., *The Pleasure Bond: A New Look at Sexuality and Contentment,* Boston: Little, Brown, 1974.

Mead, M., *The Anatomy of Love,* New York: Dell Publishing, 1960.

Meerlo, J., *Conversation and Communication* (1952), in J. McCary, *Freedom and Growth in Marriage,* New York: Hamilton/Wiley, 1975.

Perls, F., *Gestalt Therapy Verbatim,* Moab, Utah: Real People Press, 1969.

Poloma, M., "Role Conflict and the Married Professional Woman," in C. Safilios-Rothschild, ed., *Toward a Sociology of Women,* Greenwich, Conn.: Xerox College Publishing, 1972.

Ramey, J., *Intimate Friendships,* Englewood Cliffs, N.J.: Prentice-Hall, 1975.

Rapoport, R., and Rapoport, R., "The Dual-Career Family: A Variant Pattern and Social Change," in C. Safilios-Rothschild, ed., *Toward a Sociology of Women,* Greenwich, Ct: Xerox College Publishing, 1972.

Rogers, C., *Becoming Partners: Marriage and Its Alternative,* New York: Delacorte Press, 1972.

Rossi, A., "Equality Between the Sexes: An Immodest Proposal," in R. Lifton, ed., *The Woman in America,* Boston: Beacon Press, 1964a.

Rossi, A.. "Transition to Parenthood," *Journal of Marriage and the Family,* vol. 30 (1968): 26–39.

Rossi, A., "Will Science Change Marriage?"*Saturday Review* (December 5, 1964b): 75–77.

Rostow, E., "Conflict and Accommodation," in R. Lifton, ed., *The Woman in America,* Boston: Beacon Press, 1964.

Safilios-Rothschild, C., "Companionate Marriages and Sexual Inequality: Are They Compatible?"in C. Safilios-Rothschild, ed., *Toward a Sociology of Women,* Greenwich, Conn.: Xerox College Publishing, 1972.

Sorensen, R. C., *Adolescent Sexuality in Contemporary America,* New York: World Publishing, 1973.

Stein, A. H., and Bailey, M. M., "The Socialization of Achievement Orientation in Females," *Psychological Bulletin,* vol. 80 (1976): 345–66.

Tubbs, W., "Beyond Perls," *Journal of Humanistic Psychology,* vol. 12 (1972): 5.

III

ANDROGYNY AND SEX ROLES: THE REALITY

If you don't know the kind of person I am
And I don't know the kind of person you are
A pattern that others made may prevail in the world
And following the wrong god home we may miss our star.

William Stafford, *"A Ritual to Read to Each Other"*

The reality of the other person is not in what he reveals to
You, but in what he cannot reveal to you.
Therefore, if you would understand him, listen not to
What he says but rather to what he does not say.

Kahlil Gibran, *Sand and Foam*

5

The Search for Stability: Standardizing the Individual

Many individuals relinquish their freedom by seeking security in the fixed images of masculinity and femininity. However, with the continued advances of science and technology, traditional sex roles have lost much of their justification. For example, machines now perform much physical labor so that the physical strength of men is no longer required for economic survival. Similarly, contraceptives are available to prevent unwanted pregnancies so that women's functions are no longer limited to those related to child bearing. Despite these changes, the traditional forms still exist and continue to create strain and discomfort in the personal lives of many men and women. Why, then, do many of us still cling to these old forms? In Chapters 3 and 4 we explored the characteristics of individuals who were willing to govern their lives by their inner processes; such individuals illustrate the *vision* of how we might live. In Chapters 5 through 8 we will show how, if we maintain the

Gradually we form our concepts of what sorts of persons we are, and unthinkingly we assume that that is the only way we can be. . . . When we allow our reaching out to be inhibited by what we or others assume to be our fixed image, then we settle for less than is potential to us.

James Bugental, "The Self: Process or Illusion?"

The more we are threatened, fragile, vulnerable, the more we renounce freedom in favor of an expanding necessity.

Allen Wheelis, *How People Change*

traditional sex roles, we allow form to take precedence over process and we preserve the illusion of certainty and stability in a rapidly changing world. For most of us, these chapters outline the *reality* of our lives.

CHARACTERISTICS OF ROLE-ORIENTED INDIVIDUALS

When faced with freedom of choice, and the possibility of several courses of action, many of us feel vulnerable and threatened. When faced with the fact that people—and the society they compose—are constantly changing, we feel anxious and insecure. At such times, many of us choose to retreat to familiar forms that will bring some semblance of stability back into our lives. We choose to believe that relationships last forever and that the pattern of our days will continue in the customary way. Many of us choose to cling to the traditional roles of masculinity and femininity to help us to guide our lives.

We can identify several characteristics of role-oriented individuals—those individuals who choose form over process. First, role-oriented individuals tend to regard people, including themselves, as objects acted upon by their environment rather than as subjects acting upon the environment. We often hear people say: "Well, that's the way women are"; or "Boys will be boys." Such expressions overlook the uniqueness of individuals and the potential for change that is in all of us. Instead we regard men, women, and even ourselves as objects with certain fixed and unchanging characteristics. By denying the possibility of change, by accepting the historical definition of the sexes and our own personal history as a command, we forfeit freedom for the illusion of security.

Second, role-oriented individuals must limit their awareness of what goes on within themselves and in the world around them if they wish to maintain a degree of consistency. Role-oriented individuals do not really listen to statements that may change their perception of reality. How many times have we told other people a new piece of information only to have them repeat it back to us months or years later as if it were an original revelation on their part? When we protest, "But I told you that. . ." the other persons may reply, "You may have, but we never heard you." In fact, they did *hear* that particular piece of information but did not *listen* when it was spoken. Although they may have been aware of the words we spoke to them, our message never penetrated their mental defenses.

To further limit their awareness, role-oriented individuals do not invite disclosure from others or offer disclosure of themselves. The results of such open communication might require them to change their views either of others or of themselves, and changes of this nature are seldom welcome. Therefore, disclosures are kept to a minimum, governed by what we "ought" and "ought not" say. For example, as we walk down the sidewalk, one person says tersely, "How are you?" and the other replies, "Fine, thank you." We are really not concerned about the other person's health. In fact, if the other person actually replied, "I haven't been feeling well, my head aches, my throat is sore . . ." we may get annoyed. Similarly, other role-oriented behaviors also limit self-disclosure. A brilliant young woman with severe family difficulties was falling behind in her work. Smiling and composed she told me, "Well, things aren't too bad, and I've got everything under control." The next week she withdrew from school in order to deal with family crises. A good friend of mine says I tend to do the same thing. When I felt my world was beginning to fray around the edges and was losing its familiar shape, instead of admitting my fear and uncertainty, I smiled and said, "It will be all right."

In such situations most of us behave in role-oriented ways. We ignore, repress, or distort any interpretations about life that contradict our own preconceived ideas. By believing that "everything is under control" or "everything will be all right," we can dismiss any feelings of anger, sadness, or fear that may threaten our own self-image. By doing so, we can preserve the illusion of stability and continuity in our world.

Finally, the fixity and sameness role-oriented individuals attribute to themselves and others is also extended to include their interrelationships with others. If they do not perceive power within themselves, they must seek this power in the world around them—in institutions, ideologies, groups, and other individuals. Thus, role-oriented people base their interactions with others on the degree of power they perceive others to have. For example, if role-oriented individuals meet a new face at a cocktail party, they only know how to react after learning his or her occupational status: A doctor merits more respect than a salesperson; those with a high degree of power merit more respect than peers or subordinates. Students are often uncomfortable among professors who are not instantly recognizable by their dress as distinct from students. One such student remarked, "I wish teachers wouldn't look like people because then I get confused about what to say."

We can see then that the modes of relating for role-oriented individuals become fixed and consistent: They listen with deference or defiance to an authority; they exercise power—benevolently or harshly—over a subordinate. For role-oriented individuals relate the "mask" of one person's personality to the "masks" of others in an accustomed fashion; they rarely relate to the real persons.* Whatever the relationship, category and structure are regarded as being more important than the persons living within them. The pattern of

---

*The psychologist Carl Jung (1971) has developed the term *persona* to signify the mask we wear. Our *persona* is the face we turn to the outside world. Our *persona* is not our total personality but only that part of ourselves which we find acceptable for display to others. Just as actors and actresses assume various roles on the stage, role-oriented individuals adopt various *personas* or masks to fit the roles they play in everyday life.

relationship reflects our assessment of other people's places in the world rather than any personal or unique attributes they may have. These patterns of behavior are somewhat compulsive and inflexible and allow the role-oriented individual to maintain stability in the changing world.

Thus, because role-oriented people perceive power in their relationships rather than in themselves, they must fix and stabilize these relationships at all costs—even if they must surrender their freedom. In this way social ties, including marriage, religion, political orientation, and jobs, are often perceived as permanent and immutable.

We have seen how role-oriented individuals have relinquished their freedom by taking their directions from the outside world. The very process of becoming aware of the roles that guide our lives is in itself threatening enough to keep many people locked into their conventional places. The popular philosopher Alan Watts (1958) speaks of the self-doubt and insecurity caused by an awareness of the impact of roles upon our lives:

> Anyone who becomes conscious of role-playing will swiftly discover that just about all his attitudes are roles, that he cannot find out what he is genuinely, and is therefore at a loss what to do to express himself sincerely. He will find the sensation that every road is barred . . . (p. 63).

It is at this point in awareness that many individuals scuttle back to their accustomed boxes and attempt to close off the possibility that there may be other alternatives. The realization that we are so molded by society, family, or other external forces is indeed frightening. It may be greeted with genuine fear or anger.

In this connection, a young college student, Arthur, writes, "I believe that freedom could be the key to unlock the true human in both male and female. . . . But now I'm sitting here wondering what it would mean to me to be totally free. I get scared thinking about it. . . ." And another student, Brian, speaks with anger of his own realization:

> *This whole thing about roles has really got me bugged. We don't really seem to have any control over our lives. Our roles do everything for us. They cook, sew, wash, open doors, light cigarettes, speak, love, have sex, and even dress us. . . . Here we are robots. I never thought about it: 210 million robots with value systems and everything programmed, or preprogrammed to learn.*

And yet from this realization he beats a hasty retreat when just two weeks later he denies the impact of roles in his own life: "I think that I have come to an earth-shattering conclusion. I don't think that I am playing a role. . . ." Like many of us, Brian is very uncomfortable when he admits that he might not be in total control of his life. He had come to a new awareness that he, in fact, had been shaped by his masculine sex role as others have been shaped by their gender-specific sex roles. However, this new awareness produced an inner conflict in Brian and he closed himself off (at least temporarily) from this new awareness.

SEX-ROLE STEREOTYPES

Sex-role stereotypes have all the characteristics of the structures that confine role-oriented individuals. Their content comes from the past or tradition rather than from a continuing response to current situations. Sex roles tend to objectify men and women, attributing to each sex fixed and relatively unchanging traits. People confined within their sex roles thus become "end products"—finished men or women rather than human beings living in process and exploring a full range of human behavior. If we assume the validity of conventional sex-role definitions, we need not expand our awareness of the world, others, and ourselves, for we "know" what women want and what women do, and we "know" what men want and do. There is no need to look further. In fact, we should fear looking further, because new information might jostle the stability provided by our assumption that masculinity and femininity are indeed universal, either God-given or biologically determined.

Within the framework of sex-role stereotypes man is regarded as the achiever—regardless of whether any particular man at any particular moment might rather not achieve. Within this same framework woman is regarded as the nurturer—regardless of whether at any given moment she might choose not to nurture. Safilios-Rothschild (1972) translates the general behavior patterns ascribed to men and women into specific requirements imposed upon men and women in our society. The requirements she lists are no doubt more specific than our own individual experience of them. Nonetheless, they point to differing expectations of men and women.

This definite restriction of women's options in the United States does, of course, necessarily involve the restriction of men's options; however, the net result for men is not as serious a restriction of freedom and development as is experienced by women. Thus, men do not have the option to abstain from work even when they are severely disabled; they cannot study nursing or home economics, they cannot become nursery school teachers or domestics, and it is tolerated but not encouraged for them to become dancers, painters, etc. (and even then, they are under pressure to excel). They also have to marry while they are young, they must not marry a much older woman, they must become fathers, and they must support their wives and children for life, whether married, separated, or divorced from them. These "right" options do tend to curtail significantly the freedom and development of men in the following ways: they often must choose occupations that can provide them with high incomes rather than the occupations they would most be inclined to follow; they have little opportunity to "look around," grow up, and find out who they are and what they want before they are married; they do not have the chance to enjoy a stimulating and loving wife with a career and/or passionate interests and instead often must endure a psychologically tired, bored, and boring housewife and mother; and they are also never given the chance to develop, through socially approved channels, the "feminine" aspects of their minds and personalities.

Still their option restriction is much less severe than that experienced by American women, for whom the corresponding restrictions have much more devastating effects upon their freedom of choice and their chance for self-fulfillment and growth. The occupational options for women are restricted to only the four "feminine" occupations (nursing, home economics, elementary education, and social work) while most rewarding, stimulating, high-prestige and high-paying occupations are inaccessible regardless of the women's talent or ability that would qualify them for such occupations. Women as well as men have little opportunity to "look around," grow up, and find out who they are and what they want before marriage. But this restriction is much more acute in the case of women because their behavior is generally more regulated, they tend to marry earlier than boys, and they are not encouraged to develop a distinct personality or to have definite ideas and opinions in order not to restrict their field of eligibles. Their personalities must stay flexible to accommodate the man they will marry to the maximum, following his wishes and preferences as to the nature of options they should choose. Therefore, women often fail altogether to develop their identities and personalities throughout their adult lives (pp. 178–179).

The sexes are, therefore, ascribed distinct traits which cause them to be assigned separate and distinct life-styles and role options. The separation of the sexes leads to many advantages as well as disadvantages depending upon the value system applied. From the vantage point of the process-oriented individual, however, most of the results of this separation are indeed disadvantages. When men and women are seen as distinct and separate from each other there is little common ground upon which they can meet and empathize. The lack of empathy leads to the romanticization and mystification of each sex in the eyes of members of the opposite sex. As a result, through the haze of romanticization, members of each sex appear even more different and more remote. Yet at the same time the common tendency to fear what we cannot understand also operates between the sexes. Thus any romanticization of members of the opposite sex is counterbalanced by an equal amount of fear. This fear breeds more insecurity and more need for structure. Sex-role forms become even more important.

IMPACT OF SEX-ROLE STEREOTYPES

Stereotypes of masculinity and femininity mold and shape the lives of all of us today and are also shaping the lives of today's children. Men grow up and live out their lives knowing that, in some way, they must choose to be strong or pay the price of inner guilt and/or the disapproval of members of our society. Women also know that in some way they must nurture others; if they do not, they must pay the price in anxiety and conflict. Moreover, the price is higher for individuals who, in other aspects of their lives, display their need for security and their lack of inner strength and thus have a greater need to conform to the expectations of others.

The impact of these sex-role stereotypes on our culture is affirmed by the recent study of Broverman and her colleagues (1970). In this study seventy-nine clinicians of both sexes and all ages received a questionnaire which asked them to define a healthy person, a healthy man, and a healthy woman. Regardless of the age or sex of the respondent, the answers conformed to the usual sex stereotypes. A mentally healthy man was seen as aggressive, independent, objective, and autonomous. A mentally healthy woman was seen as submissive, dependent, subjective, and suggestible. What makes these two pictures particularly important is the finding that a mentally healthy adult of unspecified sex was described in the same terms as a healthy man. This implies that mental health in our society is defined by the standards of what men are and do. A woman who demonstrates the traits that define a mentally healthy adult would be considered an unhealthy woman. If, on the other hand, she demonstrates the traits that would label her a healthy woman, she would be typed an unhealthy adult. Thus the submissive stereotypes for women and the aggressive stereotypes for men are perpetuated by the clinical establishment that counsels men and women on how best to attain mental health. Small wonder then that women, comparatively speaking, experience a marked degree of ambivalence about questions of mental health and feminine identity.

The conclusions reached in the Broverman study agree with those of a slightly earlier date reached by Neulinger (1968). In his study, Neulinger found that being a healthy woman and being a healthy person were mutually contradictory. Both healthy men and healthy people were seen as dominant, achieving, and autonomous, whereas healthy women were seen as sentient, nurturant, and playful. He concludes that the female ideal of our society is one most useful to men: "namely, an affiliative, nurturant, sensuous playmate who clings to the strong, supporting male" (p. 554).

These results have been confirmed by studies using college students and nonuniversity adults as subjects. Using similar methods two groups of researchers—Rosenkrantz, Vogel, Bee, Broverman, and Broverman (1968) and Broverman, Vogel, Broverman, Clarkson, and Rosenkrantz (1972)—found that sex-role stereotypes are clearly defined by both college men and women. Both sexes see the masculine traits as more desirable. In addition, the self-concepts of men and women as individuals are very similar to the respective stereotypes. Whereas men regard themselves as strong and dominant, women see themselves as nurturant and submissive. Here we come to Bardwick's conclusion (see p. 157) that sometime in adolescence girls come to see themselves as feminine as well as inferior (1971). This is not a very promising prospect.

A more recent study (Unger & Sitar, 1974) shows that there may now be a move away from stereotyping in college students' concepts of themselves. For the most part students in this study tended to see themselves as outside the stereotyped norms. Each sex valued honesty, broadmindedness, and the ability to love, forgive, and assume responsibility. Unger and Sitar conclude that perhaps the stereotypes are diminishing in effect—in particular, the achievement-oriented stereotype for males. However, before we can agree with that conclusion, we must note that although self-concepts tended to be nonstereotyped, both sexes perceived the other sex in strongly stereotypical ways.

Apparently then the ideals of men and women upheld by our society still affect men and women. Traces of the impact of stereotypes are revealed on every level of our intellectual and emotional lives. Men are seen as having the edge intellectually, while women are seen as having the edge emotionally. Members of each sex suffer on a different plane from different disadvantages.

Differences in Intellectual Functioning Years of conditioning and training have produced different cognitive styles, that is, different ways of thinking, in men and women. Gutmann (1970) describes the male style as allocentric. This implies that men are more analytical, and that they tend to have firm ego-boundaries so that they separate themselves from any problem they may be tackling. They do not identify with a problem but rather seek to analyze it. They then proceed to solve the problem by defining a goal, restructuring the field, and abstracting principles. Women, on the other hand, are described as autocentric. They tend not to separate themselves from their problems. Because they have diffuse ego-boundaries, they tend to personalize the world and to see themselves as its focus. Consequently, women learn through the imitation of others and through interaction in interpersonal relationships.*

What are the practical implications of this research? In a well-known experiment by Goldberg (1968), men and women were requested to evaluate identical articles signed by John McKay and Joan McKay. Regardless of the topic involved, the identical articles were evaluated more highly if the author's name was John McKay. Both men and women appear to think that men are better at intellectual tasks and to put women down in achievement-oriented areas.

In addition to rating men's verbal work higher than women's, both sexes rate men's artistic work higher as well. Pheterson, Kiesler, and Goldberg (1971) performed an experiment similar to Gold-

---

*This point of view about male and female differences in cognitive styles has had wide support (Weschler, 1958; Broverman, Klaiber, Kobayashi & Vogel, 1958; Witkin, 1972). However, recently, various researchers including Maccoby and Jacklin (1974) have challenged this point of view and state that there is not enough evidence to support a conclusion that men think more analytically than women.

berg's, substituting abstract art for written articles. In this situation identical paintings were shown to both men and women. Those tagged with a male artist's name were evaluated higher than those identified as being by a female artist. One additional piece of information should be mentioned as pertinent, though: This inequality of evaluation was not apparent if all paintings were presented as winners in an art show. In this case a positive evaluation from the masculine world of art criticism removed a stigma from the women's paintings, which were then evaluated equally with the men's.

Not only are women's intellectual and artistic achievements downgraded; women are also fearful and anxious about their own successful performance in life. In a study by Horner (1970) college students were asked to complete stories relating to the academic success of their respective sexes. Whereas the academic success of men was followed by tales of fortune, many stories about successful women ended with mixed blessings—they might gain academic and professional success but at the cost of their social standing or their femininity. Thus we see that women themselves tend to view their own intellectual success with misgivings.

Further research studies reveal results somewhat different from those of Horner. Yet they substantiate her main conclusion. Hoffman (1974) and Levine and Crumrine (1975) both found that women feared success, but *not* to a greater degree than men did. However, the motives for such fears are probably different for each sex. Whereas men now have a negative response to success because they are beginning to question the value of the traditional achievement ethic, women fear success because of the damage it might do to their social lives.

When women do attain success they tend to devalue its significance. One possible explanation for this may be that women do not want to threaten what they perceive as a "fragile male ego." In addition, they may not want their success to interfere with the interpersonal relationships they have with men. Komarovsky (1973) documents the age-old practice of women "playing dumb" with men they see socially. Also, both sexes consider male accomplishments to be better than female accomplishments, and attribute this fact to different causes. In a recent study (Deaux & Emswiller, 1974), both men and women agreed that if men did well it was due to skill and intelligence, while if women did well it was due to luck. Moreover, both sexes agreed that women do not achieve as well as men, even when evidence is available that they do achieve as well as men.

Thus, most women apparently see themselves as playing a zero-sum game in which success in the arena of achievement spells defeat in the interpersonal arena. Women are trained to be second, not first. For them to take the initiative in an instrumental sense is risky.

Let's hear what two women have to say about this matter. A young student, Vicki, reflects on her own behavior:

> I follow the norms too closely. I fit the description of a success-afraid female. The idea of leaving school and actually working, accomplishing something is totally foreign to me. I'm a good student, a good follower and imitator, but an actualizer? I'm not so sure.

Beth, whose case history appears in Chapter 4 (pp. 132–134), compares her own capabilities to those of her husband and is fearful of surpassing him:

> Why is it important to me that my husband should be more competent in my mind than I? He should handle certain affairs, because I can't do as well, I reason. Yet I know that I can do as well, and perhaps even better. Am I afraid that I may come out "superior" to him in too many areas? If so, what do I fear?

Thus in areas involving assertion and achievement women are timid. As the studies of "equal" relationships show, even career women are willing to take second place. It is most likely that the roots of this timidity lie in women's fear of not pleasing men and not being favorably evaluated by men. From this evaluation they take their own self-definition.

Differences in Emotional Expression Although men are encouraged to be superior intellectually, women are their emotional superiors, according to the traditional pattern. Women have permission to feel, to cry, and to be happy and joyous. On the other hand, men are expected to be inexpressive.

In a study about self-disclosure Jourard (1964) concluded that men tended to reveal themselves much less than women. He hypothesized that this produced more internalized secrets, more tension, more expenditure of energy, and more stress. He suggested, in addition, that this lack of self-disclosure prevented men from knowing themselves or women, inhibited their ability to love, and eventually led to illness and death. To compensate for their lack of self-disclosure men tend to depend in a stereotypical way on gainful employment, enviable status, and sexual potency to give meaning to their lives. Once these achievements are gone, men have no other resources, become dispirited, and are subject to an early death.

Early training most likely accounts for the low rate of self-disclosure among men. From their earliest years males learn that "boys do not cry," that they must keep a "stiff upper lip." They learn that affection is best expressed by an "affectionate" punch to the shoulder with its built-in implication of power and strength rather than by an action implying tenderness and concern. The emphasis on achievement and strength prevents the development of such qualities as tenderness and a willingness to be vulnerable.

By referring to the popular stereotypes, Balswick and Peek (1971) delineate two types of male inexpressiveness: James Bond and John Wayne. Neither stereotypical character overtly expresses his feelings, with the possible exception of anger. Neither James Bond nor John Wayne is ever sad or fearful. There is, however, a significant difference between the two. James Bond is out of touch with his own feelings; indeed, as a result of years of learned repression, he no longer even knows what he feels. John Wayne, on the other hand, obviously struggles with internal feelings but does not permit them to surface or to influence his life. Balswick and Peek include this description of him:

> The on-screen John Wayne doesn't feel comfortable around women. He does like them sometimes—God knows he's not *queer*. But at the right time and in the right place—which he chooses. And always with his car/horse parked directly outside, in/on which he will ride away to his more important business back in Marlboro Country (p. 364).

The implication is, of course, that men's business is out in the world where strength and power are demanded. To maintain the "strong" image, men must limit their relationships with women who stereotypically represent the warm, soft, and tender aspects of life. Although these characteristics are also representative of the warm, soft, and tender side of man, this is a side he chooses not to acknowledge.

Bartolomé (1972) in his study of business executives finds that their most common characteristic is a lack of expressiveness in behavior. Often they would like to express their feelings, but fear or a sense of uncertainty prevents them from doing so. One executive remarks:

> *If I express tenderness to my wife or let her get away with it in front of my friends, they give me hell. Besides, if you express*

tenderness and don't get it back, that's also a problem. And it's also a problem because you're always trying to have some authority at home and there is often competition with the wife about who wears the pants, and you can't afford to show dependence or tenderness when these other things are going on (p. 66).

In this statement about the executive's lack of expression of "soft" feelings lies a very explicit fear that the expression of feelings might make him vulnerable and a loser in what he sees as an ongoing power struggle. Again we come back to the role-oriented individual's preoccupation with power—not genuine power but power in relation to others and, in this case, the security obtained by maintaining control over himself and his wife.

Most men who are awakening today to the possibilities of freedom find that the most severe limitation they experience is the inability to express themselves fully. Again and again they become aware of their lack of ability to communicate on a personal or emotional level. For example, Tom, a young student, reflects on his relationship with his fiancée:

I feel that at times I hide my emotions and feelings, especially from Ann. I don't know why, really. I want to tell her everything but I don't always. I can express myself and I do feel but I don't always want her to know. What it is I can't really say. Am I trying to play or live up to the manly role?

A month later he too justifies his position, moving backwards from his moment of awareness and his potential for freedom to the rigidity of role playing:

Culture needs to have some fixed ideas and values in order to persist. I know that culture is constantly changing but ... certain roles must be taken on by certain people, male and female. I pretty much have accepted society's do's and don'ts. I am open when I feel I should be. But I like to keep some things to myself when I choose to. I have chosen the way I want to be.

The next month finds him again at the other end of the seesaw, once more aware of his own inexpressiveness:

I'm trying to show my feelings more, especially toward Ann. She often remarks that she doesn't know how I feel because she can't tell. That's not good. I want her to know how I feel. But, I'm afraid to let her know. I think I can tell her. I want to tell her but maybe like so many men I can't.

The contradictions in Tom's self-reflections indicate the difficulties we experience in coming to terms with new awareness of our own being and our world. On the one hand, Tom is aware of his fear and chooses to grow. Yet a month later he justifies maintaining the traditional structures or forms because that's the only way to maintain order; in reality, of course, they provide for him a familiar and secure pattern in which to live. And then once again he tries to come to terms with his inexpressiveness. His course is not clear. The roots of the male stereotype run deep.

Other young men also complain of their lack of expressiveness. For example, three male students remark on the discomfort they experience because they do not feel free to discuss their feelings. Rodney says:

> There have been so many times that talking about personal things would have done me a great deal of good, yet no matter how hard I tried I just couldn't talk about them to others.

Another student, George, expresses his feelings of frustration in the following way:

> I'll bet I could count the times on my fingers, with a few left over, that I have cried since I was 12. . . . Do you have any idea of what it's like to get so frustrated that you could crack up but you have no release except physical violence?

These thoughts are echoed by Mike, who tells about the ongoing struggle within himself:

> I realize that I don't talk about my feelings and most of the males I am in close contact with tend to be like this also. . . . Whenever someone says something that hurts me, I try not to let it show and don't say anything about it to anyone. This is something I do automatically and it's something that really creates tension inside me and I can feel it sometimes. . . . I actually find it hard to let these feelings out.

Leonard—a serious, hardworking young man—explains specifically the sensations he experiences when he begins to talk or write about himself:

> Something I think is important to mention is how I feel when talking or writing about emotional, sensitive kinds of things. When the situation arises that I have an opportunity to write about a topic or to talk about something that would enable me to say how I feel, I usually am very excited in doing so. I want to

express myself. But as I get started I soon become very warm. I feel that I have a temperature. My hands become sweaty, and somehow I feel just awful. I then feel not "turned on" about expressing my views but instead I feel "turned off." I start to feel I am saying things that I shouldn't be saying.

Leonard describes all the symptoms of heightened anxiety. Such anxiety characterizes the majority of men when they are confronted with the expectation of disclosing themselves.

"I AM PLAYING MASCULINE AND YOU ARE PLAYING FEMININE"*

As we can see, although women are handicapped in achievement-oriented spheres, men are handicapped in emotional spheres. Both sexes are deprived by the confines of their sex roles. The results are a male who must be strong, and a female who must accept her subordinate status and develop the ability to please her superiors. Soon after or during adolescence the male usually develops a strong sense of his own identity, whereas the female, because of the ambivalence built into her role, "rarely achieves an independent sense of self and self-esteem" (Bardwick, 1971).† This is appropriate, suggests Douvan (1972), because in this way the future wife can more easily take her identity from her husband, who has taken his identity, of course, from the culture around him rather than by creating it himself.

The forms of masculinity and femininity thus affect all of us from birth to death. The impact of these forms is seen in our thinking, our feeling, and our sense of identity. Regardless of the degree to which we are role-oriented, we all have to come to terms with the traditional masculine-feminine structures or forms.

The individuals most in need of these structures are those who cling more tightly to them even when their inner and outer experience finds that they are restrictive. For these individuals who lack inner strength to accept change, the forms provide a sense of security. We will now see how these people cling to the masculine and feminine stereotypes. A poem by a student on the masculine stereotype will begin our discussion.

---

*From Roszak & Roszak, 1969, p. VII.

†This subject will be further explored in Chapter 10.

THE MASCULINE CASE

Dew speckled leaves glisten in the autumn sunlight
And as the cool breeze drifts aimlessly through its limbs
The tree sparkles like cut glass.
Is the illusion not more spectacular than the substance?
So too of many men.

Several variations of the masculine stereotype are outlined by Kaye (1974). Man may see himself in any of the following roles: as a Superman of limitless capacity; as a Neanderthal man in whom physical force rules over reason; as a sexual athlete ready and willing to perform sexually at any moment with any attractive woman; as the hero fighting insurmountable odds in the name of valor and finally triumphing in a fair fight; as the achiever seeking status and possessions; as the dominator whose goal is power; or finally as a playboy, the constant youth.

It is noteworthy that each one of these masculine stereotypes is an unambivalent expression of strength, power, and superiority in the world of achievement, on the field of honor, or in the bedroom. All reflect the notion that men have an unlimited potential for creativity, leadership, and recreation. At the same time, however, all place a burden on men who see themselves as cast in these molds, for there is little room for the feelings of inadequacy, weakness, dependency, or idleness which occur naturally among humans.

It is important to recognize that no man fulfills completely any one of these stereotypes. All of us, regardless of how role oriented, are more complex than any single characterization can portray. But, in many—if not all—men there are traces of the influence of these stereotypes. In our society, men display concern over achievement, sex, and status. Yet they are often unaware of these concerns unless they fail in any of these areas. Men who lose out in competition for a better job, or who lose their job altogether, men who suffer from temporary or chronic impotence, men who are bested in physical contests, all experience some inner conflict and some questioning of themselves. They may, if reasonably enlightened, quickly decide that such incidences are not very significant in the ongoing process of their lives. However, in almost all cases, failure in any of these areas is not accepted automatically. This is true in the case of Mark, who exemplifies the impact that male stereotypes can have on one's own life.

MARK

Mark is young and single and the product of a strongly traditional family. Like many men, he has been strongly shaped by the impact of masculine expectations. And, like most men, he has often felt inadequate as a result of not being able to measure up to this ideal. Feelings of lowered self-worth resulted when he did not excel on the job, in sports, or in the bedroom. Here is how Mark describes his situation:

> Now, let me turn to some of the stereotypes which are attributed to males and show you how I fit or tried to fit into them. As you will see, I didn't meet up to all the characteristics that prove masculinity and, when I didn't, I really felt the effects.
>
> Superman: I feel I have been conditioned to believe that I can do almost anything. "The world is yours; go out and conquer it. Your life is what you make of it. You can do anything if you put your mind to it." . . . But when I went out and faced the real world, I found that no matter how hard I tried, there were barriers blocking my progress and I was left with a feeling of despair and hopelessness.
>
> Sexual Athlete: This stereotype entails the belief that man should be ready for sex almost anytime. I have found this to be true to an extent. . . . But there are times when I am not in the mood for sex. (God what's wrong with me?) This has nothing to do with the girl but has to do with the fact that something on my mind is bothering me. . . . Since it is man's role to be potent and ready to go to bed at all times, and potency means power, a man who cannot ejaculate is powerless. The man who isn't ready to make it at all times is subject to great social pressures.
>
> Aggressor: Throughout my life I was told to be aggressive. Whether on the basketball court, the football field, or the baseball field, the key to winning was to be aggressive. Well, when it came to dealing with people of the opposite sex, I became passive. . . . In my dealings with women, I found it hard to make that big phone call. But I usually called the girl when I asked her out because it was easier to talk to her on the phone than to face her, especially if she said that most painful of all words—"No." That's hard on both sexes. . . . Why should a girl sit back and not go out or go out with somebody she doesn't really want to go out with? . . . What the hell's the difference?

There was an occasion when I went to Susan's one night, a happy man, and left feeling like a disheartened boy. She wanted to know why I didn't make a move on her and why I wasn't aggressive. She felt that everytime we are together, she is the one who initiates our love affair. I disagreed and said we both took part. I know I'm not as aggressive as other men are or as I "should be" but I told her that it shouldn't matter. . . . I took her in my arms and asked her if she knew I loved her and she said she didn't know. I know she said it in disgust but it really hurt me. I began to cry. Man, I just about ran out of the door because I didn't want her to see me cry. I was not a man: I wasn't aggressive and I didn't hide my emotions and I really felt bad.

Emotions: I have found myself involved in a dilemma nearly all men suffer whether they are aware of it or not. Men are strong and can take any physical or emotional pain. . . . Well, I can take the physical but I sure as hell have a harder time coping with the emotional. The physical pain may last for a short time but then it is over while the emotional pain keeps eating away at you the longer you keep it inside.

Many times I have felt like crying and have cried but not in the presence of a single soul. When I really get down and feel depressed I like to be alone. Do I really like to be alone? I guess I have become conditioned to withhold my emotions and keep them to myself. That is why I wish to be alone. Many times I've cried but never in front of someone. (I take that back. I cried in front of Susan that one time; but I felt like an ass.) Keeping my emotions all bottled up really tears me apart and makes me irritable as hell.

IMPLICATIONS

Mark is struggling with the male stereotypes, and he often feels inadequate because of his inability to live up to the stereotypical ideal of masculinity. He is now questioning these stereotypes, especially the societal requirement that he be inexpressive. He recognizes the difficulties of keeping his emotions in; such behavior "really tears me apart." Yet when he expresses himself he feels "really bad." Nevertheless he is subject to the common masculine dilemma created by the cultural expectation that men must never appear weak or vulnerable. Now let's take a look at the stereotypical female, beginning with a poem by Erica Jong on the function of women.

THE FEMININE CASE

I envy men who can yearn
with infinite emptiness
towards the body of a woman, . . .

Women have no illusions about this,
being at once
houses, tunnels,
cups & cupbearers,
knowing emptiness as a temporary state
between two fullnesses,
& seeing no romance in it. . . .

Sex-role stereotypes for women have a different flavor than those for men. They are ambivalent in that they divide the female stereotypes into two opposing roles. The good, or favored, role is generally the one that is the most nurturing. Strength is not favored in a woman; if it appears, the woman is cast into a counterrole that reminds her how far she is from displaying traits natural to women.

Women are seen alternately as the nurturing mother or as the witch mother. The nurturing mother is kind and giving. The witch mother is fearsome and angry. Women also may choose between being the loving and submissive wife or the dominating wife and bitch. Again submission is built into the favored role; strength is seen only in its perversion, in the bitch. Finally women are seen as the temptress-goddess or the sex object. The temptress-goddess is viewed with awe and fear, representing the sexual mysteries of women. The sex object is a passive toy that bends itself to the will of men (see Ferguson, 1973; Janeway, 1971; Lifton, 1964).

Thus, masculine stereotypes revolve around strength and domination; feminine stereotypes, around submission. There is no room within the conventional feminine stereotypes for the exercise of strength, for the need to achieve, for the desire to create. The message is clear: Women are to tend to the needs of men and children. Women are here on earth to please men.

The impact of the feminine stereotypes is somewhat less than the impact of those affecting the male, partially because the messages are not as clear and straightforward for the female. From the time that males are about 5 years old, they are encouraged to be "manly," not to be sissies or like girls. On the other hand, women are encouraged to achieve and to engage in boyish activities until early adolescence. At this time the feminine sex-role messages become intense. The earlier foundation of achievement-oriented messages is often overridden in adolescence and the early 20s as young women learn to be feminine. The following case studies illustrate the effects of sex-role stereotypes on women.

LOUISE

I am a product of my white, middle-class, Catholic background. My values and morals today have been and still are very much influenced by this fact. Upon birth I was duly baptized Louise Collins and for the next eighteen years was taught to be a "good, obedient, Catholic young lady." I learned very early and quickly what things a "good little girl" was supposed to do. . . . I always received the best of everything and was encouraged to "achieve" in grade school. . . . Achieving in the scholastic area won the reward of lots of praise. . . . I see now that the need for the approval of significant others started very early in my life. This need carried over from parental approval to that of teachers in grade school. I was a model student, always doing what I was told, following all the rules, respectful at all times. . . . I was usually quietly obedient.

In contrast to this role behavior, I was also very much a tomboy. Though I enjoyed dressing up for parties and on Sundays, my everyday play activities centered around baseball, kickball, tag, and even Army. . . . Of course when we did play Army, the boys always made me the nurse. . . . I was never afraid of getting dirty, and the messages I was getting were that this was OK.

This happy state of affairs continued until about the fifth or sixth grade. Suddenly my mother began talking about being a "little lady." . . . It was now not OK to play with boys. . . . I had to stop being a tomboy. This new set of imprints really threw me off balance, creating enormous anxiety and confusion that lasted well into my late teens. While once I had been encouraged to achieve the best grades, I now got a subtle but very strong message to be good, but not better than the boys. . . .

My all-A average dropped to Bs and Cs, especially in math and science. To this day I still have a feeling of panic whenever I am asked to do a math problem.

At the same time I was really lost as to what was the right and "in" way to behave in my peer group. . . . I soon learned though, by imitation of older girls and my mother. . . . I dated very little in my first two years of high school. I was playing two roles at this time. The first, despite lowered grades, the "good student–brainy type" girl. The second was the "dateless wallflower."

I continued to be a brainy, plain Jane till my junior year. At this point, contact lenses, a new hairstyle, and a suddenly well-rounded figure changed the whole picture. The males in my classes started talking to me more and more after class. They didn't want help with their homework, but began flirting and clowning around as if they were interested in me as a potential date. This was a new, enjoyable feeling, to be accepted and teased as other popular girls were. This seemingly overnight change sent me to the library and drugstore to read all about poise, charm, and how to be popular. I quickly internalized the sex-role stereotypes that all the teen magazines turn out. . . . I was only happy if I had at least three or four males interested in me at one time. When I was without a boyfriend, I felt lost and miserable. . . . I learned well to identify with a male and when there was not a significant male around, felt panicky.

GLORIA

Gloria's early tomboyishness, like Louise's, also began to fade with great encouragement from her mother and her peer group as she grew into early adolescence.

I was now old enough to realize that, when I grew up, I was going to be a wife and mother. That's what my mother did and that's what Bernadette's mother did and that's what we knew we were supposed to do.

But my mother first wanted me to go to college: "What if something happens to your husband, and you need to get a job and support your children until you remarry? . . ." By this time I caught on real fast to everything my mother told me, even though it helped to have it repeated a thousand times a day.

My mother had two goals picked out for me: One was nursing, the other was teaching. Teaching was good because I could work while my children were in school and be home in time to cook dinner. . . . But nursing was my mother's preference because she had wanted to become a nurse at one time. Also nursing was good because once you had your R.N. you could find a job anywhere your husband located. My parents also liked the idea of my going into nursing because I would probably meet a lot of eligible doctors. My parents have always told me (a thousand times a day) that it is just as easy to marry a rich man as a poor man. So I should leave the poor, unambitious men alone and go out with those that are going to make it in the world. The richer and more ambitious a man is, the more masculine he is.

Most of these messages came from my mother, but when I started dating my father lowered the boom: Leave the bums alone and marry a rich husband.

I started dating when I was in high school, two months before I was sixteen. My mother gave me sound advice, "Don't let him get fresh." When I asked her what that meant she just looked at me and said, "You know, don't let him get fresh." I was very naive; it was only the year before in biology class that I had figured out the reproduction cycle. I figured getting fresh meant either you are not supposed to let boys slap or pinch you, or else it meant not letting them get you pregnant. But getting pregnant was always called "getting in trouble," and I was not sure if that was considered getting fresh.

Anyway, one evening my date, Frank, put his hand on my breast. I didn't know how long to let Frank do this and what it might lead to, but at the same time I didn't want to stop him. . . . I even remember reading Ann Landers' list of ten ways to "cool it," in which she specifically states, "Don't let him get fresh." Ten times. (My mother must have read it first.) Frank's hand had moved away from my breast to inside my pants.

I had to learn to live with all this guilt . . . having no one to share it with and having my mother tell me all men want is sex; if you give it to them, they won't marry you because you aren't the marrying kind. . . . I lived with all this guilt and fear. I think I really loved Frank but, after ten months of dating, my mother accused me of having intercourse with Frank. She screamed and asked where did she go wrong. . . . I told her it wasn't true and she called me a liar. . . . I couldn't take not seeing Frank anymore . . . . I don't know if I've ever gotten over him. He married on the rebound a year later. I entered college and was going to leave my life up to my mother. I had never in my life wanted to be a nurse, but I went into nursing. Moreover, I didn't really want to do anything. I was not ambitious, I had not been programmed to be. I was only programmed to be a wife and a mother, and the only man I had ever loved was now married to someone else.

PEGGY

I don't think I had really been too concerned with role orientation up to the time of my marriage. I had always felt that I could pretty much do and be what I wanted. . . . As a young child in my own family I derived a sense of worth from my father's approval. He was proud of a little girl who was pretty, smart, and well behaved. I'm sure that all the proper "girlish" behavior was reinforced by the approval of my father. I was just happy that "Daddy" was pleased with me and I always tried hard to do what was expected of me . . . . My father was a high-school mathematics teacher and I was proud of him. . . . I can't say truthfully that I ever knew my mother really well.

In spite of the fact that I was encouraged to achieve, I did sense an ambivalence in my father's thinking about women. I felt that he put my mother down a lot, that he considered her opinions valueless. . . . As a result, my mother offered her opinions less and less, and very often had nothing to say at all. . . . Actually, my mother was a very intelligent woman who had done well in school. But she had never been encouraged to do anything with her intelligence, and I think she felt it her duty to be as my father expected and not to question her status.

I got my first "bum steer"—about which I now feel somewhat resentful—in the planning of my college career sixteen years ago. . . . It was decided, with the assistance of my high-school counselor, that I should go into home economics at a good university. By the time I was a high-school senior, I was so excited about the prospect of going away to a big school that I never questioned the fact—and neither did anyone

*else—that I no longer had any interest in fashions and abso-
lutely no other reason for going into home economics. And so I
went, hating my courses, and not doing well in them. I had no
goals at all for my future career. As a result, I did very little
studying, concentrated on my social life, and "busted out" at
the end of my sophomore year. I was horrified—what had I
done?! My father was very upset. . . .*

*Shortly afterward I met my husband. . . . He was like the
proverbial "breath of fresh air." . . . Anyway I was impressed,
my parents were impressed, my friends were impressed—and
we liked each other too, which made it even better. In time (not
very much time) we decided that we loved each other. . . .
Anyway, to make a long story short, about a month before I was
to return to school I discovered I was pregnant. . . . And so we
were married and started out our life of "happily ever after." My
father, although disappointed in the circumstances, was glad
that I would be settling down with a nice young man who
would take care of me. Besides, as Daddy put it, "Girls really
don't need a college education."*

*I entered marriage with all the usual role expectations. I
swallowed the whole line, and wanted to be "everything a good
wife should be." I must try to do all the things my mother had
told me as I was growing up. "You must always try to please
your husband. See to it that you keep a comfortable, clean, and
relaxing place for him to come home to. Always be ready for
sex when he wants it because you don't want him to go
someplace else! You must always be there when he needs
you." These, among many other things, I tried to do.*

IMPLICATIONS

Each of these women has experienced the struggle that origi-
nated in early independence followed by strong emphasis on the
need to be feminine. Despite protestations of independence and
strong achievement orientation, each of them succumbed sometime
during middle to late adolescence to one or the other of the feminine
stereotypes. Louise, in late high school, with a well-rounded figure,
revelled in the role of seductress-goddess, able to attract numerous
males but retain her power over them by being a "good girl." Gloria,
on the other hand, could not untangle the messages given her by her

parents. Without wanting to do so, she fell into the role of sex object, at least in the eyes of her parents. Guiltily she recompensed them for this by becoming the good, submissive daughter. Peggy, who for a long time thought of herself as independent and self-directed, fell into an early marriage when her plans for a career collapsed. She strove to become the submissive wife—and later the nurturing mother. None of these women, however, has reached the end of her story. All of them are now trying to reconcile their femininity with their early strivings for achievement. The trip back from the feminine stereotypes—from submission and undervaluation, from shaping their lives around the world of the men whom they wanted to please—is not an easy one.

Yet in the past ten years women have been questioning their prescribed role. They are coming to grips with their inner conflicts and are attempting to choose more favorable alternatives. However, for some the trip back is too difficult. They yield again to the traditional stereotypes. Lynn, a twice married 38-year-old woman, illustrates this point as she reaches a conclusion after months of soul searching.

After all the feelings I have had about liberation, I have had to conclude that I really am not ready to accept many of the responsibilities that go with it. I really like having a strong man around to lean on, both emotionally and financially. This has come as a surprise to me. Liberation, even in small ways, is really not what I want and I feel uncomfortable with it.

SUMMARY

Role-oriented individuals cling to the past and relinquish their freedom in an attempt to find security in a changing world. The roles of masculinity and femininity bring some semblance of stability into their lives. Yet these roles affect all of us from birth to death, depending on the degree to which we are role oriented. The impact of these forms enters all facets of our lives.

Each of the last four case histories in this chapter presents people who have moved toward an awareness of this impact. Some, like Mark, have increased their awareness. In doing so they have enlarged the scope of their freedom, but have not yet decided to what extent they want to change their behavior. Others, like Louise, Gloria, and Peggy, are now making changes in their lives as they seek to realize their inner learnings and make their own decisions apart from traditional expectations. For them, as for many of us, large parts of their lives remain traditional, often not by choice. Others like Lynn, however, choose to return to the old patterns of behavior rather than venture further on a process-oriented journey which they find, on balance, too strewn with obstacles.

EXERCISE: ENLARGING THE AREA OF FREEDOM

In every situation for every person there is a realm of freedom and a realm of constraint. One may live in either realm. One must recognize the irresistible forces, the iron fist, the stone wall—must know them for what they are in order not to fall into the sea like Icarus—but, knowing them, one may turn away and live in the realm of one's freedom. . . . However small the area of freedom, attention and devotion may expand it to occupy the whole of life (Wheelis, 1973, p. 286).

The above quotation points out that we have a choice between focusing on our freedom or on our limitations. No matter how little freedom we may have at any given moment, we can enlarge that area of freedom by recognizing that ultimately we have chosen our own circumstances, our own manner of expression, and even our attitude toward currently unchangeable restrictions.

Many Gestalt psychologists have developed short exercises to encourage us to recognize and thus expand our freedom. Such exercises may be performed alone or in pairs. Below are a few I have found most useful.

Make a mental or written list of all the things that follow from the following sentence stem:

"I have to . . . (go to school, work, etc.)"

After you have stated a number of items repeat those same items prefaced by the sentence stem:

"I choose to. . . ."

Can you recognize that at some point you made choices that led you to your current situation? Can you see that you do indeed have the freedom to choose otherwise?

Try a second pair of sentence stems:

"I can't. . . ."

and change it to:

"I won't. . . ."

Again do you perceive the enlargement of your area of freedom?

A third pair of sentence stems also includes rearranging our thinking to illuminate areas of choice:

"I need to. . . ."

and change it to:

"I want to. . . ."

Finally, make a list, as long as possible, of all the items that follow for you from the stem:

"I can. . . ."

There are many things we all can do. One student remarked that it is frightening to say, "I can . . ." because then she has to take responsibility for herself and not depend on others. Even so, the area of freedom is recognized, attended to, and enlarged. This is exciting as well as occasionally threatening.

REFERENCES

Balswick, J., and Peek, C, "The Inexpressive Male: A Tragedy of American Society," *Family Coordinator,* vol. 20 (1971): 363–68.

Bardwick, J., *The Psychology of Women: A Study of Biosocial Conflict,* New York: Harper & Row, 1971.

Bartolomé, F., "Executives as Human Beings," *Harvard Business Review,* vol. 50 (1972): 62–69.

Broverman, D. M., Klaiber, E. L., Kobayashi, Y., and Vogel, W., "Roles of Activation and Inhibition in Sex Differences in Cognitive Abilities," *Psychological Review,* vol. 75 (1968): 23–50.

Broverman, I. K., Broverman, D. M., Clarkson, F. E., Rosenkrantz, P. S., and Vogel, S. R., "Sex-Role Stereotypes and Clinical Judgments of Mental Health," *Journal of Consulting and Clinical Psychology,* vol. 34 (1970): 1–7.

Broverman, I. K., Vogel, S. R., Broverman, D. M., Clarkson, F. E., and Rosenkrantz, P. S., "Sex-Role Stereotypes: A Current Appraisal," *Journal of Social Issues,* vol. 28 (1972): 59–78.

Deaux, K. K., and Emswiller, T., "Explanations of Successful Performance on Sex-Linked Tasks: What's Skill for the Male is Luck for the Female," *Journal of Personality and Social Psychology,* vol. 29 (1974): 80–85.

Douvan, E., "Sex Differences in Adolescent Character Process," in J. Bardwick, ed., *Readings on the Psychology of Women,* New York: Harper & Row, 1972.

Ferguson, M., *Images of Women in Literature,* Boston: Houghton Mifflin, 1973.

Goldberg, P., "Are Women Prejudiced Against Women?" *Transaction* (May 1968): 28–30.

Gutmann, D., "Female Ego Style and Generational Conflict," in J. Bardwick, E. Douvan, M. Horner, and D. Gutmann, eds., *Feminine Personality and Conflict,* Monterey, Calif.: Brooks/Cole, 1970.

Hoffman, L., "Fear of Success in Women," *Journal of Consulting and Clinical Psychology,* vol. 42 (1974): 353–58.

Horner, M., "The Motive to Avoid Success and Changing Aspiration of College Women," Women on Campus, 1970, a Symposium of the Center for the Continuing Education of Women, Ann Arbor, Michigan.

Janeway, E., *Man's World, Woman's Place,* New York: William Morrow, 1971.

Jourard, S., *The Transparent Self,* New York: Van Nostrand Reinhold, 1964.

Jung, C. J., *The Portable Jung,* ed. by J. Campbell, New York: Viking, 1971.

Kaye, H., *Male Survival: Masculinity without Myth,* New York: Grosset & Dunlap, 1974.

Komarovsky, M., "Cultural Contradictions and Sex Roles: The Masculine Case," *American Journal of Sociology,* vol. 78 (1973): 873–84.

Levine, A., and Crumrine, J., "Women and the Fear of Success: A Problem in Replication," *American Journal of Sociology,* vol. 80 (1975): 964–74.

Lifton, R., "The Woman as Knower," in R. Lifton, ed., *The Woman in America,* Boston: Beacon Press, 1964.

Maccoby, E. E., and Jacklin, C., *The Psychology of Sex Differences,* Stanford, Calif.: Stanford University Press, 1974.

Neulinger, J., "Perceptions of the Optimally Integrated Person: A Redefinition of Mental Health," *Proceedings of the 76th Annual Convention of the American Psychological Association,* 1968, p. 554.

Pheterson, G., Kiesler, S., and Goldberg, P., "Evaulation of the Performance of Women as a Function of Their Sex, Achievement, and Personal

History," *Journal of Personality and Social Psychology,* vol. 19 (1971): 114–18.

Rosenkrantz, P., Vogel, S., Bee, H., Broverman, I., and Broverman, D. M., "Sex-Role Stereotypes and Self-Concepts in College Students," *Journal of Consulting and Clinical Psychology,* vol. 32 (1968): 287–95.

Roszak, B., and Roszak, T., *Masculine/Feminine: Readings in Sexual Mythology and the Liberation of Women,* New York: Harper & Row, 1969.

Safilios-Rothschild, C., "Discussion: The Options of Women," in C. Safilios-Rothschild, ed., *Toward a Sociology of Women,* Greenwich, Conn.: Xerox College Publishing, 1972.

Unger, R. K., and Sitar, R., "Sex-Role Stereotypes: The Weight of a Grain of Truth," paper presented at the Eastern Psychological Association, Philadelphia, Pennsylvania, April 1974.

Watts, A., *On the Nature of Man and Woman,* New York: Pantheon, 1958.

Weschler, D., *The Measurement and Appraisal of Adult Intelligence,* 4th ed., Baltimore: Williams & Wilkins, 1958.

Wheelis, A., *How People Change,* New York: Harper & Row, 1973.

Witkin, H., *Personality through Perception: An Experimental and Clinical Study* (1954), Westport, Conn.: Greenwood Press, 1972.

6

Masculine and Feminine Scripts: The Locus of Power and Security

The sex-role scripts ordain that men must compete and win, and that women must gain favor in the eyes of men. For men this means a preoccupation with achievement, with being first, and with being admired by women. For women this means predominantly a concern with men. In this way men gain power and women find security under the protection of men.

The script directives govern all interactions between role-oriented men and women, setting the stage and moving the relationship along to a predictable conclusion. The consequent relationship between the sexes results in some advantages for women, although they must sacrifice some of their freedom. Women are aware of this dilemma and accept the benefits of their sex role, even though they chafe at the restrictions inherent in it.

She was taught
If you don't get married you'll wind up
a very lonely person staring at the
four walls
He was taught
If you don't finish law school you'll
wind up an object of pity and contempt
selling ties in an East Orange haberdashery. . . .

Judith Viorst, "Lessons"

Roles came with costumes and speeches and stage directions. In a role, we
don't have to think, we just follow the script.

Ellen Goodman, "Flip-Flops: New Disease of the Sexes"

WOMEN'S ACCEPTANCE
OF DEPENDENT BEHAVIOR

Women are nearly unanimous in appreciating the fact that
they are protected, financially secure, and treated as something
special by men. Most women value this deferential treatment more
than the accompanying prohibitions against achievement and
power on the part of women. Suzanne, a 21-year-old student heading
toward a career, sums up the feelings of a majority of women:

> *I enjoy men catering to me, taking me out, paying the tab,*
> *opening the door, and in general treating me as someone spe-*
> *cial. I would not want to give this up.*

She is very accepting of her feminine scripting and tolerates the disadvantages in order to retain the benefits.

Other women, however, regard their having been scripted into feminine behavior from a more analytical viewpoint. They tend to view with a jaundiced eye the benefits accorded to women by the chivalrous code of men. They are aware that these benefits are only one half of a bargain and that in exchange for protection, security, and courtesy men take for themselves power, assertiveness, leadership, and the ease provided by a domestic female work force. Appreciation of the small gestures of chivalry is tempered by an awareness that, in accepting such gestures, women accept the implicit evaluation of themselves as less competent and capable than men. Some of these women forego the feeling of specialness in order to develop more assertively their own individualities.

Nevertheless, many women find themselves slipping into traditionally dependent feminine behavior when in the company of men. Vicki, a capable, sports-loving young woman whom we encountered earlier (p. 153), describes a camping trip she took with a female friend. The two managed quite well for themselves until two men joined them. Suddenly the women appeared unable to start their own campfire.

> *I guess what I'm documenting here is the noticeable shift from a feeling of competence which we experienced by ourselves to a somewhat playful spotlighting of our weaknesses (real or imagined) when we had interaction with men. We almost gratefully slipped into the helpless female role.*

This script reappears predictably in the lives of many single and divorced women, as the following statements indicate. We have already encountered these three women in Chapter 3 (Mary Beth, p. 93; Angela, pp. 89–92; and Sylvia, pp. 93–94).

MARY BETH

> *My evening out this week was really interesting. We went to eat. . . . During the meal we discussed a personal problem—my friend's family. I had a very strong view and expressed it. My male friend listened and didn't argue. All of a sudden I started to back down. I even apologized for getting so involved. Then I became very affectionate. It was amazing. I was passive*

*and motherly. I became aggressive and logical—then sorry—
and regressed to the sex object. I seemed to take a step out of
my sex role—became frightened and jumped back as far as I
could go. I've noticed that on dates I'm not very liberated.
When I'm getting to know men who are mate material I start off
very slowly. I'm very "feminine." I test for their tolerance level.
I'm as liberated as they allow me to be. This is not the case for
men with whom I just want to be friends.*

ANGELA

*I think I'm regressing. I'm going out with a guy named Jerry
who's the typical sports nut. . . . And, how I hate to admit it, I've
taken the role of the typical female who knows nothing about
sports. Naturally it's bullshit. I played baseball, basketball, and
football on our high-school teams. But do I tell him that? Not a
chance. He really gets off when I ask him about sports. . . . And
this is the worst of all and I probably shouldn't even admit it.
I've started reading the sports page. That in itself isn't bad. But
I'll purposely (can you believe it!) get the names mixed up with
the sports when I talk to him about them!*

SYLVIA

*I am beginning to realize more of the feminine stereotypes in
my own personality. After evaluating my behavior at a social
gathering recently I became aware of the emphasis on the
small feminine physique. I am 5'8 1/2" tall and on this occasion
I felt like a giant. My date measured about 5'6" with platform
shoes and all. To compensate for the difference in height I
wore shoes with no heels. . . . I slouched all evening too. . . .
My voice became high-pitched and whiney. I became very
passive, impressionable, and naive in my manner. I found
myself acting like a child! Was this for my benefit, my date's,
the others? Now in retrospect I can remember other instances
when I have tried to become less assertive, less confident, less
sophisticated when I was surrounded by men shorter than I.*

None of these women accepts such behavior in herself. Each is aware
that such behavior is manipulative and does not lead to a fully

functioning relationship. Yet the women still behave in traditionally feminine ways. Why do they continue to acquiesce?

For most women, behaving in such a manner represents a familiar and comfortable pattern. They have been trained to please men and to use their power covertly—that is, by manipulation—to get their needs met. But this pattern may not be the only reason that women behave in this way. Particularly in relationships with men, women may come to a realistic judgment that such behavior is necessary in order to maintain a relationship—which must be maintained at all costs. (They may indeed be dating men who are so immersed in the masculine role that other behavior would seem threatening and might cause the relationships to end.) This reflects the feminine viewpoint learned in early adolescence that a woman is only a woman when attached to a man—any man. The risk of having no relationship at all with men is one that even many process-oriented females today are not willing to take.

For this reason women often maintain relationships and marriages that have little chance to be more than minimally satisfactory. Sylvia speaks of her early short-lived marriage in these words:

> *All of my life I have been led to believe that the best indication of my worth is how capable I am of attracting men. Who cares? I had a terrible inferiority complex. . . . Even during my first years of college, girls knew each other by whom they were going with. Nobody ever looked at me, so when one guy finally did, I married him.*

Sylvia's *need* for male approval is representative of the feminine need to please the superior sex. Even "liberated" women fall prey to this need and engage in inauthentic relationships in order to enhance their own self-esteem; for most women their self-esteem still depends on "having a man." As Janeway (1971) states strongly, women are here on earth to please men, and most women, even today, are unwilling to do without male approval. The case study of Elise illustrates this point.

ELISE

On several occasions Elise—a highly competent, outwardly independent female—documents her own dependence on male approval:

At times I feel like a little toy doll—dressing, acting, and speaking in ways which men will be happy with. How disgusting. But I know it is the truth.

I really feel trapped! Someone has always told me, "Never be aggressive with men; you must sit quietly and wait for the guy to make the first move." Of course I got this message from my parents, and also from my school, friends, church, etc. What reinforcement! How can I break out? It seems so silly to want to be close to someone so much and yet to be so afraid. I repeatedly advance to make a move and suddenly hear echoes of the past ("Never be aggressive!"). Only this time it comes to me in a little different form—queasy stomach, cold sweat, red face, etc. Something tells me to "stay in my proper place." Why? Mentally I come on so bold, yet emotionally I drag far behind. . . .

This weekend I was asked out by a guy that all summer I had not had the courage to meet. I could hardly believe my excitement. I treated him not as a human being but as a prize to be won. . . . I have a funny feeling: truly in myself I feel no great attraction for him. Yet I dearly want to hear from him again. I want him to approve of me. I want to be accepted. Am I afraid? Friends and family expect me to develop a relationship. . . . I am being pressured by them. Do I want this guy to approve of me just to satisfy others? Yes! . . . I think that for so long I've been told that without a mate I would be lonely, isolated, etc. that I have now come to believe it!

Moreover, Elise recognizes that, just as men regard her as an object with her compliance, she in turn regards them as objects in order to meet the role expectations of her friends and family.

THE SEX-ROLE TRAP

Most of the women described in this chapter have found out that—at least on an intellectual level—they have allowed themselves to be caught in the trap of the sex-role stereotypes. Thus they have given up their freedom. They also have found that the confines of their traps are defined by men rather than by themselves. In their evaluation of themselves and of what is feminine they follow the male lead. Annette—whom we met in Chapter 1 (pp. 16–17)—

describes the continual polarizing of behavior as a "mad merry-go-round game" in which men define women's role and women accede to this definition. Then each sex becomes fearful and feels threatened by the separateness of the other sex.

Vicki analyzes our need to deal with images rather than real people:

> *It seems to me that we all sometimes want to mystify and glorify the real person. We add elegant finishing touches so that their value is partly real and partly polish. For some reason it's not easy to abandon the desire for "heightened" reality as though reality were not enough. . . . All this is related to the idea of sex roles. They are easy traps for avoiding confrontation with the real self. It may be why we still cling to them emotionally, even though we fight them intellectually for the restrictions that they are.*

The heightened reality of which she speaks is the elevation of form or role over content or process orientation. This elevation continues on the emotional level for Vicki as for most others, although at the same time she has difficulty defending her reliance on form.

How do men react to all this?

THE POWER OF MEN AND THE INCENTIVE TO ACHIEVE

Whereas women are willing to examine their own behavior, men as a rule are reluctant to do so. They fear that any role change stemming from this introspection will result in substantial losses on their part. After all, they are the ones who hold the overt power, according to the traditional sex-role stereotypes. Men are the achievers, the leaders, the creators. The white male is today probably at the pinnacle of power in the world, and wishes neither to give up this power nor to share it. Brian, who is typical of role-oriented young men, defends his masculinity in these terms:

> *I really like my sex role. In a sense it gives me power. Not so much a sense of superiority, but more a sense of attractiveness. What guy doesn't want to appeal to women?*

Brian (who periodically denies his role orientation, as illustrated in Chapter 5) attributes the sense of power he experiences as a male to his relations with women. This feeling of power is also revealed by his striving for achievement and a "significant" career. However, as with most young men, his efforts to achieve are taken for granted.

It is only when men fear that their sense of achievement is being surpassed by women that they comment on the power they derive from assumed instrumental superiority. A single male comments on the possibility that his future wife might make more money than he does:

> I do not object to a woman going out and getting a job. I know I would not mind if my wife intended on doing just that. But I can't help but feel a little hurt if she were to make more money than I. Isn't it strange that I feel that way? Yet I wouldn't know how to handle a situation like that.

He carries the situation a step further and imagines himself divorced or widowed, and having to take full-time care of his future children. He would be willing to care for these children only if a good day-care center were available. For, as he puts it, he would find it "extremely difficult to be a loving, affectionate, nurturing father twenty-four hours a day." Asked what his reaction would be if he were forced to give up his job or work part-time in order to look after the children, he replies:

> I would be tempted to say no to that. I would find the pressure to be great, and I would feel that I should be working. I too realize that what I just wrote is a result of my conditioning but all the same I would find it hard to go completely against masculine role expectations.

Thus only in the imagined situation of losing the ability to achieve do men see their power as derived from achievements. Otherwise they usually seem to take their power for granted. At times, however, men experience feelings of personal ineptness and must compensate for them. Because society does not allow men to be expressive and self-revealing, men transfer these feelings to a strong motivation to achieve in the world of work. Consequently many suffer from the disadvantages and effects of the pressure to work harder (see Jourard, 1964; Brenton, 1966). George (who previously talked about his frustration in not being able to express his feelings) does question the achievement ethic. In commenting on the disadvantages of the push to work, however, he draws a caricature, thus alleviating the full impact of what he sees as unacceptable criticism of the masculine role:

There is by far too much stress and too many demands placed on men by society. There is stress from society to be a "success," financially that is. Personal happiness is secondary. There is also stress to get married, settle down, raise a family, hold a job, and support all this. On top of this—especially now—there is the fear of losing your job, which might possibly mean the loss of all the things you have managed to obtain in your short lifetime. That's right—short lifetime. Because of all this stress, man's life expectancy is reduced by about ten years, not to mention all the nifty little things he acquires along the way like ulcers—bleeding, of course—a heart attack, or addiction to alcohol or drugs. You've got to relieve some of the pressure somehow, right? And of course lung cancer—because you smoke two packs of cigarettes a day trying to calm your nerves. So to all the men of the world, Eat, Drink, and be Merry, for tomorrow you may die— and tomorrow may come sooner than you think!

LEONARD

The disadvantages of being masculine are thus often phrased in terms of what a man *must* do whereas women often feel restricted by what they can't do. Let's now consider a 20-year-old man, Leonard, as he reflects on both the assets and deficits of his sex role.

Leonard is rather quiet and shy in nature. He displays an alert intelligence and openness to new experiences, although his openness is somewhat limited. In the following account he reacts to a new view of himself with initial surprise. This is followed by a quick acceptance, which is later converted into hostility. Finally he attains a limited commitment to change. Leonard dates only occasionally, and his thoughts revolve around his future career in business. He describes his current sex-role behavior and emphasizes both his lack of expressiveness and his need for achievement. His definition of self is taken from the cultural stereotype of masculinity. He is only somewhat uncomfortable about this, realizing that his feelings and behavior are two different things. But he sees only limited possibilities for change.

Today, I feel that my sex-role behavior is in accordance with society's view of how a man should be. But I also contend that because of my sex-role conditioning I find it extremely difficult to be the kind of man I could be or should be. There are many times when I want to be deeply expressive and show other people how much I really care about them. But while trying to be expressive I suddenly find myself at a loss for words. My father's inexpressiveness has become my own inexpressiveness. There are those many occasions when it would be appropriate to show a loving, affectionate attitude toward another individual, but I find myself literally freezing up under such circumstances.

In the future, when I marry, as I intend to do, I am surely going to be influenced by my sex-role behavior in my marital relationship. Even if I know that my wife may be well qualified for a professional career, this does not help convince me that it is perfectly all right for her to go out and achieve a higher professional status than I. It's not that I would feel that she didn't belong in such a position. But it's the kind of situation where I would find myself thinking that I have failed in my own career, that I wasn't as capable as she in climbing the social ladder. The thought of my wife making more money than I is an extremely frightening thought. Here again I realize that this is the result of my conditioning and of my feeling that the man should be the breadwinner. One change I would particularly like to make in my thinking is, in fact, this very point. I should not feel guilty or believe that I am a failure because my wife is a success.

Reality, however, often is not the way I would like things to be. I cannot fool myself into thinking I'll ever reach that level where it would be impossible to fall back into the male sex role for which I have been conditioned. At this point in my life I am now more open and honest in my relationships with others, more so than my own parents were able to be. I sincerely hope that if I have children of my own, they will be even more expressive than I can ever hope to be.

IMPLICATIONS

Leonard thus sees some forward movement in his behavior. He is more expressive than his father and has at least considered the possibility that he might have an achievement-oriented wife. However, the thought of being openly affectionate or sharing achievement equally in a male-female partnership is still highly threatening in him. He hopes that his children will do what he cannot—or rather what he chooses not to do at this time.

RELATIONSHIPS OF SINGLE PEOPLE

Sex-role scripting is thrown into high relief in the lives of young men and women who have not found a mate or a career. The uncertainty they experience as they seek to discover what, out of a multitude of possibilities, the future may hold for them, sends them retreating quickly into familiar and predictable sex-role behavior.

The Singles Bar: The Search for Male Approval One of the scenes most likely to evoke typical sex-role behavior is the singles bar. Here women undergo overt evaluation and often rejection by men for the possibility of winning the wanted prize—the company of an attractive man.

In the bars women experience themselves as objects subject to the review and evaluation of men. Most women who have described for me their reactions to singles bars report feelings of inadequacy and resentment, anger, and depression from being treated as objects. Often they are made to feel that they do not "measure up" to the type of women the men are looking for. (It is no consolation that, although men appear to have the upper hand in singles bars, many of them often feel that they themselves fall below some standard of attractiveness in the eyes of the women.) Barbara, a young, single woman, talks about her experiences in a singles bar, where she was not "chosen":

> Some of those guys think they're God's gift to women. And instead of being mad or angry at them, I internalize it into a self-rejection. I begin to feel—well, maybe I am ugly or dull or whatever. . . .

Yet, this self-evaluation, she knows, is contrary to her objective view of herself as an attractive young woman.*

---

*I was recently impressed again by the fact that even women who are generally regarded as very attractive are subject to feelings of inadequacy in regard to their appearance. In a workshop setting, one stunning young woman said that her major problem was that she wasn't attractive. A moment of silence followed reflecting the amazement of the group. *She* was probably the most attractive woman in the room. Yet her concern was genuine. We all carry with us—women as well as men—a general belief that in various ways we are not attractive enough and that if

Mary Beth's statement about the atmosphere in the singles bars also implies that women take their evaluation from men:

If a woman is in a bar, she is there to be picked up. If it's a fast crowd she'll be propositioned and she should love it secretly. She shouldn't get drunk—that's gross. She can get giggly—that's cute. Men are very masculine in bars and women are very feminine.

This woman experimented with "human" behavior in such a setting and found that she was either rejected or viewed as a "hustler." This quickly led to a change in her behavior and a retreat to the feminine stereotypes.

The Price of Male Approval In the dating world of late adolescence, and particularly for people in their 20s and 30s, the implicit assumption is made by men that women will repay them for their company and attention with sexual favors. This assumption is bitterly resented by many women. Yet there is still a residue—often nonverbalized—of the scripting which says a woman must be sexually attractive to a man. A divorced woman, Shirley, after her first date in several years, came to a rather negative evaluation of herself and correspondingly to a resentment of men in general because of this assumption:

I met, or should I say, I had a date with a new fellow recently; and as well as I can determine I am a prude. He was a terrifically nice guy—good conversation, nice dinner. Then we were alone. I really don't mind kissing but enough is enough. I should mention that this is the first new date I've had in two years. . . . But back to this person. He wanted to know—I'm trying to remember the right words—something about how I am in bed: comfortable, liberal. . . . Anyway I guess when he mentioned bed I just turned him off. I don't think I am a prude, but if I am, what the hell?

Yet women often continue to enter into such situations in the hope of fulfilling their adolescent fantasies of a glowing romance.

---

individuals look closely at us they will surely detect the flaws. This is a result of early childhood scripting in which at some times and to some people we were necessarily lacking in physical appeal, combined with leftover egocentrism from adolescence which causes us to highlight our own importance, particularly the importance of any defects. Although men and women are both subject to feelings of inadequacy in regard to their physical appearance, the feelings are often more devastating for women because traditionally there is no acceptable compensation for such a deficit.

Margaret—a young businesswoman—is well aware of this fact, but she is not yet ready to disown her fantasy and face reality. She is dissatisfied with trading sex for male chivalry and attention, but is still willing to play the game.

> *When I first "turned on" to sex, I went almost nympho. After many unfulfilling relationships I realized my "promiscuity" was an attempt to find self-worth through feeling desirable or sexually attractive. All—well, most—of these relationships were shallow and meaningless. It's taken a while to realize this. And it sort of hurts to admit it.*
>
> *I like all the traditional little "niceties," like having my doors opened, cigarettes lit, being helped with my coat, having the man foot the bill, etc. But I don't like being treated like I'm subhuman and I don't like being expected to "repay" a man with sex for an evening out. I have visions of beautiful romance. I'll meet "Mr. Wonderful" and everything will be fine. I know this is unrealistic but I still maintain the fantasy.*

Like Louise and Gloria in Chapter 5 (pp. 162–165), Margaret and women who share her feelings succumb to the traditional feminine stereotypes of seductress-goddess or sex object in their relation to men. Often they do not willingly put themselves in this role, but seem rather to be placed there by the expectations of men. The power women wield as the seductress-goddess—the mysterious woman—is suddenly given up if she becomes man's prey—the sex object. Many women, on the other hand, attempt to move away from these roles. But even the most liberated women occasionally fall back into the culturally determined slots if they believe, as they have been taught to believe, that a woman is a woman only if she has a man.

Single Men Relating to Women Just as women behave predictably in their search for male approval, men also revert to traditional sex-role behavior in their pursuit of women. We shall now hear from two men as they comment on the difficulties of dating and winning a girl. Tom, who is about to be married, recounts his former experiences:

> *I remember when I dated different girls. Going out with them was like putting on a performance. If they liked it, they'd want to come back to see me again. I was always trying for rave reviews. I didn't always get them though.*

And Brian, without revealing his own behavior, discusses that of a friend. He speaks of his friend with condemnation but possibly also with a bit of hidden envy:

> *Guys really piss me off. They put on acts and play roles just to get a girl, and then they drop her. What happens next is that the chicks clam up and close out all guys. . . . There is one person I know who does this constantly. He's been engaged for a while, but his girl is not responsive to him. Well, hell, he never spends any time with her. This one chick he drops really gets bugged with him and tells him that she doesn't even want to be friends. So he bitches about her not being fair; then she makes a friendly gesture, and he turns her off like a light in a power failure.*

The men in these passages speak of women as objects who are there to admire them and respond to their needs. There is no possibility of an authentic relationship as long as men relate to women in an "I-It" rather than "I-Thou" fashion.* Women, however, are just as likely to treat men as objects—objects that increase their prestige, serve a protective role, and confirm their own sense of self-esteem. Role-oriented patterns of behavior limit the degree to which we can have vital, loving relationships with others.

Single Men Versus Single Women From our discussion of the "singles scene," it appears that single men fare better than single women. However, according to recent studies, this is not the case. Gilder (1974) reports that men come off rather poorly unless they have a woman nearby. Men without women frequently become victims of the "single menace" syndrome, and live short, destructive lives. Gilder cites figures showing that single men, aged 25–35, usually make less money, drink more, kill themselves more often, and account for an unusually large percentage of the mental illnesses and criminal proceedings in this country. The image of the playboy, the superstar, the rich, young man free to enjoy life is indeed a fallacy. Single men, as opposed to single women, are unhappy people.

On the other hand, there are indications that single women fare rather well. Gilder points out that "women, in fact, can often do without marriage." A recent study by the Department of Health,

compared to single women or to married men?

---

*"I-Thou" and "I-It" are terms which Martin Buber used to define, respectively, a relationship in which one related to the other as a person in his or her right and a relationship in which one related to the other as an object designed solely to meet one's own needs.

Education, and Welfare (1970) also shows that single women get along favorably. From among four groups of the population—married men, married women, single men, single women—the single woman has the lowest incidence of mental illnesses. Another study (Gove, 1972) found that single women had slightly lower rates of mental illness than single men. This was confirmed in a later study (Campbell, 1975) which found that the degree of stress experienced among single women was indeed less than that of single men; however, this study also reported that the degree of satisfaction among single women was also low. Thus, single women are not entirely happy, but statistically they seem more content than single men.

[handwritten margin note: Is it because they're process-oriented + feel it more?]

In addition, Gilder's work shows that married men are satisfied and productive, while divorced men are less so. There is also some new and reassuring information about divorced women. In discussing success in graduate schools, Feldman (1973) finds that divorce appears to be a liberation from role conflicts for women: "Divorced women appear to be very productive and very involved in the student role—while divorced men have lost their psychological support and appear unhappy and less productive than their female counterparts."

The image of freedom and power surrounding the single man is therefore just not a valid picture. Nor is the image of the withdrawn, embittered man-hating spinster who was left behind. In our world it appears that women without men fare better than men without women. Yet this fact is not reflected in the stereotyped rules governing the dating game and male-female behavior.

Both men and women are willing to pretend that it is women who need men, rather than the other way around. Moreover, the pretense is gradually converted into belief. In order to maintain this belief, women thus appear to wait on the whim of men and try to become what men expect them to be. In many cases (as shown earlier) women give up the surface appearance of liberation for the fulfillment of what women see as men's expectations of their behavior.

SAME-SEX FRIENDSHIPS

Just as in the heterosexual dating arena, the stereotypes of masculinity and femininity impose expectations and restrictions among friends of the same sex. Men relate to other men in patterned and predictable ways which are very dissimilar to the patterned and predictable behavior of women with other women. Yet each pattern of interaction has a long history in our cultural and personal experience, and each pattern is weighted by the expectations of what it means to be a man or woman.

Friendships Between Women Women's friendships with other women tend to lack staying power when men are involved. Because a woman's status depends on her attachment to a male, she is willing to give up her women friends, if necessary, in order to win the approval of a man. Thus friendships among women in the role-oriented world are secondary. A study by Rapoport and Chammah (1965), for example, found that women were not loyal to each other when separated from each other. This is not surprising, for women gain little by remaining true to those who hold no power, particularly if such loyalty threatens their attachment to those who really hold power.

Therefore, women's friendships are impaired by the necessity of competing for men. From early childhood women learn to measure themselves against other women in terms of charm and poise (Pogrebin, 1972). They eye each other's men and have few compunctions about stealing another woman's man in order to gain a few points in the primary competition.

Nonetheless, outside the arena of competition for men, women quickly learn to develop intimate and meaningful relationships with other women. Women, who have long trained to be expressive and supportive, find it relatively easy to be close with other women—and supportive of them if men are not at issue. Susan, a young and very attractive woman, found her good friend most supportive and comfortable when she was hurt and disappointed. However, when Susan's disappointment was overcome by a new "catch" she had made of a man, such support vanished:

Just recently I was very hurt about some news I received and all my women friends rallied around to help me emotionally. I thought it was beautiful, and I told them how much I appreciated their help. One of my closest friends who was particularly good to me during this period was visiting me a few days ago and I told her I was no longer hurt, and that I really felt great now because I've met another guy and have been having a great time. She hardly responded when I told her this. I wanted to share my happiness with her, but she couldn't care less. When I was down, we talked for hours but now that I'm up again, she changes the subject.

With women, then, competition for men is primary and friendship with other women, secondary. Thus women tend to cut themselves off from many meaningful relationships with other women. Instead they are willing to maintain sexual relationships with men whose power and status they think will increase their own.

Friendships Between Men Men hardly fare better with other men than women fare with members of their own sex. However, the reasons are very different. Men are taught not to be expressive and find it hard to relate intimately to anyone, let alone another man. Moreover, the lifelong ethic of competition with other men for goods, status, and sexual conquests sets the tone of much of their interaction. If alone, women tend to be supportive of each other, but men tend to compete for an "invisible hierarchy," regardless of the subject at issue. Status in many male groups is determined by who makes the most money, plays the best game (sports, women, etc.), drinks the most beer, or tells the most adventurous story. There is little intimacy here nor is there personal disclosure.

Mark, whom we met in Chapter 5 (pp. 159–160), describes a personal encounter with another man. He related how their conversation quickly veered to subjects of interest to many men:

We kind of got off on the right track from the start. The first thing we talked about was our hobbies and interests, which led us into some experiences down old memory lane. Both of us are involved in sports, baseball for the most part, and we began to talk about our teams, . . . then about our vacations, our cross-country travels. . . .

Paul, another young man, also comments on his conversation with a man in a personal encounter. With much awareness and insight he compares his behavior in this situation with his behavior when he is talking with a woman:

When talking about financial situations, I was much more open with my male partner, as if it was important for us to know each other's net value in money. This, I think, is a typical male-oriented response—the competitiveness that is so obvious within us both. With my female partner, however, I played the question down. I was more realistic, and used fewer words. It didn't seem to be a pressing issue. We were not competing for an invisible hierarchy. In talking about our love life again, I suspect that my male partner and I were trying to impress each other more than relate to one another. In the male-female encounter, however, the responses about love appeared to be true and more sincere.

Again it seems clear that competition is the key to conversations between many males. Although they may learn very little about each other, the support men derive from each other's company is evident. The camaraderie and jovial competition of men's groups tend to shore up their feelings of self-esteem.

It is only in crisis situations that men can be warm and expressive to each other and really "get to know each other." Richard, another typically competitive male, recounts an incident with another man in a moment of crisis:

I had an interesting encounter this summer. I was driving down the highway doing 90 mph when I went to pass a van. . . . The other driver moved over into my lane without seeing me; then he saw me a second too late. I had to go off onto the dirt shoulder. When I hit the gravel part of the road, my car spun back off the pavement, and I was sliding sideways in both lanes at about 75 mph. Luckily I pulled out of it without an accident. We both pulled to the side of the road. . . . I got out of my car and the van driver got out of his, and we hugged each other in a tight embrace. . . . At the moment I didn't even think twice, I was just so relieved.

Such behavior is highly unusual for men in our society, because it poses a threat to men's sense of power and masculinity. The display of warmth and expressiveness—characteristics usually ascribed to women—may imply an unwanted femininity in men. Moreover, since the only time warmth and physical contact are "allowed" for men is within the context of a sexual relationship, men have come to associate most physical and emotional expressiveness with sexuality. Touching between men (outside contact sports in the athletic arena where masculinity is not in question) raises, however irrationally, the spectre of homosexuality, which is associated with femininity and lack of power in men.* The need, therefore, to maintain their superiority according to traditional norms places

---

*Recent controversies about homosexuality in the athletic world, however, may mean that even in the athletic world men's touching of each other may become somewhat suspect.

men in an emotional straitjacket where they cannot reach out to other men. They cannot learn about each other even if they are close friends. As one young man commented when his best friend committed suicide, "I don't know why he did it. I guess I never really knew him."

PLATONIC OPPOSITE-SEX RELATIONSHIPS

The association of expressiveness with sexuality also prevents the flourishing of platonic relationships between the sexes. Both men and women are afraid that their overtures to a member of the opposite sex may be interpreted as sexual. On the other hand, they are also afraid that these overtures may *not* be interpreted as sexual, since both sexes acquire their self-esteem in part from their sexual attractiveness to members of the other sex. In addition, men also enhance their self-esteem by having a woman devoted to them. This proves to a male his indispensability. Women, in turn, derive their security from men and therefore go to great lengths not to share their men with others. Thus, most men and women have invested much effort in maintaining exclusivity in their opposite-sex relationships. The fear and hope that relationships can only be sexual as well as the accompanying emphasis on exclusivity in relationships are obstacles that hinder the development of opposite-sex friendships.

The confusion encountered by many in maintaining such relationships is apparent in the accounts of Mary Beth, now divorced, who has friendships with several men but experiences a resulting uneasiness. (For previous references to Mary Beth, see Chapter 3, p. 93, and pp. 174–175, 183 in this chapter.) She has a married male friend but is nervous and suspicious about the relationship. "What if his wife finds out? . . . Does he just want friendship? . . . I'm sad and confused." Thus this relationship, which might have been beneficial to both partners, is running up against the shoals of cultural unacceptability.

In another instance Mary Beth finds a warm, human experience when she spends the night with an old friend. When she told him the next morning how much she had enjoyed herself, he replied that he felt "very down" and rejected because they had not had sexual relations. What might have been perceived as a warm and human encounter instead turned out to be a threat to sexual adequacy for the man.

Similar feelings are voiced by Robert, a reasonably open young married man. He tells of his intimate encounter with two young women, which he found very worthwhile, even though it posed a threat to his masculinity. Moreover, he feared that this platonic friendship might threaten his marital relationship because for several days afterwards he hoped that this new intimacy would not stop short of sexual relations:

A couple of weeks ago I spent almost all day with a pair of girls who had been just good friends of mine and close friends of each other. We all had tensions seething inside our bodies and minds. As a result, our standard cafeteria-time jokes kept going, building, and "decaying our minds." Finally after about three hours we had burned off all our tensions, leaving us with a mellow seriousness that feels good for personal interaction. We got down to personal problems . . . and off we went on a personal counseling session about mistresses, double standards, and so forth. . . .

What about all this? It struck me as antisexist in that I managed to fit into this typical female way of handling personal problems. At the same time I think I offered them some help. . . . Another thing, though, as I say this I feel twinges of effeminacy. This I find hard to handle, and so I reaffirmed my masculinity by creating sex fantasies about females going by in the street.

Fortunately we managed to break the confines of role —not to mention taboos against a married male's expressiveness with nonspouse females. We concluded that by the simple virtue of friendship we could share feelings, comfort one another—"even to the point of hugging" and touching each other—without communicating sexual implications. An important point to remember though is that this unfolding of intimacy did seem to me to be threatening to my marriage.

Nonetheless, this example may be only an early illustration of a new trend among process-oriented individuals in which males are able to be expressive and women come into contact with such men by leaving the domestic scene. Balswick and Peek (1971) wonder what will be the result of more expressive cross-sex encounters. Will we be able to keep the competitive sexual conditioning from rearing its ugly head? Will it be possible to maintain fully human relationships?

In the meantime we can turn to preliminary evidence for an answer. Process-oriented individuals have in some ways increased the importance of sexuality in their lives by asserting that sex is part of a loving relationship rather than primarily a physical exercise. At the same time, they have also diminished the importance of sex by not making sex and sexual fidelity the *sole* indicator of the stability and value of a relationship as most Americans have done. As Jourard (1973) points out, Americans have tended to idolatrize sex by believing (not always coincident, however, with acting) that the sexual activity itself—and its exclusivity—was a barometer of the welfare of a relationship. He continues by saying that this idolatry reflects America's preoccupation with sex per se and the lack of attention we pay to emotional understanding and communication. Perhaps these latter concerns would measure the welfare of any given relationship more accurately. Thus it seems possible that we can remove the competitive wrappings from our uses of sexuality. If we succeed in doing so we may then be able to regard sex as another means of communication among those who love and care for each other.

GROUP SETTINGS

In group settings of mixed company there is also strong evidence of masculine/feminine role-oriented behavior. In a normal setting of six to ten men and women, Farrell (1974) states that 1) men generally speak most of the time, 2) the conversation is centered on topics of interest to men, 3) women tend to smile and ask questions of the men, and 4) men tend to interrupt more often and in less supportive ways. Examples can be found at any cocktail party where clumps of men stand around chatting with each other and boasting about their achievements. The women meanwhile form a supportive and smiling periphery unless they decide to retreat to the other side of the room to talk among themselves.

Several experiments in my university classes document this pattern. In one class a student unobtrusively noted the number of student responses during the course of the semester. The men, who formed one third of that particular class, controlled the conversation three quarters of the time. In an experiment in small-group behavior, observers found that the men talked more, while the women asked supportive questions. Moreover, the women looked at the person to whom they were speaking, whereas the men tended to look at their papers or the ceiling.

Finally, in another experiment, the men were asked not to contribute to group discussion for a period of fifteen minutes; instead, they were supposed to listen to the women. The experiment was conducted in two classes. In the first, three men excused themselves to go to the restroom, saying later that they found it impossible to sit and listen to women talk. Two other men experienced great difficulty in not interrupting the conversation, and showed signs of nervous tension and agitation. In the second class several men wrote about their experiences and commented on the difficulties of listening to women. They found the conversations of women boring and dull, since women "smiled a lot and seemed to always agree with each other." They missed the competitiveness and argumentativeness that characterize all-male conversations.

Carl, an articulate member of the second class, comments on this most aptly:

I began to squirm and, even though I always considered myself a good listener, I could have gotten up and left after about five minutes of listening; their conversation just wasn't competitive enough. All they did was agree with each other. If there was disagreement, it was very mild. I do have to admit that I prefer a lively opponent in a good emotional debate. Gut issues bring out my competitive spirit, and I have a very strong competitive spirit in relation to other males.

Later after the men entered the conversation, Carl becomes aware of his part in steering the discussion away from topics of interest to women and bringing into it his preference for lively argument:

Jim went on to his usual liberal dribble about how rotten things were in this country. I reiterated that "if he didn't like it he could leave." Afterwards I think that we both realized how silly it all was: How like most males we had taken a pleasant conversation, tuned out the women, and turned the discussion into the type of argument we males really enjoy.

Women who desire male approval smile at this sort of conversation but remain attentive. They don't find it personally stimulating, however. It comes as a great surprise to men to learn that women are not listening because they are interested in men's conversations but because they have been trained to do so. On the other hand, it becomes most apparent that the men have never been trained to listen to women.

Therefore, in courtship, dating, and friendship, the personal accounts just given strongly support the stereotypes of the competitive male and the supportive female. Men's and women's expectations of each other further reinforce these stereotypes.

MEN'S AND WOMEN'S EXPECTATIONS OF EACH OTHER

Although on the surface men may feel liberal about their expectations of women, on the emotional level their attitudes are somewhat more conservative. Out of a small sample of sixty-two male college students, Komarovsky (1973) found that 30 percent experienced difficulty in dating a woman who might be more intelligent than themselves. These men dreaded risking comparisons with women that might reflect sadly on their masculine achievement-oriented capacities. At the same time many of these men appeared quite liberated if asked general questions, for example, questions about women's rights.

Yet Komarovsky's study indicates that there has been some change from previous years. Komarovsky found that men now indicated that they valued intellectual traits in women more than in the past, although her sample of males still wanted their women to be attractive. However, this change is still on a very superficial level. Despite claims that the men liked intelligent women, the men still reported gut-level negative reactions to the idea of equality with women, and the women acceded to this underlying idea of the men by often "playing dumb" on dates, as women have done in the past.

Steinmann and Fox (1966) also found that men were more liberal on general issues than on specific ones. On the one hand men agreed that women should be active, talented, and creative. On the other hand, however, they saw marriage as important in a woman's life and consequently were unanimous in vetoing the suggestion that at some time women were entitled to devote themselves to their own self-realization. Thus the evidence appears to show that on the surface men favor equality between men and women but on a more substantial level men are against such equality. Perhaps what we are finding in the research is that it is still a man's world, even though we no longer pay lip service to that fact.

Young women who feel the need to maintain a relationship with men are very aware of this fact, and, even in a very open relationship, there are still emotional reactions to inadequacy in terms of sex-role stereotypes. Vicki says of her steady boyfriend:

He sensed his defensive behavior. It bothered him but he said he couldn't help it somehow. It was as if agreeing with me or even recognizing the validity of my idea was admitting to his weakness or inferiority to me. . . . I guess if the girl is obviously inferior, the need for impressing her actively slowly fades. . . . But if the woman is not so obviously inferior, the need to establish supremacy is something which must be continually worked for—without it comes the feeling of failure.

On the basis of male supremacy and female inferiority—alas—most of us build our lives.

CONFIDENT WOMEN AND ANXIOUS MEN?

The difficulties of making changes in personal behavior have been illustrated by many personal accounts in this chapter. All of the individuals cited in this chapter are aware that the world is changing—and that changes in masculine and feminine sex roles are also undergoing change. Yet, while they manifest an attitude of "liberation" their emotional responses often reflect traditional values.

In assessing the research and the personal responses of my students, it becomes clear that men resist approaching changes in sex roles more than women. This is understandable since the immediate losses incurred by men, as traditional sex roles change, will be greater. There are many benefits to male liberation, such as greater expressiveness and the sharing of what is often a burdensome economic responsibility, but in the process of achieving these benefits men will also be dislodged from their positions of power and control over women. This is indeed cause for anxiety. As Hartley comments (1960), we may be approaching an age of more confident women and more anxious men.

An example of this anxiety is seen in the personal account written by Leonard, who earlier in this chapter examined his own inexpressiveness. In this quotation, Leonard reveals his anxiety by a *reductio ad absurdum* that threatens to throw the baby out with the bathwater:

But the point is we cannot all of a sudden drop our conditioning and all become liberated. . . . After all, would I really be happier if I were to outwardly tell my male friends that I have a need to kiss them because I feel that it is the way I should show that I

*care for them? In the same light, would it be to our advantage if
all the wives, mothers, husbands, and fathers left their unful-
filled experiences in life? That I am afraid would make an
excellent counterpart to* Future Shock, *only this book would be
called* What the Hell is Going On!

SUMMARY

Masculine and feminine scripts provide guidelines by which
most of us, often unconsciously, live out our lives. There are both
advantages and disadvantages accrued by following the sex-role
scripts. For women, there is a security in knowing that they will be
protected by males. Some women are reluctant to give this up.
Others realize that the protection they receive also implies that they
are not able to take care of themselves nor are they to be taken
seriously in worldly matters. Yet most women gear their lives to
achieve male approval even when this means a violation of self.

Men on the other hand fall heir to all the advantages of power
and dominance—at least over women. However, such power carries
with it both injunction against being dependent and vulnerable and
the requirement that men achieve in the outer world. Men are finding
today that both of these script messages are at times burdensome.
Men suffer personal discomfort because they cannot express their
feelings. Many men also find that the constant need to achieve is a
straightjacket which inhibits the development of other sides of
their personalities. Despite the confines of their role, though, they
are reluctant to give up the power that goes with being continually
strong and responsible.

Among single young men and women sex-role scripting is
thrown into high relief as each seeks to find a relationship with a
person of the other sex. Women allow men to treat them as objects in
such places as singles bars in the hopes of attracting the "right man."
Men in turn also treat women as objects, often to improve their
standing in the male peer group and often, no doubt, to cover for
their own vulnerability. As one man said, they are "trying for rave
reviews" but they often strike out.

Yet from the discussion of the "singles scene" it seems that
single men fare better than single women. Various research studies
show, however, that this is not the case. Men who live without a
steady female partner tend to be lonely and unhappy. On the other

hand, women who have not married appear to be relatively satisfied with their lives. Indeed they show less signs of mental strain than other subsets of the population. Women, trained to please men, appear to survive very well without them.

In relating to those of the same sex, we find that individuals are trapped by the traditional sex-role expectations. Women relate well to each other unless they are in competition for a man. At such times women tend to forsake their female relationships and place more emphasis on pleasing men. Men, on the other hand, only relate to each other in competitive ways. They lack the training to be open with each other and moreover are held back from attempting to do so by the fear of incurring the stigma of homosexuality.

However, there are signs that women, more quickly than men, are freeing themselves from sex-role injunctions which keep them dependent on men. Some women are discovering that they are able to live without constant male attention and that they are happy in doing so. This realization on the part of women is leading to some changes in their behavior as they begin to develop new strengths of independence and self-reliance. Such changes, however, may be threatening to men, who are slower to relinquish the overt power associated with the traditional sex role. We may question, as does Hartley, whether or not we are entering an era of more confident women and more anxious men.

EXERCISE A: SHARING OURSELVES

This is an exercise for members of the class to do in pairs. *
Each person in turn says all he or she wants to about his or her personal views and experiences on each of the topics listed below. While he or she does this, the partner listens but refrains from drawing the center of attention to himself or herself. The listener may ask clarifying questions but must not interrupt to talk about himself or herself. Neither partner may press the other to say more than he or she wishes, and a person at any time is free to state that he or she has finished talking about a given topic.

Now you are requested to talk about each of the following topics, one after the other:

---

*Modified from Jourard, 1971.

1. *Your hobbies and leisure-time activities.*
2. *Your school and job responsibilities.*
3. *Your present financial status.*
4. *Your political and religious views.*
5. *The people in your family.*
6. *Your love life.*
7. *Problems in intimate relationships.*
8. *Your partner in the present dyad or pair.*

If it is at all possible you should do this exercise twice—once with a person of the same sex, and next with a partner of the other sex. Then compare your own openness and/or nervousness in each situation.

Which topics do you find easy to talk about? Which are difficult? Is it easier to talk with a man or a woman? Why? Do you want to change any of this behavior?

EXERCISE B: THE ROLES WE PLAY

On a sheet of paper draw a large circle. After reflecting how you have spent your time in the preceding week, divide the circle as if it were a pie into sections representing the different roles in which you spent your time. Each section should be proportionate in size to the amount of energy and time you invest in that particular activity. Labels might read student, employee, friend, *etc.*

When you have done this, spend a moment reflecting on the current shape of your life as symbolized by your "role pie." If you are in a dyad or a group, exchange role pies and imagine what your life would be like if you had another's role pie. How would your life be different? Share this with the person whose role pie it is.

Now, taking your role pie, consider what sections are most important to your sense of being "you"—to your identity. Number the sections from most important one to the one of least interest. Let 1 be the section of greatest importance to you, 2 the one of next importance, etc. Note that the numbers will usually not correspond with the relative size of the sections.

If your most important roles or activities are not taking most of your time, consider why this is so. Is it due to temporary conditions? Are you undervaluing some major activities or overvaluing minor ones? Are there any changes you would like to make in the way you spend your time? You can *choose to make changes. What would be the consequences of change? Would you willingly accept the consequences?*

Now look at the least important area on your role pie, which is marked with the highest number. Lightly X it out in your paper. What would your life be like without that section? Would you still be you?

Now X out the section with the next highest number. What would your life be like without this section? Would you still be you?

Continue to do this until only one section is left. Now X out this section. Would there be anything left? Would you still be you? Know that there is a you left—you could still survive and do so profitably. We can all exist for a time, alone and without traditional or familiar definitions of ourselves.

Discuss with others what you learned. Which roles are most important to you, and which would be most difficult to give up? Which do you feel you could not give up? Do you feel at some point you would stop being you? If you answer yes, consider again the importance of roles in your life. How did others feel about roles?

REFERENCES

Balswick, J., and Peek, C., "The Inexpressive Male: A Tragedy of American Society," *Family Coordinator,* vol. 20 (1971): 363–68.

Brenton, M., *The American Male,* New York: Fawcett Publications, 1966.

Campbell, A., "The American Way of Mating: Marriage *Si,* Children Only Maybe," *Psychology Today,* vol. 8 (May 1975): 37–40.

Farrell, W., *The Liberated Man,* New York: Random House, 1974.

Feldman, S., "Impediment or Stimulant? Marital Status and Graduate Education," *American Journal of Sociology,* vol. 78 (1973): 982–95.

Gilder, G., *Detroit Free Press,* November 11, 1974.

Gove, W., "The Relationship Between Sex Roles, Marital Status, and Mental Illness," *Social Forces,* vol. 51 (1972): 34–43.

Hartley, R. E., "Some Implications of Current Changes in Sex Role Patterns," *Merrill-Palmer Quarterly,* vol. 6 (1960): 153–64.

Health, Education and Welfare (Department of), "Selected Symptoms of Psychological Distress," Public Health Services, Health Services, and Mental Health Administration, 1970.

Janeway, E., *Man's World, Woman's Place,* New York: William Morrow, 1971.

Jourard, S., "Interpersonal Yoga," in S. Jourard, *Self-Disclosure: An Experimental Analysis of the Transparent Self,* New York: John Wiley & Sons, 1971.

Jourard, S., "Marriage is for Life," paper presented at the Annual Meeting of the American Association of Marriage and Family Counselors, St. Louis, Mo., November, 1973.

Jourard, S., *The Transparent Self,* New York: Van Nostrand Reinhold, 1964.

Komarovsky, M., "Cultural Contradictions and Sex Roles: The Masculine Case," *American Journal of Sociology,* vol. 78 (1973): 673–84

Pogrebin, L., "Competing with Women," *Ms. Magazine* (July 1972): 78–81, 131.

Rapoport, A. and Chammah, A. M., "Sex Differences in Factors Contributing to the Level of Cooperation in the Prisoner's Dilemma Game," *Journal of Personality and Social Psychology,* vol. 2 (1965): 831–38.

Steinmann, A., and Fox, D., "Male-Female Perception of the Female Role in the United States," *The Journal of Psychology,* vol. 64 (1966): 265–76.

7

Marriage and Romantic Love: Sources of Marital Dissatisfaction

In Chapter 4 we explored the need for both individuality and relatedness in human experience and showed how process-oriented individuals were able to meet both these needs within their relationships. They were able to accept and enhance their own individuality and yet transcend this individuality in relating to another. This required an openness, an honesty, and a willingness to accept the change and the growth that ensued. In this chapter we will examine role-oriented relationships—those relationships in which individuals sacrifice their individuality to meet the needs of their partners. In so doing, they sacrifice their own experience and their process in order to maintain traditional forms. To set the stage for the study of such relationships, let us first look at the institution of marriage and its association with love.

In America the independence of woman is irrecoverably lost in the bonds of matrimony; if an unmarried woman is less constrained there than else-where, a wife is subjected to stricter obligations. . . . This opinion is not peculiar to one sex, and contested by the other; I never observed that the women of America consider conjugal authority as a fortunate usurpation of their rights, nor that they thought themselves degraded by submitting to it. It appeared to me, on the contrary, that they attach a sort of pride to the voluntary surrender of their own will, and make it their boast to bend themselves to the yoke, not to shake it off.

Alexis de Toqueville, **Democracy in America**

Among the most potent of apparent protection from contingency and tragedy are our relations to certain others. We learn and are encouraged to use symbiotic partnerships to disavow responsibility for our choices, to displace guilt for our failure to actualize our potentials for authentic living.

James Bugental, **The Search for Authenticity**

MARRIAGE: THE SOUGHT-AFTER INSTITUTION

In a recent book, the sociologist LeMasters quotes a current joke among the blue-collar workers that he was studying: "Marriage is a wonderful institution—but who wants to live in an institution?" (1975, p. 45). Unfortunately many Americans seem to regard marriage in this way, as evidenced by the amount of dissatisfaction reported within marriage. Colton (1974) reports that there are currently three divorces for every two marriages in California. Kahn (1973) reports that more than one fourth of all married women between the ages of 27 and 32 can expect to get divorced later in their lives. In a populous and affluent Detroit suburb a lawyer stated recently that two out of three couples were exploring the prospects of separation.

Disenchantment with the marriage state is not new. In the 1800s the historian de Toqueville spoke of the loss of independence that occurs in American marriages. Biographers remind us that such outstanding individuals as Socrates, Abraham Lincoln, and Robert Frost experienced turmoil and unhappiness in their marital relationships (see McCary, 1975). Today, psychologists such as James Bugental, speak of our intimate relationships as a way to disavow responsibility and displace guilt. Current sociologists speak of the utilitarian nature of marriage, the fact that many marriages are held together by external considerations (Cuber & Harroff, 1963) and continue over the long-term without resolving any long-standing problems (Matthews & Milhanovich, 1963).

The disenchantment with marriage outlined by social scientists is reflected in our popular culture. The verses sung by Carly Simon highlight the dark underside of marriage:

> My friends from college they're all married now.
> They have their houses on their lots.
> They have their silent noons,
> Tearful nights, angry dawns.

> Their children hate them for the things they're not.
> They hate themselves for what they are.
> And yet they drink, they laugh,
> Close the wound and hide the scar.

Carly Simon concludes her song, however, by saying that "we'll marry." And despite all the dissatisfactions that individuals incur in marriage, most Americans will do the same. Americans as a whole still believe in the necessity of marriage. They believe that the world is made for couples and that one cannot exist alone. They believe that men and women "ought" to marry, that marriages "ought" to be enduring, and that partners "ought" to be faithful and accept responsibility for the welfare of each other. Cuber and Harroff (1965) refer to this belief system as the "monolithic code":

> This monolithic code is based on precepts from Judaic and Christian tradition and has long been codified into law and buttressed by something vaguely referred to as public opinion. Few, therefore, have to be told that chastity, fidelity, parenthood and various forms of attendant responsibility and restraint, all channelled through heterosexuality, are the mainstays of proper male and female behavior (pp. 18–19).

Americans believe in marriage; moreover almost all Americans marry at least once. There is no evidence that marriage as a continuing institution is in any particular danger. Rather the evidence indicates that a significant number of individuals experience unhappiness in the institution of marriage. We might ask then, why do individuals persist in believing that marriage will bring them happiness? Why do individuals seek to enter this institution?

Individuals marry for a great many reasons: for companionship, for somebody to talk to and to do things with, and because they want to be loved. But underlying most of these reasons is one that is more fundamental: Most people enter relationships in order to bring some measure of stability to their lives and to escape from the feeling of being alone. Ernest van den Haag (1962), a sociologist and psychoanalyst, points out that particularly in the twentieth century have we turned to marriage as an answer to our aloneness.* As we have lost our sense of security previously found in extended families, in community roots, and in religious beliefs, we have turned—somewhat in desperation—to our relationships to provide us with a sense of worth. Van den Haag states:

> Thus one longs, perhaps more acutely than in the past, for somebody to be tangibly, individually and definitely one's own, body and soul (p. 43).

In our relationships we can attempt to forget our separateness and fortify our sense of worth by seeking out that "ideal other" who will make our lives worthwhile. We believe that in our relationships we find both relatedness and security.

Many other sociologists are also calling attention to this point. They find that many marriages are based on a belief system that values stability at the expense of spontaneity. This can be seen in a study of a large group of newlywed marriages by Goodrich, Ryder, and Raush (1968). They found that in these relationships, "one can discern in the marital behavior, and in the implicit values of the family as a whole, an investment in stability and rationalism, rather than in spontaneity and change" (p. 388). In such relation-

---

*In a major work, *Motivation and Personality* (1954, rev. ed., 1970), Maslow outlined a hierarchy of human needs in which he postulated that certain human needs, such as those for safety and security, must be met before others, such as those for love and self-esteem. Therefore, when individuals' needs for safety or security are not being met (which often is the case today as traditional supports crumble) they will seek stability or security in whatever ways they can—often by emphasizing the form rather than the process in their love relationships.

ships the interpersonal relationship itself often took second place to the external roles within which individuals found stability.

Yet in seeking stability at the expense of spontaneity we often structure our personal relationships so that they hinder our own personal development and that of our partner. But, we say, that is what love is all about—the two become one. We give up our own needs for each other in order to strengthen the relationship—all in the name of love. And we believe that love is inseparable from marriage. In American society love and marriage go together, as the song says, "like a horse and carriage." But the belief that "you can't have one without the other" is not common to all cultures. And in fact we have not been very successful at combining the two.

The joining of love and marriage is a relatively new phenomenon in human history. In ancient Greece, for example, love between two men was the ideal and marriage was another state altogether. In medieval Europe—and even later—love, for a man and woman, was something experienced outside of marriage. Marriage was arranged for economic and traditional reasons, not for love. In many cultures this pattern has continued into this century, although the influence of Western culture has inaugurated changes.

An example of the irrelevancy of love to marriage in cultures other than our own is given to us in the musical production *Fiddler on the Roof,* which takes place in czarist Russia.* Tevye, an Old-World patriarch, asks his wife of twenty-five years whether or not she loves him. She highlights the absurdity of the question by replying that he must either be ill or upset. She tells him to go lie down and suggests that maybe he has indigestion. After a little rest she is sure that he will feel better. However, Tevye is not satisfied with this response and repeats his question. The wife then expands on the irrelevancy of the question. She's cleaned, cooked, and washed for him for twenty-five years and he wants to talk about love? She's lived, fought, and starved with him; she's shared her bed with him. Isn't that love? Tevye concludes that it must be and hence they love each other. But this love doesn't change anything since love played such an insignificant part in their marriage from the beginning.

---

*As a musical production, *Fiddler on the Roof* does, of course, simplify the questions of love and marriage. The questioning of love and marriage and their relationship to each other, however, *did* exist for some individuals in that culture and time, just as these questions have been raised by larger numbers of individuals in our own era.

Today, however, we suppose that love changes everything and we give love a prominent place in marriage. Many writers on the subject believe that the American attempt to join love and marriage has been a disaster. Arthur Schlesinger, Jr., (1966), a historian, points out that we do not yet have evidence that love and marriage are a happy combination for most individuals:

> The American experience in love has not yet proved itself. The national attempt to unite passion and marriage led many Americans into hypocrisy in the nineteenth century and into hysteria in the twentieth.

Van den Haag (1962) also makes the same point when he states that Americans are bent on attempting to unite love and marriage despite the adverse results of the previous three thousand years. Referring to the song we quoted earlier, he comments:

> . . . love is a very unruly horse far more apt to run away and overturn the carriage than to draw it. That is why, in the past, people seldom thought of harnessing marriage to love. They felt that each has its own motive power; one primed for a life-long journey, the other for an ardent improvisation, a voyage of discovery . . . (p. 44).

Love and marriage, he concludes, are both endangered when they are combined.

Other writers, primarily sociologists, argue that although it is most difficult to find love and marriage living well together, it is indeed possible. Cuber and Harroff's (1965) study of upper-middle-class Americans is a striking example. After investigating the personal lives of over 400 highly successful Americans, they found a small percentage of marriages in which the partners had a vital, changing, and growing relationship with each other. Whether such marriages exist in smaller or larger percentages outside the upper-middle class is undetermined. Nonetheless, the documentation of such marriages is a fairly conclusive rebuttal to those who say that love and marriage cannot be united successfully.

However, in most marriages love, as a vital, caring feeling, diminishes over time. In such relationships partners do not put energy into the interpersonal dynamics of the relationship but rather invest their energy in maintaining the traditional roles of husband and wife (Kerckhoff & Bean, 1970). In the following sections we will look closely at the characteristics of such relationships and at how love is viewed in this context.

CHARACTERISTICS OF A ROLE-ORIENTED RELATIONSHIP

The primary characteristic of a role-oriented relationship is the need to maintain the appearance of stability. The appearance of sameness over time—something none of us as changing individuals can ever genuinely achieve—aids in creating an illusion of security for individuals who do not find such security elsewhere. More specifically, traditional roles, particularly those of masculinity and femininity, provide a stable frame of reference by which we chart our lives. By following these roles we also conform to cultural expectations of how men and women should behave.

Two students comment on their picture of the future and how their prescribed roles will give shape and continuity to their lives. Tom, a graduating senior majoring in business, thinks about his upcoming marriage and his hoped-for job in the business world:

I've been thinking about me. If I should get a job will I fall into that traditional role? Married, with one or two kids, a house? Will I be in debt? It seems that I will be, but I really don't mind. . . . No one can make it on their own. People need to belong somewhere with someone. For me it's going to be in the role of a husband and a worker. I think I'll like it.

Tom expects to be a husband and a provider. Here he justifies his dependence on the traditional role and his need for order and predictability by saying: "People need to belong somewhere with someone." Later he remarks: "I've always been told that the man is the provider for the family and if he doesn't provide he is in some way unsuccessful." Thus in order to meet cultural expectations, Tom plans to shape his life according to traditional stereotypes.

The feminine counterpart is voiced by Marlene, who in Chapter 1 was aware of greater choice outside her traditional sex role. Here she voices a new note of skepticism as she comes to understand but not yet accept other alternatives:

This is difficult for me to explain but a little while ago I think that I perceived myself as finishing school, working for a little while, getting married, having children, and then going back to a nonprofessional job after they grew up. I was looking for the right man whose identity I could take on. Now . . . I may follow this same pattern anyway—but at least I will be conscious of my actions and aware of the consequences.

Thus for both Marlene and Tom the prospect of a role-oriented relationship provides a semblance of security in viewing what is for all of us an uncertain future. This relationship will also enable them to escape their own sense of separateness and isolation, which is frightening to many individuals (Bugental, 1965; Fromm, 1956; Moustakas, 1961). For most of us, just as for Tom and Marlene, the institution of marriage sanctions most of our long-term relationships. It also provides a stage on which we can fully play out our traditional roles. How does love fit into this role-oriented picture?

LOVE IN A ROLE-ORIENTED RELATIONSHIP

Love in a role-oriented relationship is conditional (see Chapter 4, pp. 113–114). We give it to others with the expectation that they in return will meet our own needs. If our needs are not met, the love disappears. Thus such love always means, "I will love you if . . ." not "I love you as you are." In fact such love strikes a bargain or as Meerlo (1952) states, "it is a wish for an emotional exchange." Through such love we establish a framework that we hope will fill our needs and provide us with power, safety, and security. In this way we confuse love and power.

Love and Power Very often we use our love to try and shape others into the images we want them to maintain. We "shower" another with love so that the other person will feel wanted and in turn will make us feel wanted. We withdraw our love so that the other person will become emotionally dependent on us and will return to what we have designated as more acceptable behavior. Similarly we "sacrifice" our own needs for those of the loved one and expect that he or she will do the same in return. We spare the other person the unpleasant details or the "stark truth," and in doing so remove the power of decision from his or her hands. We do many things because they are "in the best interests" of the other or because we know that it is "for his or her good." In these ways we use our love as a cover for power with which we control and manipulate others.

Such behavior comes from a view of limited power. We realize that there is not enough power to go around. If I "wear the pants" in the family, independent decisions by other family members consequently threaten my use of power and my self-esteem. If I see myself as the "boss" and my child rebels or disobeys, my sense of power, and my esteem as a parent, are also threatened. From this view, what power you have you take from me; what power I have I must take from you. In this manner such power divides and pits one person against the other. There is always a winner and a loser. Ultimately, when such a situation exists within an intimate relationship both parties lose.

Just as there is a limited amount of power in such relationships, there is also a limited amount of love which must be carefully conserved. Love that is spent on another outside of the marital relationship (whether it is in platonic friendship or in a sexual relationship) is love that is taken from the other person. In such ways we parcel out small doses of love and jealously guard those that belong to us. Again we have created a zero-sum game in which there must be a winner and a loser. Again, in the long run, such a view of love presupposes that both parties lose.

In role-oriented relationships, therefore, we see that both power and love are limited, and each is confused with the other. Power is wielded under the name of love. Love justifies the use of power. But is this the type of love for which we married?

Romantic Love: Ecstasy and Despair Most of us strongly believe in romantic love and the possibility of romantic love leading to marriage. We believe that all our cares will disappear and that everything will change if we find the right person to love. Love makes the heart beat fast, the adrenalin speed up, and in our best moments makes all of us feel ten-feet tall. Love as we experience it is a rapturous emotion through which we react to our partner. In *My Fair Lady* Freddie sings to Eliza of his love for her:

> And oh, the towering feeling,
> Just to know somehow you are near!
> The overpowering feeling
> That any second you may suddenly appear! . . .

Yet love is also despair and disappointment. Because it relies on an idealized image of the beloved, we are inevitably disappointed and disillusioned when our partner does not live up to that image. We suffer and feel the world is coming to an end. At the same time, however, we seek with excitement a new love tomorrow. The popular song by Bacharach and David tells of the pain of love—and the compulsion to seek it out:

What do you get when you fall in love?
You only get lies and pain and sorrow.
So for at least until tomorrow,
. I'll never fall in love again.

When we examine our view of romantic love, it is perhaps not surprising that our marriages fail at an increasing rate. We have come to base our marriages on the concept of romantic love and expect this love to sustain us well into our less productive years. But often the idealized image fades and we come to see the real person behind the image. At this point many of us are disappointed and our love turns to anger. Consequently we either grow into a mature love that is based on mutual respect for each other, a responsibility for ourselves, and an acceptance of human interaction, or we resign ourselves to our disillusion, or we leave and run the same circle again.* We may question our beliefs about the compatibility of love and marriage. We may question also the roles we have assumed in the name of love.

TRADITIONAL ROLES WITHIN A MARRIAGE

Since the traditional conceptions of masculinity and femininity define man as instrumental and woman as expressive, then it follows that men and women can function in their traditional roles only in conjunction with each other. Each requires the other in order to express between them the full range of human emotions and to be able to stand together in the world. A man is incomplete without nurturing and tenderness, and when he cannot find these qualities within himself he becomes dependent on the woman in his life to provide them. A woman cannot function well without the self-

---

*An alternative explanation for marital disappointment is offered by Martha Baum (1972), who argues that we do not value romantic love in our society, but rather companionate love, which emphasizes understanding, sharing, and mutual support and affection. She states that the expectations of companionate love are realistic in terms of the personalities of the partners, but that later dissatisfaction results because of conflicts between the roles of companion and the roles related to economic achievement and child rearing. This explanation of marital dissatisfaction is well-supported in the literature and will be discussed at length later in this chapter (see pp. 222–227). However, such an explanation does not, as Baum argues, exclude the likelihood that dissatisfaction in marriage occurs due to early romanticization of the partner. In fact, both explanations add to our understanding of marital dissatisfaction. As Pineo (1961) states, there are really two separate stages of decreasing satisfaction in marriage: The first is due to the decrease in romanticization of the partner in the early years of marriage; the second is due to the increasing burdens of occupational and child-rearing roles.

assertiveness and leadership that she, if traditionally feminine, has not developed within herself. For these qualities she becomes dependent on a man. Neither can stand alone. This relationship is formalized within the institution of marriage.*

Once the relationship is formalized, tasks and behaviors become dichotomized along sex-oriented lines. The woman becomes the wife and mother with certain prescribed tasks and behaviors; the man becomes the husband and father with certain prescribed tasks and behaviors.

In this relationship power is divided rather than shared. The man is allocated the power to think, to decide, to evaluate, and to achieve status, responsibility, and material goods in the outer world. The woman, on the other hand, assumes the power to feel, to nurture, to serve and please others, and to manage the domestic and interpersonal life of the inner world—that is, the home. Women thus gain power in private in exchange for submission in public. This is the traditional bargain struck between the sexes. Let us now examine more closely the expectations surrounding the roles of wife and husband.

To Be a Wife With the acceptance of the role of wife almost all women, especially role-oriented women, accept as well the role of housewife. The deprecatory phrase "I'm just a housewife" typifies the low esteem in which this position is held in our society. Scott (1972) suggests that the following mock advertisement accurately describes the housewife role:

Help Wanted

Requirements: Intelligence, good health, energy, patience, sociability. *Skills:* at least 12 different occupations. *Hours:* 99.6 per week. *Salary:* None. *Holidays:* None (will be required to remain on stand-by 24 hours a day, 7 days a week). *Opportunities for Advancement:* None (limited transferability of skills acquired on the job). *Job Security:* None (trend is toward more layoffs, particularly as employee approaches middle age). Severance pay will depend on the discretion of the employer. *Fringe Benefits:* Food, clothing, and shelter generally provided, but any additional bonuses will depend on financial stand-

---

*This relationship reflects the role-oriented conception of marriage that most Americans have. Psychologists term this type of relationship "symbiotic" in that both partners believe they cannot live alone (Fromm, 1956, 1971). When this relationship fails, partners still adhere to role-oriented beliefs and believe that the fault lies in themselves rather than changing their systems of belief or trusting in the processes of their own experience.

ing and the good nature of the employer. No health, medical, or accident insurance, no Social Security or pension plan.

It is not a job description which would attract any person with a variety of options. Economists have classified a housewife's tasks under at least twelve occupational titles: nursemaid, housekeeper, cook, dishwasher, laundress, food buyer, chauffeur, gardener, maintenance worker, seamstress, dietitian, and practical nurse.* On the basis of these job classifications the housewife was worth at *least* $257.53 a week in 1972 (Porter, 1972). However, she receives no pay, and often has to ask her husband for money to buy a lunch or take a taxi. It is remarkable that most women still rush to fill such a position.

Scanzoni's (1975) research also outlines the tasks of the traditional wife: She puts the interests of her husband and children first; assumes that her central mission in life is to care for her husband and children; finds her major satisfaction in her family. In addition, for the traditional wife individual achievement is proscribed though she may "help" bring in the family income if it should become necessary; however, she must not bring in more money than her husband. She believes, moreover, that psychologically and biologically women are better suited for some tasks than others and that the feminine domain does not include sharing equal authority with one's mate.

Thus women seek their fulfillment in serving others within the domestic sphere. Such service leads women to highly value working and caring for others and self-sacrifice; a system of ethics built upon intense loyalties to their family and kin also results from such service. Women, within their domestic sphere, become more particularistic, more emotional, and more willing to live through the lives of others at the same time as they begin to lose the independence and achievement-oriented skills they may have developed through prior education and training.

The role of wife and mother isolates most women from any meaningful contact with the outer world. They hold a secondary position on the periphery of man's world, which controls all the tangible rewards and acknowledgments of creative labor. They have no external support for the development of domestic and interpersonal skills. They live in a private world dominated by family,

---

*For a more complete listing and discussion, see Caplow (1964).

children, and occasional neighborhood ties. All judgments become more personal, private, and emotional. They learn to be flexible instead of goal-oriented, to be responsive rather than decisive. As their world thus becomes increasingly private they become more timid in relation to outside affairs. In this outer world they accept their inadequacy and live there only vicariously through those with whom they have intimate relationships.

Moreover, women expect to find their major satisfactions in their marriage. They have no other independent sources that might yield satisfactions. Thus marriage becomes increasingly more important to women as they spend less time outside the home. "Because women have to put so many more eggs in the one basket of marriage, they have more of a stake in its stability. Because their happiness is more dependent on marriage than men's, they have to pay more for it. All the studies show that women make more concessions" (Bernard, 1971, p. 149).

A study by Renne (1970) furnishes some figures that supplement these conclusions. In a survey of 2480 marriage partners, she found that more women than men reported dissatisfaction with their marriages, said their marriages were unhappy, had regretted their marriages at some time, and were considering separation or divorce. As Bernard (1971) points out, in every marriage there are really two marriages and "hers" is decidedly less happy than "his."

Despite such reports, the majority of married women state that they are happy with their marriages. In fact, more married women than single women report a general state of well-being (Bernard, 1971, p. 150). Most married women apparently think they are happy, and yet many indicators of mental health are lower for married women than for other groups in our society.

A study by Knupfer, Clark, and Room (1966) shows that more married women than single women were bothered by feelings of depression, did not feel happy most of the time, felt that they were about to go to pieces, and experienced other symptoms of heightened anxiety. In general, more married women than single women were reported to be passive, phobic, and depressed. The same study showed that married women displayed more signs of emotional distress than did married men. Twice as many married women as married men felt that a nervous breakdown was impending and, in general, more women than men felt inadequate and unable to adjust to the demands upon them.

A study by the Department of Health, Education, and Welfare

(1970) provided similar findings. Married women ranked first in incidence of disorders in eight separate categories, and second in three others. Married women appeared to have the worst mental health of the groups studied. On the other hand, single women ranked last for ten disorders and had the best mental health. Although Gove (1972) reports that married people of both sexes have lower rates of mental illness than single people, he finds that married women have considerably higher rates of mental illness than married men. Again it is apparent that the married women do not fare well. Then why do so many married women report that they are happy?

Bernard (1971) argues that married women may be confusing "adjustment" with happiness.* Women are aware that they are expected to be good wives and mothers and have been told that, if they fulfill these duties well, they will achieve a real sense of satisfaction. They learn early that real satisfactions are to be gained in forgetting themselves and in serving others. Therefore, women who are striving to be good wives and mothers can convince themselves that they are also reaping the rewards of such occupations. If a woman is not reaping any rewards from domestic life, she is convinced that something is wrong with *her,* not with the role she is playing. If something is wrong with her, then she must just try harder. And so she does. And little by little she manages to convince herself that she *is* happy for, after all, isn't she supposed to be?

This is a case of buying into the external model or form presented by society rather than measuring our needs and satisfactions in terms of an "inner locus of evaluation." It is quite likely that many women are happy because they think they *should* be happy. In order to accept this idea, they must ignore the internal signs of discomfort, distress, and self-questioning suggesting that perhaps they are unhappy and therefore also inadequate. Since these feelings are not recognized or communicated to others, they manifest themselves in anxiety, unfounded fears, and various forms of emotional distress and mental impairment.

These feelings of discomfort and distress, however, seem inherent in the role of housewife. Mike McGrady (1975), a journalist who experimented with a role reversal for a year while his wife worked,

---

*A study by Edmonds (1967) shows that respondents to "marital happiness questionnaires" tend to conventionalize their answers. In other words they tend to respond with the conventional or expected answer (that they are happy) rather than with assessments of their real feelings.

found that many emotional problems faced by most housewives also came his way. His year as a househusband resulted in many joys but also in depression, lack of energy, and irritability since he had to adjust his schedule to nonstop demands of small children and a working wife. He reflects on another man's statement that men go crazy faster as "housewives" than do women because they have not spent a lifetime learning this role. McGrady says, "My feeling is that a person going crazy slowly is not all that better off than a person going crazy fast" (p. 212). Since it appears that woman's character (and man's) is shaped by her (and his) situation, McGrady argues that it is necessary to change the system that creates and supports this situation.

In addition to losing their individuality in service to others, traditional wives often discover another source of disappointment and disillusionment. Bernard points out that women expecting to depend upon their husbands often discover that their husbands are not the "sturdy oak" upon whom they can rely (1971, p. 153). Women respond to the recognition of men's hidden weaknesses in a number of ways: by denying that men are weak; by refusing to recognize men's weaknesses; by holding back their own potential; or, most commonly, by reinterpreting signs of weakness with the explanation that "men are just little boys grown tall" (Bernard, 1971, p. 155).

Fasteau writing in *The Male Machine* (1974) concurs in this point of view. He agrees that women are disappointed that their men are not emotionally strong and states: "Of all the areas in which men fail women, this is the one that cuts the deepest and, ultimately, evokes the most contempt" (p. 82). Thus we see that men too carry within their prescribed role certain burdens and responsibilities.

Man as Breadwinner and Financial Provider As we have seen in earlier chapters, men are traditionally inept in the interpersonal sphere. They are not in touch with their feelings or, if they are, they feel threatened by expressing them. They have not developed interpersonal resources that allow them to be responsive and flexible in an unstructured interpersonal situation. Instead of developing within themselves the capacity for interpersonal relationships, men have assigned to women all of the skills in this important area of living. First, development of such capabilities by men would imply that they are neither busy nor successful enough in the "real world." Second, the development of emotional responsiveness poses a threat to men who wish to see themselves as strong and invulnerable. Men, nonetheless, recognize the importance of emotional interpersonal sensitivity and wish to keep such sensitivity alive and well in the human race. Thus, in order to preserve their own invulnerability and yet preserve these characteristics they assign such capabilities to women (de Beauvoir, 1953; Janeway, 1971, 1975).*

Similarly, the ability to care for themselves and their homes has not been developed in most men, and such tasks, which they nonetheless regard as necessary for their own well-being, are disdained as "woman's work"—the chores of the inferior sex. Undertaking housewifery for many men is again an admission of failure, a sign announcing inadequacy in doing men's work, which, if successful and profitable, would no doubt keep them too busy for insignificant domestic tasks.

Men do, however, develop traits often not found in women. Scanzoni (1975) describes the role of the traditional husband in two dimensions: being a provider and being the head of the family.† In their competitive world men enhance their own logic and rationality. They learn to deal with problems, not people, as they inch their way up the ladder of status and prestige. External supports in this world are strong and the rewards are tangible. They seldom have to wonder if their labor is or is not noticed, appreciated, or of value. Moreover, at the same time as men's energies are engaged in this competitive milieu, they tend to lose touch with their own emotions and with those of others. They are not interested in vital interpersonal communication when they return home after a day's work. Overworked and preoccupied, they desire only relief from those they have left at the office.

A successful lawyer told me recently that he wanted peace when he returned to his family, as he had been fighting a war all day —a day which often lasts eighteen hours—and one war was enough. Later, he described inadvertently the focus of his life as his career; his interpersonal relationships with a wife and three children were

---

*It is true that recently and predominantly in younger men we are seeing a heightened sensitivity and expressiveness but even here such expressiveness often produces an internal conflict with their masculine socialization.

†The traditional husband so defined, however, has begun to yield to what Scanzoni describes as the "problematic husband" who believes that his interest is basically superior to that of his wife but is willing to adjust to her needs and to allow them to temporarily intrude in family decisions. All the same, the wife still maintains control of the domestic environment.

described as "filler." This response is not uncommon in successful males. Very much in need of emotional support, they still regard the interpersonal realm as secondary to the major business of life. Few women, including this lawyer's wife, find satisfaction in occupying such a secondary position. This man's wife, who feels the need for companionship and communication, has filed for a divorce.

The dilemma of the successful male who sees his career as having primary importance, while love and friendship are regarded merely as "filler" in life, is described by Fasteau, who outlines the parameters of the life of the "male machine":

> The male machine is a special kind of being, different from women, children, and men who don't measure up. He is functional, designed mainly for work. He is programmed to tackle jobs, override obstacles, attack problems, overcome difficulties, and always seize the offensive. He will take on any task that can be presented to him in a competitive framework, and his most important positive reinforcement is victory. He has armor plating which is virtually impregnable. His circuits are never scrambled or overrun by irrelevant personal signals. He dominates and outperforms his fellows, although without excessive flashing of lights or clashing of gears. His relationship with other male machines is one of respect but not intimacy; it is difficult for him to connect his internal circuits to those of others. In fact, his internal circuitry is something of a mystery to him and is maintained primarily by humans of the opposite sex (1974, p. 1).

Fasteau's reference to "men who don't measure up" is a reminder that few men indeed fill adequately the image of the successful provider. There is room at the pinnacle of income and power in our society for only a very few. Thus most men have feelings of inadequacy and insecurity about their ability to fulfill the achievement-oriented aspects of the masculine role. To compensate for this insecurity they must align themselves with the powerful males, and thus against the females and whatever smacks of the "feminine." If they did not do so, their failures and inadequacies might come to light and reveal that they are no more powerful than women. For such men, maintaining the myth of masculinity, and disdaining the feminine side of life within themselves, are even more important than for the successful male. It is necessary to display in mannerisms, behaviors, and attitudes that one is a member of the superior sex.

Traditional men, therefore, leave the emotional side of life to women, and traditional women likewise leave the action-oriented side of life to men. After years within this traditional framework, it is hardly surprising that such men and women have very little to say to each other. What needs to be said can apparently be communicated in twenty-seven and a half minutes of conversation a week (Birdwhistle cited in Ramey, 1975, p. 73)!

Examples of Role-Oriented Marriages Let us now look at examples of role-oriented marriages. Two individuals both in their early 30s write of their expectations of marriage, the well-defined roles which they expected to play and the disillusionment resulting from the disappointment of their expectations.

DOROTHY

Now I am a married woman. I cook, clean, wash the clothes, support my husband and continue working to supplement the family income. I present myself in public in an attractive way when accompanied by my husband. It is important that I impress his colleagues and boss with intelligent conversation and an attractive appearance. I find that in public it is necessary for me to support his decisions and beliefs. As he said once, "Dorothy, you're not supposed to be on their side; you're supposed to be on my side." (Hell, what about Dorothy's side?) Let me backtrack a little. I first met my husband at college ten years ago. He was a highly opinionated person, on the rebound from a troublesome relationship. He was jilted. Likewise at the same time so was I. He was looking for someone who could totally immerse herself in him and I needed a strong opinionated person to love and guide me. What a beautifully symbiotic relationship. He was a fraternity brother, mentally impressive, analytical, instrumental, and emotionally empty. I was intelligent, but weak, attractive, expressive, and emotionally empty. He was my male ideal, and I his female ideal.

He and his friends were used to going out often and after we married it continued. The men felt security and recognition from their constant contact and played important roles in boosting each other's egos. We wives were allowed to share our husband's identity and not too much of our own. . . . What little importance I had was swallowed up by marriage. . . . My husband is clearly an authoritative figure in his own eyes, in his peer group's, and to an extent in mine. Ours is a role-oriented relationship with my husband at the helm. I feel stifled. Jim loves to talk and tries to coach me in the art of analytical and abstract thinking, constantly pointing out how I should do this or go about doing that. I've become so aware of what I do and say wrong, that I've stopped saying much for the sheer fear that it might be wrong. Now communication with each other is closed to a great degree because of my fear of being wrong.

We have discovered that after the romantic glow faded we are each faced with a partner really not like the one we thought we married.

ALEX

Alex, 30 years old, married eight years, is very honest about his premarriage fantasies about a future relationship.

I remember entertaining myself by thinking about and longing for the day that I would be married and at last have someone to take care of these "needs" and provide me with these "services." How nice, I thought. How neat! I'll go off to my job, be a breadwinner, make money and return in the evening to my beautiful, sympathetic, understanding wife, who will meet me with a drink, have my meal all ready, have the house as neat as a pin and be ready to listen to "what a hard day" I had at the office. I can even recall making a mental list of items that I expected to be taken care of by my wife in return for my "slaving" away all day at some job.

Both of us would know what our duties were to be. There would be no doubts, no need for questions; certain responsibilities would fall into certain categories and we would only need three headings: hers, mine, and ours although ours was probably just an extension of mine.

But above all else I was determined that I would have an ideal marriage that would be filled with love, happiness and eternal bliss. . . . I thought I had a healthy outlook as to what my role should be as a husband with the usual provider image. I wanted my wife to be dependent on me, to be able to confide, find strength in me and be able to look up to me. . . . I anticipated certain responses arising from a particular situation and felt that I had all the right answers and would be able to deal effectively with whatever kind of problem presented itself. I really didn't think at the time that this was one-sided and that I was being selfish and egotistical but rather that this was the way I was expected to react, that this was the way my wife would expect me to react.

He turned these fantasies into reality in the first years of his marriage but found them shaken by his wife's "waking up and saying, 'Hey, I've got needs too.' "

When Alice mentioned earlier in our marriage that she would like to seek a career in nursing I thought, "That's great, that'll be like an insurance policy for her and the kids in the event anything should happen to me." Things were great until our first child arrived. Alice hadn't started her training yet and I thought she would just forget about it now that the baby was here and obviously her place was in the home. About six months later when she again expressed a desire to get started in school I wasn't all that enthused. "What," I said, "you want to go off and leave our baby?" She assured me that she had no intention of leaving the baby, that I was perfectly capable of attending to his needs and as I didn't leave for work until late in the afternoon she would be home in plenty of time to say goodbye.... I said I didn't think it would work out although I had really made up my mind that I wouldn't let it work.

All the same I decided to try it.... However, I began making unwarranted demands—expecting her to do things for me that I had always done for myself (getting meals, washing clothes, etc.). I found fault with the housekeeping and was getting more lax at this myself. I began to expect things of her that I knew could only be accomplished during the hours she was in class. One thing led to another until her frustrations finally boiled over and she dropped out of training, adopting a "what's the use" attitude.

I consoled her and sympathized with her and assured her that she had made the right decision. I was really hung up on the notion that mother's place is with the baby and reaffirmed my conviction and thought that she agreed with me.

Things seemed to fall back into their normal patterns.... I went merrily along knocking myself out in one business venture after another, trying to make something of myself, hoping to amount to something someday and still feeling I wasn't doing enough to provide for my family. We were com-

fortable enough but I was caught up in measuring my worth by how much I could make.

We began to grow apart. Alice got more and more tuned in to herself and I got more and more involved in outside interests. . . . Alice completed her nurse's training and worked for a year, returned to school and is now on her way to law school. . . . I am fiercely proud of her. I wish that I had undergone some degree of awakening earlier in my marriage. . . . The most immediate task lying before me right now is to convince Alice of my sincerity in attempting to restructure my values and attitudes and reorder my priorities. I know these attitudes won't disappear in a flash and I anticipate they will be painful but I have a firm conviction that I will be able to adapt to and grow with the ensuing changes.

IMPLICATIONS

Both Dorothy and Alex entered role-oriented marriages with traditional expectations. Dorothy believed in her own weakness and need to lean on somebody. She wanted somebody to cling to and found such a person in a man who wanted to dominate. Alex on the other hand also had needs which he wanted met. He wanted to be served and waited on but more importantly he needed someone else to affirm his strength, his ability as a provider, someone who would prove his indispensability by her dependence on him. Both entered a relationship, not to give to another, but to complete themselves. Both have come to the conclusion that they cannot complete themselves by merging with another. As Erica Jong writes in *Fear of Flying,* completion of self is never the result of such an alliance.

> People don't complete us. We complete ourselves. The search for love becomes a search for self-annihilation and then we try to convince ourselves that self-annihilation is love (1973, pp. 299–300).

MAINTAINING THE FORM AND LOSING THE PROCESS

Unfortunately, not all partners in role-oriented marriages come to a realization of the roles they are playing. Once locked into their respective roles, partners in a traditional marriage often find themselves losing whatever common ground they formerly shared. Indeed, at this point the distinctions between men and women increase so much that it may appear that biological differences or the hand of God had some part in creating the disparity.

From these observations many social scientists conclude that traditional marriage forms are dysfunctional in our society. They focus their critique on evidence that suggests the lessening of companionship, communication, and understanding between the partners, and the impoverishment of the sexual relationship.

Companionship, Communication, and Empathy In the twentieth century, most Americans expect to find companionship and friendship in the marriage relationship (Baum, 1972; Komarovsky, 1967).* However, numerous social scientists are pointing out that traditional role orientations mitigate against this ideal. As the men become more involved with their work and the women become more involved with their children the common ground which the couple once shared diminishes. Thus, Bailyn (1970) finds that for more conventional couples, to the degree that they are alternately absorbed in their careers or their children, marital happiness is lessened. Pollak also states that "neither husband nor wife can find satisfaction or security in a division of labor between the sexes" (1967). The point is further reemphasized by Baum: "To the extent that each partner gets involved in spheres which drain off resources from the couple relationship a strain is put on the marriage" (1972, p. 101).

The strain is largely felt in diminished communication between the couple. Men are primarily preoccupied with their work, a topic which wives tend to find boring and sometimes incomprehensible (Komarovsky, 1967). On the other hand, men are not vastly interested in their wives' conversation about home and family (Feldman, 1965, pp. 14–16). In fact, when the couple has preadolescent children, the husband and wife are most involved in their separate worlds. Numerous studies show that marital satisfaction is lowest at this point, particularly for the wife, and that marital satisfaction increases as the children grow into adolescence and especially when they leave home (Burr, 1970; Renne, 1970; Rollins & Feldman, 1970).

This strain is further amplified by the different styles of com-

---

*These ideals are generally accepted by most individuals of the middle and upper-middle classes and by a proportion of the working class. Instances in which these ideals are not accepted will be discussed in the next chapter.

munication utilized by men and women. Women, trained to be expressive, often feel bludgeoned by the rational argumentativeness of men (de Beauvoir, 1953). In contrast men are often embarrassed and, I might add, frightened by the more emotionally expressive communication of women (Bernard, 1968). The consequence is that after years of marriage men and women may have little to say to each other. In fact Cuber and Harroff (1963) find in their study of upper-middle-class marriages that the major source of marital difficulty is a communication impasse. This finding has considerable bearing on other social classes as well (Komarovsky, 1967; LeMasters, 1975).

Just as the separate spheres of work and home life tend to diminish communication between husbands and wives, so also do they lead to a decrease in understanding between them. As individuals hold back part of themselves in order to fit into separate roles, they naturally come to have less understanding of the part of them that is being repressed. And this is the very part that is *not* being repressed in their partner. Moreover, this lack of understanding often breeds resentment toward one's partner and toward the opposite sex in general. Several social scientists (Horney, 1969; Rossi, 1964) have discussed this resentment in terms of the latent hostility between the sexes. The necessity of men suppressing their feminine aspects and women suppressing their masculine aspects leads not only to inner conflict but to a tendency to displace this conflict onto others. For example, men who fear the feminine within will be, to one degree or another, resentful of the feminine characteristics embodied in women. Similarly, women who suppress their masculine tendencies will resent the expression of such tendencies in men.

Sexual Relationships When two partners share increasingly little of their lives, when communication decreases, it is perhaps not surprising that the sexual relationship deteriorates as well (Jourard, 1964). Minimal sharing and communication is not likely to lead to the full, total fusion of two complete selves which may be experienced in sexual intercourse in the process-oriented relationship.

Once again, writers on the subject emphasize difficulties in the sexual relationship arising from suppression of feminine and masculine aspects of partners, occurring in men and women respectively (Fasteau, 1974; Rossi, 1964). Fasteau points out that the sexual act is the closest many men come to intimate contact with women. In this act they also come closest to their own feminine side, the side of emotion and tenderness. Thus for many men "one of the ultimate tests of their masculinity" is "to get this close to a woman, to the feminine in her and—because of the emotions evoked—in oneself, and still be in command" (1974, p. 21).

Moreover, the man's need to remain in command imposes traditional constraints on the sexual act. With the man on top and the woman beneath him,* with the man active and the woman passive, there is little of the joyful interplay of assertiveness and tenderness found in the process-oriented relationship. Instead, even in sexual intercourse, roles are prescribed and functions allotted on the basis of masculinity and femininity.

The woman's passivity in the sexual act has been shown to diminish her pleasure and delight. The man's traditional inability to be tender and expressive focuses—for him, and thus for the woman too—greatest attention on the physical and genital aspects of the act, in which successful orgasm is the main and perhaps only goal. The loving play, the caring interaction, the full communication found between strong individualities in sexual intercourse are missing. The transcendent quality is not to be found. Sex is limited to the physical level.

Thus in the traditional relationship there is a strong tendency, created by the separate roles and situations in which men and women find themselves, for men and women not to fully know each other. If they do not experience each other totally in an ongoing process of change, the constant excitement and stimulation of change are missing. Instead the relationship becomes an uninteresting but safe preserve in the background of people's lives.

Diminishing Returns in the Role-Oriented Marriage The diminished satisfaction that many couples experience over the years of marriage has been well-documented by recent research. Cuber and Harroff (1965) find that many marriages which began as vital relationships become devitalized with the passage of time. Dizard

---

*Again, it is not the adherence to a particular form, but the adherence to any externally imposed form which indicates role orientation. Thus, couples may adopt traditional sexual positions or follow other less conventional sexual techniques because they are adhering to external forms. The emphasis on sexual experimentation in the mass media has led many individuals to be as concerned about the perfection of innovative techniques as they previously have been about traditional practices. Such experimentation does not necessarily indicate both individuals are escaping a role orientation. In fact traditional or nontraditional sexual practices may be process oriented *if* the individuals are behaving in ways which are satisfactory to them and grow out of the relationship—not if they are adopting traditional and nontraditional norms.

(1968), reviewing a longitudinal study of over 400 families in the Chicago area, also found that marital unhappiness increased with time. Finally, Pineo (1961) states:

> Simply put, we argue that the grounds upon which one decides to marry deteriorate; the fit between two individuals which leads them to marry reduces with time (p. 7).

In other words, the relationship between a couple after marriage has nowhere to go but down.*

Numerous social scientists attribute much of this dissatisfaction to the belief in traditional forms and the impact of these forms upon people's lives. Komarovsky (1967) and LeMasters (1975) find that the traditional forms, particularly those of masculinity and femininity, increase the strain that blue-collar workers experience in their marriages. Cuber and Harroff (1965) document the discrepancy found in upper-middle-class couples between what they actually do and their outward adherence to traditional forms. Pollak states that traditional distinctions between men and women are dysfunctional in marriage because "in the realm of intimacy there are only equals" (1967). Slater (1961) also suggests that such forms are dysfunctional and that we must develop less differentiated expectations for men and women in order to accommodate current societal changes.

Pratt (1972) made a strong case against traditional norms when she studied the health maintenance and health care in married couples. She found that those who were *not* in role-oriented marriages rated themselves as healthier and maintained better health care than those who were in more traditional relationships:

> The data permit us to conclude that marriages characterized by a relatively egalitarian power pattern, flexible division of labor, and a high degree of companionship are associated with a higher level of health and health behavior among both husbands and wives than are marriages which are characterized by relatively unequal power, strict sex role differentiation, and lower companionship (p. 92).

Therefore, traditional roles in our society apparently not only affect our psychological state but affect our physical well-being as well.

Marital dissatisfaction results from a number of causes but the adherence to concepts of traditional masculine and feminine roles

---

*This is not true in all relationships, as discussed in Chapter 4. There are exciting, growing relationships, the above statements to the contrary.

appears to be predominant among them. If individuals are more satisfied when they cross role boundaries and allow themselves to be more fully human, and yet we know that many individuals do not, there must be a large reservoir of dissatisfaction among married individuals. What happens when they are not satisfied?

Many couples do not even realize the degree of their dissatisfaction, for they simply lower their expectations and accept their disillusionments. Others disturb the balance, at least covertly, by seeking variety and stimulation elsewhere: for men in their work, for women in their children, and for both sexes in sexual relationships with others. Often such external sexual relationships are accepted and tolerated if the form of the relationship can be maintained.* Whatever discomforts experienced by partners may all be accepted in order to maintain the security offered by the sameness and predictability of the relationship.

EXPECTATIONS OF YOUNG MEN AND WOMEN

From this picture of role-oriented marriages we find that dissatisfaction is often inevitable. We seem to face a pretty grim picture of the future. However, recent studies of young people show that although very few anticipate a process-oriented relationship, at least they are moving away from the traditional conventional pattern.

In a survey of young men at an Ivy League college Komarovsky (1973) finds that they anticipate marrying young women who have some career orientation but are willing to interrupt their work during the child-rearing years. At the same time, these men are willing to assist in domestic routines. Thus the common ground between the two sexes would be enlarged. Yet, this is not a free-flowing equal partnership since men still have the primary responsibility for achievement and women the primary responsibility for the home. Moreover, the young men surveyed here reveal views of a partnership that is not process oriented but is a structured, though moderate, view of the appropriate roles of both sexes.

---

*External sexual relationships may sometimes be chosen in process-oriented relationships and integrated into the flow of the relationship. This is generally not the case for role-oriented couples who tend to adhere to the "monolithic standard" described by Cuber and Harroff (1963) and therefore believe that extramarital sexual relations are not acceptable. Thus extramarital sex in this case is something to be *tolerated* but not invited or welcomed or integrated into the marriage pattern.

In this study 48 percent of the sample hold this view, whereas only 24 percent value the traditional conventional pattern and a very minute 7 percent look forward to a process-oriented relationship in which they are willing to moderate and mesh their needs with those of a partner, depending on the particular needs of each.

Thus, as the circumstances of life have changed, individuals have created life-styles more appropriate to the content of their lives. The danger is, of course, that those who follow their footsteps will cling as tenaciously to these new and more moderate patterns as to the old ones. Again, the degree to which one clings to form, regardless of how traditional or how liberated, indicates the degree of role orientation.

In a written parody of the early months of marriage Paul, a young man of 23, highlights the ease with which many of us take on the coloration of our roles. Here he indicates some of the difficulties that emerge even from a more moderate marriage pattern. Recently married to a working wife, he tells how they both allowed the institution of marriage to shape their relationship.

> *The greatest modifications (in one's relationship) take place immediately after one says "I do." I was automatically given the right to be the decision maker, protector, provider, and King of the castle. Chris wasn't quite as lucky as I; she became Queen sure enough, but she still was given the task of dealing with the shit-jobs. Because neither of us accepted our responsibilities gracefully, there were a lot of inner stresses. Seemingly insignificant things would start battles. The greatest problem we had was the realization that nine times out of ten we were arguing for the wrong reasons. . . . Playing the role-game was making life difficult for me. Conversations began to start, but many times I cut them short. . . . Finally, Chris and I began interacting on a personal level and together we made progress.*

Paul and Chris are now sharing more equally, communicating openly, and working on being more "fully human." As we have seen, couples who continue to be molded by the traditional roles of husband and wife often find themselves living in two separate worlds as their marriage progresses. After years of doing their respective duties, the King of the Castle and the Queen of the Shit-Jobs may indeed have little to say to each other.

SUMMARY

Many of us enter into marriage as an escape from our aloneness. We hope to find stability and security but very often we find disenchantment instead. Yet we are willing to enter such a relationship that hinders our own personal development and that of our partner, all in the name of love. We continue to try to unite love and marriage despite evidence that this attempt has been unsuccessful throughout history.

Such marriages come under the heading of role-oriented relationships. In these relationships we attempt to maintain stability at all costs. While doing so we assign certain characteristics to love. Love in role-oriented relationships is conditional: It provides a framework in which we hope to fill our needs of power, safety, and security. In role-oriented relationships we confuse love and power. This is not the romantic love for which we married.

As we formalize our love within the institution of marriage, tasks and behaviors become dichotomized along sex-oriented lines. The woman assumes the role of housewife and the man takes on the role of breadwinner and financial provider. Partners often find that their expectations are not met and eventually they often experience a lessening in companionship, communication, and understanding, and an impoverishment of the sexual relationship.

Yet our future is not as grim as it seems. Although very few young people anticipate entering into a process-oriented relationship, at least they are moving away from the traditional conventional pattern.

EXERCISE: OUR IDEAL MAN AND IDEAL WOMAN

Sit back and clear your mind of all thoughts. As you relax let your mind picture a blank television screen. Now let appear on this screen whatever image comes first when you as a man think of "woman" or you as a woman think of "man." Notice carefully the person on your own particular screen. Describe him or her to yourself. Share this description with another if you are in a group setting.

Now return to your fantasized image of man or woman. If you were to know, love, or be loved by such a person, how would you feel? Would you feel better or worse than you do now? What would this person do for you? What would you do for this person?

To what extent was your fantasy composed of those qualities which you do not now possess? To what extent would such a fantasy person complete yourself? Would you really like to know such a person?

Now go back to your television screen and picture a person of the opposite sex about whom you care in your real life. What qualities does he or she have that were not part of your fantasy? Are these qualities disadvantages? In what way? Now allow yourself to see how these qualities can be advantages in your relationship with this person. Perhaps these qualities require that you think more for yourself, or that you develop a greater empathy for others. Finish by remembering all the things you like about this real person on the screen.

REFERENCES

Bailyn, L., "Career and Family Orientations of Husbands and Wives in Relation to Marital Happiness," *Human Relations,* vol. 2 (1970): 97–114.

Baum, M., "Love, Marriage and the Division of Labor," in P. Dreitzel, ed., *Family, Marriage and the Struggle of the Sexes,* New York: Macmillan, 1972.

Bernard, J., "The Paradox of the Happy Marriage," in V. Gornick and B. Moran, eds., *Woman in Sexist Society,* New York: Signet Books, 1971. See also J. Bernard, *The Future of Marriage,* New York: Macmillan, 1972.

Bernard, J., *The Sex Game,* Englewood Cliffs, N.J.: Prentice-Hall, 1968.

Birdwhistle, R., cited in J. Ramey, *Intimate Friendships,* Englewood Cliffs, N.J.: Prentice-Hall, 1975.

Bugental, J., *The Search for Authenticity,* New York: Holt, Rinehart & Winston, 1965.

Burr, W., "Satisfaction with Various Aspects of Marriage over the Life Cycle: A Random Middle-Class Sample," *Journal of Marriage and the Family,* vol. 32 (1970): 29–37.

Caplow, T., *The Sociology of Work,* New York: McGraw-Hill, 1964.

Colton, H., *Sex after the Sexual Revolution* (1974), cited in J. Ramey, *Intimate Friendships,* Englewood Cliffs, N.J.: Prentice-Hall, 1975.

Cuber, J. F., and Harroff, P. B., "The More Total View: Relationships among Men and Women of the Upper Middle Class," *Marriage and Family Living,* vol. 25 (1963): 140–45.

Cuber, J. F., and Harroff, P. B., *Sex and the Significant Americans,* New York: Penguin, 1965.

de Beauvoir, S., *The Second Sex,* New York: Alfred A. Knopf, 1953.

Dizard, J., *Social Change in the Family,* Community and Family Study Center, University of Chicago, 1968.

Edmonds, V., "Marital Conventionalization: Definition and Measurement," *Journal of Marriage and the Family,* vol. 29 (1967): 681–88.

Fasteau, M., *The Male Machine,* New York: McGraw-Hill, 1974.

Feldman, H., *Development of the Husband-Wife Relationship,* Department of Child Development and the Family, Cornell University, 1965.

Fromm, E., *Art of Loving,* New York: Harper & Row, 1956.

Fromm, E., *Escape from Freedom* (1941), New York: Avon Books, 1971.

Goode, W. J., "The Theoretical Importance of Love," *American Sociological Review,* vol. 24 (1959): 37–48.

Goodrich, W., Ryder, R., and Raush, H., "Patterns of Newlywed Marriage," *Journal of Marriage and the Family,* vol. 30 (1968): 383–90.

Gove, W., "The Relationship Between Sex Roles, Marital Status, and Mental Illness," *Social Forces,* vol. 51 (1972): 34–43.

Health, Education and Welfare (Department of), "Selected Symptoms of Psychological Distress," Public Health Services, Health Services, and Mental Health Administration, 1970.

Horney, K., *Neurosis and Human Growth,* New York: W. W. Norton, 1950.

Horney, K., "Distrust Between the Sexes," in B. Roszak and T. Roszak, eds., *Masculine/Feminine: Readings in Sexual Mythology and the Liberation of Women,* New York: Harper & Row, 1969.

Janeway, E., *Between Myth and Morning: Women Awakening,* New York: William Morrow, 1975.

Janeway, E., *Man's World, Woman's Place,* New York: William Morrow, 1971.

Jong, E., *Fear of Flying,* New York: Holt, Rinehart & Winston, 1973.

Jourard, S., *The Transparent Self,* New York: Van Nostrand Reinhold, 1964.

Kahn, E. J., *The American People,* New York: Penguin, 1973.

Kerckhoff, A., and Bean, F., "Social Status and Interpersonal Patterns among Married Couples," *Social Forces,* vol. 49 (1970): 264–76.

Knupfer, G., Clark, W., and Room, R., "The Mental Health of the Unmarried," *American Journal of Psychiatry,* vol. 122 (1966): 844.

Komarovsky, M., *Blue-Collar Marriage.* New York: Vintage, 1967.

Komarovsky, M., "Cultural Contradictions and Sex Roles: The Masculine Case," *American Journal of Sociology,* vol. 78 (1973): 873–84.

LeMasters, E. E., *Blue-Collar Aristocrats,* Madison, Wis.: University of Wisconsin Press, 1975.

Maslow, A., *Motivation and Personality* (1954), New York: Harper & Row, 1970.

Matthews, V., and Milhanovich, C., "New Orientations on Marital Maladjustment," *Journal of Marriage and the Family,* vol. 25 (1963): 300–04.

McCary, J., *Freedom and Growth in Marriage,* New York: Hamilton/Wiley, 1975.

McGrady, M., *The Kitchen Sink Papers,* New York: Signet Books, 1975.

Meerlo, J., *Conversation and Communication* (1952), in J. McCary, *Freedom and Growth in Marriage,* New York: Hamilton/Wiley, 1975.

Moustakas, C., *Loneliness,* Englewood Cliffs, N.J.: Prentice-Hall, 1961.

Pineo, P. C., "Disenchantment in the Later Years of Marriage," *Marriage and Family Living,* vol. 23 (1961): 3–11.

Pollak, O., "Outlook for the American Family," *Journal of Marriage and the Family,* vol. 29 (1967): 193–205.

Porter, S., *The New York Post,* February 14, 1972.

Pratt, L., "Conjugal Organization and Health," *Journal of Marriage and the Family,* vol. 34 (1972): 85–95.

Renne, K., "Correlates of Dissatisfaction in Marriage," *Journal of Marriage and the Family,* vol. 32 (1970): 56.

Rollins, B., and Feldman, H., "Marital Satisfaction over the Family Life Cycle," *Journal of Marriage and the Family,* vol. 32 (1970): 20–28.

Rossi, A., "Equality Between the Sexes: An Immodest Proposal," in R. J. Lifton, ed., *The Woman in America,* Boston: Beacon Press, 1964.

Scanzoni, J., *Sex Roles, Life Styles, and Childbearing,* New York: Free Press, 1975.

Schlesinger, A., Jr., "An Informal History of Love, USA," *The Saturday Evening Post,* vol. 239 (December 31, 1966): 30–32.

Scott, A., "The Value of Housework," *Ms. Magazine* (July 1972): 56–59.

Slater, P., "Parental Role Differentiation," *American Journal of Sociology,* vol. 67 (1961): 296–311.

van den Haag, E., "Love or Marriage?" Harpers Magazine (May 1962): 43–47.

8

Social Class and Role Expectations: Marriage and External Forms

As de Toqueville reminds us, Americans believe in self-direction rather than tradition. Yet, at all levels of the social strata, sociologists find strong evidence that tradition influences human behavior. For example, in the upper-middle class sociologists find that tradition affects the beliefs of individuals even though they may act independently of these beliefs (Cuber & Harroff, 1965). At the working-class level tradition has a strong influence in shaping both actions and beliefs (Komarovsky, 1967). Thus, although we may believe along with John Locke that "all men are naturally in ... a state of perfect freedom to order their actions, and dispose of their possessions and persons as they think fit," our behavior belies this. What has caused us to depend on tradition when we claim otherwise?

The environment in which we live strongly affects our behavior. It influences our perception of the world and shapes the ways by

[A]ll men are naturally in ... a state of perfect freedom to order their actions, and dispose of their possessions and persons as they think fit, within the bounds of the law of Nature, without asking leave or depending upon the will of any other man.

John Locke, *Two Treatises of Government*

To evade the bondage of system and habit, of family maxims, class opinions, and in some degree, of national prejudices; to accept tradition only as a means of information, and existing facts only as a lesson used in doing otherwise and doing better; to see the reason of things for one's self, and in oneself alone; to tend to results without being bound to means, and to aim at the substance through the form—such are the principal characteristics of what I shall call the philosophical method of the Americans.

Alexis de Toqueville, *Democracy in America*

---

which we react to the world's demands. As has been shown in earlier chapters, very often we react by creating internal and external constraints. By doing so we become bound to traditional forms of behavior. However, not all of us are bound to traditional forms to the same degree. We must conclude that our environment must account for this somewhat.

The environment in which we live is partially determined by our social class—that is, by our occupational, economic, and educational levels. Our social class, in turn, leads to various cultural and economic restrictions that prevent us from choosing varying alternative life patterns. For example, a lower-class woman might not feed her family a balanced diet because the need for such was not stressed in her upbringing. On the other hand, an upper-middle-class man might ignore options for developing recreational and leisure activities because he is so strongly involved with the achievement ethic in regard to his career. These leisure options become secondary to him. Thus social class bears heavily on the shaping of our lives, both in the influence social class norms have on our expectations and beliefs and in the economic and cultural restraints that limit our options.

In this chapter we will examine how our expectations, beliefs, and behavior are shaped by our social class. We are particularly interested in our expectations and beliefs concerning the institution of marriage. But first let us turn to a brief description of characteristics of various social classes and ethnic groups.

SOCIAL CLASSES AND ETHNIC GROUPS

Kahl (1957) has broken down the class structure of America in the following manner:

Social Class	Percent of the Population
Upper Class	1%
Upper-Middle Class	9%
Lower-Middle Class	40%
Working Class	40%
Lower Class	10%

Neither these percentages nor the distinctions among classes, however, clearly define all parts of the population. They are not to be taken as hard-and-fast categories, but instead they should be taken as guidelines for isolating groups of beliefs and attitudes that differentiate the American population. Nevertheless, as we will see in the following sections, the impact of tradition in terms of sex roles can be seen in all social classes. Almost all families maintain some division of labor according to the sexes, though this division is less rigid in the middle classes, and in almost all families the male maintains at least the pretense of dominance.

The Upper Class In the small upper class, Hollingshead (1950) points out that there are two separate subclasses: the established upper class and the new upper class. In the established upper class, position is defined by inherited wealth and a long family tradition of high social standing. In this class patriarchal trends are extremely strong, in part because fortunes are passed down from father to son. Marriage is not always a matter of choice, but requires the approval and permission of both families. In some ways marriage for the upper class is more of a merger than a love match. In such marriages, moreover, the wife loses her identity and takes on that of her husband. She is a showpiece, a helpmate, and a companion. She does not work at home or in the marketplace. Her role in life is determined by the customs inherent in the patriarchal family into which she has married.

Established upper-class families tend to be very stable and are not often disrupted by divorce or desertion. Much of this is due to the weight of tradition in determining the behavior of individuals in this class (Hollingshead, 1950). Such tradition and the stability derived from it are both a source of power and a source of restriction for individuals in this class (McKinley, 1964).

On the other hand, the new upper class, as defined by Hollingshead (1950), is composed of individuals who have recently acquired a great amount of wealth and so belong to this class because of economic success and not because of established lineage and tradition. Such individuals, moreover, are more self-directing and independent than individuals in the established upper class. The sudden accumulation of wealth, however, and the economic freedom that goes with it are also attained without any traditional normative patterns to guide attitudes and behavior. Thus such individuals manifest highly unstable family patterns and are typified by "fast living, insecurity, and instability" (Hollingshead, 1950). The common attribute of the "jet set" is undoubtedly a suitable label for much of this class.

The Upper-Middle Class In our society, the upper-middle class, small in number as it may be, tends to reflect the dominant orientation of American values. This group tends to be the innovative section of society that takes the lead in adopting new norms.* Members of the upper-middle class are not hindered by tradition or entrenched family patterns as are people in the upper class. Neither is the upper-middle class preoccupied with economic struggles, as is most of the remainder of the population. Consequently, the upper-

---

*It is not true, however, that the innovative forms of the upper-middle class remain there—a privilege and perhaps eccentricity of the elite. As Yankelovitch's (1974) study shows, many beliefs and attitudes of upper-middle class university students in the 1960s are now being adopted by their nonuniversity counterparts in the working classes.

middle class has had the "greatest material and psychological freedom to work out its own life-styles" (Hacker, 1975, p. 141). In particular, women in the upper-middle class have had the most freedom to choose what might be called "deviant" life-styles, such as that of the married career woman.*

Regarding marriage relationships in the upper-middle class, partners tend to be selected by individual choice and marriages remain fairly stable over a long period of time (McKinley, 1964). However, a wide variety of man-woman relationships proliferate outside of marriage: Some of these may be platonic, such as the close association that often develops between an executive and his secretary or "office wife"; but others are sexual relationships of long or short duration. Many of these relationships, as noted earlier, are not accepted in terms of the common belief in the "monolithic code" and occur in spite of the belief that one man and one woman can satisfy each other's needs without other relationships (Cuber & Harroff, 1965).

Although sex-role distinctions play a part in determining the behavior of men and women in this class, they are applied less rigidly than in other classes. Elizabeth Bott's (1957) study of families in England found that upper-middle-class partners did not automatically assume that men and women had separate functions but that the question of sex-role differences was a lively topic of discussion in all the homes of this status. Nonetheless, men are generally expected to support their families whereas women usually occupy themselves with domestic and community affairs.

 Nevertheless, because of the psychological freedom prevalent in this class, many women *choose* to work, and they often choose a career orientation rather than just taking a "job." Work is regarded as an opportunity to fulfill oneself, not as a means of putting bread on the table. Despite the fact that they are making a choice, however, these women suffer the greatest role conflicts. The greater latitude they have in action appears to go along with the greater doubts and frustrations they feel as they attempt to fulfill their chosen roles. Moreover, such women generally put their work second to that of

---

*McKinley specifies, in several examples, how this same freedom is extended to men. An upper-stratum unemployed man might be called a "playboy" whereas an unemployed man in the lower strata is a "bum." Hostile behavior from a higher class individual might be attributed to his eccentricity whereas in the lower classes such behavior would be labeled "just plain meanness." The economic and social standing of the upper classes creates tolerance for nonconventional behavior which would not be found in other classes (1964, pp. 56–57 fn.)

their husbands. If these women choose not to work they may become occupational assistants to their husbands, acting in partnership with them to further their careers. They derive little recognition from this endeavor, the credit for any accomplishments usually going to the husbands. Two instances in which this is particularly likely are noteworthy.

The first case involves women who function as helpmates to their husbands, both in their careers and at home. Papenak (1973) studies this phenomenon under the term "Two-Person Careers." Her research indicates that many women, particularly those who are well-educated and have had previous work experience, function as unseen partners in their husbands' careers. She points to women who assist their academic husbands in conducting research and writing articles. Nonetheless, when the material is published, usually only the husbands' names appear. Papenak does not comment at any length on the wives' perception of their roles. But because of the high value that women in general place on self-sacrifice, it seems they accept this role as a palatable means of using their talents.

The second case, an offshoot of the first, involves the executive wife. Here, too, the male has the upper hand in the partnership. Because the wife is married to a rising executive, there are certain behavioral guidelines that she must follow. A good executive wife is highly adaptable and gregarious, recognizing that her husband belongs to the corporation (Hacker, 1975, p. 140). Seidenberg has devoted an entire book entitled *Corporate Wives—Corporate Casualties?* (1973) to the difficulties wives of corporate executives encounter. This book focuses on the rootlessness of women who willingly merge their identity with that of their husbands and who are also required to lose whatever local moorings they may have attained as a result of frequent moves required by their husbands' positions. Seidenberg, a psychiatrist, is increasingly concerned with the "feelings of loneliness and helplessness that women develop over time from having little or no say in their destinies" (p. 28).

Thus although women of the upper-middle class have much psychological freedom, at the same time they suffer much stress. The price of freedom comes high.

The Lower-Middle Class In contrast to the upper-middle-class emphasis on career interests, whether this be shared or individual, the lower-middle class is more concerned with family interests. In addition, the lower-middle class emphasizes respectability (McKinley, 1964) and conformity to traditional concepts of duty, decency, responsibility, and morality. McKinley (1964) points out that the upper strata regard members of this class as "fearful and unimaginative conformists," whereas in the eyes of the lower strata they "get nowhere and get no fun out of life .either" (p. 21). The preoccupation with doing things as they should be done may be a response to what they view as their sometimes tenuous hold on middle-class status. Yet as McKinley points out, the lower-middle class enjoys greater status and respectability than individuals in lower social classes as well as freedom from the economic striving of the upper-middle class (1964, p. 21).

In terms of sex roles and marriage, in the lower-middle class both husband and wife share many obligations. These couples are primarily home-centered with a joint social and recreational life. Nevertheless the husband is definitely head of the house and the wife caters to his wishes. If she works, she is only "helping out," not seeking individual fulfillment. Couples in this class tend to adopt the usual instrumental role for the man and the expressive role for the woman. Moreover, wives appear relatively content with this division of function. Their husbands are generally better educated than they and are also reasonably successful in the "man's world." Thus the women are happy to accept a subordinate position. Hacker suggests that women in this class may experience a higher satisfaction with their role than women in any other social class (1975, p. 145).

The Working Class The working class is largely insulated from the mainstream of American intellectual life and lives under the mandates of fairly rigidly defined traditions (Komarovsky, 1967; LeMasters, 1975). Sex roles are tightly prescribed, boys and girls are raised differently, and men and women are expected to take on completely different functions. Men provide for the family and women undertake most of the domestic tasks with less help from their husbands than middle-class wives receive from theirs. In addition, because of the separate spheres of men and women, husbands and wives often engage in separate social lives, each having their separate same-sexed circle of friends and relatives. There is often little communication or sharing between individuals who live in such different worlds (Komarovsky, 1967; LeMasters, 1975).

The views that the sexes hold of each other are more disparate than in the middle classes.* Men tend to think of women as temperamental, emotional, demanding, and irrational (Rainwater, 1960, p. 77). In LeMasters' study of blue-collar men who gathered regularly in a particular tavern, the men said that they regarded women as crafty, tricky, and sly. On the other hand, women told LeMasters that men were "dumb," implying that, at least in home matters, the men acted like children but expected to be treated like adults (1975).

The economic situation of these individuals has a large impact on their home lives. Hollingshead (1950) points out that there is more instability and divorce in this group than in the social classes above them. In part this is due to these families' dependence on wage-earning and the business cycle. In addition, men have a relatively low occupational status and to some extent this affects their status in the home. Many commentators have pointed to the "rule of woman" in these homes and the matriarchal norms thus adopted by the working class (Hacker, 1975). Other writers, however, have pointed out that as in the other classes, the males are still dominant, though perhaps more at the mercy of the wiles of their women. LeMasters' blue-collar men, almost all well-employed and well-paid, did not yield dominance to their women, although they were not interested in the day-to-day running of the home—a sphere controlled by their wives. Komarovsky (1967) also found that the largest percentage of homes in her study were male-dominated, and that this male domination *increased* as one moved *down* the social ladder. Apparently, again, individuals who have less power in the outer world may compensate for this deficiency by claiming more power at home—if at all possible. Nonetheless, regardless of who rules the home, the fiction is maintained that the man is king in his house.

In terms of satisfaction, women in this class appear to be less happy than their middle-class neighbors. Despite their influence in the home, working-class women tend to have a pervasive anxiety and feelings of helplessness (Hacker, 1975). The women married to LeMasters' blue-collar men were not content but felt that they had made the best of alternative choices, which were meager at best. The women in Komarovsky's study were less satisfied than the men but felt that they had accepted what was offered. Both men and

---

*However, this situation may be subject to change. LeMasters (1975) points out that upper-middle-class feminist attitudes are beginning to affect some of the women in the working class. Some of these women, like many of their upper-middle-class sisters, are beginning to question the traditional division of sex-role tasks and obligations.

women said that they looked forward to marriage as a liberation from the restrictions of the parental home. Marriage thus viewed, however, sometimes fell short of expectations. As one woman commented, she had escaped from the frying pan into the fire. All in all, for both sexes, Komarovsky sums up the blue-collar life-style of her sample as "drab and impoverished."

Despite this view, satisfactions are indeed possible in this life-style, as evidenced by LeMasters' study. Most of the men in his study made good incomes and liked their work. They took satisfaction not only from their work—usually construction work or truck driving—but also from their camaraderie with each other. In the almost exclusively male social and occupational world in which they lived, there was a sense of both productivity and companionship. However, their reactionary attitudes toward social change left them little resiliency with which to face our changing society. Their satisfaction may be the satisfaction of those who have protected themselves from change—and thus a satisfaction that is very vulnerable to outside events. LeMasters sums up his views of these "blue-collar aristocrats:"

> And yet one has the feeling that eventually these men are going to lose their fight against social change. . . . They are opposed to sexual equality, racial equality, mass production of houses, and many other features of modern life. In a very real (or literal) sense these men are reactionary—that is, they yearn for the America that began to disappear yesterday or the day before. . . . Perhaps this generation of blue-collar aristocrats can survive free and undomesticated in their marriages, but their sons may be in for a rude awakening a few years hence (1975, p. 90).

The Lower Class The lower class is composed of individuals who generally do not have any stable, continuous means of support, or who have very low-paying jobs. Instability, both in and out of the family, is a byword of lower-class life. Hollingshead (1950) points out that in some areas "50 to 60 percent of lower-class family groups are broken once, and often more, by desertion, divorce, death, or separation, often due to imprisonment of the man." A recent University of Michigan study, moreover, reports that this class is not composed of a stable group of individuals but that individuals move in and out of this class as their economic situation improves or deteriorates (*Detroit Free Press*, 1977).

Much of this instability can be traced to the difficult economic struggle of the lower class, which places them out of reach of any legitimate channels to power. Cut off from legitimate sources of status and power, the lower class becomes apathetic in those areas of life that members of other classes see as serious business. Lower-class individuals therefore live more in the emotional and physical present. "Drinking, dancing, exciting movies, sexual adventure, physical conflict, horseplay, sports and gossip all weave a kind of riotously rich and disorganized tapestry out of the demands of the situation and the 'libido'" (McKinley, 1964, p. 22).* McKinley (1964) also points out that the lower class in general is defined by society as "immoral, unintelligent, irresponsible, and unproductive" and in accord with this definition, they indeed become so (p. 22).

Moreover, in addition to living in the present, lower-class individuals often turn against the system and become ineffective rebels who flagrantly flaunt violations of the social code accepted by the rest of society. And yet they have little hope for the future or comfort in the present. It is perhaps not surprising that any pleasure that can be obtained at the moment is worth any long-term risk, for the future promises no more and perhaps less than the present.

The Black Culture In common stereotypes held by many Americans, black race and lower class go together. Therefore many adjectives applied to blacks are stereotypically associated with members of the lower class and not with the black race itself. Although large proportions of blacks still comprise the lower class, however, a large and significant minority have moved into other strata of American society. As they do so, there is evidence that they are adopting the norms created and maintained by the white middle class (Scanzoni, 1975). In fact, Frazier (1957) and others have commented that the black bourgeoisie are more middle class than whites in their pursuit of status and adoption of white American norms.

Among lower-class blacks, moreover, the norms for behavior do not differ markedly from those of lower-class whites. Class, not race, appears to be the determining variable in understanding much of the behavior patterns of blacks in America. In the lower class, for example, whites as well as blacks develop families that are run by

---

*Libido is a Freudian term for the instinctual drive for pleasure which Freud saw as a major motivating force in human lives.

women, whether or not a husband is currently present.* However, although lower-class black women often run the family home, they are less concerned about maintaining the pretense that the man is in charge. Whereas white lower-class women tend to be intimidated by their husbands, black lower-class women are not. As Rainwater states, they "give as good as they get" (1965). If the man steps out on his wife, she will step out on him. If the man loses his job, the wife stops cooking. Marriage, tentative and short-lived as it may be, is not a joint operation in the black, lower-class world but rather a conditional arrangement: "As long as you do your share, I'll do mine and when you quit, I quit."

In part, such lack of intimidation on the part of women comes from a general ambivalence toward marriage, which is created by the expectation that men will be irresponsible. Not only do black women expect their husbands not to provide for the family, they also expect them to drain off resources needed for raising the children. And these expectations are somewhat realistic: Lower-class black men may not have regular employment and, in fact, may be unable to provide for their families. Moreover, when they are unemployed, they may use the family resources for their own amusements and street adventures. Thus lower-class black men have little credit with their wives and consequently do not come first in their wives' concerns (Rainwater, 1965). This supports the general conclusions of researchers who state that black women are more concerned with being mothers than wives (Bell, 1971).

Black men, in addition, are not heavily invested in either the marital or parental role (Bell, 1971), and thus leave many decisions about and responsibility for family life in the hands of the women. Staples (1970) is careful to point out here that women in this class do not dominate their husbands but rather make decisions in the absence of decision making by their men. As Blood and Wolfe (1969) point out, black husbands are not henpecked but rather segregated. They lead much of their existence on the periphery of the major undertakings of family life.

Because of the antagonism toward marriage in the black culture (although, as Rainwater (1965) points out, most blacks eventually marry), there is a tendency to have more open standards of

---

*Rainwater (1965) points out that in the black culture this pattern is exaggerated, in part because of the less stable economic situation of the black man.

sexual gratification, which are based on mutual satisfaction rather than on institutional obligations. In addition, among both sexes there is a greater allowance for emotional expressiveness, particularly among the men. This emotional expressiveness, in part due to the emphasis on living in the present, contrasts with the reserve of the white American male.

The lack of promise in the lives of the black lower class, and of the lower class in general, lies at the root of most attitudes adopted by this class. As Rainwater (1965) points out, identity in this culture involves the strength to defend oneself against debasement by others but not the strength to embark wholeheartedly on any future-oriented program. At heart, lower-class blacks accept the teachings of their experience: Human beings are evil and the world is hostile and chaotic. From this basic learning, all other attitudes, behaviors, and expectations become understandable. Meers sums up the relevance of this belief system to the marriage of the lower-class black: "The ghetto marriage is an unsacred institution, an attempt at intimacy fraught with insecurity, in which distrust is endemic and ambivalence explodes into nightmare wrath" (1972, p. 109). This is not a picture with which most middle-class Americans are comfortable.

Other Ethnic Groups The contrast in expressiveness between white and black men is also found when white American men are contrasted with men from Latin, Mediterranean, and Arabic cultures. Men from these cultures are open and expressive and easily moved to emotion as contrasted with the American male. However, they are not necessarily more liberated from sex-role stereotypes. Individuals from such cultures come from a long tradition of *assured* male dominance. In cultures such as these with a history of caste stratification, where for centuries men have been superior and women inferior, men have less need to struggle to prove their masculinity. This contrasts with American men who must struggle to prove their masculinity by achievement and in the process must shun all that appears to be feminine.

However, this greater expressiveness rests not only on a basis of assured superiority, but also covers an underlying contempt for the female half of the population. Thus in these countries men and women are more apt to know their place in life—and the places of each are even more distant than in the competitive American culture.

The Influence of Social Class and Ethnic Group From the preceding discussion we see that just as most people are largely influenced by whether they are men or women, they are also shaped by the expectations of the social class or ethnic group to which they belong. Yet the question may be raised, do those of us who succumb to traditional roles do so because the pressures from our class orientation leave no other choice or because we choose to do so? No assortment of facts can totally decide the issue, although I believe that there is a component of choice in the way all of us conduct our lives. Yet for some of us the impact of external circumstances is so overpowering that our capacity to choose is limited if not nearly nonexistent.

On the other hand, most middle-class Americans and a large proportion of working-class Americans have more freedom than they utilize. When a skilled factory worker who makes more money than most college professors tells me that he has to stay in his current job for economic reasons, I disagree. Surely he has enough money to tide him over until he can find another job—even though his new employment might be very much like his last one. Nonetheless, what keeps him from making a change are his beliefs that (1) he cannot exist at less than his current standard of living; (2) he cannot move to another part of the country because he would have to leave his friends and relatives; (3) he may not find a better—or even equal—job so that he must not lose the one he has; and (4) ultimately he is doing what he sees he has to do, and any other alternative course would have little meaning for him. All these beliefs are understandable in terms of the worker's class origins and his resulting expectations about occupations, friends, and marriage. However, these beliefs do not have the same impact as constricting external circumstance. He *could* move without necessarily bringing economic havoc on his family. For various reasons, one being social class, he *chooses* to stay where he is. We will now examine the influence of social class on love and marriage.

THE INFLUENCE OF SOCIAL CLASS ON MARRIAGE

As we have seen in preceding chapters, process-oriented individuals are able to combine love and power in such a way that they become both expressive and instrumental, compassionate and strong. We also found these same traits carried thorugh when these individuals entered process-oriented relationships. However, most individuals are not process oriented and therefore they tend to mold themselves to the norms of their particular culture, which in America vary by social class. Consequently, depending on our life situation, our occupational orientations, and our values, we tend to develop varied expectations of love and marriage.

Two patterns are of particular concern here: One has been identified with the upper strata of society and the other with the lower. The two patterns have been typed respectively by Elizabeth Bott (1957) as a "joint conjugal role relationship" and a "segregated conjugal role relationship." Jessie Bernard (1964) refers to them as an "interactional pattern" and a "parallel pattern." Each pattern is woven out of the strands that form the total life situation of the middle and upper-middle classes or that shape the life situation of the working class.

The interactional pattern is the one most common among the middle classes. It is most often referred to in discussing "companionate marriages"—that is, marriages in which the partners expect that they will be friends with each other. The idea of companionship and friendship involves a concern for one's mate *as a person,* a value that is part of the socialization of the middle classes. Moreover, in being concerned with this value, which entails personal development and understanding of psychological needs, there is a greater tendency in such marriages to move away from the traditional roles.

This tendency is reinforced by certain sociological characteristics of these individuals. Generally they are upwardly mobile and are concerned with occupational success. In addition, because they are upwardly mobile, they are often geographically mobile as well. Thus they frequently move away from their original community, their early friends, and their relatives. They become isolated from customary traditional supports and tend to rely more on their spouses in order to meet their needs.

Couples who expect companionship in marriage demand a great deal more of themselves, each other, and their relationship than individuals in the historical past and in other subcultures. They emphasize communication, sharing, and understanding of the other. At its best the companionship pattern described here typifies the process-oriented relationship. At its worst (which perhaps occurs more frequently), it typifies the "empty shell" marriage described by Goode (1962) in which the reality of the relationship falls far short of the couple's expectations. As Kerckhoff and Bean

(1970) state, individuals adhering to this pattern "must be constantly 'finding' or 'creating' the bases of a satisfying relationship. This is a trying business and requires constant attention to both one's own and the other's behavior and its meaning" (p. 270).

In contrast to the interactional or companionate pattern, which is much more common among the middle classes, the parallel or segregated pattern is more typical of those in the working class. Working-class individuals, in general, view life more objectively, focusing on external and situational characteristics rather than on interpersonal development (Komarovsky, 1967). Therefore, they are more concerned with what one will *do* instead of who one *is*. They focus more on the roles one will play rather than on the process of the relationship itself. This concern, in turn, leads to expectations of marriage that focus more on roles—generally traditional roles—that clearly state what it is one will do and not do. Moreover, for men and women these expectations are very different, thus resulting in a "segregated" rather than in a "joint" marital pattern.

As in the interactional pattern, sociological factors once again reinforce the psychological tendencies that lead many individuals of the working class to prefer the segregated marriage model. Generally working-class individuals are neither occupationally nor geographically mobile and thus tend to reside in the community of birth. Consequently they are surrounded by the emotional supports and the early relationships that sustained them prior to marriage. The continuation of contacts—often very frequent contacts—with former friends and especially with relatives means that the couple does not *need* to turn to each other for companionship as does the more mobile and more isolated middle-class couple. Rather, each partner moves within a separate social world usually composed of members of the same sex. Such separate social connections continue throughout marriage, for marriage itself is not expected to provide intimacy but is regarded as a functional framework in which to raise children and establish a home.

Jessie Bernard describes the pattern of the segregated marriage as follows:

> If the man is a good provider, not excessive in his sexual demands, sober most of the time, and good to the children, this is about all a woman can reasonably ask. Similarly, if the woman is a good housekeeper and cook, not too nagging, a willing sex partner, and a good mother, this is all a man can really expect. Each lives his or her own

life primarily in a male or female world. There are sometimes even strong mystic barriers between the sexes in such a pattern, and neither violates the boundaries of the other's world. . . . Companionship in the sense of exchange of ideas or opinions or the enhancement of personality by verbal play or conversation is not considered a basic component of this pattern (1964, p. 687).

Thus, according to this pattern, men and women live separate lives: They have separate circles of friends, and are content to share their confidences, worries, and needs with their friends and kinfolk rather than with their mates. They adopt, even if unconsciously, the traditional norms, and thus maintain role-oriented relationships.

What are the strains associated with this pattern? Obviously the expectations are less, so the chances of disappointment are also less. Bott (1957) describes one couple in her study who adhere to this pattern and appear to be very happy. LeMasters (1975), however, points out that though the men in his sample are content with both their jobs and their marriages, and often describe their wives (in their better moments) as "good sports," the women appear to be less content. In Komarovsky's (1967) sample of working-class marriages, she finds that although one third of her couples are happy, one third are very dissatisfied. She attributes this dissatisfaction to the lack of sharing and communication in these partnerships as a result of the segregated life men and women lead within the confines of their traditional sex roles.

In addition, both LeMasters (1975) and Komarovsky (1967) find that these couples are insulated from the mainstream of intellectual thought in America and to some degree suffer from a lack of the sociological and psychological options available to the middle class. For some of these couples, however, this insulation has been protective and has preserved their satisfaction with themselves and their relationships. Expecting little of life, they achieve little but remain content. When this insulation disappears, as inevitably with the erosion of time it must, the traditional sex-role patterns and the "segregated conjugal life-style" of these individuals may prove less satisfactory.

Thus, we have seen how social classes affect the relationships we develop. But more than that, we are affected by the psychological expectations arising from our class. The major limitations on our growth are therefore psychological and thus internal rather than physical and external. Yet we must recognize that the hand of external circumstance lies more heavily on some than on others. The varied circumstances of our lives will be illustrated in the following case histories.

CASE HISTORIES

Since we tend to be rather myopic about white American middle-class culture and since most case histories in this book feed into that myopia, the case histories in this chapter are drawn from a variety of classes and cultures. In the comments of an upper-class Latin American we see traces of the "graceful living" that has been a hallmark of the American upper class. In the lower-middle-class upbringing of a Middle Eastern young man there are traces of the strong male dominance that characterizes the American middle class, seen here, however, in the context of a country at war. In the story of a young black woman we see the ethics of the working class emboldened by the fire, emotionalism, and violence endemic in inner-city culture. These case histories are written by men and women who are not married. Thus they are reporting on the families in which they were raised. Finally the chapter concludes with the self-searching of Andrea, a corporate wife.

LUIS

Luis, a man in his 30s, recalls his background as a member of the upper class in Mexico City.

My education took place in a fine old school that was run . . . on the principle of making you something of which they could be proud, regardless of the costs to almost anyone involved. We marched, kept silent, obeyed, and gave back to them exactly what they expected. . . .

At home things were quite different. I was shown how to be a gentleman, I did well, and I loved it. In the doing of those things a young Roman Catholic boy is supposed to do, I excelled, and my parents were delighted. . . .

As I grew older, I was introduced to the arts in every form that was available. My parents took me to plays when I was 3, to the opera when I was 11, and I was introduced to the Art

Institute, drawing, and music lessons at whatever age they thought best. Reading was second nature in our house. . . .

When the matter came to my dealings with ladies, there was never any doubt what my behavior was to be. I was taught that my conduct with them was to have almost a sacred quality, and that there could never be any reason for not adhering to the strict code that I was taught and shown. Needless to say, once again I excelled, to the delight of my parents but often to the anguish of my peers.

As I grew into manhood, the baseball bat was replaced with the golf club, and the birthday party gave way to the dance. Girls grew into womanhood and became even more untouchable and commanded greater respect, whether they liked it or not. . . . Around age 15 it began to dawn on me that young ladies were great for other things that did not take place on the dance floor or at the dinner table. . . . Though I often wondered about my new discoveries, I knew one thing for sure, I must never discuss them with anyone, so I didn't.

Two strong messages came out of my early training: first, be a gentleman; and second, right is right and to be done regardless of the cost.

Very strong in Luis's background are elements of respect for women who, just as in the Victorian age, were put on a pedestal. Thus women were out of competition for the material rewards found in the world of men. He remarks that it was never considered that a woman might have a career: Women would naturally marry, be supportive and companionable partners for their husbands, and also be mothers of their children. The man generally ruled the world *and* the home.

TONY

Tony grew up in the war-torn Middle East in an "average" family. Many elements of the American lower-middle class are apparent in his story, though these elements are thrown into high relief by the long tradition of male dominance and the crisis conditions under which this family was beginning to live.

Let me tell you a little bit about my family. My father took the role of the dominant man—possessive, demanding, unemo-

tional, and overpowering. My mother took the role of the submissive woman—sensitive, soft, loving, and nurturing. . . . I was brought up during wartime, a war that left many scars in my parents' hearts. . . . My father would hold me and look deeply in my eyes, saying, "This world is yours—you are going to be a strong man and I'm going to do all I can to help you be so." I spent my spare time studying politics and working to help other people. . . . I wanted to heal the injured heart of my father by fulfilling his dream and I wanted to rebel against him to make him see his hypocrisy.

One of the first things I learned was that a man does not cry—no more tears. I learned that crying is for women because they are weak. I learned to take responsibility for myself and not depend on others. I felt that I had to be always right and never wrong. I learned to smoke cigarettes and hang around cafes and talk with other men about politics, society, and women. I learned from them that women are only for sex and housecleaning.

It was very confusing trying to cover my fragile self with a tough, steel shell. . . . I had to act and behave in such a way to show others that I was a man. But deep in my heart I did not believe in the things I was acting.

I learned to admire women because I loved my mother. I admired her beauty, sincerity, and strength. She used to work from sunrise until sunset, making sure that our home was beautiful and happy. . . . She used to tell me that to be a man is not an easy thing to do. It is a lot of love, tears, sweat, and smiles. She advised, "You must always be strong inside, be free, be open-minded and helpful to others. . . ."

In adolescence I took advantage of feeling strong and found it easy to slip into the illusion of the man my father wanted me to be. . . . I wanted to screw every woman that I desired. I found it easy. . . . I dominated everyone I was with.

Later after being rejected by a girl I loved, I realized I was still trying to build an artificial tough shell around a fragile center. I could not bear the pain and broke into tears. . . . I got in touch with my loneliness. . . . After that I began to open up and get in touch with my feelings and thoughts. I would have to start anew.

Katz (1973) speaks of the contempt men feel for women. If contempt is not readily apparent in many American men, it is highly visible in Tony's story. Yet the masculine scripting that taught him to treat women as objects is in conflict with his own admiration of his mother and in the end with his recognition of his own vulnerable side. Underlying this struggle, however, is a portrait of a family in which the father is strongly dominant and the mother warm and supportive. But beneath this overt domination there are hints that the strength of the father may be partly pretense, maintained by the warm support of the woman.

CHRISTINE

Christine has grown up in an inner-city black community. With love and pathos she writes of her family:

Both my parents came up poor and hard, working while still children. Unlike many of their peers, they both had the ability and determination to make it during the Depression, even though they were black. My father is a true artisan. He can do anything he wants with his hands. . . . My mother has always worked, despite her husband desiring that matters be handled otherwise. Momma is a liberated woman although she does not know it, and I will never tell her for the simple reason she likes to think Daddy is the king of his home. He ain't.

Men are supposed to be analytical in thinking, huh? Ain't none of those experts that ever came up with my father's thinking. I am a Clark, and the Clarks have no connection between brain and heart. Emotions, according to the Clark creed, are unaffected by the thought patterns emitting from the gray matter. They are damn emotional people and are ruled by their emotions. All of them. Momma says she was afraid for a long time that I would turn out like the Clark side of the family. During my middle teens, me and her went at it so heavy, she arranged for me to move into a motel. I was determined to leave this overbearing woman behind me. We chickened out at the last moment. We do that.

In my childhood, what with five brothers at home, four boys next door, and six other boys on the other side, all the other boys in the neighborhood came our way. My sister, Angela, and I were literally forced to take care of ourselves among a multitude of sickies. I learned to whip anybody my age regardless of size. (The trick was to find a handy stick or any other weapon if the opponent was older and more experienced in these matters. If that was not possible, I was not ashamed to run like hell.) I adapted to the situation by becoming just as bad as the boys. Angela got even badder. While I did not go for a rock until the odds were out of hand, Angela came with a rock in her hand.

Angela is, at a distance, a lady. She dresses like some fashion plate. My clothes actively repulse her. Angela can talk circles around most dudes, while I muddle around and end up missing the ones I want and getting the creeps.

My mother and father do not take much from other people. Daddy is a yeller, a screamer, with flashing black eyes that used to scare me half to death until I realized eyes never hurt anybody. Momma looks at you evil and doesn't say anything, just sticks her lip out. I guess you might say they are opposites. . . . My father is a selfish man, likes his own way, and will protect what is his with all sorts of deadly anger. He has never shot anybody like most of his brothers and sisters, but he's hit his fair share with bricks, hammers, etc. . . . I do believe he would die for us, not because we are Angela or Christine, but because we belong to him and he loves us, if you understand what I mean. Momma is worse because she'd rather handle everything for us including all our troubles. . . . Daddy calls taking care of his family putting bread on the table, a roof over their heads, and clothes on their backs. He does that very well. Momma calls taking care of us doing everything else. Forever.

I can talk about my family all day long. I think it is a very fantastic family to have come from. I love it from Grandpapa, who is now 110 years old (he thinks) to Bobby, my 17-year-old cousin who thinks he is so cool he can barely stand himself. It's a tough group of people to live with. I have missing teeth from the time my uncle hit me accidentally with a baseball bat he was throwing at his son-in-law. A cousin named Vince . . . was racing with some white dudes down the freeway and that got me the scar above my left eye and the one on the bridge of my nose. Grandma slammed a car door on my hand, breaking two fingers. My own mother let her 2-year-old daughter stick her fingers in a tub of scalding water . . . so that I got these dark marks. All the same, I am crazy about my family and I would not change it for nothing, although, considering the bodily damage they have done to people, I should.

This story is especially moving. In spite of hardships, fighting, and violence, the love flowing in this family is apparent. Neither love nor anger is hidden: There is no trace of white middle-class male inexpressiveness—nor of white middle-class female timidity. Typical of working-class families, the mother rules the roost but all believe that the father is king. At the moment this arrangement appears to satisfy everybody in this particular family.

ANDREA

Andrea is a white, upper-middle-class woman in her late 30s, married, with five children. Her life up to the time she returned to school fitted smoothly into the traditional role patterns. Although she has broken these molds in order to further her education, her behavior in other ways remains highly role oriented. The freedom won in returning to school appears a large victory for her, and asking for more now would be too much.

Andrea married soon after completing high school. Her adolescent hopes revolved around finding a "tall, dark, and handsome man, getting married and living in a lovely home with four lovely children." These hopes became reality, including even an extra child. Andrea had everything she thought she wanted. However, she found, as do many women, that the life of wife and mother was not entirely fulfilling. But she was certain that her lack of fulfillment was her own problem; she held her feelings back and tried to do even more for the people around her.

She comments on the isolation and unhappiness of the early child-rearing years:

The isolation for me at that time was devastating, which at the time seemed abnormal. I felt I should be happy doing what I had planned since I was a child. Of course, I could have been happier if I didn't feel so alone all of the time.

This situation was compounded when her husband developed a stomach disorder and the doctor recommended that she make life easier for him:

He said he noticed on the chart that we had five very young children, and he suggested that I start a program to protect my husband from some of the daily domestic problems. . . . So I

*added being the perfect wife to being the perfect mother and
housekeeper. It never occurred to me that I could have used
some protection from the children also. . . . Then the migraines
came. . . .*

The dissatisfactions that broke through in migraine headaches
were partially resolved by Andrea's return to school, which she finds
stimulating and exciting. She is a highly intelligent woman. She
reads a lot, her thinking is thoughtful and organized, and her writing
excellent. In the classroom she has found external rewards for her
talents. Yet, though Andrea is aware of the benefits of a more
liberated life-style, she does not choose to carry her new behaviors,
or view of herself, into the home.

In her life outside of school Andrea still follows the traditional
norms. Her husband still controls her behavior and is reluctant that
she spend time away from home. She acts as hostess for a busy
corporation executive. Moreover, she picks up after all the children,
now teenagers, and takes full responsibility for domestic chores.
Although she finds all this cause for complaint, she sees no prospect of changing this situation substantially in her own life.

She has, however, made some attempts at change and then
retreated:

*Yesterday my 18-year-old son sitting at the dinner table asked if
we had another bottle of catsup. I answered yes. He just sat
there. Eventually I laughed and he smiled but we both continued to sit. Finally, still laughing, I got up to get it. Old habits are
hard to break.*

*At the same meal my husband knocked over a glass of
water. He quickly said: "Honey, I'm sorry." I said, "Don't be
sorry. Clean it up!" The look on his face was beautiful. He was
startled. I could almost read his mind: "Was she mad at me for
something?" It was funny. He was genuinely sorry for making
extra work for me, but it didn't occur to him that he could have
cleaned it up himself. I mentioned this to him as I cleaned up
the water.*

Thus, although Andrea suggests that changes might be made, she
smilingly goes along with the familiar patterns. She herself is not
ready for change. Deeply ingrained in her are society's expectations
of what a wife and mother should do.

In another instance she examines this behavior particularly in relation to her children:

The question is what am I going to do about it. The answer is, first stop being afraid of the children's negative feelings. As it stands now, they think I'm a pretty cool mom. Good. That's today. Tomorrow, if I'm after them to be contributing members of the family, I will be a mean old son-of-a-bitch. This will make me feel bad and guilty. Then I'll back off.

The resistance to change that Andrea finds within herself is the guilt and anxiety that surface when traditional norms are not met. For many this guilt is countered by the desire to seek the rewards of a strengthened individuality. For Andrea, however, who is a "good wife" and a "cool mom," the risk involved in seeking further personal freedom is not worth losing the comforts of a familiar and traditional role. Thus at this point she is willing to surrender the potential of freedom for the security she has built within the confines of her family. School and intellectual pursuits, however, as long as they do not interfere with family needs, are a necessary outlet for her.

The lessened value Andrea places on her own personal needs is reflective of the place of many women in our society. Women generally tend to undervalue themselves as people and find their measure in the approval of their husband and children. This is currently Andrea's view of herself. She is, however, very aware that she is acquiescing to this system and that it is not being imposed on her. In comparing her husband's day with hers she finds that she diminishes her own activities and elevates his. In part, as she reflects, this is because he is paid for his work and she is not, and the value put on money by our society causes this to be a crucial difference at this time.

SUMMARY

To the extent that we are shaped by our roles, we adopt role-oriented patterns in our individual lives and in our relationships with others. However, the roles to which we are shaped vary not only according to sex but also according to social class. The beliefs and expectations surrounding life, and particularly the institution of marriage, are demonstrably different if one is a member of the working class or if one is a member of the upper-middle class.

Specific psychological and sociological factors in the upper-middle class, for example, predispose individuals to value a companionate marriage with high expectations for intimacy and sharing. In their work as well as their relationships, upper-middle-class individuals place less stress on traditional roles and more emphasis on self-direction and individual responsibility. On the other hand, the psychological and sociological factors associated with the working class lead to a greater emphasis on conformity, decency, and a segregated-role marriage in which individuals adhere to traditional roles with lowered expectations of marital communication. In such ways our class origins predispose us to value process-oriented or role-oriented life-styles, the former more strongly suggested by middle-class values and the latter more closely associated with working-class patterns.

Various critiques of American life, however, point to the difficulty members of any class have in achieving process-oriented life-styles and process-oriented relationships. Those of the upper strata of our society who have more freedom from external, role-oriented constraints are more restricted by internal, psychological restraints. Individuals in the lower strata are undoubtedly more restrained by the limitations of external circumstances but more particularly by the value complexes woven from their external circumstances. Although the weight of external limitations may press more heavily on those in the lower strata of our society, there is sufficient evidence that the attainment of a process-oriented approach to life is very difficult for *all* strata of American society.

In the interplay of individual personalities and class factors, however, the impact of sex roles—as well as the traditional superiority of men—are still noticeable. At all levels of society, the theme of male dominance, or at least the pretense of male dominance, is maintained. Except in the lower class, men continue to rule the roost in all social classes—or at least their women allow them to think they do.

Case histories from various cultures illustrate, in a variety of forms, the continuing motif of male dominance and feminine submission in disparate social classes and ethnic groups. Men still believe that women are here on earth to please the superior sex and in that belief most women concur.

EXERCISE: SEX ROLES, SOCIAL CLASS, AND FAMILY BELIEF SYSTEMS

This is an exercise designed to help us get in touch with the nonverbalized assumptions we make about life. On a piece of paper write the heading: "My family believes . . ."

Under this heading write quickly, without much thought, general beliefs that most members of your family have in common.* Such beliefs need not be formally stated, or even beliefs with which you intellectually agree. Rather these statements should reflect general "gut-level" reactions that your family tends to reflect toward the world.

Topics you might consider include attitudes toward work, education, marriage, health, cleanliness, religion, politics, food, social occasions, and so forth. They may include beliefs about people who make a lot of money, those who are on welfare, those who don't work—or those who live next door. Other topics to consider are safety (at home, at school, or on the streets at night), sex, love, and even personal appearance. All families have innumerable beliefs on these topics. Even when such beliefs are not accepted by every member of the family, they are attitudes that are an issue in the home. So—write them down!

When you are finished, compare your list of statements with those of others. Notice similarities and differences. How many beliefs have to do with traditional sex roles? How many beliefs are similar to those described for specific social classes? How many beliefs can you attribute to other circumstances in your life situation? In your own personal evaluation, how many of these beliefs are ones which you accept? Reject? Accept with qualification? How many of these beliefs do you act out in your interactions with others? Do you choose to do so?

REFERENCES

Bell, R., "The Related Importance of Mother and Wife Roles among Black Lower-Class Women," in R. Staples, ed., *The Black Family: Essays and Studies*, Belmont, Calif.: Wadsworth, 1971.

---

*If you are married, you may choose to work with your current family, or your family of origin. However, since most of our beliefs about the world are shaped by our family of origin, more benefit may be derived from thinking of one's parental family.

Bernard, J., "The Adjustments of Married Mates," in H. T. Christensen, ed., *Handbook of Marriage and the Family,* Skokie, Ill.: Rand McNally, 1964.

Blood, R. O., and Wolfe, D. M., "Negro-White Differences in Blue-Collar Marriages in a Northern Metropolis," *Social Forces,* vol. 48 (1969): 59–63.

Bott, E., *Family and Social Networks* (1957), 2nd ed., New York: Free Press, 1972.

Cuber, J. F., and Harroff, P. B., *Sex and the Significant Americans,* New York: Penguin, 1965.

Detroit Free Press, Report on University of Michigan Study on Poverty, July 26, 1977, p. 1A.

Frazier, E., *The Black Bourgeoisie* (1957), New York: Macmillan, 1962.

Goode, W., "Marital Satisfaction and Instability: A Cross-Cultural Analysis of Divorce Rates," *International Social Science Journal,* vol. 14 (1962): 507–26.

Hacker, H., "Class and Race Differences in Gender Roles," in L. Duberman, ed., *Gender and Sex in Society,* New York: Praeger, 1975.

Hollingshead, A. B., "Class Differences in Family Stability," *The Annals of the American Academy of Political and Social Sciences,* vol. 272 (1950): 39–46.

Kahl, J., *The American Class Structure,* New York: Holt, Rinehart & Winston, 1957.

Katz, B., "Women's Lib Auxiliaries?" *The National Observer* (December 29, 1973): 8.

Kerckhoff, A. C., and Bean, F. D., "Social Status and Interpersonal Patterns among Married Couples," *Social Forces,* vol. 49 (1970): 264–71.

Komarovsky, M., *Blue-Collar Marriage,* New York: Vintage, 1967.

LeMasters, E. E., *Blue-Collar Aristocrats,* Madison, Wis.: University of Wisconsin Press, 1975.

McKinley, D. B., *Social Class and Family Life,* New York: Free Press, 1964.

Meers, D., "Crucible of Ambivalence: Sexual Identity in the Ghetto," in W. Muensterberger and A. Esman, eds., *The Psychoanalytic Study of Society,* vol. 5, New York: International Universities Press, 1972.

Papenak, H., "Men, Women, and Work: Reflections on the Two-Person Career," *American Journal of Sociology,* vol. 78 (1973): 852–71.

Rainwater, L., *And the Poor Get Children,* New York: Quadrangle Books, 1960.

Rainwater, L., "The Crucible of Identity: The Negro Lower-Class Family," *Daedalus,* vol. 95 (1965): 251–64.

Scanzoni, J., *Sex Roles, Life Styles and Childbearing,* New York: Free Press, 1975.

Seidenberg, R., *Corporate Wives—Corporate Casualties?,* New York: Anchor/ Doubleday, 1973.

Staples, R., "The Myth of the Black Matriarchy," *The Black Scholar,* vol. 1 (1970): 8–16.

Yankelovitch, D., *The New Morality: A Profile of American Youth in the 70's,* New York: McGraw-Hill, 1974.

9

Androgynous Individuals in a Masculine/ Feminine World: Barriers to Being Fully Human

In previous chapters we have described process-oriented and role-oriented directions for living and have explored the impact of traditional sex roles and social-class influences in shaping our choices. In this chapter we turn to another sphere and examine the world of work and its impact on process and role orientation. Specifically, it is suggested that the work world will create obstacles in the path of those choosing a process-oriented, androgynous life-style, particularly women.

In our society many still maintain the belief that women must stay home and men must go to work. Psychologists, sociologists, and other social commentators have produced a great body of material that justifies maintaining the status quo. Many prominent people (generally men) in our society have also given theoretical and empirical support to this notion. Adler's statement, made in 1931, is not without strong support today. His views imply that a woman who does not like being a mother is deviant:

*Why does American society persist in maintaining erroneous myths ...
urging women to believe their children's development requires their daily
attendance upon them? ... I believe the answer lies in the economic
demand that men work at persistent levels of high efficiency and creativity.
To free men to do this requires a social arrangement in which the family
system serves as the shock-absorbing handmaiden of the occupational
system.*

Alice Rossi, "Sex Equality: The Beginning of Ideology"

---

*The development of this economic system was no longer determined by the
question:* What is good for Man? *but by the question:* What is good for the
growth of the system? *One tried to hide the sharpness of this conflict by
making the assumption that what was good for the growth of the system ...
was also good for the people.*

Erich Fromm, *To Have or To Be?*

> If we are to help [a girl] we must find the way to reconcile her to her
> feminine role. ... Girls must be educated for motherhood and edu-
> cated in such a way that they like the prospect of being a mother,
> consider it a creative activity, and are not disappointed by their role
> when they face it in later life (in Janeway, 1975, p. 109).

Speaking of men, Rossi comments on the societal injunctions dictating that they should remain heavily invested in the work force:

> ... our society ... expects men to aspire to jobs of the highest occupa-
> tional prestige consistent with their abilities; indeed, his job should
> tax and stretch his ability or it will not be "challenging" enough. If it
> does not, if a man settles for a job below his abilities, we tend to
> consider this a "social problem," a "talent loss" ... (1972, p. 125).

Clearly, men who do *not* work to the limit of their capacities are
deviant. Numerous writers tell us that masculinity is measured by
the size of a man's paycheck (e.g., Gould, 1973), and that if he works

at less than his capacity or earns less than is possible, society will enforce social sanctions designed to curb such deviance.* How have we allowed ourselves to be led by such beliefs?

It may indeed be that such a view was created, and assumed true, by those who had a vested interest in maintaining our current economic system. It is, no doubt, at least partially true that in order for our current technological industrial system to continue—at what many see as a breakneck pace hurtling toward self-destruction—a substantial proportion of the population must work most of their waking hours. If this is true then, as Rossi states above, it is also necessary that another part of the population must provide the upkeep, maintenance, and wherewithal of the daily lives of these workers. Individuals working 50–70 hours a week have little time for domestic tasks or, it might be added, for interpersonal relationships.† Somebody else must take over the maintenance and development of both. In our system the task of producing tangible products has been allotted to men, while the maintenance tasks for such a work force have been allotted to women. Thus, the traditional sex-role division of labor supports our current economic system. In such a system, division of tasks is accomplished with a view toward what is good for the system. But this does not necessarily coincide, as Fromm points out, with what is good for individuals in the system. Evidence compiled in recent years very strongly suggests, in fact, that what is good for the system may not be good for people. For example, the lives of many men are shortened by the workings of our economic system, while the lives of many women are characterized by mental and emotional difficulties because they are following the course that most profits the system. The imposition of masculine and feminine sex-role structures on human individuals, in many cases, wreaks more havoc than it relieves.

Finally, it appears that what has been thought to be good for the system itself may indeed no longer be so. Economists, biologists, and psychologists are joining an ever-growing chorus warning us of

---

*There is little in the way of traditional social sanctions, such as social approval, prestige, or status, offered to those who work at less than their capacity. Such individuals are often termed "lazy" or "irresponsible" and give evidence of "lack of commitment."

†It is true of course that many individuals do not work more than 35–40 hours a week. However, Whyte (1954) points out that most executives do work 57–80 hours a week—as do many other professionals. Even among blue-collar workers who may work only 40 hours a week plus occasional overtime, "the world of work has retained its basic significance" (LeMasters, 1975, p. 20).

our own physical peril if we continue to develop explosive weapons, pollute our environment, strip our mountains, and crowd our cities. We may be approaching a time when only radical change toward a more humanistic mode of being can provide us with the opportunity for physical survival. The individual's need for change may be converging with society's increasingly insistent need for social change. The new *necessity* may be that we must all stop yearning to *have* so much; instead, we must learn to *be* ourselves. In so doing, we may develop compassion, cooperation, responsibility, and concerned caring both for ourselves and for others:

> The need for profound human change emerges not only as an ethical or religious demand, not only as a psychological demand arising from the pathogenic nature of our present social character, but also as a condition for the sheer survival of the human race. . . . For the first time in history the physical survival of the human race depends on a radical change of the human heart (Fromm, 1976, pp. 9–10).

The pace of social change, however, is not so rapid as that of individual change, nor does the individual change as rapidly as we might hope. Therefore, individuals who choose to change, in particular individuals who opt for a process-oriented androgynous lifestyle, will encounter opposition and will have to sort out for themselves whether that opposition comes from within or from society.

THE ECONOMIC SPHERE AND PRETENSIONS OF POWER

Since our society elevates production, power, and material goods over other denominators of human well-being, men (and some women) tend to derive their sense of self-esteem and inner security from their capacity to produce and acquire material possessions.* In our society money and production are power, and men are its primary controllers. The strength of such power is measured in comparison to the power of other men; among men some have more

---

*Women, in many ways, are as concerned about material possessions as are men, but their concerns differ in emphasis from those of men. Whereas women's concerns about material possessions often center around being a consumer, men's concerns revolve more around being a producer. More specifically, whereas women are more concerned with their skill or good taste in buying, men are more concerned with the amount of money they make, a reflection of their ability to produce.

power, while others have less. To the extent that women are excluded from the economy, men are consistently regarded as more powerful than women. As Janeway (1975) remarks, this is a great source of comfort for men: Though there will always be other men in the "real world" with more power—i.e., status and money—men could always be certain that they control the power in the domestic world.

In more than material terms, women's entrance into the work force poses a threat to men who fear the loss of the power attached to money as well as the competition for jobs, advancement, and material goods. It is not surprising, then, that men have put up signs saying "Keep out" and have sent women back to the home. If men succeed in such tactics, not only do they cut the competition in half, but they effectively keep power, as societally determined, in the hands of men.

Despite discriminatory measures seeking to keep women out of the work force, women *are* managing to enter the world of work in ever-increasing numbers, and the women who enter the higher echelons of prestige and power do indeed pose a threat to men. In what have traditionally been male occupations, women are still thought of as "bitches" and "castrating females," even though the thought is less often voiced now than in the past (Rossi, 1970). For example, a man remarked in reference to a competent woman who was going about her business, "You need to wear a steel jockstrap when she's around!" The literal threat against which he felt the need to defend himself was not actually present. All the same, that man saw the woman as a real *threat* to himself, for as women gain status, they also gain money and power, which have been for years the chief symbols of masculinity. To a man who knows that he is a man only because he can earn money and hence gain power, competent women in the work force are seen as a threat to his masculinity.

The way out of this dilemma, of course, is for us to move beyond the need to measure our self-esteem by the size of our paychecks. We must *give up* what is only an illusion: the idea that how much we *have* determines who we *are*. If we move to a process orientation in which our sense of security comes from within us, then outward props are no longer necessary. But if the props appear necessary and someone shakes them, the world appears to us to be on the edge of chaos. In line with this thinking, a male student writes:

Each person's own façade is propped up by a weak foundation. However, if we lean our façades together, we have the feeling that we are very strong. Yet suppose somebody's façade falls apart?

The answer is that at this point we all must change. The change will be easier and more profitable—in human, not monetary, terms—if we give up our need for façades and find the growing human being within all of us.

Such change, however, has not yet come about. In the latter half of the twentieth century we still live in a world that is dominated by what we believe is good for the economic, industrial, and technological system. Men are encouraged to achieve and those who choose not to achieve to their capacity are penalized. Women, on the other hand, are still restricted in terms of opportunities in the work world. The remainder of this chapter will focus primarily on the difficulties women encounter in actualizing their potential in the world of work.

WOMEN AND WORK

The percentage of women in the work force has risen markedly in this century in the United States. In 1900, 20 percent of women were working; today 43.8 percent are a part of the work force. In 1900, 18.1 percent of those employed were women, whereas in 1974 the figure had risen to 47 percent (Bureau of the Census, 1976). Most striking is the increasing percentage of mothers at work, particularly mothers of young children. The increase of mothers in the work force represents the most dramatic change in the nature of employment in the last thirty years (Nye & Berardo, 1973, p. 271). Whereas in 1948, 32 percent of mothers of school-age children and 13 percent of mothers of preschool children were working, in 1975 these figures had climbed to 52 percent for mothers of school-age children and 32 percent for mothers of preschool children (Bureau of the Census, 1976).* This is consistent with the fact that over two thirds of American wives are employed outside the home at some time in their married lives (Amundson, 1971, p. 15).

Several factors have contributed to the increased number of women at work: (1) Since 1900 women's life expectancy has increased from 48 years to 74 years. Because most women have

---

*It is still true, however, that women in the age group from 25 to 34—the traditional child-rearing years—have the lowest representation among women workers (Kreps, 1974).

given birth to their last child by age 30, this means that approximately forty years of an adult woman's life will not be occupied by the care of small children. (2) The level of education for women has increased, although the gap between higher education for men and women still continues to widen. (3) Women now have more experience in the marketplace, and are beginning to reap the rewards of working for pay. The increase in women's self-esteem resulting from their entrance into the work world appears to keep more women at work and to encourage others to join them. (4) Although many areas of the work world are still largely sex-segregated, other areas in it have been desegregated, thus providing more opportunities for women. (5) Finally, warnings about the dangers of the population explosion have been a factor causing women to have fewer children (Suelzle, 1970).

Although women are rapidly becoming a permanent and significant part of the work force, they do not receive the same rewards as men. If jobs are matched for status and seniority, women are paid, on the average, one third less than men (Kreps, 1974). This gap has been increasing in recent years. Even in prestigious occupations, such as law and university professorship, women tend to be in the lower-paying and lower-status subfields of their professions (Epstein, 1970, p. 163). In addition, one third of all women workers are employed in typically feminine jobs—clerical and sales positions, domestic service, elementary school teaching, and nursing. These fields generally do not pay as well as men's fields (Fox, 1973). Moreover, the fields women are now entering in larger numbers may lose prestige as a result (Touhey, 1974). The general picture, therefore, shows women in lower-paying jobs than men or in similar jobs but being paid less than men for the same work. This is part of a general phenomenon of devaluing what women do.

Despite this picture, most employed women are committed to their jobs. For example, women Ph.D.s stay in the work force in nearly the same percentages as their male counterparts. Harris (1970, p. 284) found that 90 percent of women Ph.D.s were still employed ten years after completing their degree. Furthermore, if the job statuses of women are equalized with those of men, women do not drop out or quit sooner than men, nor do they take more absences than men (Mead & Kaplan, 1965, p. 52; Suelzle, 1970, p. 55). It is primarily in jobs for which women are overqualified— which in many instances are the only jobs available to them—that women demonstrate a lack of commitment. This would no doubt be true for men as well. In short, in all instances where the different variables of employment are equalized, women appear to be as committed to their work as men are.

One of the reasons that women are committed to their jobs—the way men are—is financial. A large number of working women support their own families or are in other ways financially independent of men. Crowley, Levitin, and Quinn (1973) report that 40 percent of working women in their sample were economically independent, while one third of them were the sole wage-earners in the household. In the last several years the number of families headed by women has risen dramatically: 37 percent of low-income families are now headed by women (Kreps, 1974), and the number of families dependent on two paychecks has also increased. A recent article in the *Detroit Free Press* stated that the average middle-class family could no longer afford to buy its own home without two incomes in the family. Therefore women are not just working to earn "pin money" (Chafetz, 1974; Crowley, Levitin, & Quinn, 1973; Peterson, 1964) but are committed to working. They remain a significant part of the work force, of which they may comprise 50 percent by 1985 (Ferris, 1971, pp. 85–87).

Yet even though women are an integral part of the job market, they suffer many problems when looking for a job and also once they have found one. Let us now hear from two women as they recount these difficulties.

LORRAINE

Lorraine is a young divorced woman, whose story illustrates many of the difficulties of women suddenly faced by the necessity to earn an income. Her story also illustrates differing attitudes toward work: At first, she was a married woman to whom the job was a secondary consideration, and as a result the indignities she received on the job seemed unimportant. But later, after separating from her husband, she approached work as a single woman who expects a reasonable income and some "mental stimulation" to accrue from her job. Indeed, I would argue that her increased expectations are a by-product of seeing herself as a more fully functioning person rather than as a person typified by the roles of wife and mother-to-be. Lorraine writes:

After I was separated, I went job hunting. I had a 3-month-old baby and very little in the way of job skills. So I finally decided to go back and work where I had been employed before Michelle was born, as I had enjoyed the work there and the people were familiar. Then, and this sounds a little dramatic, I was awakened to the world with a bolt of lightning. No, I was told, I could not be paid more because I had a child to support: One hundred and twenty dollars a week was "good money for a woman." For this amount of money I was expected to make coffee, pick up lunches, joke with the men, do my work, and be quiet.

Now obviously all of these things had gone on when I worked there before. But I had been there as a married woman. What did I care? My mind was occupied with housecleaning, cooking, and planning for a baby, and these "annoyances"—if I even thought of them as that—were trivial. I had more important things to worry about.

Yet now it seemed different. I was head of a household, and I wanted more mental stimulation and more money than I had been satisfied with before. I knew my income was a vital concern now, so I decided to go to night school and learn shorthand. That certainly would help me get a better job, or at least more money. So I went, and I learned, and I didn't get a better job or more money. I worked hard, tried to get by, but simply could not afford to support myself and my baby. So, against all of my moral principles—and my parents' advice—I quit my job and went on welfare.

I felt worse at that point than I had in my whole life. I was convinced it was all my fault that I couldn't handle my situation. . . . It began to seem more and more unfair to me that just because I was a woman I couldn't make enough money to support myself and a child. This was demoralizing, but the remarks people made were even worse: "A woman should stay home anyway"; "Why did you get a divorce?"; "You need to find a man to take care of you"; "Of course, women don't make as much money as men because they aren't as smart, reliable, or capable as men. . . ."

Eventually, Lorraine returned to school and has gone on to medical school with full hopes of becoming a successful professional. Nonetheless, it wasn't until she faced the "outside world" that she emerged from her role-oriented cocoon and began to discover her own talents and abilities. The transition was not easy.

SYLVIA

Sylvia, who has appeared in Chapter 3 (pp. 93–94) and Chapter 6 (p. 175), also recounts many of the difficulties women find in trying to enter the world of work. The break-up of an early marriage forced her to leave college and return to the work force. Although more qualified for a job than Lorraine, she encountered similar difficulties.

I set out to find that job. Sensing my own capabilities, I presented prospective employers with good college grades and an adequate job record. Much to my dismay, the first question interviewers asked was, "How fast can you type?" Eventually, I yielded to the employers' views of women on the job and learned to type. Again I went in search of employment. This time my skills were sufficient, but employers regarded me as undependable. . . . They felt I would have frequent absences because of physical and emotional difficulties. Since I was recently divorced, their views were reinforced. If I couldn't handle a marriage, chances were I couldn't handle a job either. Further, pregnancy was always an important factor when hiring women employees, regardless of marital status. I walked out during one interview when I was asked whether I was taking birth-control pills.

I attempted to convince employers that I had abandoned my life with a man to pursue a career. However, my inner feelings never really supported this idea. Somehow, I felt cheated if required to give up all my interest in the opposite sex. . . . Who said I had to choose between a man and a career?

Finally, I secured the job of my dreams. It was a position of responsibility, glamour, and rewards. I worked for one of the local television stations, where I met celebrities and received praise for my ability to run operations smoothly. I rediscovered my confidence in myself and found a great deal of satisfaction in my work. I made enough money to move into my own apartment and establish a life separate from my parents. Unfortunately, my freedom began to have conditions imposed upon it. My boss was determined to get more from me than my work, and sex became a requirement for keeping my job. So I quit. . . . I began my search again—for a job, for love.

I worked as a secretary in a police department next. I met officers in every phase of the criminal-justice system, and became extremely interested in their work. The department had a policy of not accepting female applicants for the police officer position. Although I learned a lot about police procedures, I had no way of utilizing them. Finally, I was accepted as a volunteer on the reserve force. . . . I became actively involved in most of the department's programs. I worked on detective cases and undercover activities. In addition, I openly challenged the administration regarding their discriminatory practices. I was determined to be a pioneer in a field which had not previously admitted women. . . . Unfortunately, vigorous competition and aggression were not elements present in my prior conditioning. I became tense and irritable. . . . I found I was making enemies. . . . I began to wonder if I could only deal with the world as a woman, in the traditional sense. . . . I needed men; but I wanted to be free to be my "self." Freedom now meant breaking the bonds which held me to my feminine role. . . .

From the preceding accounts we can see that women are often subjected to many difficulties—both inner and outer—in the job market. Very often they become confused about how to cope with these difficulties. At the same time they want to retain their femininity but still be competent in a career. Let us now examine one of these difficulties—discrimination—more closely.

DISCRIMINATION AGAINST WOMEN

Overt discrimination in the job market on the basis of sex has been illegal in the United States since 1964, although this law was only applied to universities in 1972 (Chafetz, 1974, p. 137). Nonetheless, in more subtle ways, discrimination against women is still a real part of our current world. Women are not hired for many jobs because they are "unqualified." Often their lack of qualification pertains to things other than skills and education: Very often they are accused of alleged unreliability, irrationality, or emotionality.

Women are not, however, less reliable than men when performing a job for which they are qualified and which holds their interest. A woman with a college degree cannot be expected to remain entranced for long by hours of filing insurance claims and sorting office magazines. It is not surprising that many women defect from such jobs because they find them of little interest. If a complaint is raised against women for being irrational and emotional, we would agree that this is the case. Yet some men are emotional and irrational too, but their behavior is often condoned. A man who has temperamental outbursts is often excused on the grounds that his emotionality can be attributed to his creativity. On the other hand, a woman's emotionality is often attributed to her psychological "imbalance" or to the vagaries of the female menstrual cycle. There is no evidence that women in decisive positions are more emotional than men or that their emotions are in any way detrimental to their on-the-job performance.

A number of other, usually nonverbalized reasons explain why women are often not recognized as capable individuals. Most of these reasons stem from an underlying belief that a woman has to be "masculine" to succeed in a male world. McGregor (1967) states that in our culture the model of a successful manager is a masculine one. The good manager is aggressive, competitive, firm, and just (p. 23). Two other writers describe the effective male (read employee, employer, executive, or whatever) as follows: " . . . men are supposed to be tough, concerned for the dollar, practical, and objective enough to face the facts and act accordingly. Even if someone gets hurt in the process, a man is supposed to be strong enough to do what has to be done. Such strength, toughness, and total responsibility, even occasional, necessary violence are attributed to men as 'natural' " (Loring & Wells, 1972, p. 92). This, then, represents the model of the successful person—male—in our society. Small wonder that women are told they do not measure up to it! Yet toughness and competitiveness may not be, as most people assume, the only, or even the best, way to get a job done today.

It must be admitted, however, that many women have fought their way up the ladder of success by learning how to be tough and competitive in the process. They have adopted the "masculine" approach. Such women may be labeled brazen and difficult, whereas men in their shoes would be praised for their "hard-headedness." On the other hand a woman who attains her goals without being "tough" is thought to be too soft for the world of men. Either way she may lose marks in congeniality. Either way, it is a no-win situation for the woman. The old assumption underlying this evaluation of women, however disguised, is that women really belong in the home. A natural woman cannot operate in the world of men, whereas an unnatural woman *can* operate in such a world, but she may be damned for her unseemly, unnatural behavior.

Women are, therefore, often judged unqualified for a position because unwritten addenda to job descriptions generally add personality factors that are typically "masculine" in our society. A woman may also find herself unqualified for a high-level job in other ways. Potential executives, chairpersons, and leaders in other fields rarely emerge suddenly from a pool of young talent. They are subtly trained, encouraged, and then finally promoted through an unofficial protégé system in which those who "have made it" select out and groom specific protégés. As Epstein (1970) points out, such protégé arrangements are difficult to establish between a man and a woman, particularly if the woman is either attractive or young. Thus those groomed for and hence qualified for high positions are generally male.

In addition, many steps in the informal selection process occur in informal settings from which women are excluded (Safilios-Rothschild, 1972). A great deal of business is often transacted in bars, cocktail lounges, or clubs unfrequented by women (Epstein, 1970, pp. 169–173). Or the women may simply not be invited to an informal gathering at which the guidelines for the formal meeting are laid down. (Many, if not most, important decision-making meetings are simply dramas that act out scripts already written at earlier, informal conferences.) If a woman is included in such conferences she is generally either older or unattractive and thus may be regarded as "one of the guys." A young, attractive woman, on the other hand, is seen in such informal settings primarily as a potential sexual partner or as a distraction from the "real business." Thus sexism continues to pervade the power structure.

The exclusion of women from the elite is documented by numerous behavioral scientists. White (1970) shows that women have limited access to the professional socialization procedure in the scientific world. Gumperz (1967) argues that women are excluded from the elite on the basis of arbitrary restrictions. Janeway sums up the difficulty women face in being recognized as *persons* by those with whom they work or with whom they might (if employed) work: "Men see other men as individuals, each with distinguishable character traits. They see women as a set of people who share certain character traits which can be summed up under the label 'feminine'" (1975, p. 47). Men tend to relate then to the "femininity" of women, regarding either the potential or actual young woman professional as a sex object or as a vulnerable individual needing their protection. The sense of treating people—men and women—as human beings is slow in coming. Women are up against real discrimination despite legislation that outlaws it.

Discrimination in the Business World A study (Bowman, Worthy, & Greyser, 1965) published in the *Harvard Business Review* examined the attitudes of executives toward women in the executive ranks. Six percent admitted to being strongly opposed to the idea of women executives; 41 percent claimed to be somewhat unfavorable to the idea; and 35 percent indicated that they favored having women in management. But those who were favorable to the idea said that they preferred older women in management to younger women, thus obviating the sex-object stereotypes and implied difficulties in the sexual sphere. Furthermore, 33 percent of the men said that women had a "bad" effect on employee morale; 51 percent said women were temperamentally unfit for management jobs; and 81 percent believed that they would be uncomfortable working for a woman. Overall, there was universal agreement that only the exceptional woman—probably an overqualified woman—can hope to succeed in management.

In this study some men made a few favorable comments about women executives. Most men, however, reflected at least some skepticism about women in business. A number of men were quoted as saying that women could not stand the pressure and would turn into little "kittens" if the going got rough, or that they would try to prove themselves by being overly dogmatic, overprotective, and unduly perfectionist. Women surveyed in the article also had mixed feelings about women in business, although all of them were themselves employed in managerial positions. They were against women "acting like men," and they did not like women to act as if they were "smarter than any man." These women also commented on the difficulties a woman executive encounters in trying to hire a staff of able men. Others said that they had had to fight against being labeled "temperamental," even though emotional behavior in men executives is often overlooked. They believed that a woman executive must "be dedicated, have a flair for what she's doing, and work a little harder than a man." Other women clearly indicated that although they had successful careers, their home and family came first.

The underlying biases of the masculine world apparently are still very antifemale, and women—even successful women—react to this bias in a variety of ways: by exalting their femininity, by giving it up, by relying on men rather than making decisions themselves, or by just working harder than everybody else.

The following account by a male police officer named Neil tells of a woman who chose to be feminine rather than competent. Most likely because of male patronage, she was promoted ahead of other men, including Neil. The situation has caused Neil to be most unhappy about the use of women in his department and to generalize his feelings to *most* women in traditionally male jobs. After reading his account, we must admit he does so with some justification. Neil writes bitterly:

> *To further enhance my image of the police woman, yours truly was recently passed over for promotion. . . . Following a written exam, I was Number 1 and she was Number 5. This ratio was reversed after an oral examination by a board which had among its members a man who occasionally bangs, if you will, this woman. She is now a Lieutenant, and her primary duties consist of watering plants and brewing coffee for the former oral board member. As a supervisor she is indecisive and passive.*
>
> *I must say that of three women employed by this particular police agency, all are undeniable failures. It has been necessary to send a "back-up" on occasions where normally a single man can perform quite competently. Or shall we "sacrifice" a few to prove the point? Women in police work are challenged by men, women, and children on even the most minor confrontations. To avoid assistance, they must overreact. . . .*

As we can see, women's reactions to masculine pressures are not always exemplary. Instead of regarding this fact as a point against women, however, we should regard such behavior as evidence that the game has been rigged against women ahead of time. Since women undergo psychological pressures not felt by their male colleagues, women should not be condemned outright because of their reactions to these pressures. In our evaluations of working women we should take into account the pressures that women alone sustain. The choices women must make are more ambivalent, and the guidelines for them are less clear-cut. As a result, their behavior sometimes suffers from this psychological ambiguity.

The Ivory Tower: For Males Only? In the academic world as well as the world of business, women suffer the consequences of being born female. Although academic discrimination may be more muted, it is still omnipresent. The ladder into the higher realms of academe can be climbed for the most part only by persons who succeed within the educational system. It is well-known that females do well at the lower educational levels, yet males begin to emerge as academic leaders by the university years. (This subject will be discussed at greater length in Chapter 10.) Although more females than males complete high school, only 43 percent of women high-school graduates enter college compared to 46 percent of male graduates (Epstein, 1970, p. 57). Moreover, proportionately fewer women than men complete college. This is partially due to the extent of discrimination against women at the university level. In 1972 Stanford University reportedly required its entering class to be 60 percent male, whereas Princeton and Harvard admit only 25 percent females. To gain admittance to the best universities, therefore, women need higher grades, and they also receive less scholarship money than men (*Time,* 1972). In addition, parents are less willing to pay for their daughters' college education than for their sons' (Roby, 1972, p. 123).

Several examples of faculty and administration prejudice against females in academic life were collected by Harris (1970, pp. 284–285). The following comments all came from faculty and administrators of universities:

> I know you're competent and your thesis advisor knows you're competent. The question in our minds is are you *really serious* about what you're doing.

> The admissions committee didn't do their job. There is not one good-looking girl in the entering class.

> We expect women who come here to be competent, good students, but we don't expect them to be brilliant or original.

> President Pusey of Harvard spoke on the effects of the draft in the 1960's: "We shall be left with the blind, the lame, and the women."

> President Carlo of Sarah Lawrence College (formerly for women only): "Feminine instincts are characterized by caring qualities, con-

cern for beauty and form, reverence for life, empathy in human relations, and a demand that men be better than they are."

An administrator at Bryn Mawr College (recently admitting men): "Our general admissions policy has been, if the body is warm and male, take it, if it's female make sure it's an A-."

Women have less than an even chance in graduate school. The more advanced the level of training, the more discrimination exists (Roby, 1972, pp. 122–123). Consequently, women earned only 10 percent of Ph.D.s given in 1966, which represents a decline from the percentage of the 1930s (Epstein, 1970, p. 58). After obtaining an advanced degree, moreover, females are hired less frequently and by less prestigious institutions. They are not promoted and are paid substantially less than their male colleagues (Roby, 1972, pp. 123–130). For example, female sociologists, matched with male sociologists by rank, earned $1700 a year less on the average (Hughes, 1972). In addition, Rossi (1970) reports that after twenty years in professorial rank 90 percent of the men are full professors, whereas only 53 percent of the single women and 43 percent of the married women have attained this status.

Rossi's report also shows that women in sociology departments are more likely than men to teach undergraduates and to teach on a part-time basis. This is in spite of the fact that female junior professors tend to publish more than their male colleagues, although this ratio is reversed for upper-level professors. Fidell (1970) substantiates a similar discrimination in psychology departments. In sending out a number of "fake" applications for positions in various universities, she prepared ten pairs of similar biographies, but one half of the pair carried a male name, the other a female name, as shown below:

... Patrick (Patricia) Clavel received his (her) doctorate in clinical psychology from Western Reserve University. He (She) is considered both highly intelligent and very serious about his (her) academic goals. His (Her) students feel that he (she) is more interested in them than in his (her) research. He (She) works well with his (her) colleagues on committees, but has added only three articles to his (her) vita since graduation. These articles have, however, been well received professionally. Dr. Clavell is married.

When results were in they showed that Patrick was offered a full professorship in 1 percent of the replies; an associate professorship in 59 percent; and an assistant professorship in 34 percent. By way of contrast, Patricia was not offered a full professorship by any university; 44 percent offered her a position of associate professor; and fully 50 percent made their offer at the assistant professor's level. Fidell's results revealed that more men than women were offered appointments; more men than women were offered appointments of high rank; and full professorships were offered only to men.

Once in the classroom as teachers, women tend to be evaluated by different standards than the men. Siskel (1976) found that competent, attractive women—in contrast to less attractive women— were evaluated more highly by males than by other females, whereas Kaschak (1976) found that women on the whole were evaluated less highly than men. These results corroborate the findings of Ferber and Huber (1974), who found that men and women students tend to prefer male teachers, at least for large classes. On the other hand, a recent study (Hesselbart, Tieche, & Blakey, 1975) showed that student evaluations tended to differ more according to the subject taught than according to the gender of the professor.

My own observations in many cases reinforce the findings of studies showing that male and female professors are evaluated on different bases. After male guest speakers had come to our class, several young women students commented that they preferred listening to a man than to a woman. Moreover, after hearing a male guest speaker, a male student named Allan discovered that his early resistance to my ideas had been due to my gender rather than to my ideas or way of presenting them. Consequently, with this realization, he did an about-face in the middle of the semester. Here is what Allan states about his reactions to the guest speaker:

The thing that struck me most was that I accepted what he said more freely just because he was a man (who could be taken seriously). I look back at my resentment and reluctance to accept the things our female teacher has said, and I think a lot of my cynicism was a result of her being a woman. It had nothing to do with what she was saying, but just the fact that she was a woman. I felt challenged by what she said because, if I would admit to myself that she was right, part of my socialized maleness would be cut down. . . . The real irony of it all is that our female teacher was not in any way challenging me directly but was simply asking me to do some self-examination. It had nothing to do with any power or male ego but just a sort of invitation to examine my own values in directing my life. . . . I have a lot of questions in my mind with very few answers. . . .

Evaluation of the Work of Women Evaluation of the work of women who have obtained key positions is also affected by the discrimination women receive. Several studies have assessed the performance of women. Taynor and Deaux (1973) found, for example, that both men and women rated a woman higher than a man if she operated well in a masculine situation; it was assumed that the woman's performance was inflated in value to balance the increased merit of her reward. In this case women were profiting from a subtle discrimination by being rewarded for overcoming the discrimination against them. Feldman-Summers and Kiesler (1974), however, found that this response was applicable only to the evaluation of females by other females. In contrast, they found that males, when evaluating female students and successful female physicians who performed the same tasks as men, perceived the women as having an easier task generally than the men and as performing less competently than them. Thus in this situation the evaluation of women's performances was deflated instead of inflated. The authors argued that this evidence suggested that, in the eyes of both males and females, success is cognitively linked to "maleness." A female's work performance will be either inflated or deflated depending upon who is doing the evaluating. In either case she is being treated differentially. These writers also stated that "in that survey and in further work at a later time, the investigators have not been able to find a single occupation in which females are expected to be more successful than males" (p. 854).

Perceptions of Discrimination Women themselves often perceive that they are discriminated against and report such discrimination. In fact, the women perceiving and reporting the most discrimination are (1) the most successful women, and (2) married women. It may be, of course, that such women do suffer and perceive that they suffer more discrimination. For example, successful women who run into difficulties in their careers may have found more opposition at the upper levels of their professions. They would have more difficulty than less successful women in attributing this opposition to lack of competence on their part. Married women, on the other hand, may find that professional organizations—particularly if husband and wife are in the same profession—tend to defer to their husbands (Simon, Clark, & Galway, 1967). Because they have a visible male model with which to compare themselves, they therefore may be more aware of differences in treatment (Bryson, Bryson, Licht, & Licht, 1976). Yet at the same time, research supports the fact that married women themselves choose to defer to their husbands (Rossi, 1965).

Women who publish more, go to more professional meetings, and have higher salaries are the ones who report higher levels of discrimination (Astin, 1967; Simon, Clark, & Galway, 1967). There is evidence also that married women tend to publish more than their single colleagues, though they reap fewer rewards (Simon, Clark, & Galway, 1967). In fact, married women in general earn less commensurate rewards than single women (Ferber & Loeb, 1973). Apparently for women to be married and successful—that is, to succeed both in the masculine and feminine worlds—poses a contradiction that the "establishment" does not understand, accept, or reward. The double success of such women flies in the face of a generally unspoken assumption that women who succeed in their careers are "marital rejects" (Havens, 1971) and therefore not "feminine." Thus their success in a masculine sphere may be regarded as a compensation for their lack of femininity. In fact, such assumptions were widely accepted in the 1950s and 1960s. Helson (1972) reviews the beliefs about working women of those decades:

> ... a girl with strong career aspirations was said by several of the investigators to be very rare and the unfortunate victim of childhood traumata. The very term "career woman" suggested pretentiousness or hard-boiled insensitivity and rejection of femininity (p. 36).

Helson continues her review by quoting Edwin Lewis in *Developing Women's Potential*, which was published in 1968:

> ... the girl who aims for a career is likely to be frustrated and dissatisfied with herself as a person.... [She is] less well-adjusted than those who are content to become housewives. Not only is [she] likely to have a poor self-concept, but she also probably lacks a close relationship with her family.... There is still the possibility that a career orientation among girls grows out of personal dissatisfactions, so that the career becomes a frustration outlet.... (pp. 33 & 35).

Even in the 1960s the ethic of the housewife remained strong. It was firmly believed that the best use of woman's intelligence was in keeping house and raising children. Terman and Oden said in 1959: "There are many intangible kinds of accomplishment and success open to the housewife, and it is debatable whether the fact that a majority of gifted women prefer housewifery to more intellectual pursuits represents a net waste of manpower" (p. 145). Obviously very few at that time challenged the assumption that only unnatural women would prefer not to remain at home. Something was wrong with a woman who "sublimated her desires" in her work. She had most likely failed in the most important arena of life—that of pleasing men.

Fortunately, this assumption has been challenged recently. Havens (1971) suggests that perhaps the healthier women are the ones who have found the strength to live alone and compete in the masculine world. She points out that in 1960 there was indeed a strong direct relationship between economic attainment and unmarried status for women. But it is as reasonable to assume that these women chose not to get married as it is to assume that they were marital rejects. Let us now take a look at the "career woman."

CAREER WOMEN: WHERE DO THEY COME FROM AND WHAT ARE THEY LIKE?

Most studies show that the backgrounds of career women are indeed somewhat different from those of women who choose to be full-time homemakers. But there is no reason to assume that the backgrounds of career women are unhealthy or unnatural. It has been shown, for example, that a large percentage of female medical students come from "intellectually harmonious" homes rather than from conflict-ridden homes, and that such women students are "conscientious, deliberate, determined, industrious, persevering, and thorough" (Cartwright, 1970, p. 208). Other research has found female Ph.D.s lower in neuroticism and anxiety than more traditionally oriented female populations (Bachtold & Werner, 1970; O'Leary & Braun, 1972). Furthermore, such women do not appear to feel socially rejected, for generally the "significant men in their lives" see femininity in much the same terms as the career women do (Hawley, 1972). From the above studies and others (see Safilios-Rothschild, 1972; Tangri, 1972), career women have been characterized as autonomous, individualistic, confident, dominant, and self-sufficient. In sum, the studies on career women suggest that these women portray a picture of fully functioning human beings, developing the positive masculine traits valued in our culture without necessarily sacrificing the positive feminine traits. According to our definition they are androgynous. Cartwright's (1970) statement about her sample of medical students may very likely be generalized to apply to many career women: They are positive, effective persons with a strong desire to use their capabilities and to be helpful to others.

Yet not all autonomous, self-sufficient women are career women. Many women, autonomous and otherwise, choose to remain at home. In reviewing the backgrounds of women who have made different life choices, researchers have attempted to determine why some choose to go to work and others choose to become homemakers.* In a large study of women graduating from college in 1961 (Rossi, 1965), it was found that three years later 20 percent of them had chosen to be full-time homemakers, while 7 percent were pioneers who had opted for a full-time career in a "masculine" field.† The family backgrounds of the homemakers were characterized by intense and extensive family relationships and a conservative image of the traditional sex roles. These women were both nurturant and dependent, and saw marriage, for which they had been trained, as the turning point in their lives. On the other hand, the pioneers had grown up with less intense ties in families more oriented to the world of ideas. They were less nurturant and less dependent than the homemakers, and did not find marriage a pivotal point in their lives. Instead, they said that the introduction of children into the home had critically changed their lives. One assumes that the relatively egalitarian husband-wife relationship among the pioneer group had not greatly affected their ability to carry out their individual goals, while the added responsibility of children required a major adjustment in their life scheduling. Nonetheless, the pioneers, like the homemakers, tended to value their marriage first, and to put other concerns second. Astin (1969) also found that family concerns continued to affect women's decision to work, although in her sample of Ph.D.s the majority did choose to work full-time.

---

*We must remember from Chapter 8 that varied social backgrounds may predispose groups of individuals toward a given point of view or life-style, but that such conditions are not *predictive* for any given individual.

†In 1964, 90 percent of the homemakers and 50 percent of the pioneers were married. In the descriptions of characteristics given here, no distinction is made between single and married women.

Other studies support the fact that career women tend to come from different backgrounds than noncareer women. One such study (Almquist & Angrist, 1971) finds that working women generally had working mothers, had more work experience themselves, and were more likely to see themselves as highly evaluated in their academic world and to choose goals similar to those of their male peers. These data also suggest a picture of career women as less entrenched in past, current, and potential family relationships and as tending to draw their models both from working family members and professionals in the academic world.

It would appear also that these women have had closer relationships with their fathers, often because there was not a brother in the family who competed with them for the father's attention (Hennig & Jardim, 1977). Moreover, many of these women describe their fathers as supportive and encouraging them to achieve (Ginzberg, 1971). In addition, then, to the fact that the mothers of career women often worked themselves, there is also evidence of a closer relationship with the father, a relationship that encouraged independent achievement.

In their approach to their work, career women do not differ greatly from men. Women are concerned with competence on the job, *not* interpersonal relations (Crowley, Levitin, & Quinn, 1973) and tend to approach their work with motivations similar to those of men (O'Leary, 1974).* Both successful men and women tend to demonstrate similar traits. Neugarten (1968) finds that successful adults, regardless of sex, are competent, creative, and able to learn from experience. Furthermore, there is no definitive evidence that women who work are more or less feminine than women who don't (Safilios-Rothschild, 1972).

Despite high marks for autonomy, self-sufficiency, self-confidence, and other traits contributing to emotional well-being, working women suffer from conflicts as they move away from the traditional sex roles. *Interrole conflict* is generated by committing

---

*Women who are successful in the occupational world generally put a task orientation ahead of a concern for interpersonal relationships. Women who continue to emphasize interpersonal relationships in their work, *at the expense* of a task orientation, often find themselves passed over for promotion at the upper levels. This does not mean, however, that interpersonal relationships—or marriage—are necessarily secondary in their lives, particularly their nonwork lives. It only suggests that women who put interpersonal relationships first, when operating in a task-centered system, are generally not those who become "successful" career women. For further development of this point see Hennig and Jardim (1977).

themselves to filling two disparate and full-time roles—in this case, the roles of working woman and homemaker. As noted earlier (Garland, 1972; Poloma, 1972; Rapoport & Rapoport, 1972; Rossi, 1965), women who work still tend to take on the major responsibility for the home, and many exhaust themselves by working at what are literally two full-time jobs.

Some women resolve the conflict by adopting a sequential pattern; they interrupt their work for a period of years in order to bear children and care for the home, returning to work when the household responsibilities have lessened. Bernard (1973) comments on several patterns women follow in arranging sequentially the four major contingencies (marriage, children, education, and a profession) in their lives. Bernard finds that the worst possible pattern in terms of establishing a successful career is the one in which the woman leaves work for marriage and/or child rearing between completing her education and beginning her career. Such a break interrupts the woman's career at a time when her career is least stable, and temporary defection has serious consequences. Even for men there is evidence that interrupting a career at such times—usually for military duty—results in men who rarely make creative and original contributions to their demanding professions. In the case of women, a lengthy stay at home also tends to create familial dependence upon her, which in the long run makes it harder to pull out and go back to her career.

Many sociologists argue strongly against the sequential pattern for women, although this is the current choice of nearly half of young American women (Rossi, 1965). Rossi has been one of the strongest opponents of this pattern, pointing out that the most creative period in the life of professional men and women is likely to be during the very years that the contemporary woman is encouraged to stay at home and raise a family. Moreover, when these women return to the labor force, they do not return as leading professionals but rather are an "important reservoir for assistants and technicians and the less demanding professions." They come back "only rarely for creative and original contributions to the more demanding professional fields" (Rossi, 1965, pp. 102–3, 107). Gillespie echoes this point of view by pointing out that the isolation and emotional dependency of the young mother/housewife are handicaps in returning to work. Furthermore, the woman who returns to work has lost her prior position, has not kept up with developments in her field, and has lost seniority. "If she returns to work, and most women do, she must begin again at a low-status job and she stays there—underemployed and underpaid" (1971, p. 756).

Women, therefore, who want both a career and marriage are faced with the incompatibility of maintaining both at the same time. The common choice is to allow the career to suffer by dropping out of the work force during the time a person is most likely to be creative. The woman who chooses not to drop out may choose not to get married or at least not to have children. Again, the choice is either/or—a choice not faced by men. On the other hand, the woman who chooses to commit herself both to career and family is very likely handicapped by the need to be a superwoman who can handle dual responsibilities. Such responsibilities, except in the case of the most exceptional and energetic women, do "constitute another barrier to their ascendency into higher level occupational positions" (O'Leary, 1974).

The *intrarole conflict* experienced by women results from the fact that feminine training is not applicable in a masculine world. Many women thus tend to behave one way at work and another way at home. Chafetz refers to this as a Catch 22, a tightrope between maintaining traditionally feminine characteristics and those that enable women to succeed (1974, p. 121). In addition, women are subject to lowered expectations: Little is expected of women, and many women respond by producing little. Women, in fact, are often not taken seriously in the world of work, and often respond by behaving in such a way as to fulfill that belief. Moreover, women have two options: They may work or remain at home, so that remaining in the work world requires a continual renewal of choice (Epstein, 1970). Women may quit work without social criticism and thus must convince themselves and others that their work *is* a serious matter to them.

The difficulty women experience in integrating masculine and feminine traits has been illustrated in the stories of Sylvia (pp. 271–272) and Neil (p. 276). It is a problem that most of the women's case histories in this book document. Do women really want to be masculine? How can women be assertive, yet not ostracized for unfeminine behavior? How ready are women to retreat to the safe preserve of femininity when the going gets rough? Arlene, a student in business management, voices the confusion many women experience over this issue. She discusses her success in feminine areas (e.g., social popularity and excellence in aesthetic pursuits); but her last parenthetical remark indicates that she is not sure whether the development of masculine characteristics required by the business world may not entail a sacrifice of some of the benefits of femininity:

> *At this point in my life, I have a need to be "masculine" because of my career interest in business administration and therefore I try to project an image of aggressiveness and independence. . . . I also feel inferior to men. By becoming more like a man, I feel as though I'm on an equal basis with them. My feelings of inferiority stem from always being compared with men. The standard is male; women are compared against that standard. . . . This feeling of second-ratedness has been reinforced in almost all areas of my socialization. . . . I am trying to break away from being feminine and resent others commenting on my feminine behaviors. That's what I'm trying to get away from! (Or is it?)*

IS A CAREER REALLY GOOD FOR ANYBODY?

Arlene's confusion, which reflects that of many women, stems from her acceptance of the traditional definitions of success. Most people, including the researchers cited earlier, assume that success in a career is to be determined according to our existing norms, i.e., masculine production-oriented norms. But there are suggestions from numerous authors that success needs to be redefined; that it is not healthy for a *human being* to work 60–70 hours a week on a career to the exclusion of other interests, including relationships with people. Slater (1970) has written such a criticism of our concept of "career" and proposes a redefinition that would have some rather far-reaching societal consequences.

"Career" is in itself a masculine concept (i.e., designed for males in our society). When we say "career" it connotes a demanding, rigorous, preordained life pattern, to whose goals everything else is ruthlessly subordinated—everything pleasurable, human, emotional, bodily, frivolous. It is a stern Calvinistic word. When a man asks a woman if she wants a career, it is intimidating. He is saying, are you willing to suppress half of your being as I am, neglect your family as I do, exploit personal relationships as I do, renounce all personal spontaneity as I do? Naturally she shudders a bit and shuffles back to the broom closet. She even feels a little sorry for him and bewails the unkind fate that has forced him against his will to become such a despicable person. The perennial success of this hoax perhaps contributes to the low opinion that men so often have of feminine intelligence (an opinion which, as any teacher knows, is otherwise utterly unfounded) (p. 72).

Slater's criticism of "career" is based on the way many men pursue their work, often conforming to the demands of the institutions for which they work. Such demands are based on the assumption that the most important things in life are found in the world of work. Therefore, people who spend their lives almost exclusively in the world of work are regarded as the most important individuals in our society. Because of their importance, it follows then that other less important activities will be taken care of by less important individuals—women. Thus we return to the traditional view of sex roles: The superior men work in the marketplace while the inferior women remain at home. The counterpoint to this is that women, who accept the "inferior" role, silently observe that any individuals who allow themselves to be so enslaved to the marketplace, with all its destructive side effects, must indeed be inferior to those who have the good sense to stay home.

Instead of struggling over the relative merits of disparate functions, Slater suggests that we redefine the concept of career so that it is not such a suffocating and pernicious activity. Rather, it would be meaningful and stimulating, and would provide excitement, challenge, and social satisfactions. This redefinition would be beneficial to both sexes, freeing them from their enslavements to traditional role definitions (1970, p. 73).

The work role, as it applies to work outside the home, *is* definitely structured for males. People can hardly excel in a demanding field "if they are diverted constantly by worries about what to defrost for dinner, running noses, dry cleaning, the plumbing and so forth" (Chafetz, 1974, p. 120). Yet if these concerns interfere with excelling, then perhaps we need to redefine what "excelling" means. If we are all to have equal chances to excel, who then is going to worry about the dinner, wipe runny noses, and tend to the plumbing? It may be that no one should have a career but rather a stimulating and fulfilling "job" or "position" that still allows both men and women to tend to the necessities of domestic living on an equal basis. Would such lowered "career" expectations humanize our society? If so, would this occur at a cost of lowered production? It is not at all certain that production must give way to humanization. This may represent a false dichotomy, a case of saying either/or, when in fact we can have both. Fulfilled human beings may indeed be creative, capable, "contributing members of society" to an even greater extent than the harried, ulcer-ridden, overworked, and underloved men who dominate prime positions in every sphere. The answer will not be known, however, unless we choose to experiment and accept whatever the consequences may be.

WOMEN'S EXPECTATIONS

Women are, however, as much victims of their own expectations as they are victims of the external system controlled by men. "The movement of women into a wider range of occupations has thus been impeded by the young woman's expectations: expectations that have been quite realistic, given the employer's view of women's limited worth in the marketplace and the woman's view of her family responsibilities" (Kreps, 1974). Women expect to be in charge of a household and to raise children. From this expectation, they have been taught to derive self-esteem. Moreover, most women do not expect equal success in the work world as a whole and, as Slater (1970) points out, they have a tendency to shuffle back to their broom closets. There are two approaches to changing these expectations: The first is to raise women's consciousness so that they *know* they can be creative and competent individuals; the second may involve convincing women—and eventually men—that a career does not have to be defined solely on a man's terms, and that the notion of career can be redefined so that women as well as men do not become slaves to the system in which they work. Obviously, the second is the harder and more long-term approach. The first—the task of raising women's consciousness—is essential, however. Such change can be effected, and has been already effected on the individual level.

Research reflecting where women's "heads are at" reveals definite ambivalence on the subject of careers and marriage. A large study of high-school seniors in 1964 showed that only 12 percent of the women had "realistic" hopes of combining a career and marriage. In the same study only 4 percent opted for a lifetime career, whereas the rest divided themselves between full-time homemaking and the sequential pattern discussed earlier. Male students surveyed were even less willing for their wives to work (Turner, 1964). Another study of college women found that 55 percent of them expected to derive primary satisfaction from family and marriage

(Cross, 1968). A survey in the late 1960s found that 50 percent of a large sample of college women at both Berkeley and Stanford expected to work part- or full-time when they had young children, and that 87 percent expected to work after the children reached the age of 12. The males in this sample expressed the same pattern of willingness for the women to work (Katz, 1968). Similar results were found when a group of 1968 National Merit Scholars were questioned. In this sample 50 to 60 percent of the women students had either begun a career or had immediate plans to do so, whereas 86 percent planned to work when their children were older (Watley, 1969). This represents an increase in women's expectations from the decade of the 50s when there was much less career aspiration, even among highly talented women (Bunting, 1961; Gruenberg & Krech, 1952; Heist, 1962).

Helson (1972), in summarizing much of the research on career women, finds that very recently the image of the career woman has begun to change. It is true that at the moment no social image exists of woman as creative in the world of work (Helson, 1971). However, she also points out that psychologists of the 1970s are now working away like billboard artists to revise the image of the career woman. Recent studies, such as those previously summarized, all show the highly educated woman as serious, competent, committed, and individualistic.

POWER FOR SELF-ENHANCEMENT OR SELF-DESTRUCTION

Successful working women have "made it" in the man's world in the traditional sense. In so doing they have gained the symbols of power in our society: money, status, positions of influence and productive skills. Such women have gained the tools with which they can bargain from a position of equality, both in the marketplace and within their domestic circle. It is true that most current career women have acceded to the masculine definition of success. They have developed the qualifications that allow entry into the masculine marketplace. Yet it is not necessary for women, or men, to "sell out" to the dehumanizing impact of the system.

Hoffman (1960) points out that the capacity to earn money enhances our sense of power in what we term both process-oriented and role-oriented ways. Women who work gain power, control, greater respect in societal terms, and independence. Moreover, in interaction with others outside the home, women develop greater social skills and self-confidence, gain knowledge of psychological alternatives, and develop a higher estimation of themselves.* Such factors increase an individual's power inside the home as well as in the marketplace. To the degree to which women become dependent upon money and status for their self-esteem, as men traditionally have done, they become slaves of our socioeconomic system and slip into the role-oriented trap. However, to the degree that they come to recognize a new level of personal worth and self-esteem that are viewed as *internal* rather than *external,* they may retain their own freedom.

What our discussion suggests is that at the moment it is necessary for women to enter the working world on masculine terms. We cannot expect men to accept more humanitarian terms on their own. Such entrance into the masculine world increases the power of women. As Helson remarks, there is no "equality" when the traditional symbols of power are unequal (1972, p. 44). This may in fact be unfortunate, but at the moment it is true. If women wish to increase their bargaining position and use their skills to produce a more humanized work world—and egalitarian, intimate relationships—they must first accept the masculine definitions of power, and yet not "sell out" to the pursuit of power. They must use the tools of the system without enslaving themselves. This is a large order, but one in which women will be joined by many men who also wish to remain productive while being fully human. Eventually, we may hope, the male marketplace will become a *human* marketplace for which the standards of entry will be *human* standards, and the power people wield will enhance the humanness of themselves and others instead of becoming a goal in itself in whose pursuit we dehumanize ourselves and others. Success in the work force can give us the tools to wield power over others, or it can aid us in standing more firmly on our own feet, retaining our productiveness as well as our compassion, understanding, and concern for those about us. It is

---

*The learning of new social skills by women builds upon their prior acquisition of interpersonal skills emphasized in the training of most females in our society. Thus, the skills they learn in the outer world do not teach them "to be like men" but add to their interpersonal repertoire— something that is often denied women during the child-rearing years. On the other hand, the skills men learn in the outer world also teach them to deal with people; however, such skills do not rest on a foundation of interpersonal understanding but are more objectively viewed as ways to "get ahead" or "get what one wants" in the outer world.

our choice. Let us now see how the points brought up in this discussion affected an individual's life.

JANINE

The story of Janine exemplifies the positive benefits that can accrue to a working woman, even in a nonprofessional sense.

For ten years . . . the fact that I had a husband to support me and didn't have to "work" was something of which I was very proud, but I was bored by the routine of cooking, housework, and child care. Also I was in an inferior position in my own home. . . . I was required to state the previous day specific reasons why I needed money and how much I needed. At times I didn't even have a quarter to buy a Coke if I took the kids for a walk because, of course, I had not requested it the previous day. This inequality was just beginning to sink into my consciousness when my husband got laid off and I was able to secure a good-paying job on an assembly line. Since I refused to do two jobs, Allan took over the home and we began a role reversal which changed my life completely.

At first I hated working away from home. I would cry because I missed the kids. . . . The work was also hard and exhausted me, but I was determined to do it. As I became acquainted with people all over the plant, I began to enjoy going to work. After I got used to getting up at 5:00 A.M., I no longer was exhausted and I did better on the job. My first paycheck was like a miracle. I never expected to earn that much money. My ideas and attitudes began to change with that first paycheck. . . .

One very important change was in my attitude toward myself as a contributing family member. Previously, I had viewed my role as rather insignificant next to my husband's. Since I was now the provider, I began to act and feel somewhat the way my spouse had felt before the switch. Money became more important to me, as I saw for the first time that I was capable of supporting my family. . . .

One trait that I felt was desirable and have retained from this period is my feeling of independence. . . . I will never again feel the need to request permission to go where I want to go. I now try to be considerate about making plans but while I was asserting my independence I did not even do this. . . . I was not balancing all considerations at the time, but felt that I had to go through this period.

Another realization was also coming to me. . . . The men at work thought I was attractive! All my life I had felt that I was ugly and I had been raised in a family where looks were very important, which made my feelings of inferiority in this even worse. In addition, my husband is an extremely handsome man who was constantly complimenting other women on their appearance and telling me I didn't measure up. When the men at work went out of their way to come and talk to me on their break, I started to feel better about the way I looked, and as I felt better I actually looked better. Even my husband began to compliment me. . . .

All told I have become an extroverted, outgoing person and I like myself much better.

IMPLICATIONS

When Janine entered the work force, her sense of power increased. For a while she used this power to dominate her family but later as her self-esteem grew she recognized that the power she now had could be used to assert her own independence in a caring way; it did not have to be a tool to be used against others. Janine's story dramatically illustrates the positive factors Hoffman (1960) has named as the benefits of wage-earning.

ENEMIES AND FRIENDS WITHIN: CHANGING OURSELVES

When women enter the masculine world of work, they find many obstacles to overcome, many of which have been documented here. However, the most difficult obstacles are those women create within themselves. It is possible for women to go to work; they have done so for years. It is also apparent that the most committed and talented women have been very successful. Yet many women find themselves "shuffling back to the broom closet" when they face the outer world. They feel unable to distinguish the pernicious aspects of the marketplace from the positive ones, and end up by giving it up altogether. The marketplace will never be a more humanitarian place unless women take the responsibility for making it so. To do this, women must have the courage to face the outer world, with all its hassles, as it is.

Janeway (1975) has emphasized that social change will follow only with a change in women's images of themselves. She comes back to the old axiom that women are, after all, their own worst enemies:

> I think [the enemies] are the creatures present in our minds who say, why fight? who say, why go after that job? it will mean a hassle, who say, well, maybe I could have got it if I'd tried harder but I really did not want it anyway. That's the woman in us—the old-fashioned, programmed-to-please woman—and we all contain some of her (p. 131).

Women have indeed been programmed to please, and the ones they have learned to please are men. To develop masculine skills, to withstand the social pressures that still surround working women, to sustain the interrole and intrarole conflicts that are the lot of many working women, are all barriers that are indeed formidable. But many women are also frightened about losing the approval of the men upon whom they have learned to base their self-evaluation. However, dependence on the approval of men is as much a role-oriented trap for women as dependence on status and money is for men. Women who fear affronting men are still saying that their self-esteem lies outside themselves. By finding the source of their self-esteem within themselves in their own ability to care and to work, women will be less subject to either the approval or disapproval of men. Women will indeed be more process-oriented individuals and less the puppets of those in the external environment. It is true, of course, that such working women are going to meet resentment.

> We actually want to be treated as equals by men, we want to compete openly for their jobs, if we can do them as well, we want our opinions to be listened to and our applications to medical school to be processed as if we were our brothers. Do you really imagine we aren't going to run into resentment? Of course we are. So what? (Janeway, 1975, p. 137).

Yes, so what? To the extent that women internalize the resentment of others, and allow it to guide their actions, they are confusing external necessity and internal necessity. They are saying, "The others won't let us. . . ." But what women mean is, "We won't let ourselves incur their disapproval. . . ." Recognizing the internal necessity, then, allows women to change whatever appears to need changing. Women can free themselves from bondage by recognizing their own internal limitations; by enhancing their own self-esteem and power-to-be, women can remove such limitations. If women work and earn power and money, some men will approve while others will not. Let's put the problem where it belongs: Such approval or disapproval is the problem of men, not of women. Process-oriented women, like process-oriented men, will be more fully human. They will no doubt grow to like themselves better as they face and overcome their own fears and expand their area of freedom.

To the extent to which women submit to their fears, they allow themselves to be bound to their past conditioning—the heritage of our society and our culture. They are clinging to what they have, rather than reaching out to create what they might become.

> Not to move forward, to stay where we are, to regress, in other words to rely on what we have, is very tempting, for what we *have,* we know; we can hold on to it, feel secure in it. We fear, and consequently avoid, taking a step into the unknown, the uncertain; for indeed, while the *step* may not appear risky to us *after* we have taken it, *before* we take that step the new aspects beyond it appear very risky, and hence frightening. . . . Every new step contains the danger of failure (Fromm, 1976, p. 108).

SUMMARY

This chapter has been primarily about women and the difficulties they face in enlarging their sphere of freedom. Many of these difficulties are, indeed, external and revolve around discrimination that bars women from full acceptance in the marketplace. Women who work—and more and more of them do—have less interesting jobs than men, have less access to positions of power, and in general are paid less than men. Moreover, the subtle discrimination that keeps women in the lower echelons is difficult to recognize and difficult to fight: Women are excluded from jobs because of an unconscious masculinization of job descriptions so that women cannot be "qualified"; because unconscious bias causes those in positions of power to undervalue women's competence; because women are not heirs to the informal cliques and protégé systems that elevate men to key positions. Such discrimination stems from the conscious or unconscious assumption on the part of many that women can be competent or feminine but not both at the same time. In some cases women's reactions to this prejudice only give further evidence with which to support it.

All the same, women have achieved success in the world of work and have met "masculine" evaluation standards. Yet not all women have succumbed to the lust for power and status prevalent in the world of men. Such women can lead other women, with the cooperation of sympathetic men, to a more humanitarian socioeconomic system. However, this will not happen if women persist in becoming victims of their own fears, if women retreat from power, if women fear the disapproval of men.

Ultimately, therefore, the basis of social change lies in our ability—the ability of men as well as women—to change our images of ourselves, to become more process-oriented individuals who do not cling to the past but can move toward the future. However, the ties of the past are strong, and moving forward will take all the courage we can call to our command.

EXERCISE: CHOOSING OUR LIFE DIRECTIONS

In a brief paragraph, write down a description of your life as it is now. You may want to talk about your occupational and financial situation, your status as a student, important relationships in your life, and any other aspects of your situation or your personality that are important in your current view of yourself.

In a second paragraph, describe yourself as you would like to *be in five years.* Again, pay attention to the same aspects of your situation and personality that you noted earlier.*

Now, make a list of the changes that you would anticipate occurring if you were as you would like to be five years from now. Be

---

*It is important, in terms of this exercise, to be aware of a distinction between process-oriented and role-oriented approaches to planning and formulating goals. In order for us to plan goals in a process-oriented way we must enjoy the intermediate steps toward a goal as well as the goal itself. For example, we must enjoy going to school as well as getting a degree. If we do not enjoy the process of what we are doing, maybe the goal is wrong for us. Thus, from a process-oriented viewpoint goals must take into account our desire to enjoy the intermediary stages—and we ought to be able to change our goals when we find that they don't fit our current needs. This is not to say that we will necessarily enjoy everything that we do, but rather that there is some balance and flexibility required in setting goals that takes account of both the intermediate process and the possibilities of change.

as specific as you can and include both situational and personality variables (e.g. get a better job and gain more self-confidence, respectively).

Now what are the possibilities of such changes occurring?

(1) What are the strengths you have that would facilitate such changes? You might mention such things as specific talents and abilities and also external factors such as financial and emotional support from others.

(2) What difficulties do you foresee that might impede your making such changes? How many of these difficulties are psychological? How many of these difficulties are possible external restrictions? How many of these external restrictions can be transformed into more deep-rooted psychological fears (such as things you really don't want to give up in order to make these changes)?

Having considered all these factors, are there any ways in which you would revise your self-portrait of five years from now? If so, go ahead and do so and revise your other lists accordingly.

What are you doing now that will help you to be where you want to be in five years? What else might you be doing? You might choose to make a contract with yourself about some small behavioral changes that you can make now in order to facilitate your growth toward your own goals.

REFERENCES

Adler, A. (1931) cited in E. Janeway, *Between Myth and Morning: Women Awakening,* New York: William Morrow, 1975.

Almquist, E., and Angrist, S., "Role Model Influences and College Women's Career Aspirations," *Merrill-Palmer Quarterly,* vol. 17 (1971):263–79.

Amundson, K., *The Silenced Majority,* Englewood Cliffs, N.J.: Prentice-Hall, 1971.

Astin, H., "Factors Associated with the Participation of Women Doctorates in the Labor Force," *Personnel and Guidance Journal,* vol. 46 (1967):240–46.

Bachtold, L. M., and Werner, E. E., "Personality Profiles of Gifted Women Psychologists," *American Psychologist,* vol. 25 (1970):234–43.

Bernard, J., "Adjusting the Lives of Women to the Establishment," in C. Stoll, ed., *Sexism: Scientific Debates,* Reading, Mass.: Addison-Wesley, 1973.

Bowman, G. W., Worthy, N. B., and Greyser, S. A., "Are Women Executives People?" *Harvard Business Review,* vol. 43 (July-August 1965): 14–16.

Bryson, R., Bryson, J., Licht, M., and Licht, B., "The Professional Pair: Husband and Wife Psychologists," *American Psychologist,* vol. 31 (1976):10–16.

Bunting, M., "A Huge Waste: Educated Woman Power," *New York Times Magazine,* May 7, 1961.

Bureau of the Census, "A Statistical Portrait of Women in the United States," Washington, D.C.: U.S. Department of Commerce, 1976.

Cartwright, L., "Women in Medical School," unpublished doctoral dissertation, University of California, Berkeley, 1970.

Chafetz, J., *Masculine/Feminine or Human? An Overview of the Sociology of Sex Roles,* Itasca, Ill.: F. E. Peacock, 1974.

Cross, P. A., "College Women: A Research Description," paper presented at the annual meeting of the National Association of Women Deans and Counselors, 1968.

Crowley, J. E., Levitin, J. E., and Quinn, R. P., "Seven Deadly Half-Truths about Women," *Psychology Today,* vol. 6 (March 1973):94–96.

Epstein, C. F., *Woman's Place: Options and Limits in Professional Careers,* Berkeley, Calif.: University of California Press, 1970.

Feldman-Summers, C., and Kiesler, S. B., "Those Who Are Number Two Try Harder: The Effect of Sex on Attributions of Causality," *Journal of Personality and Social Psychology,* vol. 30 (1974):846–55.

Ferber, M., and Huber, J., "Sex of Student and Instructor: A Study of Student Bias," paper presented at the annual meetings of the American Sociological Association, 1974.

Ferber, M., and Loeb, J., "Performance, Rewards, and Perceptions of Sex Discrimination among Male and Female Faculty," *American Journal of Sociology,* vol. 78 (1973):995.

Ferris, A., *Indicators of Trends in the Status of American Women,* New York: Russell Sage Foundation, 1971.

Fidell, L. S., "Empirical Verification of Sex Discrimination in Hiring Practices in Psychology," *American Psychologist,* vol. 25 (1970):1074–98.

Fox, M. F., "Sex-Related Income Differential among Academic Employees at the University of Michigan," unpublished report, 1973.

Fromm, E. *Revolution of Hope,* New York: Harper & Row, 1968.

Fromm, E. *To Have or To Be?* New York: Harper & Row, 1976.

Garland, T. N., "The Better Half?: The Male in the Dual Profession Family," in C. Safilios-Rothschild, ed., *Toward a Sociology of Women,* Greenwich, Conn.: Xerox College Publishing, 1972.

Gillespie, D., "Who Has the Power?: The Marital Struggle," *Journal of Marriage and the Family,* vol. 33 (1971):445–58.

Ginzberg, E., *Educated American Women: Life-Styles and Self-Portraits,* New York: Columbia University Press, 1971.

Gould, R., "Measuring Masculinity by the Size of the Paycheck," *Ms. Magazine,* vol. 1 (June 1973):18.

Gruenberg, S., and Krech, H. *The Many Lives of Modern Women,* New York: Doubleday, 1952.

Gumperz, E., "Women: The Last Minority?" *Columbia University Forum,* vol. 11 (1967):30–34.

Harris, A. S., "The Second Sex in Academe," *AAUP Bulletin,* vol. 56 (Summer 1970):283–95.

Havens, E., "Women, Work and Wedlock: A Note on Female Marital Patterns in the United States," *American Journal of Sociology,* vol. 78 (1971):975–81.

Hawley, P., "Perceptions of Male Models of Femininity Related to Career Choice," *Journal of Counseling Psychology,* vol. 19 (1972):343–47.

Heist, P., "A Commentary on the Motivation and Education of College Women," *Journal of the National Association of Women Deans and Counselors,* vol. 25 (1962):51–59.

Helson, R., "The Changing Image of the Career Woman," *Journal of Social Issues,* vol. 28 (1972):33–46.

Helson, R., "Women Mathematicians and the Creative Personality," *Journal of Consulting and Clinical Psychology,* vol. 36 (1971):210–20.

Hennig, M., and Jardim, A., *The Managerial Woman,* New York: Anchor/ Doubleday, 1977.

Hesselbart, S., Tieche, R., and Blakey, L., "Sex-Role and Occupational Stereotypes: Three Studies in Impression Formation," paper presented at the annual meeting of the American Sociological Association, San Francisco, 1975.

Hoffman, L., "Effects of the Employment of Mothers on Parental Power Relations and the Division of Household Tasks," *Marriage and Family Living,* vol. 22 (1960):33.

Hughes, H. M., ed., *The Status of Women in Sociology,* The American Sociological Association, Washington, D.C., 1972.

Janeway, E., *Between Myth and Morning: Women Awakening,* New York: William Morrow, 1975.

Jourard, S., *The Transparent Self,* New York: Van Nostrand Reinhold, 1964.

Kaschak, E., cited in "Sexist Ratings," *Human Behavior,* vol. 5 (November 1976):50.

Katz, J., ed., *No Time for Youth,* San Francisco: Jossey-Bass, 1968.

Kreps, J., "The Occupations: Wider Economic Opportunity," in M. McBee and K. Blake, eds., *The American Woman: Who Will She Be?,* Encino, Calif.: Glencoe, 1974.

LeMasters, E. E., *Blue-Collar Aristocrats,* Madison, Wis.: University of Wisconsin Press, 1975.

Loring, R., and Wells, T., *Breakthrough: Women in Management,* New York: Van Nostrand Reinhold, 1972.

McGregor, D., *The Professional Manager,* New York: McGraw-Hill, 1967.

Mead, M., and Kaplan, F. B., eds., *American Women: The Report of the President's Commission on the Status of Women,* New York: Charles Scribner's Sons, 1965.

Neugarten, B., ed., *Middle Age and Aging,* Chicago: University of Chicago Press, 1968.

Nye, F. I., and Berardo, F. M., *The Family: Its Structure and Interaction,* New York: Macmillan, 1973.

O'Leary, V., "Some Attitudinal Barriers to Occupational Aspirations in Women," *Psychological Bulletin,* vol. 81 (1974):809–26.

O'Leary, V., and Braun, J. S., "Antecedents and Correlates of Academic Careerism in Women," *Proceedings of the 80th Annual Convention of the American Psychological Association,* vol. 7 (1972):279.

Peterson, E., "Working Women," in R. J. Lifton, ed., *The Woman in America,* Boston: Beacon Press, 1964.

Poloma, M., "Role Conflict and the Married Professional Woman," in C. Safilios-Rothschild, ed., *Toward a Sociology of Women,* Greenwich, Conn.: Xerox College Publishing, 1972.

Rapoport, R., and Rapoport, R., "The Dual-Career Family: A Variant Pattern and Social Change," in C. Safilios-Rothschild, ed., *Toward a Sociology of Women,* Greenwich, Conn.: Xerox College Publishing, 1972.

Roby, P., "Structured and Internalized Barriers to Women in Higher Education," in C. Safilios-Rothschild, ed., *Toward a Sociology of Women,* Greenwich, Conn.: Xerox College Publishing, 1972.

Rossi, A., "Barriers to the Career Choice of Engineering, Medicine or Science among American Women," in J. Mattfield and C. Van Anken, eds., *Women and the Scientific Professions,* Cambridge, Mass.: Massachusetts Institute of Technology Press, 1965.

Rossi, A., "Job Discrimination and What Women Can Do About It," *Atlantic Monthly,* vol. 225 (March 1970):99–103.

Rossi, A., "The Roots of Ambivalence in American Women," in J. Bardwick, ed., *Readings in the Psychology of Women,* New York: Harper & Row, 1972.

Rossi, A., "Sexual Equality: The Beginnings of Ideology," *The Humanist,* vol. 24 (1969):3–6, 16.

Safilios-Rothschild, C., ed., *Toward a Sociology of Women,* Greenwich, Conn.: Xerox College Publishing, 1972.

Simon, R. S., Clark, S. M., and Galway, K., "The Woman Ph.D.: A Recent Profile," *Social Problems,* vol. 15 (1967):221–36.

Siskel, F., cited in "The Beauty Bias," *Human Behavior,* vol. 5 (November 1976):51.

Slater, P., *The Pursuit of Loneliness: American Culture at the Breaking Point,* Boston: Beacon Press, 1970.

Suelzle, M., "Women in Labor," *Transaction,* vol. 8 (November/December 1970): 50–58.

Tangri, S., "Determinants of Occupational Role-Innovation among College Women," *Journal of Social Issues,* vol. 28 (1972):177.

Taynor, J., and Deaux, K., "When Women are More Deserving than Men: Equity, Attribution, and Perceived Sex Differences," *Journal of Personality and Social Psychology,* vol. 28 (1973):360–67.

Terman, L. J., and Oden, M., *The Gifted Groups at Mid-Life,* Stanford, Calif.: Stanford University Press, 1959.

Time Magazine Staff, Special edition on the American woman, March 20, 1972.

Touhey, J. C., "Effects of Additional Women Professionals on Ratings of Occupational Prestige and Desirability," *Journal of Personality and Social Psychology,* vol. 29 (1974):86–89.

Turner, R., "Some Aspects of Women's Ambition," *American Journal of Sociology,* vol. 70 (1964):271–85.

Watley, D. J., "Career or Marriage?: A Longitudinal Study of Able Young Women," *National Merit Scholarship Corporation Research Reports,* vol. 5 (1969):1–16.

White, M., "Psychological Barriers to Women in Science," *Science,* vol. 170 (1970):413–16.

Whyte, W. H., "How Hard Do Executives Work?" *Fortune,* vol. 49 (January 1954):108.

IV

THE PAST: SPRINGBOARD TO FREEDOM OR RATIONALE FOR RESIGNATION?

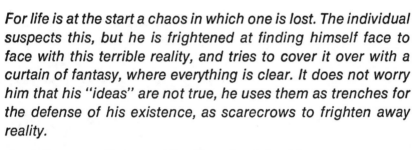

For life is at the start a chaos in which one is lost. The individual suspects this, but he is frightened at finding himself face to face with this terrible reality, and tries to cover it over with a curtain of fantasy, where everything is clear. It does not worry him that his "ideas" are not true, he uses them as trenches for the defense of his existence, as scarecrows to frighten away reality.

José Ortega y Gassett, ***The Revolt of the Masses***

... our concern must be to live *while we're alive—to release our inner selves from the spiritual death that comes with living behind a façade designed to conform to external definitions of who and what we are.*

Elizabeth Kubler-Ross, ***Death: The Final Stage of Growth***

10

Socialization of Boys and Girls: Examining Our Personal Heritage

Our emotional heritage, which we carry forward from our personal past, has been influential in shaping our present personalities. From our parents we learned who we were *supposed* to be and obediently most of us molded ourselves into these images.* Very early we learned which behaviors met with approval or, at worst, escaped retribution, and we took these behaviors into ourselves until they *became* ourselves. We continued this pattern into adulthood without realizing that in large part the selves that we became are the selves that we were persuaded to be in order to meet with

---

*Other factors such as heredity, social class, environmental surroundings, and influence of peers, teachers, and others also have an impact on our growth and development. However, one of the most important variables, and one to which we all need to be alerted, is the influence of parents and other authority figures in our lives. This chapter, therefore, emphasizes this particular area of influence. The absence of lengthy discussion of other factors does *not* imply their insignificance or lack of impact.

As infants—and later children—begin to discover and interpret reality, they are acquiring a vision that is largely shaped by parents and other family members. Children may distort some family messages. . . . They may not hear what others intended to say. . . . However, for better or for worse, a child's first tentative vision will by and large be that of his or her parents and family.

John Powell, **Fully Human, Fully Alive**

Being the product of conditioning and being free to change do not war with each other. Both are true. They coexist, grow together in an upward spiral, and the growth of one furthers the growth of the other. The more cogently we prove ourselves to have been shaped by causes, the more opportunities we create for changing. The more we change, the more possible it becomes to see how determined we were in that which we have just ceased to be.

Allen Wheelis, **How People Change**

---

love, support, and/or protection. As a result, the selves that we might have been still rest within, undiscovered and undeveloped. At least this is true for most of us. We are, to a large degree, products of our environment—our early environment—and rarely do we break from this mold or leave these early role behaviors to utilize our freedom. Leontine Young, in her book about children—and their difficulties with adults—states:

> Not many adults ever grow up that completely. Like a patchwork quilt, we are made up of pieces from every age and stage. We carry a residue from those early passions that were somehow not so transient as they had seemed. We seek from others those controls that may prop up our own creaking ones and protect us from the terrors of those feelings that overwhelmed us long ago. For this spontaneity is turned into a commercial and what is masquerades as what is not (1965, p. 20).

Thus we live behind a façade to protect us from the terrors of the past. We may not be happy with this state of affairs but we do not allow ourselves to risk stepping from these roles to live up to our full potential. We put off such risks, if we do indeed contemplate them, until tomorrow, deluding ourselves with the belief that tomorrow will always come and that some "magic helper" will intercede to improve our affairs and thus give us a second chance. There is, however, no second chance. Now is *all* we have and even as the moment passes it is lost.*

Yet we do not recognize or accept this ultimate reality and consequently we avoid full commitment in the present. Instead we live partly in the past and partly in the future. As Kubler-Ross states, we choose without choosing and value without evaluating. We accept the extrinsic judgments of others rather than of ourselves, and continually search for *their* approval, whoever *they* may be (1976, pp. 164–165). (*They* may represent our parents, our neighbors, our church, or our country.) We circumscribe our lives to meet *their* demands, while at the same time we ignore the ongoing processes within. Why do we allow this to occur?

ROLE-ORIENTED FAMILIES: THE SEPARATION OF POWER AND LOVE

Most (if not all) of us grew up in homes that were to one degree or another role oriented, since our parents, while coping with their fears and insecurities, attempted to bring some stability to their world. In many homes the impact of parental insecurities is balanced by genuine love and concern; in other homes this is not the case. But to one degree or another we bring into our adult lives not only the sense of worth we developed as a result of parental love, but the emotional restrictions molded by parental fears. We carry with us the residue of the past, the effects of which will mold our behavior and that of our children. Because this is so, the picture of a role-oriented home does have some application for all of us. However, for many of us this applicability is limited to subtler nuances, not the broad strokes.

---

*There is no second chance to *relive* the *present* moment. This does not imply that later in time we do not have opportunities to correct past errors or to develop untouched potential. Yet, as each moment passes, the opportunity to utilize that moment in time is irrevocably lost.

As in role-oriented relationships (see pages 209–210), power in role-oriented families becomes separated from love. We realize that there is not enough power to go around. Consequently, "If I have more, you have less" and "If you win, then I lose."* Thus, those wielding this power generally do not surrender their position easily or allow others to share equally in the power. Rather they use this power to boost their self-esteem.

Power in such families is derived from the status of the parent rather than from inner strength or from the greater knowledge of the parent. For example, in the traditional family, the father is the "boss" *because* he is the father and not because he knows more or is wiser than his wife or his children. His rules, then, often become assertions of his will and manipulate and restrict his family. In this manner, power is linked to domination and is recognized by the submission or obedience of others.

Although power used in such a way may appear benevolent and "for the good of all," such power is wielded for power's sake. Therefore it must be separated from caring and genuine concern. As a result, in the traditional family the father wields the power and the mother assumes the functions left vacant by the father—she loves, nurtures, and comforts the other family members. In such a situation the mother is also submitting to the father, and may be viewed as lacking power. The implicit message in such a family arrangement is that power belongs to the strong (generally males) and love is the virtue of the weak (generally females). Furthermore, the weak use love as a tool of power in covert ways, and give and withhold love as a means of meeting their own needs.

This traditional arrangement is subject to a variety of permutations. The strength of the "woman behind the throne" may indeed be recognized as more powerful than the overt power of the throned king. This recognition, however, is nonverbal. On the other hand, the power of the mother may be overtly stronger than that of the father, which leads to stories of "hen-pecked husbands," passive men, and pushy wives. Yet another permutation may occur if the children by default usurp the power and tyrannize over their parents. Nevertheless, whatever the allocation of power, such power is seen as a goal in its own right, not a by-product of inner strength.

Children growing up in such families soon learn the "machina-

---

*This is the origin of the proverbial "power struggles" between family members as each struggles to attain his or her own share of the limited resource.

tions of power" (Lowen, 1972, p. 164). Power is perceived as valuable and the children, who are relatively helpless in the face of adults, learn how to comply with or outmaneuver the demands of the person in power. Often they assume the roles of pint-sized persecutors, small mother-hens, bullying father-figures, or incapable, clinging whiners. Sometimes, however, children learn ways to manipulate power that are not obvious, noisy, or necessarily offensive. Often the most successful tactics are the most subtle and the outfoxed parent does not even know that he or she has lost. Leontine Young speaks of the pleasing but manipulative aspects of childhood guile:

> The pathos of helplessness, the wistful charm of a smile, the pathetic glint of a tear, the feel of a soft, young cheek against your own, the moist whisper of a kiss and almost any adult with a heart feels that it is no less than virtue to succumb to so charming a suppliant (1965, pp. 89–90).

Parents often give in to such maneuvers as well as to childish whining or bullying tactics. In the process children are learning how to manipulate others.

The Negative Effects of Power The problem, however, is that these same behavior patterns continue to characterize adult behavior, often without conscious awareness. Adults continue to manipulate, bully, cajole, and outwit others, as if they were still outnumbered and overwhelmed by the power of others. They fail to recognize that if they are inherently powerful, such tactics are indeed unnecessary. Anaïs Nin remarks: "If a person continues to see only giants, it means he is still looking at the world through the eyes of a child" (1966, p. 53).

Adults who still see themselves as small persons in a world where everyone else is big grasp for power and utilize that power to counter fears of their own weakness. Such power is seen as external to themselves; it must be wrested from others—and then used against them. The negative impact of such power when wielded within the home is documented in both empirical and clinical writings.

Empirical research substantiates the hypothesis that children from rigid homes in which power is used in an authoritarian manner tend to rank lower on the personality variables valued by our society. Hoffman (1960) finds that if parents assert power in an unqualified manner, children tend to develop hostility and power needs. Lefkowitz, Walder, and Eron (1963) show that physical punishment, which is often a manifestation of unloving power, increases aggression in children. Starr (1965) carries the case further by showing that parents with authoritarian attitudes raise children with the same attitudes. Lang (1969) studies power systems in families and finds that power exercised solely by the parents rather than shared by both parents and children leads the children to experience responsibility as external to themselves. In other words; the children do not see themselves as responsible for what happens to them. On the other hand, the same study reports that children who usurp the power of their parents tend to become self-serving and insensitive to the needs of others. In short, homes that are highly restrictive as well as those that are highly permissive miss the mark of sharing power between parents and children. Instead they allow one side to tyrannize over the other.

Clinicians report that such use of power for power's sake results in patterns that continue into adult life. Children who grow up at the mercy of powerful parents often bide their time until they, in turn, can exert power over their own children. Moreover, children who learn that power is valued for its own sake tend to devalue love, which is seen as the polar opposite. Such perceptions, if carried into adult life, make it difficult to form rewarding interpersonal relationships. For example, a love relationship becomes either a trap in which we lose all power or a preserve where we exercise power over another. In either case a warm, intimate relationship becomes relatively impossible. By learning to separate power from love we learn to manipulate power but we rarely learn to love.

Other Characteristics of Role-Oriented Families In addition to separating power and love, role-oriented families are dominated by form and structure rather than by the ongoing process of people's lives. In such a system communication is indirect and often unclear. The family is operating by rules that are not specified but that take priority over our changing needs. The outcome of such a system tends to be diminished self-esteem at best and chaos at worst, whether or not such chaos is covered by a polite veneer (Satir, 1972, p. 116).

Examples of indirect communication and unspecified rules come from my own experience and that of my students. For example, many families believe that everybody should be doing physical work most of the time—household maintenance, yard work, or whatever. In such families an individual who lies around reading books is called "lazy" and "irresponsible" and sometimes "no good." No one states clearly the belief that "all *good* people work most of the time" or the rule that comes from that belief, which is: "You must work as long as there is work to do." Yet individuals who do not abide by this unspoken dictum are often castigated by other family members.

Other common beliefs held by families include such ideas as: "If our family goes someplace together, everybody goes." If an individual chooses not to go for some personal reasons of his or her own, then the family members may assume that this person is "not good" or "doesn't love" them.

From these examples then it seems that role-oriented families pay more attention to outward appearances than inner feelings. They teach their children to say "please" and "thank you" and fail to teach them to trust themselves, to listen to their inner feelings, and to develop their own unique capacities (even if such development is discomfiting to those around them). In this manner we suppress the spontaneity of children in favor of sameness and conventional norms. In so doing we serve our own interests to have a little peace and quiet and lack of conflict. We also avoid the nervous wear-and-tear of adjusting to, responding to, and furthering the willful desires of small persons intent on "doing their own thing."

Such young people will grow up to be parents themselves who "do not even notice how much enthusiasm, zest for living, spontaneity, and self-honesty have vanished with the unimportant past" (Young, 1965, p. 4). As parents they will have buried their own childhoods and will teach their children to bury theirs. They will live their lives according to external rules and regulations, teaching their children to do the same; they have long been separated from their inner sources of strength, security, spontaneity, and uniquely personalized feelings.

The outcome of such role-oriented socialization procedures, however, is not entirely negative. Sometimes, but not always, such instruction fits the inclination of the child. Often though, this is not the case, and as adults we are all living testaments to the suffering caused by the buried feelings of the past. Eda LeShan in her book for children *What Makes Me Feel This Way?* gives a concrete example of some of the psychological difficulties that ensue when the real feelings of a child are suppressed. The book, though written for children, is also instructive for adults. She writes as follows about one boy:

> In Tony's house, certain kinds of feelings aren't allowed. His mother and father were taught by their parents that it is bad to be angry, and that nice people never have such feelings. They are wrong, but that is what they have learned, and that is what they are teaching Tony. When a person has feelings that he is very much ashamed of, and feels he is a bad person because he has them, he sometimes pushes away the whole idea of those feelings. He just won't let them come into his mind. But feelings don't give up that easily. They have to go somewhere. Feelings that have nowhere to go often become bellyaches and headaches and make us feel dizzy or very tired. Sometimes they come out all of a sudden, so fast that we can't do anything about them (1972, p. 21).

Thus, due to the suppression of feelings, children often punch each other, whereas adults verbally assault each other or perform character assassination on their neighbors. Is the chronic discomfort that many of us experience a necessary accompaniment to living in a necessarily frantic world? It is if we choose to treat ourselves and our children as objects, subject to the imposition of external forms rather than as fully human people, growing and choosing from within ourselves.

Pressures Toward Role Orientation Yet the very process of raising children often pressures us toward role orientation. Probably in few other situations are our insecurities—and our defenses against them—brought more fully into play. Initially, children are accurate perceivers of their environment, and they can demonstrate a devastating candor. Thus they point out exactly what they see—the pleasant as well as the unpleasant—and have little regard for the social sensitivities of adults. For parents and other adults who have learned to subdue their feelings, who have learned to leave their own inner desires behind, who have rigorously learned what they ought and ought not to feel, the results can be devastating. After a lifetime of building a façade, who wants a knee-high person to point out that there are evidences of faulty construction? Who wants this small person to arouse the long suppressed voices that lie within? It is hardly any wonder that we teach our children to be like us.

However, in teaching our children to be like us, we inevitably teach them to reflect our faults as well as our virtues. Naturally, we would prefer that the children be trained to demonstrate only our virtues. After all, "Who wants to look at a certified copy of his own faults?" (Young, 1965, p. 10). And so we bring all our power to bear in order to shape the child as we would like. In this manner we try to suppress in the child what we have been unable to suppress in ourselves.

Eda LeShan gives children the following advice: "Sometimes parents can get very upset about something that is happening to *you,* but the upset is really about something that happened to *them*" (1972, p. 86). A boy's father may be very upset that his son didn't stand up to a neighborhood bully because he remembers how *he* didn't stand up to *his* neighborhood bully when he was young. A mother who was a wallflower as a young girl may push her attractive daughter into early dating in order to make up for what she (the mother) perceives as her own adolescent inadequacies. LeShan provides another concrete example:

> There is something else that is very confusing about parents. The feelings they have about themselves often make them behave in a strange way towards their children. Mrs. Montgomery has a little girl who is seven years old. One day Mrs. Montgomery came to school to see Pat's teacher because Pat was behaving very badly at home. Mrs. Montgomery told the teacher, "I don't know what it is, but that child is driving me wild. I see red every time she gets fresh or doesn't do what I tell her to do." The teacher asked, "What sort of person is Pat?" Her mother answered, "She's very strong-willed and she has a quick temper, a great sense of humor, and she's stubborn as a mule." Then, looking very shocked, Mrs. Montgomery said, "Gee—I could be describing *myself!* I guess the reason I get so shook up is because she's just like me, and I want her to be better!" (1972, pp. 84–85).

From this example we see that often our strongest reactions about others (especially our children) are provoked by inadequacies perceived in ourselves. We push our children to overcome our own inadequacies rather than recognizing them inside ourselves. We treat our children as objects who will fulfill our needs at the expense of fulfilling their own. Our children are often a substitute for therapy, a means of rectifying our own failings. In using children this way—as therapeutic tools—we will objectify our children and they in turn will objectify others. In so doing we are perpetuating role-oriented behavior from generation to generation. Let us now examine the different theories of development of childhood behavior.

THEORIES OF DEVELOPMENT

Explanations of the development of childhood behavior and attitudes have been attempted from several different theoretical points of view. _Social learning theorists_ (e.g., Mischel, 1966) feel that behavior patterns are developed through reinforcement in the environment. Thus children who whine, are subsequently slapped, and then cuddled may find the contact to be a reinforcement for whining. Consequently they may develop a pattern of complaining, sulking, and whining that they will carry into their adult lives. On the other hand, _psychoanalytic theorists_ (e.g., Bronfenbrenner, 1960) believe that learning patterns are innate and that learning occurs through identification with our parents. Traditionally children identify with the parent of the same sex. Thus girls at age 4 may mimic their mothers by scolding their dolls or their little brothers. Although not directly reinforced for such behavior, they may reward themselves with the knowledge that they are acting appropriately—like their mothers. A third group, _cognitive theorists_ (Kohlberg, 1966), postulate that after the age of 3 or so children develop cognitive maps of what boys or girls do and apply these maps as guides for their own behavior. This latter theory goes beyond the influences of environment and parents. Although children rely on the environment to guide their behavior, they then construct their own interpretations of the world.

Possibly a combination of all three processes constitutes sex-role learning (see Maccoby & Jacklin, 1974). We are rewarded, or reinforced, for "appropriate" behavior; we identify with same-sex models; and we eventually develop concepts of masculinity and femininity to which we try to conform. Nonetheless, most of the literature relies on the theory of identification as a guide to sex-role learning.

The effectiveness of identification has been attributed both to the power of the person with whom we identify (Bandura & Walters, 1963; Bronfenbrenner, 1960) and to his or her warmth and affection (Sanford, 1955; Sears, 1957). In all cases, however, the emphasis in identification appears to revolve around the two polarities of power and love. Children identify both with those adults who appear powerful to them and with those who love and support them.

It is generally accepted that for both sexes the earliest identification is generally with the mother, who is the most powerful and loving figure in the infant's environment. For girls, this feminine identification occurs throughout life and is, as Lynn (1969) remarks, in the nature of a "lesson" accompanied by large doses of positive reinforcement. On the other hand, little boys must learn to shift their early feminine identification to a masculine authority figure. This shift is accomplished through negative reinforcement by the parents ("Don't be a sissy") and through the boy's perception that his father indeed has greater status and power. The dominance and power of the father act as an attraction to the young male child, counterbalancing the attractiveness of the warm, supportive atmosphere provided by the mother. From this it follows (in traditional thinking*) that it is important for the father to maintain dominance within the household in order to provide a desirable identification model for the male child.

If the father is strong and the mother is loving, then all is well with the world—and the children. Boys come to identify with the power of the father and girls more with the love of the mother. As a result, both grow up to be appropriately sex-identified—just as their parents. We create powerful men and loving women. Or so we think.

Actually the mechanisms of identification are more complex than stated above. For example, boys do not identify solely with the father nor girls solely with the mother. Moulton, Burnstein, Liberty, and Altucher (1966) point out that both children identify with the dominant *parent*. Lynn (1966) carries this a step further by showing that children identify both with parents who are powerful and with those who are warm and supportive. Block, von der Lippe, and Block (1973) point out that children also learn in counterpoint to the opposite-sex parent, adopting those behavioral patterns—and sex identification—that are appropriate in order to *interact with* the parent of the other sex. Thus children respond both to power and love, both in their identification with—and interaction with—powerful and loving parents.

In part because of the complexity of the identification process, there are various ways in which this pattern goes awry. Because children tend to identify with the dominant parent, within the

---

*"Traditional" in this context refers to theoretical orientations which assume that men ought to be masculine and women ought to be feminine, and further that masculine and feminine roles are mutually exclusive to a large degree. Most psychoanalytic theorists and many social learning theorists subscribe to this set of assumptions. Such traditional thinking leads logically to a belief in the separation of love and power and the limited availability of each, and thus provides theoretical foundations for a role-oriented model of behavior.

traditional theory, the children suffer if, for example, the mother has "usurped" the rightful power of the father. In these instances the boys will identify with the mother and become inappropriately "feminine" and thus experience ambivalence around the value of being a man. Girls in such a home will also identify primarily with the mother, developing her strength as well as more typically feminine attributes. Such girls may benefit from the strength in many ways but at the same time may suffer in their relationships with men. The girls will not have learned in interaction with a powerful and attractive father (traditionalists assume that the father is not powerful if the mother is) how to play the counterrole—the feminine role to his masculine one (Johnson, 1963).

On the other hand, an overly strong, authoritarian father who is paired with a weak, rejecting, and unloving mother also can create difficulties for children according to traditional theorists. In such a home the boy may identify with his father, become supermasculine himself, but demonstrate the rigidity associated with the "macho" role and its accompanying contempt for women. Girls in such a home may either become exaggeratedly feminine as they play the counterrole to their father, or exaggeratedly masculine as they model themselves after his characteristics in the absence of a loving feminine model (Block, 1973). In neither case do boys and girls become appropriately "masculine" or "feminine."

As is also the case with other theories, the traditional theory itself is open to question. In a home in which the father is powerful and the mother is loving boys may grow up to be "masculine" and girls "feminine," but each may disown the characteristics of the other sex. Men from such families may be raised appropriately for the sex-typed society in which we live. Yet they may be out of touch with their emotions and unable to fully share themselves in an intimate relationship. As Komarovsky (1967) comments about working-class men, their training in masculinity has resulted in a "trained incapacity to share." Women who are raised in such homes moreover become relatively loving—but docile (Block, 1973). Again, such development may be "normal" for our culture but is it healthy?

From the point of view of this book, neither the traditional patterns nor the traditional patterns-gone-awry facilitate the development of process-oriented individuals. In these examples power and love are not equally shared between the parents. Thus the children tend either to identify more with one parent than the other, or to adopt traditional masculine and feminine roles with the deficits inherent in each. In neither situation does the child find both parents powerful and loving so that the child can identify with desirable characteristics of both. Instead, the child perceives, at best, one parent as powerful and the other as loving. Acting as models, the parents have shown the separation of power and love—a separation that the child will probably carry along into the next generation.

The fact that children seem to perceive their parents as either loving or powerful rather than both is reported in two research studies cited below. In these studies children saw their parents in terms of traditional sex-role stereotypes and as very different from each other. In addition, although the children tended to emulate the parent of the same sex, they also tended to agree that the person who has the power—generally the father—is the one who is most highly valued.

In questioning children aged 3 to 8 Kagan and Lemkin (1960) found that fathers are perceived as more fear-arousing, more confident, and more punitive whereas mothers are perceived as "nicer" and more likely to give presents to the children. In this study the girls tended to see the father as both more punitive and more affectionate than did the boys. In slightly older children Kagan, Hosken, and Watson (1968) found that boys and girls from 6 to 8 years of age assigned different symbolic terms to each parent. Both sexes agreed that the father in relation to the mother was stronger, larger, more dangerous, dirtier, darker, and more angular. In this study, however, girls tended to see the father as more hostile and the mother as more nurturing than did the boys. Yet in both studies children of both sexes agreed that the mother is the weaker and less able sex.

These views of the unequal separation of the sexes fit with the role-oriented model. Individuals adopt the prescribed sex-role stereotypes and mold themselves to fit them. Boys then hasten to identify primarily with the more powerful male even though they regard their father as fear-arousing and dangerous while girls identify primarily with the weaker mother.* In the process love and

---

*When all the complexities are considered, girls too identify with their fathers and boys with their mothers. However, in homes where traditional sex-role stereotypes are maintained the girls shun the power of the father in order to maintain the earlier feminine identification. (Unlike boys, girls are never given any reason to dissociate themselves from their earlier feminine identification.) They associate power with the counterrole and not their own. Similarly, boys learn to avoid or repress feminine identifications since their masculine role is seen as mutually

power become separated from each other. Is this the only alternative?

What if love and power could be found equally in each parent? What if both parents were powerful and loving, hence also androgynous? Then children could identify with both parents and adopt a combination of male and female characteristics. Several researchers (e.g., Bardwick, 1971; Maccoby, 1966) believe that identification with both parents in a relatively egalitarian home in which power and love are shared is highly beneficial. Let us now examine this process-oriented alternative.

THE PROCESS-ORIENTED ALTERNATIVE: THE BALANCE OF POWER AND LOVE

Within a process-oriented home power is combined with love and is regarded as a limited resource to be wielded by only one parent. In such homes children may come to identify with both parents. Identification with both sexes generally leads to higher intellectual skills and higher creativity (Bardwick, 1971; Barron, 1963; Helson, 1971; Maccoby, 1966). Bardwick states:

> Children whose personalities are like those of the opposite sex in some important ways are likely to have needs, conflicts, and defenses similar to those of the opposite sex. Personality characteristics reflect the sex of rearing and a basic temperamental disposition. Children whose personalities are closer to the norms of the opposite sex may suffer anxiety about it, but if not pathologically extreme, it may be of advantage. The intuitive, empathic boy or the competitive, independent girl, if they also have characteristics appropriate to their sex, are often more creative than the more rigidly sex-typed personalities (Bardwick, 1971, p. 130).

It seems likely that the development of the positive characteristics of both sexes would be facilitated in a process-oriented home where the parents were both powerful and loving. In such a home the focus of attention would be on the changing needs, desires, and capabilities of the individual members rather than on the forms that determine what family members "ought" to do. In such a family one

---

exclusive with such an identification. The feminine identification which they may experience is relegated to the outside and kept in the counterrole for their feminine counterpart to assume and act out for them.

would expect an openness of communication and a genuine acceptance of the uniqueness of each individual. Hence all subjects would be talked about without taboos or embarrassment. One would also expect that rules would develop based on the individual and group needs of the family. Moreover such rules would be open to change to match the changing needs of individuals.

In such a family individuals, as a rule, would not engage in power struggles in which they would manipulate others to fit their own needs. Rather each family member could openly ask for that which he or she needs; such requests would be well received and would be negotiable in terms of the needs of other family members or of the whole family. Moreover in such a family love would not be used as a weapon. It would be something freely offered by each individual with recognition of the fact that we usually experience both positive and negative feelings toward people with whom we live closely. Love would not have any strings attached; if I say that I love you, this does not mean that you must do something for me.

Thus, in a process-oriented family each individual would be respected as an autonomous human being with his or her own needs and desires as well as rights and privileges. Such needs, desires, and rights would be respected and met insofar as they did not infringe on those of other members of the family.

The basic premise of such a family is the realization that change is inevitable. Parents change, children grow up, and each day all of us present a slightly different face to the world. With the recognition of change there is less need to mold the present to the past or to treat the adolescent as if he or she were still a toddler in need of constant supervision. In such a family people accept change and do not seek the illusion of security in each other. In such a family people find strength within—strength in their own power— and from this central point of strength can give freely to others. Such a family combines within each individual and within the system the process-oriented balance of power and love. Thus each parent can nurture and can discipline, can be compassionate and can establish rules, and can be both merciful and just.

Research supports the view that love and power emanating from both parents produces relatively healthy children. A major study by Diana Baumrind (1967) sorted preschool children into three groups. The first group, which was evaluated most positively, was described as self-reliant, self-controlled, explorative, and content. A second group of children were perceived as discontent, withdrawn, and distrustful while the third showed little self-control or self-reliance and tended to retreat from new experience. The parents of the first group of self-reliant youngsters were found to be significantly more consistent, loving, and secure in handling their children than the parents of children in the other groups. Parents in the first group tended to explain reasons for rules, to communicate clearly with their children, and to enforce consistently their directives and resist giving in to the children's demands. Baumrind found that these parents, in contrast to the parents of the other two groups of children, combined control with warmth—in other words, power with love.

These results are confirmed by other studies. Clapp (1967) found that parents of 4-year-old boys described as "competent" were themselves competent and consistent in philosophy and action. Moreover, they were also warmer to their sons and less hostile than parents of more dependent children. In the field of academic achievement, Walters and Stinnett (1971) point out that "achievement leadership and creative thinking of children was positively related to warm, accepting, understanding, and autonomy-granting parent-child relationships." Esty (1968), in studying college students, found that college leaders perceived their parents as both loving and moderately controlling and neither neglecting, rejecting, nor overprotecting. In conclusion, children appear to benefit from warm, democratic, controlling but not restrictive parent-child relationships.

Unfortunately, our traditional sex roles mitigate against the development of the process-oriented family. Instead of raising individuals who are fully human, we raise children to be men and women almost as if they were members of separate species. In a book of children's writings, *Male and Female Under 18* (1973), Larrick and Merriam present strong evidence that children perceive extreme differences between the sexes. One poem by a 9-year-old boy, Mark Swan, is illustrative of this:

> Boys
> strong, slaves
> daring, smarter, workers
> warriors, astronauts
> more creative
> men.

Girls
fearful, goodies
long hair, soft voices
come to me for help.
lazy
Its!

And so by age 9, Mark differentiates the sexes, assigns the higher value to the male, and in the last word objectifies the female!

THE TRAINING OF MEN AND WOMEN

Mark's reaction is not surprising when we consider that from the moment that the child arrives in this world he or she is bombarded with messages about being male or female. The first words spoken about the child are "It's a boy!" or "It's a girl!" In part this early differentiation is forced by a language that does not recognize a human being until it (a particularly unhuman pronoun) can be referred to as "he" or "she." So with this early differentiation the process of rearing boys and girls begins. This socialization continues as relatives coo at the little girls and jostle the little boys, and as visitors speak of "dainty girls" and "husky boys." All come with gifts—either pink ruffly dresses or little blue overalls—depending on the sex of the child.

We begin with the birth of the child to create two different worlds, and this process of differentiation continues through toddlerhood, through the schoolroom, and into the adult world. Of the infant wrapped in blue we may fantasize that he may become a truckdriver, an executive, or even president of the United States! Of the small infant wrapped in pink, we pray for a happy marriage and motherhood. Her course, to a large extent, is already predetermined. Millett speaks of these differential worlds and the shaping of lives that is yet to come:

> Because of our social circumstances, male and female are really two cultures and their life experiences are utterly different. . . . Implicit in all the gender identity development which takes place through childhood is the total of the parents', the peers', and the culture's notions of what is appropriate to each gender by way of temperament, character, interests, status, worth, gesture, and expression. Every moment of the child's life is a clue as to how he or she must think and behave to

attain or satisfy the demands which gender places upon one (1970, p. 31).

Despite the different worlds we create, we know (stereotypes to the contrary) that men and women demonstrate more similarities than differences (see pp. 25–28). Thus, if we indeed set out to create two different species we are unsuccessful in our task. Yet we *do* treat boys and girls differently and such differences are apparent in the children as they grow to be men and women.

Differential Treatment of Boys and Girls There is evidence, for example, that parents tend to *perceive* boys differently from girls and that this perception colors their behavior toward young children. Such differences in perception are apparent in the ways in which they describe the newborn child. One study finds that within twenty-four hours of birth infant sons were described as big, tough, and active whereas daughters were described as little, beautiful, pretty, and cute. These different descriptions bore no resemblance to any observable differences in the infants (Rubin, Provenzano & Luria, 1974). In another study, the same differences were observed in regard to a 17-month-old baby depending on whether adults were told the baby was a boy or a girl. If the infant was labeled a boy, the adults responded that the child was aggressive, active, and alert. If told that the infant was a girl, the adults described the child as cuddly, passive, and delicate (Meyer & Sobieszek, 1972). In both of the above instances, men were more pronounced in differentiating the sexes than were females.

However, not only do parents describe infants differently according to their sex, they also tend to treat their infants differently. In one study parents were asked to "test" their 7-week-old infants. If they were asked to make their infants smile and vocalize, parents spent considerably more time with their daughters than with their sons. On this task, mothers spent much more time than fathers. On the other hand, if parents were asked to have their child "grab for the bell," the fathers participated significantly more than did the mothers (Moss, 1974). Such results suggest that very early we begin to train girls for interpersonal relations and boys for more achievement-oriented tasks. In such cases mothers and fathers play sex-typed roles.

Parents also relate to their infants differently in terms of physical contact. Boys are picked up more, played with more roughly, and in general receive more physical stimulation than girls. On the other hand, female infants are talked to more and imitated more. Such differences are significant at 3 weeks of age and still noticeable at 3 months (Lewis & Weinraub, 1974; Moss, 1974). In part, this may be due to the parental expectation that boys will be more active and physical and girls quieter and more verbal.

By the age of 4 or 5 there are some definite differences in socialization. Whereas girls are allowed to continue in either feminine or masculine play ("She's just a little tomboy"), boys are strongly discouraged from being "sissies." Hartley's (1959) early work demonstrates that parents impose earlier and more rigorous demands on boys than they do on girls. Boys have to conform by kindergarten to what is manly, whereas girls do not need to be feminine until they enter adolescence. Moreover, demands for appropriate sex-role behavior in boys are enforced more harshly than they are for girls. The behavior for boys is generally defined in terms of negative sanctions: For example, "Don't be a girl," "Don't be a sissy," "Don't play with girl things," and so forth. We rarely say to a boy: "Be a boy!" Instead we say, "Don't be a girl!"

Such early pressures on boys in our society are very much like giving people a destination but not giving them a roadmap. Moreover, if boys fail to reach the destination punishment is certain. Little boys, therefore, have difficulty in knowing what they must do to be masculine. They know, however, that they must be masculine, and that they must *never* be like a girl. Yet in most cases boys grow up in our society in what is mostly a feminine world, and have few masculine role-models for their behavior. In our society most fathers are away at work most of the time and cannot provide an adequate model of masculine behavior. Consequently little boys turn to their peers and to stereotypes in the larger culture in order to draw a model of "what it means to be a man." Therefore they learn the caricatured features of the stereotypes that tend to emphasize physical strength and athletic skills; in adolescence they emphasize the ability to "hold one's liquor" and heterosexual conquest. This model misses all the nuances of personal behavior that boys might observe in close association with an older male and emphasizes, instead, the more blatant features of what it means to be masculine.

Hartley (1959), like others (Bardwick, 1971; Lynn, 1969; Skolnick & Skolnick, 1971), comments on the difficulties of growing up male in a situation largely dominated by women: Boys are ruled and governed by what they must not yield to. They must repress in themselves all that they observe and interact with on a daily basis. Moreover, those who do not succeed in doing so are punished by the peer group that values the stereotypical traits of physical strength and emotional control. One of the consequences of this difficult situation is that athletics becomes for many boys the test of their masculinity: In this area they demonstrate physical skills and show that they are *not* feminine. Boys who succeed in sports find a great many other things coming their way. But for those who are too weak or too small or interested in other things, the disapproval of the peer group provides emotional and physical penalties. Sports and one's success or failure at them provide an easy access to heaven or hell regardless of the development of other attributes.

In the process of imposing negative sanctions on boys, fathers from the early weeks on play a stronger role than mothers do. Fathers "seem to take the lead in activity discouraging any interest a son might have in feminine toys, activities, or attire" (Maccoby & Jacklin, 1974, p. 362). Fathers also tend to "teach" their sons more and are concerned that they develop "masculine" skills. In addition, boys are on the receiving end of the mother's affection more than girls are. They also are praised and criticized more by both parents (Bardwick, 1971; Block, 1973; Maccoby & Jacklin, 1974). Thus, the greater attention paid to the developing skills of boys by the father and the greater nurturance given by the mother contribute to the heavier and more severe indoctrination of boys into appropriate roles.

On the other hand, parents pay less attention to both the skill-learning and the expressive qualities of their daughters. Rather than being hampered by this, girls may indeed benefit instead. They can then experiment with their talents and their skills to explore alternative ways of life. Often, however, this freedom to explore results in lowered levels of feminine development. Such freedom is permitted because "nobody expects much of a girl." A girl is expected to become a wife and mother and is therefore not urged to develop her skills to a high degree. Because many girls sense this expectation early, they do not focus on any particular area of endeavor and thus fall short of developing their talents in areas that require dedication and perseverance. Talented females often become "jacks-of-all-trades" (or should it be jills?) rather than "experts" in any one field.

Boys also receive mixed advantages and disadvantages from

the more intense attention paid to their development. Boys are forced to explore their talents and abilities and are urged to become independent, self-reliant, and adventuresome. Whereas some boys are challenged by such expectations and focus on one area of endeavor with satisfying occupational and personal results, many (if not most) boys find these expectations a burden. Consequently they suffer from this undue pressure and often feel inadequate in the face of high demands. Thus, while girls are allowed more freedom, there is little expectation that they will fully develop any one area. Boys, on the other hand, are constantly urged to "try harder." This leads to greater success for some and greater failure for others.

In adolescence, the emphasis on boys' achievement continues with added emphasis on success in sports and in sexual experience (or at least the ability to talk among their peers about such experience). At this developmental stage sex-role indoctrination is also stepped up for girls. Relatively free to pursue their own interests— whether termed "masculine" or "feminine"—until adolescence, girls are for the first time strongly urged to become "feminine" (Bardwick, 1971). These increased pressures for both sexes show up early in the adolescent years.

Bronfenbrenner (1961) reports that girls in the tenth grade are especially likely to be overprotected whereas boys are more likely to reap the negative effects of parental discipline. Such treatment often results in the girls being "overly socialized" (too concerned about and compliant with the expectations of others) while the boys suffer from being loved too little, or only in a conditional way. Block sums up the differences in socialization:

> The leitmotiv of socialization practices for boys across the several age levels studied reflects an emphasis on the virtues of the Protestant Ethic: an emphasis on achievement and competition, the insistence on control of feelings and expressions of affect, and a concern for rule conformity. There is differential emphasis in enforcing the "thou shalt nots" of child rearing: authority and control seem to power the vital issues between parents, particularly fathers, and their sons at this age.
>
> For girls, on the other hand, emphasis is placed, particularly by their fathers, on developing and maintaining close interpersonal relationships: they are encouraged to talk about their troubles and to reflect upon life, are shown affection physically, and are given comfort and reassurance... (1973, p. 517).

It is hardly surprising, considering such accounts, that girls grow up trying to please men while boys grow up trying to conquer the world. In case history after case history one sees the results today of this belief of yesterday: Girls tone down their minds and tone up their appearance as they come into adolescence while boys focus on the middle-class rites of passage. These are sports, drinking, and sex. Often this results in equal proportions of happiness and unhappiness in the young people's views of themselves. Yet they assume (at least in adolescence) that such behavior is necessary in order to be a "proper" man or woman.

What It Means To Be a Man In the personal accounts of my students several themes are reiterated time and again: In adolescence males *had* to be good at sports; they had to smoke and drink as well as act as if they knew about sex; and they had to fight well if the occasion demanded. Those who were successful in these tasks were considered "popular" and "leaders." One man, now in his late 20s, recounts that he took part in all these endeavors because they were "manly" things to do. Consequently "dating opportunities abounded." He also gave up his interest in tennis when he discovered that "tennis was a 'sissy' sport."

Other young men who were on the football team talked about the liberties this assurance of their masculinity gave them to pursue other interests. Two young men discussing their "liberation" said that they had joined the dance club in high school, though its members were predominantly female, and had enjoyed it. However, in further discussion, they said there was another guy in the dance club who they thought was "weird" and a "little flaky." When asked why, they replied, "Well, we were both on the football team so we knew we were OK, but he wasn't so we wondered if maybe he was queer." Apparently in recent years young men who have *proven* their masculinity can enjoy the more "feminine" arts, but woe betide those who dally with femininity without football letters to their credit! This impression is reinforced by another self-styled liberated male. Although he spent a lot of his early years cleaning house and doing other domestic tasks, he was still respected by his peer group. "How come?" "Well, I could knock down any guy on the block!"

Judging by the restricted membership of most football teams, however, we must assume that most boys do not acquire this symbol of masculinity. Indeed, in most of the case histories of males that reflect feelings of inadequacy, these feelings stem from lack of success at sports. Bruce's story is only one among many:

One of the most shattering experiences to my male ego in my whole lifetime occurred when I was cut from the ninth-grade basketball team. I went to public schools until the eighth grade and participated in basketball and baseball (my junior high didn't have football). I was a starter on the seventh- and eighth-grade basketball teams. In ninth grade I entered an all-boys private high school. The competition became very fierce but I still thought I was as good as anyone (maybe I was), but I was somewhat handicapped because as of the ninth grade I was 5'5" and 130 lbs. (a good deal shorter than many of the others). Up until this time I had gained much of my identity from the fact that I was a basketball player. There was some consolation in the fact that I was the last one to be cut from the team, but I still was in a state of shock and disbelief for a good two weeks, if not a month. My whole identity and self-image had been crushed. I don't think that anything could happen to me now or in the future that could crush me the way that being cut from the ninth-grade basketball team did. This may sound a little strong, but it shows how much this meant to me at the time.

Another common test of masculinity is the ability to drink—and to drink a lot. Drinking shows that one is "cool" and "one of the guys." Bruce again talks of his experiences:

Drinking can become a test of maleness during high school. . . . In order to prove your "maleness" you had to drink a certain number of beers without getting sick. The "best" drinker was the one who would drink the most without getting sick. There can be many arguments as to who can drink whom under the table.

In my first drinking experiences, a group of us (about three to six) would go to the liquor store and wait outside until we could find somebody to buy for us and then we would go somewhere to drink. We would either go to someone's house whose parents weren't home or else we would go to the park. We would all go to great lengths telling each other how good the beer tasted while we actually hated the taste and would rather have been drinking Pepsi. Beer is not a beverage that has a pleasing taste right from the start. However, after a while you can acquire quite a taste for it, as I did. At first, though, we were all forcing ourselves to drink so that we wouldn't be ridiculed. . . .

The third "rite of passage" into manhood among adolescent

boys is the possession (or at least the appearance of possession) of sexual knowledge. Steve, a student in his late 20s, states that in order to prove masculinity among your peers you had to prove that "you knew what you were talking about in front of someone who already knew everything about sex and therefore could test you to see if you made an ass out of yourself." His humorous postscript to this comment is that the one boy who everyone assumed was "the designated mentor of sexology" later said that he didn't know any more than anybody else!

A similar story is told by Brad:

I was most confused in my high school days. As usual, I heard a lot of the guys bragging about scoring or going all the way with some of the "chicks" in our class. I was really gullible! I thought that all of the guys were telling the truth and I felt real weird because I didn't do those things—partly because of personal convictions and partly because I was scared to death. This really frustrated me and I began to investigate. I found out that most of the stuff I heard was pure B.S. and nothing else. Was I ever relieved!

To these young men masculinity meant sports, liquor, and sex. Regardless of whether they were good in sports, agreed to drink, or had sexual experiences, they tended to measure their worth by these three measuring sticks. The stereotypical nature of these criteria is highly self-evident.

This view of adolescent men is shared not only by the young men themselves but also by the young women they know. However, although many adolescent women reinforce this behavior by dating men who excel at sports, drinking, and sex, others experience an ambivalence about such feats as measures of masculinity. Another short verse in the Larrick and Merriam collection (1973) was written by a 16-year-old young woman, Debbie Milne. It highlights the negative side of this ambivalence:

Do you really think that
by
slapping each other on the back
swearing
grunting
boxing
going to wars
getting a sports car and driving it
300 mph . . . letting your animal

instincts have more say than your brains
having a new girl every week
flexing your muscles as much as
your mouth tells the latest great
feats accomplished. Ex.—drinking 2
bottles of wine in ¾ of an hour
beating your chest
afraid of letting yourselves be gentle
and getting mad when a woman is better
than you
IS REALLY BEING A MAN??????????

Yes, they do.

What It Means To Be a Woman Young females apply very different standards of measurement to themselves: Their concerns revolve around their appearance and their interpersonal skills. Their success in meeting both these standards is measured by how many boys they can attract. For many adolescent girls this is a switch from their preadolescent behavior when they played with boys and were not concerned as to whether their behavior was feminine. This change in behavior at adolescence is in some ways more abrupt for girls than for boys, who have been pressured into sex-appropriate behavior from their early years. There are dozens of stories like Linda's:

When I was little, I was a typical tomboy. I played with all the guys in the neighborhood and enjoyed every minute of it. I also played with the girls in the neighborhood, but there were only a few. Yet a couple of the girls rejected me because I'd play with and stand up for my brothers and their male friends. And then I remember quite suddenly—it wasn't too long after I started my period—that I started getting messages to stop acting like a boy and start acting like a young lady. I remember a couple of things specifically, like my mom saying to me that I had to stop playing football because it was too rough and not a proper thing for a girl my age to do. Next, I can remember that all of a sudden I became interested (or someone interested me) in women's arts like embroidery and knitting. . . . Another thing was that I had a harder time in getting the guys in the neighborhood to let me play in their games. It was like I'd all of a sudden become fragile.

Other young women comment on the need to appear feminine by having lots of "pretty dresses," by being shy and sweet, and by smiling a lot. Moreover, as stated earlier in this book, adolescent (and postadolescent) women are not too discriminating about the men they date; the important thing is to be going out with someone. One woman says, "I went out with a lot of boys I really didn't like because I *couldn't* stay home on Saturday night." Success with the boys leads to acceptance by the other girls and, in general, is the primary status symbol in feminine adolescence.

In order to maintain this status, young women devote a lot of time to their appearance, emulating a standard set by the peer group and reinforced by the mass media. Liz, now in her early 20s, still works to meet the standards she adopted in adolescence:

> *Another thing that I am very much aware of is my need to appear feminine, both to myself and others. . . . This is achieved by wearing a feminine hairstyle, feminine clothes, perfume, and jewelry, and acting like a gentle, tender person. . . . I do this because I feel that this is what men look for in women.*

Obviously, the different parental and cultural expectations of masculinity and femininity have become the standards by which young people evaluate not only their behavior but their own worthiness. Adolescents know that men must be strong, in a variety of ways, and women must please men. Two centuries ago Jean Jacques Rousseau made the following comment:

> The whole education of women ought to be relative to men. To please them, to be useful to them, to make themselves loved and honored by them, to educate them when young, to care for them when grown, to counsel them, to make life sweet and agreeable to them—these are the duties of women at all times, and what should be taught them from their infancy (Rousseau in Millett, 1970, p. 74).

And more than sixty years ago a guidance book by Shannon (1913) stated: "A girl's ambition is to be beautiful; a boy's ambition is to be strong." Although a popular commercial may say to women today, "You've come a long way, Baby," is it really so?

ARE BOYS AND GIRLS REALLY DIFFERENT?

We have seen that the stereotypes of boys and girls *are* different, that parents reflect some of this stereotypic thinking in their handling of the young, and that by adolescence the behavior of young people is adjusted to the predominant stereotypes. However, we also have reasons to believe that in many respects boys and girls are very similar: Despite the stereotypes, they enjoy many of the same things, have the same needs, and are searching for ways to find both love and meaningful work. What differences do, in fact, exist? This section will review the research on this question.

At birth there are some slight differences in the average abilities of boy and girl infants. The male physiological system at birth is less integrated than that of the female; this may explain why male infants fuss and cry more and are generally more irritable. In addition, male infants tend to persist in their fussiness unless attended to, whereas female infants tend to soothe themselves or respond to someone's voice (Lewis & Weinraub, 1974; Moss, 1974). These differences seem to diminish by 3 months, although at 6 months girls are still more able to quiet themselves, show less motor activity, and are more attentive to visual stimuli than boys, who tend to be less attentive, more easily distracted, and more active (Bardwick, 1971).

A landmark study (Goldberg & Lewis, 1969) demonstrates marked differences in children by the age of 13 months. In this study each child was placed with his or her mother in a large room filled with toys. The girls were found to be more reluctant to leave their mothers, wished to return to their mothers, vocalized to the mothers more, and touched their mothers more than did the boys. When placed behind a net barrier and removed from their mothers, the girls tended to stay near the center of the barrier, to cry, and to motion for help. In contrast, the boys were found more often at the ends of the barrier trying to get around it.

In addition, there were differences between boys and girls in the selection of toys. All the toddlers preferred toys that could be manipulated, but the girls preferred toys requiring fine motor coordination. On the other hand the boys chose toys requiring gross motor activity as well as noisy toys. The boys selected more nontoys (such as electric outlets and doorknobs) to play with than did the girls and many of the boys chose, as their favorite activity, rolling the toy lawn mower. The authors concluded, therefore, that girls seemed to be more dependent, to explore less, and to be quieter than boys, who were more independent, more exploratory, and more vigorous.

A follow-up study by Lewis and Weinraub (1974) included fathers as well as mothers and studied infants of 2 years as well as 1 year of age. At age 1 the earlier conclusions were confirmed and extended to show that more physical and verbal behavior was directed at mothers than at fathers. Boys, however, *looked* at their fathers more than at their mothers. At 2 years there was a tendency for both sexes to spend more time in proximity to their fathers and to use more verbal than physical measures in maintaining contact.

It is apparent from such studies that children are closer initially to their mothers, but that their view of the "family" grows to include their fathers by the age of 2 years. By that age boys have also moved farther away from actual physical contact with their parents than have the girls. Beginning at this age there is also evidence, though not definitive, that little boys are more dominant and competitive while little girls are more compliant, especially toward the demands of adults (Maccoby & Jacklin, 1974). Further, there is definitive evidence that by the age of 2 or 2½ little boys are more aggressive than little girls (Maccoby & Jacklin, 1974).

Many of these personality differences are reflected in the friendship patterns of small children that continue into adulthood. Boys tend to collect in gangs where struggles for dominance take place and where they tend to develop a "team spirit." Girls, on the other hand, tend to move in groups of two or three where dominance is not an issue and where intimate conversation is encouraged. These early groupings are forerunners of the later social groupings: Men say they are going "out with the guys"—generally a large enough group so that intimate conversation is discouraged and so that they vie for dominance by telling heroic stories. In contrast, women congregate in "coffee klatches" where two or three women share confidences about their personal lives.

The heavier impact of male socialization is also apparent in the early school years. In a study of 613 elementary-school-age children, Brown (1957) found that the boys showed more consistent preference for masculine activities than girls did for feminine activities. In all attributes of sex-role typing the girls were more variable than the boys. However, by the fourth grade the girls were learning to prefer feminine activities as much as masculine activities, and by the fifth grade the transition was complete, with the girls choosing feminine tasks. A more recent study (Stein, Pohly, & Mueller, 1971) shows that girls are not adversely affected when performing tasks labeled "masculine" whereas boys' achievement motivation drops when confronted with a task labeled "feminine." The knowledge that "it's okay to be a tomboy" allows girls much more latitude than the injunction "*not* to be a *sissy*."

Cognitive Differences and Personality In her earlier work Maccoby (1966) asserts that sex differences in cognitive functioning emerge from the already *acquired* tendencies of girls to be more passive and dependent as well as for boys to be more aggressive and independent. Although in her later review of the literature (Maccoby & Jacklin, 1974) she reneges on this position, her earlier view has had a profound influence on other psychologists. Bardwick (1971) shades this position somewhat by inferring more of a biological predisposition, but nonetheless traces later cognitive differences to early behavioral differences. She argues that girls are quieter and more responsive from infancy and thus develop a personalized, responsive approach to the world whereas the more active, more easily distracted boys rely more on their own explorations and develop a more objective, more internalized pattern of learning. This point of view has been elaborated by Gutmann (1970) in his explanation of two different cognitive styles: the autocentric (personalized and subjective) feminine style and the allocentric (detached and objective) masculine style.

In part such differences coincide with the popular view that girls do better in school than boys because they are more passive and more responsive. Girls, in much of educational thinking, tend to give way sooner to pressures toward conformity than do boys. Margaret Mead is quoted as saying that the trouble with our schools is that they're planned for "nice little girls who want to help the teacher pass out pencils" (in Hughes, 1976, p. 2). Another educational commentator also highlights the same point when he remarks on his own experience as a teacher:

> The difference between teaching an all-boys class and an all-girls class is that when you enter a class of boys and say "Good Morning," half the hands shoot up demanding to know what you mean by "good" and the other half what you mean by "morning." When you say "Good morning" to a class of girls, they all write it down in their notebooks... (Freedman, 1968).

The view illustrated here has for some time been the dominant one in the literature; it emphasizes the compliance of girls and the rebelliousness of boys, the former being much preferred by school systems.

On the other hand, Maccoby and Jacklin's (1974) recent review of the literature suggests that this point of view may have been overemphasized in the past. Maccoby and Jacklin assert that girls are not necessarily more suggestible or responsive than boys, and that boys are not necessarily more analytical or objective. However, they find definite evidence that girls are more verbal and begin to learn a great many things earlier than boys. But the girls lose out to the boys as both mature, and boys are better at visual-spatial and mathematical abilities.

Despite Maccoby and Jacklin's results, few educators are willing to yield their beliefs that boys and girls are different in an educational situation, and that girls are generally easier to get along with than boys. Is it possible that our belief in the differences between boys and girls really creates the appearance of such differences in the classroom? Or is it possible that the girls' earlier maturation and earlier acquisition of verbal and numerical skills provide a means for them to adapt more easily to the school environment in the early years—a pattern that then continues throughout school? Despite the recent testimony of Maccoby and Jacklin, these questions have not yet been clearly answered.

There is some as yet unchallenged evidence from other studies, however, pointing to personality and cognitive differences in boys and girls who are unusually high achievers and/or highly creative individuals. For example, boys who excel at cognitive, analytic tasks tend to be quieter than their peers, to demonstrate more emotional control and attentiveness, and to be more cautious. Indeed, many of these boys might be described as "timid" in their elementary school years. Girls who excel at cognitive tasks, on the other hand, tend to be more impulsive, more aggressive, and louder than their same-sex peers (Kagan & Moss, 1962; Sigel, 1964; Sutton-Smith & Rosenberg, 1961). In fact, possession of higher intellectual and creative interests correlates with the possession of traits commonly attributed to the other sex (Oetzel, 1961).

A secondary conclusion of a creativity study (Fitzgerald, 1966), in fact, suggests that creative women are outgoing and dominant whereas creative men tend to be moody and introspective. My own personal experience as well as a reading of case studies tends to confirm this conclusion: Liz, a creative, intelligent woman is dominant and outgoing whereas Bruce, a creative, intelligent man, is quieter and more introspective. Although deviation from the typical sex role does appear to lead to greater intellectual and creative activity for both sexes, the personalities of intellectual and creative men and women differ. *Cross-sex identification for men and women

---

*They did not, however, vary on the variables discussed by Neugarten (1968) in Chapter 9.

does not result in homogenized human beings nor in a pattern that could be described as *unisex.*

The Need To Achieve The need to achieve has often been assumed to be a masculine trait thereby justifying the greater percentages of men in higher education and the job market. Women, after all, are supposedly fulfilled by creating children and therefore *need* little else by way of achievement. This point of view was recently stated to me by one of my male students who finds it abnormal for women to want anything more than the capacity to create new life.

Despite this accusation there is no evidence that women are lower in achievement motivation than men, although women tend to be less motivated by competition (Maccoby & Jacklin, 1974). The patterns surrounding achievement motivation, however, appear to be different. Girls tend to achieve in order to meet the expectations of others whereas boys tend to adopt patterns of internal evaluation. The result of this is that girls who do well in school do so in *all* subjects whereas boys tend to do well only in subjects that interest them (Bardwick, 1971). Stein and Bailey (1976) sum up the available evidence on the striving for achievement of women by stating that females achieve well by being careful and cautious in their work and by assuming responsibility for failure; in addition, women value achievement but are less confident about it and more anxious about failure than males. Again there appears to be a tie-in for girls and women with meeting or not meeting others' expectations, and this shows up in more concern about failure on their part.

Stein and Baily (1976) point out that as girls reach adolescence, they tone down academic achievement partially as a result of the pressure of feminine role expectations and partially because of realistic expectations of discrimination in the job world. At this point many young girls stop achieving and turn their achievement needs toward the social sphere. They realize that status now comes from attracting an achievement-oriented man and they attempt to do so. This doesn't reflect a lowered need for achievement but rather a sex-appropriate way of obtaining vicarious achievement satisfaction from a world that is still to a large extent closed to females.

Many of these differences between male and female achievement-motivation patterns are reflected in a study of adolescence conducted by Douvan (1972). In this study she assessed "core" character traits in adolescent boys and girls. She found that for a boy to be high in achievement, energy, independence, self-confidence, and realistic self-criticism, he also had to develop an internalized system of values. This system may or may not be a partial internalization of the culture, but it appears to be under the internal control of the adolescent boy. He has developed his own measuring stick and is relatively immune to social approval in his achievement strivings. Thus such a boy may do well in whatever he chooses to do by assessing the situation realistically and accomplishing his goals.

On the other hand, young girls have self-confidence, organized ideas, a high energy level, and a positive feminine identification *if* they have well-developed interpersonal skills. There is no correlation of such traits with an internalized value standard. These girls do well in school, almost *regardless* of their own particular interests, for they are skilled at meeting the expectations of others. Douvan concludes by stating that the lack of a feeling of identity among girls is possibly desirable so that they may more easily take on the identity of their future husbands.

The socialization of achieving women, as Stein and Bailey (1976) point out, does not coincide with current standards of healthy child rearing. Achievement-oriented women are produced by only moderate levels of warmth, a fair amount of permissiveness, and a reinforcement for achievement efforts. Such parental behavior, however, does not produce achievement-oriented men; they come from homes where warmth and parental control are higher (Block, 1973). The difficulties of raising children to achieve in a home where there are children of both sexes are thus highlighted. Well-socialized men with warm, controlling parents achieve; well-socialized women with warm, controlling parents become housewives.

SOCIALIZING MEN AND WOMEN VERSUS SOCIALIZING HUMAN BEINGS

Clearly we raise our children, as we have been raised, to be two different species—the one masculine, the other feminine. Very early little boys are labeled active and aggressive, and most men become so. Little girls are labeled cute and cuddly; by restraining their intellectual aggressiveness and emphasizing their helplessness and with the artificial aids of our fashion and cosmetic industries, most women become so. Much of our differential training of men and women is conveyed by subtle cues about what men and women ought to do. Some of this conditioning process is thrown into high relief by the fictional story of Baby X written by Lois Gould (1972).

In this delightful fantasy scientists have selected one set of parents, Ms. and Mr. Jones, to raise a truly non-sex-typed human being. Such rearing, in our stereotyped culture, requires intensive training and instruction of the parents. This training and instruction is written down in the *Official Instruction Manual* numbering thousands of pages, all of which are necessary to enumerate the sex-typing pressure of our society and to instruct the parents how to avoid such sex typing. The parents are also instructed how to react in the face of the frustration, fear, and anger of well-meaning aunts, uncles, neighbors, "properly" raised children, outraged store clerks, *everybody* else's parents, and the entire school system. In our culture the rearing of an androgynous child is obviously not easy.

In the first weeks of the child's life, the parents upset numerous relatives and other visitors by refusing to term the infant a boy or a girl. The parents themselves had to be *very* careful how they handled their new baby:

> Ms. and Mr. Jones had to be Xtra careful about how they played with little X. They knew if they kept bouncing it up in the air and saying how *strong* and *active* it was, they'd be treating it more like a boy than an X. But if all they did was cuddle it and kiss it and tell it how *sweet* and *dainty* it was, they'd be treating it more like a girl than an X.
>
> On page 1654 of the *Official Instruction Manual,* the scientists prescribed: "plenty of bouncing and plenty of cuddling, *both.* X ought to be strong and sweet and active. Forget about dainty altogether."

As X grew, the scientists gave further instructions to the Joneses:

> They reminded the Joneses to see page 4629 of the Manual, where it said, "Never make Baby X feel *embarrassed* or *ashamed* about what it wants to play with. And if X gets dirty climbing rocks, never say "Nice little Xes don't get dirty climbing rocks."
>
> Likewise, it said, "If X falls down and cries, never say 'Brave little Xes don't cry.' Because, of course, nice little Xes *do* get dirty, and brave little Xes *do* cry. No matter how dirty X gets, or how hard it cries, don't worry. It's all part of the Xperiment."

Finally little X was ready for school. This adventure posed many new difficulties: segregated bathrooms, segregated play, and the problem of "appropriately raised" *other children.* Little X negotiated all these hurdles, finally winning the admiration of the other children by being very good at both boys' and girls' things. Soon the other children were also doing both boys' and girls' things and wearing unisex red-and-white checked overalls to school. This elicited the wrath of their parents, who termed X a disturbing influence and requested its examination by a psychiatrist. All waited with bated breath for the conclusions of this examiner, who finally pronounced, with tears in his eyes, that little X was just about "the *least* mixed-up child he had ever seen!"

This story illustrates well the advantages of being androgynous, and thus fully human; it also illustrates the numerous roadblocks we all put in the way of such a development. Little girls grow up to love and little boys grow up to be strong: How remarkable and yet frightening it is to be confronted with a human being who can both love and be strong. Here is the juncture of the qualities of love and power that mark the process-oriented individual.

SUMMARY

Once again the role-oriented approach and traditional sex roles go hand in hand. Traditional sex roles tend to see the father as the more powerful, authoritative figure and the mother as the more loving and nurturing one. Traditional sex roles thus facilitate the separation of love and power, which is one of the hallmarks of role orientation. In families that divide love and power other characteristics of role orientation also are seen. Communication is limited to what "ought" to be said, rules are determined by what "ought" to be done, and generally the spontaneity and expressiveness of all the family members are limited. This has a particular impact on children as they grow up in such a home; they learn early not to trust their own behavior but to adopt the norms and behaviors of authority figures in their environment. This is a characteristic that continues into adult life. Thus the children learn to yield to those in power, and to try to wield power themselves. The pursuit of power is often at the expense of love.

On the other hand, in process-oriented homes love and power balance each other. Individuals communicate freely with each other without the fear of retribution for stepping outside of expectations. Rules are followed, but the rules are flexible and based on the needs and desires of individuals within the family. In such homes the unique personality of each individual is respected. Moreover, such flexibility and openness do not facilitate the development of traditional sex roles but rather an androgynous approach in which each individual, regardless of sex, is regarded as strong, loving, and capable of devising a life course that best suits his or her talents and abilities regardless of gender. Individuals living in such homes develop in this way despite the heavy sex-role socialization procedures in our society which urge us to be otherwise.

From birth human beings in our society are subjected to the masculine and feminine scripting messages of sex-role stereotypes. Little boys must be strong and active, little girls must be cute and cuddly. These parental injunctions play a large part in early differentiation of the two sexes. By the end of the first year girls are quieter, more dependent, and more attentive than their noisier, exploring, and distractable brothers. By school age, boys are more aggressive whereas girls are more verbal. Differential expectations, in part, lead boys to continue their independent explorations into academic fields in which they begin to excel in high school. On the other hand, girls in high school have learned to tone down their academic abilities and to accent their interpersonal skills. Boys are learning how to be strong while girls are learning how to be caring. This demonstrates the dichotomous development of power and love in the two sexes.

The story of Baby X illustrates that such a dichotomy need not exist. At least in fantasy we can conceive of the blending of power and love in a process-oriented individual. This story also illustrates, however, the difficulties that such child-rearing methods and the children themselves will encounter in our role-oriented society. For the fictional Baby X and its parents such struggles were well worth the reward: a healthy, strong, caring human being. Are any of us willing to risk raising children who will encounter societal opposition so that these children may become fully functioning human beings? It will clearly not be easy.

EXERCISE: RELIVING OUR CHILDHOOD*

The purpose of this exercise is to illuminate the patterns we have learned in our childhood and brought with us into our adult lives. On a piece of paper write down: "The worst thing that ever

---

*Adapted from B. Duhl "The Vulnerability Contract," paper presented at a conference on the family, University of Illinois, Champaign-Urbana, Illinois, February 1977.

*happened to me was. . . ." Then give at least five possible comple-
tions to the sentence.*

*Go back as early in your childhood as possible. Remember
times when you were mad or sad or otherwise upset. Recalling such
incidents does not mean that you did not have a "happy childhood,"
or that there was necessarily anything the matter with yourself or
your parents. We have all had times when we simply did not fit into
the adult pattern going on around us. With a child's understanding
we just could not comprehend why we were being ignored, punished, hurt, left behind, etc. And thus we had an unhappy
experience.*

*Next to each of those five occasions, write down the feelings
you had at that time. Were you sad, scared, or angry? What specific
emotions accompanied those events?*

*Next make a list of things or events that may have upset you
recently. What feelings did you experience when they occurred?*

*Can you see a pattern or connection between your early child-
hood experiences and your current ones? Is there a pattern common to your childhood and your adult life, such as your never
wanting to be ignored or left behind?*

*Finally, if you can recognize the origin of that pattern, can you
do something to change it? According to Wheelis (1973), we enlarge
our sphere of freedom through knowledge. Thus if you are always
unhappy about not being included, for example, in a social event,
and if you can tie this feeling to your childhood feeling of being left
behind, you may be able to reason with yourself. Perhaps you do not
really care about not going to every social event, but you mind
reexperiencing your childhood feeling of being disregarded. Our
experience as an adult and the knowledge we have of our own past
may enable us to reshape our world.*

REFERENCES

Bandura, A., and Walters, R. H., *Social Learning and Personality Development*, New York: Holt, Rinehart & Winston, 1963.

Bardwick, J., *The Psychology of Women: A Study of Biosocial Conflict*, New
York: Harper & Row, 1971.

Barron, F., *Creativity and Psychological Health*, New York: D. Van Nostrand, 1963.

Baumrind, D., "Child Care Practices Anteceding Three Patterns of Preschool Behavior," *Genetic Psychology Monographs,* vol. 75 (1967): 345–88.

Block, J., von der Lippe, A., and Block, J. H., "Sex-Role and Socialization Patterns: Some Personality Concomitants and Environmental Antecedents," *Journal of Consulting and Clinical Psychology,* vol. 41 (1973): 321–41.

Block, J. H., "Conceptions of Sex Role: Some Cross-Cultural and Longitudinal Perspectives," *American Psychologist,* vol. 28 (1973): 512–26.

Bronfenbrenner, U., "Freudian Theories of Identification and Their Derivatives," *Child Development,* vol. 31 (1960): 15–40.

Bronfenbrenner, U., "Toward a Theoretical Model for the Analysis of Parent-Child Relationships in a Social Context," in J. Glidewell, ed., *Parental Attitude and Child Behavior,* Conference of Community Mental Health Research, Washington University, St. Louis, Mo., 1961, pp. 90–109.

Brown, D. G., "Masculinity-Femininity Development in Children," *Journal of Consulting Psychology,* vol. 21 (1957): 197–202.

Clapp, W. F., "Dependence and Competence in Children: Parental Treatment of Four Year Old Boys," unpublished dissertation, University of Colorado, 1967.

Douvan, E., "Sex Differences in Adolescent Character Process," in J. Bardwick, ed., *Readings on the Psychology of Women,* New York: Harper & Row, 1972.

Esty, J. F., "Early and Current Parent-Child Relationships Perceived by College Student Leaders and Non-Leaders," unpublished dissertation, Purdue University, Lafayette, Ind., 1968.

Fitzgerald, E., "The Measurement of Openness to Experience: A Study of Regression in the Service of the Ego," unpublished dissertation, University of California, Berkeley, 1966.

Freedman, R., "Lines from a Ladies' Seminary," in *Book World, The Washington Post,* August 18, 1968.

Goldberg, S., and Lewis, M., "Play Behavior in the Year-Old Infant: Early Sex Differences," *Child Development,* vol. 40 (1969): 21–31.

Gould, L. X., "A Fabulous Child's Story," *Ms. Magazine,* vol. 1 (December 1972): 74–77+.

Gutmann, D., "Female Ego Styles and Generational Conflict," in J. Bardwick, E. Douvan, M. Horner, and D. Gutmann, eds., *Feminine Personality and Conflict,* Brooks/Cole, 1970.

Hartley, R. E., "Sex Role Pressures and the Socialization of the Male Child," *Psychological Reports*, vol. 5 (1959): 457–63.

Helson, R., "Women Mathematicians and the Creative Personality," *Journal of Consulting and Clinical Psychology*, vol. 36 (1971): 210–20.

Hoffman, M., " Power Assertion by the Parent and Its Impact on the Child," *Child Development*, vol. 31 (1960): 129–43.

Hughes, H., "Women's Creativity: The State of Knowledge about the Creative Process—A Feminist Perspective," paper presented at the American Association of University Women, Chicago, April 30, 1976.

Johnson, M. M., "Sex Role Learning in the Nuclear Family," *Child Development*, vol. 34 (1963): 319–33.

Kagan, J., Hosken, B., and Watson, S., "The Child's Symbolic Conceptualization of the Parents," *Child Development*, vol. 39 (1968): 625–36.

Kagan, J., and Lemkin, J., "The Child's Differential Perception of Parental Attributes," *Journal of Abnormal and Social Psychology*, vol. 61 (1960): 440.

Kagan, J., and Moss, H. A., *Birth to Maturity*, New York: John Wiley & Sons, 1962.

Kohlberg, L., "A Cognitive Developmental Analysis of Children's Sex Role Concepts and Attitudes," in E. E. Maccoby, ed., *The Development of Sex Differences*, Stanford, Calif.: Stanford University Press, 1966.

Komarovsky, M., *Blue-Collar Marriage*, New York: Vintage, 1967.

Kubler-Ross, E., *Death: The Final Stage of Growth*, Englewood Cliffs, N.J.: Prentice-Hall, 1976.

Lang, L. J., "Responsibility as a Function of Authority in Family Relationships," unpublished dissertation, Columbia University, 1969.

Larrick, N., and Merriam, E., *Male and Female Under 18*, New York: Avon, 1973.

Lefkowitz, M., Walder, L., and Eron, L., "Punishment, Identification, and Aggression," *Merrill-Palmer Quarterly*, vol. 9 (1963): 159–74.

LeShan, E., *What Makes Me Feel This Way?*, New York: Collier Books, 1972.

Lewis, M., and Weinraub, M., "Sex of Parent and Sex of Child: Socioemotional Development," in R. C. Friedman, R. M. Richart, and R. L. Van de Wiele, eds., *Sex Differences in Behavior*, New York: John Wiley & Sons, 1974.

Lowen, A., *Depression and the Body,* New York: Coward, McCann & Geoghegan, 1972.

Lynn, D., *Parental and Sex Role Identification,* McCutcheon, 1969.

Lynn, D. B., "The Process of Learning Parental and Sex-Role Identification," *Journal of Marriage and the Family,* vol. 28 (1966): 446–70.

Maccoby, E., "Sex Differences in Intellectual Functioning," in E. E. Maccoby, ed., *The Development of Sex Differences,* Stanford, Calif.: Stanford University Press, 1966.

Maccoby, E. E., and Jacklin, C. N., *The Psychology of Sex Differences,* Stanford, Calif.: Stanford University Press, 1974.

Meyer, J., and Sobieszek, B., "Effect of a Child's Sex on Adult Interpretations of Its Behavior," *Developmental Psychology,* vol. 6 (1972): 42–48.

Millett, K., *Sexual Politics,* New York: Avon Books, 1970.

Mischel, W., "A Social-Learning View of Sex Differences in Behavior," in E. E. Maccoby, ed., *The Development of Sex Differences,* Stanford, Calif.: Stanford University Press, 1966.

Moss, H. A., "Early Sex Differences and Mother-Infant Interaction," in R. C. Friedman, R. M. Richart, and R. L. Van de Wiele, eds., *Sex Differences in Behavior,* New York: John Wiley & Sons, 1974.

Moulton, R. W., Burnstein, E., Liberty, P. G., and Altucher, N., "Patterning of Parental Affection and Disciplinary Dominance as a Determinant of Guilt and Sex Typing," *Journal of Personality and Social Psychology,* vol. 4 (1966): 356–63.

Nin, A., *Diary, 1931–1934,* New York: The Swallow Press, 1966.

Oetzel, R., "The Relationship between Sex Role Acceptance and Cognitive Abilities," unpublished master's thesis, Stanford University, 1961.

Rubin, J. Z., Provenzano, F. J., and Luria, Z., "The Eye of the Beholder: Parents' Views on Sex of Newborns," *American Journal of Orthopsychiatry,* vol. 44 (1974): 512–19.

Sanford, R. N., "The Dynamics of Identification," *Psychological Review,* vol. 62 (1955): 106–18.

Satir, V., *Peoplemaking,* Palo Alto, Calif.: Science and Behavior Books, 1972.

Sears, R. R., "Identification as a Form of Behavior Development," in D. B. Harris, ed., *The Concept of Development,* Minneapolis: University of Minnesota Press, 1957.

Shannon, T. W., *Self Knowledge,* S. A. Mullikin, 1913.

Sigel, I., "Sex Differences in Cognitive Functioning Re-Examined: A Functional Point of View," paper presented at the Society for Research in Child Development, Berkeley, California, 1964.

Skolnick, A. S., and Skolnick, J. H., *Family in Transition,* Boston: Little, Brown, 1971.

Starr, B. D., "Disciplinary Attitudes of Both Parents and Authoritarianism in Their Children," unpublished dissertation, Yeshiva University, New York, 1965.

Stein, A. H., and Bailey, M. M., "The Socialization of Achievement Orientation in Females," *Psychological Bulletin,* vol. 80 (1976): 345–66.

Stein, A. H., Pohly, S. R., and Mueller, E., "The Influence of Masculine, Feminine, and Neutral Tasks on Children's Achievement Behavior, Expectancies of Success, and Attainment Values," *Child Development,* vol. 42 (1971): 195–207.

Sutton-Smith, B., and Rosenberg, B. G., "Peer Perceptions of Impulsive Behavior," *Merrill-Palmer Quarterly,* vol. 7 (1961): 233–38.

Walters, J., and Stinnett, N., "Parent-Child Relationships: A Decade Review of the Research," *Journal of Marriage and the Family,* vol. 33 (1971): 70–111.

Wheelis, A., *How People Change,* New York: Harper & Row, 1973.

Young, L., *Life among the Giants,* New York: McGraw-Hill, 1965.

11

Ever-Present Mothers and Peripheral Fathers: Is the Traditional Pattern Changing?

In the last chapter we examined the results of rearing children in role-oriented homes in which power and love are separated from each other. Such role orientation is more likely to occur in homes where traditional sex-role stereotypes are upheld and men and women perform very different tasks. Similarly, it is likely that nontraditional sex-role beliefs, which lead to the sharing of tasks, would facilitate the development of a more egalitarian power structure in the home, a more balanced view of love and power, and a process-oriented home environment. Moreover, such a power structure is more likely to occur in homes in which the mother and father both work. In this chapter, we shall examine what happens to children whose parents do not follow the traditional patterns.

Several reasons account for the fact that many women stay home rather than go to work. One such reason is based on the belief (verbalized more often by men than women) that children must

Among humans, too, it appears that there are alternatives to the mother's feeding function, but no alternative to the sustained physical presence of a mothering one in the life of the infant. There is no evidence that the father's physical contact with the child provides any special "paternal" quality. . . .

Leonard Benson, **Fatherhood: A Sociological Perspective**

[The mother/child attachment] begins before the moment of birth, when mother and child are still one, although they are two. Birth changes the situation in some respects, but not as much as it would appear. The child, while now living outside of the womb, is still completely dependent on the mother.

Erich Fromm, **The Art of Loving**

have their mothers available twenty-four hours a day. The assumption of "oneness" between mother and child has provided a relatively stable pivot point around which men have built their theories of the family and the world. There is predictability and continuity in "knowing" that children need women to care for them. Such a theory frees men from the responsibility of child care so that they can build their empires in the larger world and return to the domestic hearth only at times of their own choosing. Furthermore, the nucleus of mother-child provides a circle of warmth, at least in fantasy, from which men can draw assistance and reassurance in their own times of need. There is no necessity for developing such qualities of warmth within themselves since these qualities are already "naturally" provided by the women who remain at home. Finally, the belief that women must care for children not only effectively cuts competition in half by barring women from the "real" world but it also means that, no matter how badly men fare in the male occupational arena, they can still see themselves as superior to the women at home who have not been allowed to enter the contest.

According to some people, women have a "maternal instinct" that leads them to "choose" to remove themselves from real competition and to provide a warm "nest" from which men can sally forth each morning and to which they can return each evening. This belief has been a great comfort to role-oriented men—and some women—who prefer to see masculine and feminine sex roles as stable and unchanging. Such a belief has been supported also by numerous theorists. For example, Benson (1968) comments that there is no substitute for a "mothering one," and I assume he means to say "the mother" since he makes it quite clear that he is not referring to the father. Moreover, Fromm in his earlier publications subscribed, as other psychoanalysts have done and still do, to the notion that something about the birth process creates a unique, supposedly biologically based, relationship between mother and child. This relationship could not be supplanted by any other caretaker, particularly not by a male caretaker who did not have the capacity to give the child the required unconditional love. Talcott Parsons also argues for the necessity of motherhood based on biological factors:

> ... a certain importance may well attach to the biological fact that, except for relatively rare plural births, it is unusual for human births to the same mother to follow each other at intervals of less than a year with any regularity. It is, we feel, broadly in the first year of life that a critical phase of the socialization process, which requires the most exclusive attention of a certain sort from the mother, takes place (Parsons & Bales, 1955, p. 18).

We might assume that, according to Parsons, this year was not provided to assist the mother's recovery after childbirth nor was it supposed to give her a respite—physiologically and psychologically—from her involvement with child bearing. Instead, Parsons argues specifically that the mother was to devote herself to her child during its first year of life.

There are, however, a great array of arguments today that challenge the prevalent assumption that children need their mothers. Many studies of child rearing have found that the American child is overmothered and overmanaged and grows up "lacking in initiative, excessively dependent on others and physically soft" (Rossi, 1964, p. 119). A mother with little to do but supervise her children may smother them with her attentions, allowing little room for independence and self-sufficiency. "Full-time motherhood is neither sufficiently absorbing to the woman nor beneficial to the child to justify it as an exclusive occupation" (Rossi, 1964, p. 119).

Other evidence points to the fact that mothering may not even be innate. The number of children who are neglected, battered, and abused indeed stands as evidence against the "naturalness" of the maternal instinct.* Many women, pushed into motherhood by others' expectations, which they have absorbed as their own, are *definitely* not good mothers. They either leave their children to meet their own needs or expect them to meet the needs of the mother. When the vulnerable and dependent infants are unable to do so, they often serve as objects for the mother's wrath. Is this evidence of a "maternal instinct"?

There is evidence, on the other hand, that "mothering" is learned. One learns how to be responsive to, concerned about, and protective of another human being. For example, mothers of premature infants who are deprived of their babies for a substantial period of time following birth do not appear to mother as well as those not so deprived. Such deprived mothers hold and smile at the baby less, and show less attachment for their child (Leifer, Leiderman, Barnett, & Williams, 1972). Even Harlow's female monkeys (see Chapter 2, p. 53) which had themselves been deprived of mothers, were unable to mother their own infants when they could be enticed into conceiving and bearing them (Harlow, Harlow, Dodsworth, & Arling, 1966). All the evidence is not in, but it seems safe to conclude that there is no such thing as a "maternal instinct."

Yet men still use the "maternal instinct" argument and contend that since women must care for children, real power belongs in the hands of men. They have built their power base on the premise that women's place is in the home. As early as 1916, a sociologist commented on the social implications of the motherhood myth:

> There is, to be sure, a strong and fervid insistence on the "maternal instinct," which is popularly supposed to characterize all women equally, and to furnish them with an all-consuming desire for parent-

---

*These are the most obvious instances of poor mothering. Many other instances might include examples of emotional neglect, lack of interest, and lack of warmth.

hood, regardless of the personal pain, sacrifice, and disadvantage involved. In the absence of all verifiable data, however, it is only common sense to guard against accepting as a fact of human nature a doctrine which we might well expect to find in use as a means of social control (Hollingworth, 1916).

Indeed men do use the "maternal instinct" as a means of social control. Power in our society, which is associated with tangible income and production, is also controlled by men. It has been a comfort to many men—as stated earlier—to limit competition for this power to men only. Komarovsky's (1973) Ivy League college men (see Chapter 7, pp. 227–228), who were liberated on the surface, believed that they would not encounter problems in their domestic lives, since their wives, however bright or competent, would naturally care for their children. In this manner men have been able to free themselves of child-rearing responsibilities and yet have progeny to carry on their name. What will happen if the underpinnings are pulled out from beneath this point of view? Perhaps men as well as women will accept the fact that we all become more fully human if we all learn to care for each other and for our children and if we all can seek satisfaction in the exercise of our other talents. Incidentally, in such a way we will more closely approximate a process-oriented approach to living.

LEARNING BY WHAT WE DO

Individuals learn certain characteristics as they accommodate themselves to the job at hand. In their occupational lives men currently learn to become rational, objective, and detached. In their domestic lives women learn to become emotional, subjective, and involved with the daily lives of other human beings. In a process-oriented life-style both sexes would have the opportunity to develop both sets of characteristics. However, in the traditional role-oriented model, men develop their rationality and women their emotionality as they suit their personalities to their circumstances.

The qualities required for successful "mothering" are generally believed to be beneficial ones. Women who care for children develop responsiveness and flexibility. They develop the capacity for doing several things at once. They learn, or they are continually reminded of the fact, that we are all human and subject to the tragedies of the human condition as well as to its joys. Such characteristics broaden and deepen the personality: We are more truly human creatures when we know both our potential and our limitations. Janeway stresses this point:

> One learns (or learns to use) patience, intuitive insight and imagination, to enjoy the immediate moment in anticipation of change. . . . One learns a good deal about time—that it passes, even if one sits still. . . . Most of all, one learns other people's and one's own limits. . . . It is the kind of knowledge that is learned on the way to maturity no matter how the path winds (1971, p. 150).

These beneficial character traits, however, do not develop in all women who rear children. Child rearing is a "heavy-duty job," and many women find themselves snowed under by the demands of the task. Arlene, a student of mine who has managed to stay on top of her child-rearing duties and go to school as well—she is divorced and has six children—is most emphatic about the demands of raising children. Incensed by a patronizing male remark referring to her nonworking status, she replied, "I am a mother and I work like hell and I hope to alleviate this strenuous situation soon by getting a 'job'!"

From Arlene's comment we can guess that many women do not survive the task of child rearing. They never learn to balance the insistent demands of others against their own. They do not learn how to carry out a task or pursue a thought in spite of constant interruptions. Such women succumb to lassitude and accept defeat. Their needs and their desires are not important. In the uproar of daily domestic life they lose their spirit, their self-control, and their self-esteem. They accept the societal injunction that they have no function but to serve others, and often do so without appreciation. The message is obvious: Others are important and the woman's self counts for little.

Men who stay at home to rear children have become aware of both the benefits and disadvantages of raising children. Those fathers who have survived the desperation of living with interruptions have learned increased flexibility and developed an automatic tuning system that can filter through many conflicting sounds, sensations, and ideas at once (see Roache, 1972). Indeed, this is not a bad trait to possess in a complex world.

Most fathers, however, in avoiding child rearing because of its disadvantages have also missed the advantages. They fail, therefore, to develop the flexibility learned by most women. As Fasteau (1974) states:

Being a father, in the sense of having sired and having children, is part of the masculine image; but fathering, the actual care of children, is not. Men who spend a lot of time taking care of their children— washing, dressing, feeding, teaching, comforting, and playing with them—aren't doing quite what they should be.

Therefore, many men never learn to be responsive or flexible or to do more than one thing at a time.

How exasperating it is for a woman, for example, to watch her supposedly liberated husband working in the kitchen. He feels free to insist that he be granted absolute peace, silence, and an absence of interruptions from children, animals, and telephones. "But I can only do one thing at a time," he barks to intruders. Or what should we say about another husband, doing his stint of child care, who turns to an 18-month-old infant, hands her a bottle and a blanket as the mother departs, and says firmly, "You don't bother me, kid, and I won't bother you." He then returns to the writing of a historical masterpiece. It is my firm opinion that all of us—men as well as women—benefit from a few years of child care. It makes us flexible, it makes us responsive, and it removes any illusion that we are superhuman or can control and manage our environment through increasingly more abstract scientific techniques. Child care is one of the institutions that reminds us of our humanity—for those who survive its more desperate moments.* And humanity is one thing our entire race can profit from. Why should women alone reap the benefits?

THE IMPACT OF FULL-TIME MOTHERING

Rossi (1964) points out that in the United States, "for the first time in the history of any known society, motherhood has become a full-time occupation for adult women" (p. 106). In earlier times

---

*Since some of us at any given task do not "survive"—that is, acquire increased skills and adaptability to the task—it needs to be reemphasized that child care—just as any other function—may not be for everybody. This is true, however, for women as well as men and *not* more true for men than women. The problem is that men tend to argue that they are less fit for this task than women. A recent conversation comes to mind that is relevant to this point. A 30-year-old father of three young children in my class was arguing that his wife was more suited to child care than he, and that he simply didn't have the personality for this task, because after four or five hours with the kids he became nervous and jumpy. This being so, he needed to explore what he could do in the world of work while his wife remained at home. I asked him to describe his wife when he returned home after a long day and he replied, "The other day, for example, she did get a little tired and was sitting in the dining room crying and screaming at the kids; she'd had a bad day." And yet, he maintains that he is unsuited for child care because he becomes "nervous and jumpy"? Who doesn't at times?

women were absorbed in tasks beyond the narrow confines of the modern-day suburban home. The merchant's wife and the pioneer farmer's wife of the eighteenth and nineteenth centuries were busy with their spinning, planting, churning, and preserving, and often left their children on their own. Such women did not have time to worry about their children's development, organize their play, or discuss their problems. However, in the mid-twentieth century this is not the case. American women are preoccupied with their children and with their housewifery ten to twelve hours a day.

Has this been beneficial? Rossi (1964) states that it has not been. She refers to the lack of initiative, independence, and stamina of American middle-class children, and goes on to point out that although our children have more toys, more amusements, and more attention than children in other societies, past or present, they show more boredom, more rebellion, and more delinquency than children in any number of other societies. Much, but not all, of this can be traced to the mother-child tie, which is initially too strong and thus does not lead to easy separation or growth toward independence. We may, in fact, be "smothering" our children. Other psychologists, such as Hartley (1959), suggest that this may be the case and urge mothers to get out and work at least part of the time. A moderate amount of distance from our children may benefit them in a number of ways.

CHILDREN OF THE WORKING MOTHER

Numerous studies have assessed the impact of working mothers on children. Their findings are not totally conclusive, but they suggest that if the mother likes working—which often means she is middle-class and working at a job of her choice—the effects on the child are relatively beneficial. Rossi states that in general there is "no evidence of negative effects traceable to maternal employment"; that there are no negative effects after 8 years of age; and that, it appears at the moment, there are no negative effects before that (1964, pp. 108–109). Hoffman, after a thorough review of the literature, arrives at the same conclusion:

> Thus the data about the mother's emotional state indicate that the working mother who obtains satisfaction from her work, who has adequate arrangements so that her dual role does not involve undue strain, and who does not feel so guilty that she overcompensates is

likely to do quite well (at mothering) and, under certain conditions, better than the nonworking mother (1974, p. 142).

A major study in 1962 (Yarrow, Scott, DeLeeuw, & Heinig) found that satisfied homemakers were the best mothers, dissatisfied homemakers the worst mothers, and that working women fell somewhere in-between. However, women who liked their work were more satisfied with their mothering than those who did not. The next question is, who is likely to be a dissatisfied homemaker? Birnbaum (1971) gives a partial answer to this question in a study that compares working women and homemakers, both of whom had graduated from college "with distinction" fifteen to twenty-five years prior to the study. Among these bright women it was found that the professional women were clearly higher in morale, and that the homemakers had lower self-esteem and a lower sense of personal competence even with respect to child care. The homemakers felt less attractive, expressed more concern over "who they were," and indicated greater feelings of loneliness. Homemakers were more insecure than both married professional women and professional women who had never married. Whereas professional women who had children said they lacked time, the homemakers complained of a lack of challenge and creative involvement. Finally, married professional women said that their children enriched their lives and heightened their self-fulfillment; the homemakers saw their children more in the light of a personal sacrifice. The conclusion from the data is that able, educated homemakers probably tend to be "dissatisfied." In the light of these two studies, it may be suggested that such a homemaker would be doing both herself and her children a favor if she went to work.

Other evidence supports this point of view. Kligler (1954) found that women who worked because of their interest in their job were more likely than those who worked for financial reasons to feel that their children's behavior improved as a result of their work. Kappell and Lambert (1972) found that 9–16-year-old daughters of full-time working mothers who liked their work had higher self-esteem than the daughters of women who worked for financial reasons or of women who stayed home. Hoffman (1974) stated that a woman who feels positive about her job has better interaction with her family. However, liking one's work and working because one wishes to are not necessarily the same. Thus Coopersmith (1967) found higher self-esteem in children of working mothers who worked because they wanted to, whereas Hoffman (1974) found the evidence on this point inconclusive.

Two earlier reviews of the literature also failed to find anything particularly negative about working mothers, even though these studies were done at a time when the social climate was not conducive to maternal employment. Stolz (1961), in reviewing studies between 1946 and 1960, found no significant relationships between maternal employment and delinquency, adolescent adjustment, grades in high school, or dependent and independent behavior of 5-year-old children. She concluded that "maternal employment is less important to the behavior of children than the psychological condition within the home." Siegel and Haas (1963) also found no negative effects upon children as a result of maternal employment nor any differences in child-rearing practices between working and nonworking mothers.

Working mothers do not neglect their children or allow them to run free, entirely without supervision. On the contrary, there is evidence that working professional mothers "try harder" to be good mothers as a compensation for the hours they have to devote to their jobs. Such overcompensation may result in lowered independence and responsibility for their children, as the mothers may indeed require too little of their children. Yet this does not appear to be the case with lower-middle-class working women who expect their children to assume more household responsibilities (Hoffman, 1974). Thus the young children of working mothers are not necessarily more dependent or independent than other children. In fact, in adolescence there appears to be little difficulty for these youngsters to attain independence, whereas children with mothers at home often encounter difficulties in growing up (Hoffman, 1974).

Research on Infants and Children Although as Rossi (1964) stated, we do not know enough about the effects of maternal employment on small infants, to date we know nothing negative. Hoffman concurs:

> Obviously the effects of maternal employment on the infant depend on the extent of the mother's absence and the nature of the substitute care—whether it is warm, stimulating, and stable. . . . We have little solid evidence concerning the effect on the younger child (1974, p. 157).

We do have a few studies on the small child in day-care settings.

Usually the results are good and the infant appears in at least as good physical and emotional shape as the home-reared child. However, most of this evidence is gathered at university-located, well-run day-care centers and the results may not be applicable to the nonuniversity population or the run-of-the-mill day-care center.

Bee (1974), in a review of the available literature, found that there are no anxious behaviors, nor does less familial attachment occur, in infants raised in *good* day-care centers if there are no other factors involved, such as troubled homes. In fact, Bee stated that such children are more assertive than mother-reared children; this should be a positive factor in their growth. Moreover, she goes on to state that, on the basis of the current evidence, there is no reason to think that the age at which the child is placed in a day-care center makes any difference. This opinion finds some support from a study showing that children reared in day-care centers from before the age of 1 did not differ from their home-reared peers on measures of attachment to the mother. However, the *quality* of the relationship with the mother was critical (Caldwell, Wright, Honig, & Tannenbaum, 1970).

In addition, cross-cultural studies on group-reared children showed no evidence of emotional problems. Kaffman (1965) found no greater incidence of emotional problems in kibbutz children than in home-reared children, although this situation may differ from our day-care situation in that the Israeli parents are available on a more regular basis than the American parents, who may work a great distance from home. In a similar study, Rabin (1958) found some difficulties in interpersonal relationships in kibbutz-raised children, but these disappeared by the age of 10.

We might hypothesize, particularly in relation to the Israeli studies, that group-reared children may have a less intense relationship with *one* adult—generally the mother—and that the capacity for intense intimate relationships may thus never exist to the same extent that it does in middle-class America. Nevertheless, if we consider the difficulties many of our marriages are undergoing, and if we also consider the high rate of divorce in the United States, the tendency to put less pressure for intimacy on a single relationship may not be altogether a bad thing.

The literature, though, is too sparse to allow us to draw any firm conclusions. But it is reassuring to note that no negative effects have been noted (Bee, 1974). We can finally lay to rest the conclusion Bowlby (1951) came to in his study of institutionalized infants, whom he found emotionally, physically, and cognitively deprived: His conclusion was that children must have their mother at home. However, Bowlby's infants lived in drab institutions without much holding, cuddling, or stimulation, and as a result they really suffered. We are not speaking here of institutionalizing our children but rather of putting them in a reasonably comfortable and stimulating environment for several hours a day. This is *in addition to* and *not a substitute for* the loving care of one or both parents.

Small children *need* love, attention, and physical contact as well as an opportunity to enlarge their cognitive framework in a stimulating environment. Small children also require some stability in the child-care situation. However, we have no evidence that such love, stimulation, and stability must be provided solely by the mother—or the father.

Differential Effects on Boys and Girls Although the results are far from conclusive, mothers working appears to have differential effects on boys and girls. Daughters of working mothers seem frequently to be more responsible and independent as well as self-reliant, aggressive, dominant, and disobedient (Siegel & Haas, 1963); as we have seen, many of these characteristics are considered masculine. Other researchers report that the daughters of working women are relatively independent, autonomous, and active (Douvan, 1963). However, the effect on boys is less clear-cut. Some evidence suggests that perhaps boys benefit in the same way as girls (Dizard, 1968; Hoffman, 1961). On the other hand, other evidence suggests that boys may become more dependent and obedient if the mother works and if the masculine side of the family reflects a generally diminished status (Nye & Hoffman, 1963).

There are two possible explanations of the varying findings on the sons of working mothers. On the basis of the identification theory, Hartley (1959) suggests that children are most responsible and independent when the same-sex parent has a full-time job and the opposite-sex parent a part-time job. This assumes again a balance of power in the home so that the full-time working parent is dominant and the same-sex child benefits by identification with the dominant parent. At the same time this child should enjoy the support and affection of the other parent.

The second explanation is really part and parcel of the first. On the basis of a general assumption that power in the home is limited and that the full-time working parent has more of this power, we might argue that if the mother works, the father loses power and esteem. In fact, some studies of lower-class families show this to be the case: If the mother works, the children are less likely to admire the father (Douvan, 1963; Kappell & Lambert, 1972; Propper, 1972). However, this situation is complicated by the fact that the mother in this family is probably working for financial reasons, thereby implying that the father is inadequate as a breadwinner. If the father is not admired in his home, then the sons will suffer, and the negative effects of working mothers are explainable.

But if we assume that the father does not suffer when the mother works, and that the mother and father both work because they *want* to, it might be possible for both to be powerful figures as well as loving people to their children. In terms of a process-oriented theory—in which power expands as people feel better about themselves—two working, fully functioning parents should have beneficial effects on children of both sexes. The assumption that power is limited and that the mother, by working, takes something away from her husband and other males in the house is a very harmful one: Such an assumption can become a self-fulfilling prophecy. Then, indeed, there would be little hope that we could raise fully functioning men and women in the same nuclear family, for one sex would always be more dominant than the other. In other words, the husband or wife would be more dominant than his or her spouse.

Adolescents and Youths: Effects of Maternal Employment In contrast to the small amount of data available on the effects of maternal employment on infants, we have a lot of data on the effects that maternal employment may have had on adolescents and young people in their early 20s. In general, the results appear to be beneficial: Both sexes have less traditional sex-role stereotypes and women, in particular, have a higher self-esteem. Hoffman sums up the current findings:

> ... the data indicate that maternal employment is associated with less traditional sex-role concepts, more approval of maternal employment, and a higher evaluation of female competence. These in turn should imply a more positive self-concept for the daughters of working compared with non-working mothers and better social adjustment, but there are only indirect data on this (1974, p. 136).

Hoffman goes on to state that daughters of working mothers seem to have higher achievement aspirations. Various studies have shown that these young women have both higher academic and career aspirations (Almquist & Angrist, 1971; Ginzberg, 1971; Tangri, 1969). These daughters also have scored lower on measures of femininity (Douvan, 1963), and are more likely than daughters of nonworking mothers to name their mothers as the women they most admire (Baruch, 1972b; Douvan, 1963). Again the literature shows that young women profit from having a working mother, whereas the evidence on the impact of working mothers on young men is less clear-cut.

One study (Vogel, Broverman, Broverman, Clarkson, & Rosenkrantz, 1970), however, showed that men who were sons of working mothers did perceive significantly smaller differences between men and women, and that men whose mothers worked had a higher estimate of their own sex than men whose mothers did not work. These men saw their fathers as expressive as well as competent and thus thought better of them. We must note, though, that these young men are middle-class university students, and thus we might assume that the working mothers were often working because they *wanted* to and not because they had to. Therefore, as compared to the studies cited earlier on lower-class youth, there was perhaps no denigration of the father as a result of the mother's working. This suggests a more process-oriented view of unlimited power where parents are not engaged in a zero-sum game requiring that if one is strong, the other must be weak.

In this same study, similar but stronger results were found for females so that women with employed mothers differed more from women with nonemployed mothers than men in similar situations differed from each other. Again, sex-role stereotypes were less obvious; women had an enhanced perception of the value of women and saw that men could be expressive and women competent without either sex losing the traditional traits. Similar results for women were found in Baruch's (1972a) replication of Goldberg's (1968) experiment in which female students were asked to evaluate articles signed alternately by Joan and John McKay. Unlike the women in Goldberg's experiment, the daughters of working mothers did not downgrade the articles by women: "It is women whose mothers have not worked who devalue feminine competence." In addition, Meier (1972) found that daughters of working women, particularly of high-status working women, were strongly in favor of social equality and did not hold the traditional views of feminine subservience.

In conclusion, it appears that in homes that function well, where both parents work and enjoy working, and where both parents share the housework even though women probably do most of it, the children are less susceptible to traditional, stereotyped sex-role perceptions. We might suppose that both parents are similarly competent and expressive, and that the children thus identify with adults who balance rather than separate the capacities for power and love. We might assume that this was so in the case of a woman named Cynthia who is the daughter of a working mother. Let's now listen to Cynthia's story.

CYNTHIA

A month or so before I was born, my father, then a carpenter, had an accident in which he almost lost his life. He and my mother were both in the hospital at the time I was born. Both my parents, but particularly my father, were expecting a boy. In fact, the cigars they bought to announce my birth, each with a band reading "It's a boy," had to be tied with pink ribbons.

Because of the seriousness of the accident, my father was unable to leave the house for several months after his release from the hospital. He, with the help of a female cousin, took care of me for the first year or so of life, while my mother went to work to support us. I therefore received most of my early upbringing from my father. When he recovered, he returned to work in a different field. My mother at this point did not quit, but retained her job, leaving me in the care of my grandmother and later of babysitters. I can never remember feeling neglected by this arrangement, because I could feel the love and concern of my parents when they were with me. When we spent time together as a family, I was never left out of anything and my every want and need were catered to.

My mother, careerwise, has always been more successful than my father. She is extremely intelligent and because of this, rose quickly through the ranks of her company, becoming a manager and the highest-paid woman ever in the company. Besides her job, she takes care of all the household tasks, including housework, cooking, and paying the bills. She also attends college classes a couple of nights a week and is working toward a business degree.

My father, on the other hand, has also risen in his company, but not to the degree of my mother. He seems to be not as ambitious as my mother, possibly because his company offers him no further hope of advancement. In viewing my dad in comparison with other men I've known, he seems to relate on a more personal basis. He also enjoys cooking and will not balk at doing the dishes or other tasks so that my mother can rest.

Being an only child, raised within the framework of this type of family relationship, it is quite strange for me to conceive of a woman's place being in the home and the man's world being his career. I feel there is no question as to whether I will have a career. That I will work is taken for granted. I can't imagine having to sit at home all day and take care of children. I feel that if I do have children, I will probably return to work immediately, leaving their care to a babysitter, knowing that the love and nurture I give them when at home will be great enough to sustain them, as it was in my life.

Although I was raised in what many would call a liberated setting, there were still signs of sex-role typing. When I was young, I was much more concerned with cowboys than I was with dolls. This may be because I was used to watching T.V. with my dad—mother was often too busy—or because of the great number of little boys in our neighborhood. When I started hauling my cowboys and Indians around in my doll carriage, my parents decided that I needed more dolls, and although they never said anything, every Christmas there were one or two new dolls under the tree.

My mother, although she may be considered in many ways liberated, was willing to give up her well-paying job when my father talked about moving and going into a new field of work. She believed it was the right thing to do and conveyed this feeling to me. I know that in speaking of equality the woman's career should not take the backseat to the man's career, but I feel that if faced with the same choice, my husband's career would probably take precedence over mine.

One aspect of my upbringing with which I am particularly upset is the high degree of dependence I have on my parents. Being an only child and a girl, I'm sure, influenced my parents to overprotect me and cater to me. Instead of rebelling against them, I have let them rule many aspects of my life. I'm con-

vinced that everything they want me to do is for my own good and that by obeying their rules I can secure their love and affection, which is very important to me. In many ways I would like to be free and make a life of my own, yet I'm afraid of losing everything I have now, especially the degree of closeness we share. Deep down I enjoy being protected, and perhaps I will remain dependent on others by choice, for the rest of my life.

IMPLICATIONS

Cynthia's case illustrates many of the benefits and at least one of the disadvantages that might accrue from having a working mother. She is more egalitarian in her outlook on the roles of men and women than many individuals, and takes it for granted that she will have a career. However, she also believes that she is more dependent on her parents than are her peers. In part this may be accounted for by the fact that she was an only child and thus received more adult attention when she was younger than do children in a larger family. But such dependence may also be due to overcompensation on the part of her parents. Hoffman (1974) states that working mothers often do more for their children to make up for the fact that they are working. In Cynthia's case, both parents, in fact, appeared to have catered to her—a response that could have been motivated by their desire to make up for the time they were at work. Cynthia recognizes the conflict between her desire for a career and her desire to remain dependent. This is a dilemma that she has not yet resolved.

THE FATHER PROBLEM

It is not clear whether relationships with fathers cause problems for their children. In fact, it is not easy to decipher the research literature on fathering. Until quite recently most research on fathering has apparently been based on certain unstated assumptions that would necessarily tend to bias the results. These assumptions are the traditional sex-typed views about families in general and fathers in particular. First, it is assumed, as stated earlier, that one parent is necessarily dominant, and that children of the same sex as the dominant parent profit by that parent's dominance. There appears to be little openness to the view that both parents may be equal in a positive sense. Instead, egalitarian families are viewed as those in which there is *no* leadership, thus resulting in chaos and confusion, and providing a poor setting for the developing child (Bronfenbrenner, 1961). Second, it is assumed that in most families the father is the symbol of competence, independence, and strength, and that without his interaction these qualities are necessarily missing from the home. Finally, it is assumed that being masculine for a boy and being feminine for a girl are necessarily good. Much of the literature is directed towards determining what induces masculinity in boys rather than toward determining whether masculinity, as commonly defined, is necessarily the best measuring stick of mental and emotional well-being for males. The assumption about masculinity bears some validity in terms of the emotional well-being of young boys who receive enormous peer-group pressure if they are not masculine. However, the evidence on adult men is not clear: For adults it may, indeed, be healthier to be "less masculine" (Mussen, 1962). The complementary assumption that femininity is necessarily good for girls does not, even taking into consideration peer-group pressure, find support. In study after study the less feminine girls have the higher sense of self-esteem, self-confidence, and self-worth (e.g., Forisha & Farber, 1976; Williams, 1973).

The above assumptions underlie a large amount of the research on fathering. Consequently, the results do not always shed light on the question of raising process-oriented as opposed to role-oriented (i.e., masculine and feminine) children. With this in mind, let's examine the literature to see what it tells us about the importance of fathers.

Father Availability Studies on "available" fathers presuppose that the father is working but that he is not so absorbed in his work that he seldom sees his children. It is important to note, though; that such assumptions do not include any sharing of household tasks or an egalitarian power structure. Rather, the father is generally seen as the limitsetter in the home (Biller, 1974) and the dominant parent (Bee, 1974; Biller, 1974). When the father sets consistent limits, boys develop more independence and girls more interpersonal skills (Baumrind & Black, 1967). When the father is dominant in the home, boys are more masculine, particularly if the father is warm and nurturing (Bee, 1974; Biller, 1974; Hetherington & Deur, 1971). If the father is both warm and masculine, the sons tend to be warm and masculine, often having affectionate relationships with their fathers (Mussen & Distler, 1959).

In addition, father availability is related to more exploratory behavior in very young children, though more so in boys than in girls (Biller, 1974). In an analysis of cross-cultural data Romney (1965) also found that father availability is related to higher assertion levels in children. This is implied by the statement that "frequent availability of an active, involved father makes it more likely for individuals to actualize their potentialities" (Biller, 1974, p. 3). The question, though, is whether "individuals" here refers primarily to the male sex. Since we noted above that father availability tends to increase the feminine development of interpersonal skills rather than assertion, does this not imply that only through the development of interpersonal skills can women develop their "potentialities"? In other words, do only men develop their potentialities through assertion? We suspect that the traditional view of femininity is creeping into this conclusion.

Moreover, if father dominance is eulogized, mother dominance within the home is viewed negatively. (I hear in the background undertones of "A strong woman/wife is necessarily a bitch!") Various studies show that mother dominance leads to low masculinity in boys, even if the father is available (Altucher, 1967; Bronfenbrenner, 1961). Young boys who are low in aggression—a primary masculine trait—tend to perceive their mothers as boss (Kagan, 1958). Mother dominance, therefore, is viewed as having negative effects on male development.

The conclusions drawn from the above literature can be summed up by saying that the best-adjusted children—boys in particular—come from homes in which the father is available, dominant, consistent, and nurturing. Moreover, if this is not the case various symptoms of poor emotional health result in the children. We must assume that "best-adjusted" means masculine boys and feminine girls, and that poor mental health occurs in the absence of masculinity in boys and femininity in girls. Polatnick (1973–1974) comments on this assumption:

> It is worth noting, in this connection, how sociological definitions of the "normal" family situation and "normal" personality development for sons versus daughters sanction the status quo of male power and female powerlessness. Healthy families are those which produce strong, independent *sons,* ready to take on strong, independent "mas-

culine roles." (Strong, independent daughters are not a goal; they're a symptom of deviance.)

The literature cited in this section tends to overlook the possibility that masculinity and femininity per se may be damaging, and that we might all benefit by searching out other alternatives. Such a suggestion, however, for a great many, appears to be an attack on all that holds our world together. Do we really believe that if traditions are not kept sacred the world will fall apart? Are we unwilling to explore alternatives? For a great many people, scientists as well as others, it would appear so.

Father Absence Father absence is more the norm than not, for absence need not be solely in the physical sense. A father who is inexpressive and absorbed in his work is often emotionally absent from the home. There are data, of course, showing that fathers interact less with their children than mothers do. This is particularly so in the early years but continues through middle childhood. Before the baby is 3½ months old, fathers average less than forty seconds per day of verbal interaction with their infants and in general spend less time with girl infants than boy infants (Rebelsky & Hanks, 1971). Father absence, whether physical or emotional, does appear to be detrimental to children—more detrimental for boys than girls, and more detrimental if the absence occurs before 5 years of age.

Early father absence for boys tends to lead to significantly less masculine self-concepts (Biller & Bahm, 1971). Boys whose fathers are absent in their early years tend to be more dependent on their peers, less aggressive, and in other ways show considerable deviation from "appropriate" sex-typed behavior (Hetherington, 1966). Father-absent boys also tend to develop a more "feminine" cognitive pattern, displaying greater skill at verbal than quantitative tasks (Carlsmith, 1964). Other research shows that low father availability for males leads to poorer sexual adjustment as an adult as well as to less assertion, greater compliance, and a higher crime rate (Romney, 1965; Stephens, 1962).

In girls, the effects of father absence are less marked and tend to be seen in adolescent heterosexual relationships rather than personality development per se. Biller and Weiss (1970), however, magnify these results by stating that the father-daughter relationship appears to affect feminine development profoundly and to have lasting effects upon a girl's personality and social adjustment, with negative self-concepts ensuing from poor father-daughter relationships (Fish & Biller, 1973).

A study by Hetherington (1972) demonstrates that father absence, if not mitigated by other variables, affects females' adolescent relationships with men. In this study, lower- and lower-middle-class, first-born, white adolescent females were observed in their relationship to a male interviewer and to a group of male peers. Depending on the circumstances these girls either overdid or underdid their approach to men. The daughters of divorcées sought proximity to males and exhibited early heterosexual behavior. Moreover, their nonverbal behavior indicated openness and responsiveness to males. Daughters of widows, on the other hand, manifested disruptions in interaction with males through inhibition, rigidity, avoidance, and restraint. These differences were magnified if separation from the father occurred when the child was very young. No differences in behavior were observed in these adolescent girls' reactions to a female interviewer and female peers. It is apparent that these girls were responding in different ways to father absence.

Various factors may mitigate against the effects of father absence. Children may find other male models in the home in grandparents, uncles, and male siblings (Sutton-Smith, Rosenberg, & Landy, 1968). Moreover, the mother herself may lessen the impact of father absence, particularly on sons, by encouraging masculine development and demonstrating a positive attitude to males in general (Biller, 1969, 1971; Biller & Bahm, 1971). In fact, Nye (1959) suggests that the mother can minimize the impact of an overdose of femininity by going to work and thereby not overmothering her children. Biller (1974) also suggests that strong mothers can facilitate masculine development in the absence of fathers. We might suspect indeed that this is often the case: It is not only the father who can provide a model of competence, although our traditional beliefs lead us to think this is so.

Nonetheless, this evidence suggests that fathers are necessary in order to develop "appropriate" masculine and feminine traits in children. Masculine boys need a masculine role model and feminine girls learn from interaction with a positive male figure. However, what would be the results if the fathers were *more* available? (Evidence suggests that fathers are somewhat peripheral in the home.) What if the fathers were themselves less sex-typed, more nurturing, and expressive than the stereotyped male? Bell and Vogel state:

> ... a child whose father performs the mothering functions both tangibly and emotionally while the mother is preoccupied with her career can easily gain a distorted image of masculinity and femininity (1968, p. 586).

If this is so, is this unhealthy? Perhaps it is not.

FATHERS AS EQUAL OR PRIMARY CARETAKERS

Fathers who share equally in the tasks of child rearing, or fathers who assume the major responsibility for child rearing, are still a rare breed. However, there are indications that their number is growing. Since the movement toward egalitarian marriages is based on the maintenance of dual careers, it also assumes more male participation in the home. Moreover, the number of single-parent fathers also seems to be increasing. Whereas in 1972 it was estimated that single-parent fathers formed only 1 percent of the child-rearing population (George & Wilding, 1972), there is evidence that this number is on the rise. By 1974, divorce courts in four states had eliminated any sex bias in awarding custody of the children to either parent. Recently an article in *The New York Times* (Friedman, 1973) pointed out that 38 percent of the contested custody cases in Minnesota were decided in favor of the father. Although the percentage is still relatively small, more and more fathers are caring for children.

As more fathers care for children, there has been a corresponding flood of research investigating this phenomenon. One study showed that single-parent fathers feel quite capable and successful in their ability to be the primary and nurturing parent of their children (Orthner, Brown, & Ferguson, 1976). Another study found that divorced fathers showed better adjustment than did widowed fathers, and the divorced fathers felt that their home situation and child-rearing practices were much improved since the departure of the mother (Gasser & Taylor, 1976). Most of these fathers were carrying the responsibilities of home management alone, which implies a greater interchange of former role stereotypes. More than one study (Mendes, 1976; Orthner, Brown, & Ferguson, 1976) argues for an increased number of support facilities for single fathers to help overcome problems encountered in pursuing a nontraditional role. Such facilities include more comprehensive day-care centers, baby-sitting cooperatives, school transportation, and education in single parenthood. It is mildly surprising to find that these facilities are now urged to help single-parent *fathers,* whereas working mothers, single or married, have been pleading for such assistance for a number of years. It may be that the entrance of men into the domestic circle will upgrade the evaluation of domestic life and hasten the improvement of facilities for child-care support.

These recent studies are mostly concerned with the well-being of fathers rather than with the well-being of children under their care. In light of the paucity of evidence on this question, we may speculate on what the effects on children might be. As suggested above, fathers taking over management of home and children will necessarily have to adopt some of the feminine role characteristics unless they hire someone to do this for them. Therefore, we might expect to see less stereotyped behavior in the male parent managing the home by himself than in the traditional home. We would expect to find that boys in such a home might feel comfortable adopting the expressive and nurturing traits modeled by the father as well as his cluster of male competency traits. Wouldn't boys, therefore, be less stereotypically masculine and more androgynous?

The same might be true of girls who have more opportunity to interact with a nurturing opposite-sex parent, modeling both the competency and expressive traits displayed by a single-parent father. As Rossi (1964) states, girls benefit from interaction with their fathers, and greater father-daughter interaction "could help to counteract the narrow confines of the feminine models daughters have" (p. 133). Such a viewpoint certainly receives a modicum of support from the study by Vogel, Broverman, Broverman, Clarkson, and Rosenkrantz (1970) concerning children of working parents; in this study it is assumed that the father played a larger role within the home. These children, both male and female, were less stereotyped in their sex-role attitudes and each group tended to value its own sex more highly than their peers from more traditional families did. Such an androgynous orientation may be more common as fathers participate more actively in the home management— whether to share the domestic arena with their working wives, or to care for their children as single parents. In either case, the fathers' greater participation in the home management is to be welcomed, even at the risk of distorting traditional concepts of masculinity and femininity, as Bell and Vogel warned. We may thus all grow more fully human.

GROWING UP WITH FATHER

Examples of fathers caring for children are surprisingly plentiful among my students. Many students who now have children have experimented with this arrangement. However, their evaluation of this role reversal varies. One man who stayed home with his children for several years objected not to housework or child care but to his financial dependence upon his wife. Another male finds staying home liberating: He claims that the housework is all done by noon, and the rest of the day is his to read and think (one assumes until the three children return home from school). Another woman, heading toward a career, says that her husband very much enjoys being home, that she "can't stand it!" and that this arrangement has worked well for them both. One wonders whether the enthusiasm of the last two students is partially due to the recentness of the arrangement and, indeed, if this role reversal will stand the test of time. I would hope so but would expect that such role switches would also meet with difficulties, as do all other long-term human activities, and that a later evaluation of this arrangement would be more judicious than "It's just marvelous!"

Some more enduring arrangements are described by other students who have experienced the father as the primary caretaker for some time in their early years. All these students remark positively on their association with their fathers, and all of them evidence less stereotyped sex-role attitudes. All, that is, but one: A female student comments on the fact that she and her sisters were put in the father's custody after a divorce and that her father is "bound and determined to make women of us, something our mother failed to do because she was always so busy with her work." Apparently traditional views of masculinity and femininity are still alive and well, even in some single-father families. However, in my sample this is a minority of one, and all the other case histories attest to less stereotypical, more androgynous attitudes. Let's now take up the case histories of a woman and a man that help illustrate the points we have just discussed.

EVELYN

Now approaching 50, Evelyn is a vibrant, alive woman who is very enthusiastic about her entrance into the "helping professions." After twenty years of maintaining a traditional marriage and raising four children, she has returned to the university to complete her graduate training. Her changed view of herself and her new career direction have increased friction in her family life, and even at this time (nearly three years after she wrote the following case history), her husband has not completely adjusted to her new life. Nonetheless, she is still committed both to her marriage and to her work.

Her early background, prior to the age of 8, was highly untraditional. But her life after 8 began to conform to the traditional norms. In such a background are the foundations for living in two worlds. Is her "second adolescence"—as she now refers to her recent years—a result to some extent of her early androgynous world? Do other women, from a more traditional background, have the motivation to persevere in a new career direction in mid-life? I suspect the early memories of a working mother and domestic father have opened some psychological doors for Evelyn. She speaks of her early years and the excitement and difficulties of her current life:

> My parents were both living flexible roles at the time I was growing up. . . . It is a warm memory to recall my father, a big muscular man, folding clothes, ironing, or doing any number of things around the house while treating me with warmth and love. . . . My mother also was the prime contributor to the family income and took her work seriously. . . . I saw her life as full of adventure, yet she was there when I needed her. . . . I realized the rest of the world did not live this way and was hurt by the criticism of other family members who did not like my fishing trips with my father. When I visited other children their mothers hovered over the stoves in aprons and seemed to be constantly available to satisfy every whim. This appealed to my selfish nature, but for some reason these mothers seemed at the same time to be dull.
>
> When I was about 8 my parents went back to the traditional behavior: Mother gave up her work for full-time homemaking and my father returned to work. I'm not sure if they chose to do this or if they felt the pressure to return to more traditional roles. I too started to become more like a "girl" and

began to imagine having a warm kitchen of my own, just like my now-mother and my aunts. . . .

Many things contributed to what I call a second adolescence, my time of self-searching, self-knowledge, and reevaluation. . . . It has been difficult. It took two years for my husband to realize that going to school was not just a passing fancy for me—something to fit into the household routine—but a serious goal involved in what would be my final commitment and work. It took as long for him to realize that taking over some of the household duties was not an impossible thing for him and that he could get some satisfaction from the accomplishment of thrifty shopping or a newly vacuumed carpet. I have grown too in struggling with the world outside home, and have found that I can be a whole person and care for myself.

Today, when Evelyn talks about her life, she does appear to be a "whole person." She is a wife, a mother, and a professional. She travels alone and with her family. She has come to the realization that she does not *need* her family but that she enjoys their company—but not all of the time.

JOHN

John is a striking man of about 30, forthright and open. In the words of a colleague of mine, he "makes good contact" with others. He is actively involved in a very demanding career, goes to school at night, and has a wife with her own career and a small child. The energy required to carry out John's daily activities is more than most people possess, but he seems excited and stimulated by the activity rather than tired or worn down. His background has some parallels to Evelyn's: He too grew up in two different worlds.

As the son of an athletic hero and a warm mother, he spent the first eight years of his life in a traditional home, growing into what others referred to as "a fine young man." He liked sports, outdoor play, and helping his father around the house. However, the summer that he was 8, his mother died suddenly and his life changed completely. In addition to the loss of his mother, which John still experiences as painful, the family had spent their financial reserves on hospital expenses. In order for the family to stay together, all four children had to take over the household maintenance.

When Dad got back from the hospital that time he called the kids together and said things were going to be tough. . . . There was no money and everybody would have to help. . . . Everybody learned to take care of the house. . . . My older brother and I found that doing those things normally referred to as "women's work" did not seem at all unnatural. We did them because we knew they had to be done. Cooking in particular was fun because there was room for imagination and creativity.

In the image of his father, John and his brother continued to be active in sports and also took over the domestic routine with help from their younger sisters. John's needs for self-esteem were, for many years, met by his participation in the athletic world, but at the same time he knew how to cook, sew, and clean house. He found this a fortuitous combination.

John had an early and disastrous marriage, which he attributes, in part, to his desire to be mothered by a woman. The marriage resulted in one child, much pain, and a divorce. John is now married to a woman he met after his separation, and he also has custody of his child by his first marriage. He speaks of his current marriage as liberated and exciting. He is amazed at the openness with which he and his wife share with each other. Moreover, his second wife, Susan, is also a career woman, and they both, with paid help, share equally in housework and child care. It appears inconceivable to John that anyone would choose to live a more traditional life-style.

However, he did not arrive at this point with ease. The transition between marriages was a painful one because of the financial demands of his first wife and his concern about the welfare of his daughter, who was then living with her mother. Learning that his child had been seriously injured, he flew to the Southwest to retrieve her from her suicidal mother. At the time he had just begun his relationship with Susan:

This period of time was one of the most painful of my life. . . . We were instant parents of a very messed-up 2½-year-old. . . . Being totally broke, having a kid, being very much into a dynamite new relationship, all these things don't work very well together.

Nonetheless, after a six-month period, the difficulties subsided and John, Susan, and their daughter began to work out a life-style that suited all of them. Their marriage, which appears to encompass all their needs, is now four years old.

IMPLICATIONS

Among my students and peers, the degree to which John has adopted a nontraditional life-style is rather unique. Certainly, his self-confidence, high energy level, and self-sufficiency are outstanding. Is this at all attributable to his background? It seems likely that, through identification with his father, he achieved a firm male identity and then, because of the changes in his life circumstances, was able to learn many feminine skills. He is comfortable not only with cooking and cleaning but also with the writing of poetry. One wonders if this may be due in part to growing up with a concerned and caring father who also shared in the domestic side of life.

The case histories of Evelyn and John are unusual in the degree of contact that each child has had with his or her father. Despite other difficulties in their lives, the contact with a warm, caring, but strong father appears to have been very beneficial. It is unfortunate that, except in unusual circumstances, children have little contact with their male parent. As Young remarks, we do not value the man who pays much attention to his children and rather give our respect to the man "who succeeds in the really serious business of making better mousetraps" (1965, p. 5). It will be a more human world when we value the welfare of children more than the production of mousetraps—however, we are not there yet.

SUMMARY

The role-oriented parental pattern dictates that the mother be ever present and the father relatively distant. Such a pattern has evolved, in part, to suit the convenience of men who wish to have children but be free of caring for them. Such a pattern has been further supported by a wide-spread belief in a "maternal instinct" that particularly suits a woman for child rearing and domesticity. There is no evidence that such an instinct exists. There is evidence, however, that women learn to be mothers while men learn to operate in the occupational world. This system is not necessarily good for either the father, the mother, or the children.

There are many changes occurring now in the traditional pattern. Women are going to work, and the research shows that this does not have a negative effect on their children. A few men are now staying home and participating in the parenting of their children. There is little research yet on families in which the father is the primary or only parent, but what we do have indicates that this can be a positive experience for the child. Certainly for some children, such as John whose story just appeared, this is beneficial. If the trends continue, we may indeed be moving toward a more process-oriented mode of being in which each individual can choose whether to go to work or to stay home or to find some combination of the two. We would expect, certainly, that satisfied, autonomous parents will eventually breed satisfied, autonomous children, all of whom will be fully developed human beings.

In conclusion, I return to LeShan's (1972) book for children in which she states that we can all explore our own potential and be whoever it is that we are:

> Even today, some grownups still seem to have the idea that boys have to behave one way and girls another, and that girls must only like to do the things their mothers do, and boys only what their fathers do. But all this is changing. By the time you are grown up, you will be able to do anything you want, and still be the same sex you now are. We have learned that a man can be a dancer, a painter, a nurse, a cook, or a fashion designer, and still enjoy being a man and a husband and a father. We have learned that a girl can be an engineer or a doctor or a lawyer or a newspaper reporter, and still enjoy being a woman, a wife and a mother. Most of all, we have learned that the only way to really enjoy being a man or a woman, is to do the thing that makes you feel good about being who and what you are.

There *is* evidence that we are better off being *who* we are. Can we have the courage to implement this in our lives? It is not as easy as LeShan—or I—have made it sound.

EXERCISE: ATTITUDES TOWARD FATHERS AND MOTHERS

This exercise is designed to elicit our attitudes toward fathers and mothers.

Write down all adjectives that come quickly to your mind when you think of the word father. *The references may be literal or symbolic. They do not need to refer to your father or to fathers that you know. Only allow yourself to write whatever comes to mind.*

Now write down all the words that come to your mind when you think of the word mother. *Again, these words need not refer to your mother or to other mothers that you know.*

Now be analytical and answer the following questions:

1. *How many of these adjectives are those stereotypically associated with mothers and fathers? How did you come to choose these adjectives (exposure to media, books, personal examples, etc.)?*

2. *How many of these adjectives applied to your own mother and father when you were growing up? How did you respond to these characteristics in your parents, positively or negatively?*

3. *Does your total list of adjectives for fathers and mothers reflect more a process orientation or a role orientation? How do you feel about that?*

4. *Which adjectives on your list reflect qualities you would like to see in yourself? Do you find more highly valued characteristics under the heading of* father *or* mother? *What does this say about societal valuing of men and women? What does this say about you?*

5. *In what ways would you like to change your list of adjectives to more adequately reflect your own view of mothers and fathers (either as you are now or expect to be—or expect others to be)?*

Having done all this, compare your lists and your responses to the questions with others. Notice any similarities or differences? Can you account for the differences and similarities in terms of your own backgrounds and experiences? Finally, discuss the impact of sex-role scripting on your view of parental roles and family life. Do you find this satisfactory or unsatisfactory? Are you going to do anything about it?

REFERENCES

Almquist, E. M., and Angrist, S. S., "Role Model Influences on College Women's Career Aspirations," *Merrill-Palmer Quarterly*, vol. 3 (1971): 263–79.

Altucher, N., "Conflict in Sex Identification in Boys," unpublished doctoral dissertation, University of Michigan, 1967.

Baruch, G. K., "Maternal Influences upon College Women's Attitudes toward Women and Work," *Developmental Psychology,* vol. 6 (1972): 32–37(a).

Baruch, G. K., "Maternal Role Pattern as Related to Self-Esteem and Parental Identification in College Women," paper presented at the Meeting of the Eastern Psychological Association, Boston, Mass., April 1972(b).

Baumrind, D., and Black, A. E., "Socialization Practices Associated with Dimensions of Competence in Preschool Boys and Girls," *Child Development,* vol. 38 (1967): 291–327.

Bee, H., *Social Issues in Developmental Psychology,* New York: Harper & Row, 1974.

Bell, N., and Vogel, E., eds., *A Modern Introduction to the Family,* rev. ed., New York: Free Press, 1968.

Benson, L., *Fatherhood: A Sociological Perspective,* New York: Random House, 1968.

Biller, H. B., "Father Absence, Maternal Encouragement, and Sex-Role Development in Kindergarten-Age Boys," *Child Development,* vol. 40 (1969): 539–46.

Biller, H. B., "The Mother-Child Relationship and the Father-Absent Boy's Personality Development," *Merrill-Palmer Quarterly,* vol. 17 (1971): 227–41.

Biller, H. B., *Paternal Deprivation,* Lexington, Mass.: D. C. Heath, 1974.

Biller, H. B., and Bahm, R. M., "Father Absence, Perceived Maternal Behavior, and Masculinity of Self-Concept among Junior High School Boys," *Developmental Psychology,* vol. 4 (1971): 178–81.

Biller, H. B., and Weiss, S. D., "The Father-Daughter Relationship and the Personality Development of the Female," *Journal of Genetic Psychology,* vol. 116 (1970): 79–93.

Birnbaum, J. A., "Life Patterns, Personality Style and Self-Esteem in Gifted Family-Oriented and Career Committed Women," unpublished doctoral dissertation, University of Michigan, 1971.

Bowlby, J., "Maternal Care and Mental Health," Monograph Series, No. 2, Geneva: World Health Organization, 1951.

Bronfenbrenner, U., "Some Familial Antecedents of Responsibility and Leadership in Adolescents," in L. Petrullo and B. Bass, eds., *Leadership and Interpersonal Behavior,* New York: Holt, Rinehart & Winston, 1961.

Caldwell, B. M., Wright, C. M., Honig, A. S., and Tannenbaum, J., "Infant Day Care and Attachment," *American Journal of Orthopsychiatry*, vol. 40 (1970): 3.

Carlsmith, L., "Effect of Early Father-Absence on Scholastic Aptitude," *Harvard Educational Review*, vol. 34 (1964): 3–21.

Coopersmith, S., *The Antecedents of Self-Esteem*, New York: Basic Books, 1967.

Dizard, J., *Social Change in the Family*, Community and Family Study Center, University of Chicago, 1968.

Douvan, E., "Employment and the Adolescent," in F. I. Nye and L. W. Hoffman, eds., *The Employed Mother in America*, Chicago: Rand McNally, 1963.

Fasteau, M. F., *The Male Machine*, New York: McGraw-Hill, 1974.

Fish, K. D., and Biller, H. B., "Perceived Childhood Paternal Relationships and College Females' Personal Adjustment," *Adolescence*, vol. 8 (1973): 415–20.

Forisha, B., and Farber, R., "Sex-Role Orientation and Self-Esteem: The Value of Masculinity," unpublished study, 1976.

Friedman, L., "Fathers Don't Make Good Mothers, Said the Judge," *The New York Times*, January 28, 1973.

Gasser, R. D., and Taylor, C. M., "Role Adjustment of Single Parent Fathers with Dependent Children," *The Family Coordinator*, vol. 25 (1976): 397–401.

George, V., and Wilding, P., *Motherless Families*, Boston: Routledge and Kegan Paul, 1972.

Ginzberg, E., *Educated American Women: Life Styles and Self Portraits*, New York: Columbia University Press, 1971.

Goldberg, P., "Are Women Prejudiced Against Women?," *Transaction*, vol. 5 (1968): 28–30.

Harlow, H. F., Harlow, M. K., Dodsworth, R. O., and Arling, G. I., "Maternal Behavior of Rhesus Monkeys Deprived of Mothering and Peer Association in Infancy," *Proceedings of the American Philosophical Society*, vol. 110 (1966).

Hartley, R. E., "Sex Role Pressures and the Socialization of the Male Child," *Psychological Reports*, vol. 5 (1959): 457–63.

Hetherington, E. M., "Effects of Father Absence on Personality Development in Adolescent Daughters," *Development Psychology*, vol. 7 (1972): 313–26.

Hetherington, E. M., "Effects of Paternal Absence on Sex-Typed Behaviors in Negro and White Preadolescent Males," *Journal of Personality and Social Psychology,* vol. 4 (1966): 87–91.

Hetherington, E. ..., and Deur, J. L., "The Effects of Father Absence on Child Development," *Young Children,* vol. 26 (1971):233–48.

Hoffman, L. W., "Effects on Child," in F. I. Nye and L. W. Hoffman, eds., *Working Mothers,* San Francisco: Jossey-Bass Publishers, 1974.

Hoffman, L. W., "The Father's Role in the Family and the Child's Peer Group Adjustment," *Merrill-Palmer Quarterly,* vol. 7 (1961): 97–105.

Hollingworth, L. S., "Social Devices for Impelling Women to Bear and Rear Children, *The American Journal of Sociology,* vol. 22 (1916): 20.

Janeway, E., *Man's World, Woman's Place,* New York: William Morrow, 1971.

Kaffman, M., "Comparative Psychopathology of Kibbutz and Urban Children," in P. Neuberger, ed., *Children in Collectives,* Springfield, Ill.: Charles C. Thomas, 1965.

Kagan, J., "Socialization of Aggression and the Perception of Parents in Fantasy," *Child Development,* vol. 29 (1958): 311–20.

Kappell, B. E., and Lambert, R. D., "Self-Worth among the Children of Working Mothers," unpublished manuscript, University of Waterloo, Ontario, 1972.

Kligler, D., "The Effects of Employment of Married Women on Husband and Wife Roles: A Study in Culture Change," unpublished doctoral dissertation, Yale University, 1954.

Komarovsky, M., "Cultural Contradictions and Sex Roles: The Masculine Case," *American Journal of Sociology,* vol. 78 (1973): 873–84.

Leifer, A., Leiderman, P. H., Barnett, C. R., and Williams, A., "Effects of Mother-Infant Separation on Maternal Attachment Behavior," *Child Development,* vol. 43 (1972): 1203–18.

LeShan, E., *What Makes Me Feel This Way?,* New York: Collier Books, 1972.

Meier, H. C., "Mother-Centeredness and College Youths' Attitudes Toward Social Equality for Women: Some Empirical Findings," *Journal of Marriage and the Family,* vol. 34 (1972): 115–21.

Mendes, H. A., "Single Fathers," *The Family Coordinator,* vol. 4 (1976): 439–44.

Mussen, P. H., "Long-Term Consequents of Masculinity of Interests in Adolescence," *Journal of Consulting Psychology,* vol. 26 (1962): 435–40.

Mussen, P. H., and Distler, L., "Masculinity, Identification and Father-Son Relationships," *Journal of Abnormal and Social Psychology,* vol. 59 (1959): 350–56.

Nye, F. I., "Employment Status of Mother and Adjustment of Adolescent Children," *Marriage and Family Living,* vol. 21 (1959): 240–44.

Nye, F. I., and Hoffman, L. W., *The Employed Mother in America,* Chicago: Rand McNally, 1963.

Orthner, D. K., Brown, T., and Ferguson, D., "Single-Parent Fatherhood: An Emerging Family Life Style," *The Family Coordinator,* vol. 25 (1976): 429–37.

Parsons, T., and Bales, R. F., *Family Socialization and Interaction Process,* Glencoe, Ill.: Glencoe Free Press, 1955.

Polatnick, M., "Why Men Don't Rear Children: A Power Analysis," *Berkeley Journal of Sociology,* vol. 18 (1973–74): 45–86.

Propper, A. M., "The Relationship of Maternal Employment to Adolescent Roles, Activities and Parental Relationalysis," *Journal of Marriage and the Family,* vol. 34 (1972): 417–21.

Rabin, A. I., "Infants and Children under Conditions of Intermittent Mothering in the Kibbutz," *American Journal of Orthopsychiatry,* vol. 28 (1958): 577.

Rebelsky, F., and Hanks, C., "Fathers' Verbal Interaction with Infants in the First Three Months of Life," *Child Development,* vol. 42 (1971): 63–68.

Roache, J., "Confessions of a Househusband," *Ms. Magazine,* vol. 1 (November 1972): 25–27.

Romney, A. K., "Variations in Household Structure as Determinants of Sex-Typed Behavior," in F. Beach, ed., *Sex and Behavior,* New York: John Wiley & Sons, 1965.

Rossi, A. S., "Equality Between the Sexes: An Immodest Proposal," in R. J. Lifton, ed., *The Woman in America,* Boston: Beacon Press, 1964.

Siegel, A. E., and Haas, M. B., "The Working Mother: A Review of Research," *Child Development,* vol. 34 (1963): 513–42.

Stephens, W. N., *The Oedipus Complex: Crossculture Evidence,* Glencoe, Ill.: Free Press, 1962.

Stolz, L. M., "Effects of Maternal Employment on Children: Evidence from Research," *Child Development,* vol. 31 (1961): 749–82.

Sutton-Smith, B., Rosenberg, B. G., and Landy, F., "Father-Absence Effects in Families of Different Siblings Composition," *Child Development,* vol. 39 (1968): 1213–21.

Tangri, S. S., "Role Innovation in Occupational Choice among College Women," unpublished doctoral dissertation, University of Michigan, 1969.

Vogel, S. R., Broverman, I. K., Broverman, D. H., Clarkson, F. E., and Rosenkrantz, P. S., "Maternal Employment and Perception of Sex Roles among College Students," *Developmental Psychology*, vol. 3 (1970): 584–91.

Williams, J. H., "Sexual Roles Identification and Personality Functioning in Girls: A Theory Revisited," *Journal of Personality*, vol. 1 (1973): 1–80.

Yarrow, M. R., Scott, P., DeLeeuw, L., and Heinig, C., "Childrearing in Families of Working and Non-Working Mothers," *Sociometry*, vol. 25 (1962): 122–40.

Young, L., *Life Among the Giants*, New York: McGraw-Hill, 1965.

Epilogue: Toward Androgyny — Integrating the Vision and the Reality

In this book we have examined the process-oriented, androgynous approach to life and contrasted it with the more typical masculine and feminine role-oriented approach. We have looked at the impact of traditional concepts of masculinity and femininity on people's lives as they work and play, love and fight, marry and raise children. For the most part we have seen that individuals, often unknowingly, accept the categories of masculine and feminine given at birth, and allow these categories to shape their lives. These individuals never become aware of or else choose to ignore the advantages of the androgynous, process-oriented life-style. Instead, they

A basic assumption is that, although there may be biological factors predisposing some degree of overall sex differences, both males and females can be judged as more competent if they possess both positive masculine and positive feminine characteristics.

Henry Biller, **Paternal Deprivation**

The two principles, the feminine-motherly and the masculine-fatherly, correspond not only to the presence of a masculine and feminine side in any human being but specifically to the need for mercy and justice in every man and woman. The deepest yearning of human beings seems to be a constellation in which the two poles (motherliness and fatherliness, female and male, mercy and justice, feeling and thought, nature and intellect) are united in a synthesis, in which both sides of the polarity lose their antagonism and, instead, color each other.

Erich Fromm, **To Have or To Be?**

---

transmit their sex-role beliefs to their children, and so we perpetuate the sex-role cycle.

THE SEX-ROLE CYCLE: LEARNING AND TRANSMITTING SEX ROLES

We have seen that boys and girls do not differ from each other at birth in significant ways other than anatomically. Yet despite such findings, from birth onward boys and girls tend to be perceived differently by the adults around them and thus tend to be treated differently. Boys are expected to be aggressive and rebellious whereas girls are expected to be passive and obedient. Parents shape their children's behavior in subtle ways according to these expectations. Teachers also regard boys and girls differently. Although they know that the well-behaved, obedient girl is the better student, they give more of their attention—and their criticism—to the rebellious, less studious boy. Accordingly, by the time children have completed the elementary-school years, boys and girls are very different indeed—or at least they are perceived as being so.

In adolescence the sex-role messages directed at the growing person become even stronger. Boys are ostracized from their peer groups if they do not behave in acceptably masculine ways: They must be good at sports and at least appear to know about liquor and "women." Girls, on the other hand, who have been governed with a much freer hand up to this point, begin to learn that they must now give up their "masculine" pursuits and learn to be feminine. They are told that their purpose in life is to be receptive, understanding companions of men, not intellectual or sports-minded competitors. Thus they learn to give up or reorient their achievement strivings to fit into the interpersonal world they must now inhabit. In adolescence it is clear that boys and girls are taught to be two almost different species—the ones who "do" (or achieve) and the ones who "be" (or love).

As adolescents pass into adulthood, they carry their beliefs about masculinity and femininity into their marriages—and traditional sex-role concepts fit well into the traditional marriage. The woman who has learned to "be" stays at home and takes care of the children and the house, providing a cozy nest for the man to return to each day. The man, on the other hand, spends his day "doing" things in the outer world, where his capacity for rational endeavors, for analytic thought, and for leadership allows him to compete in the world of men and to provide for his family. In such families nurturance and love come to be associated with the woman and competence and power with the man. The separation of love and power prevents either partner from becoming fully human.

With the arrival of children, these differences are given new life. Children come to meet the expectations of their parents and so mold themselves into the preordained shapes—just as generations did before them. And so the sex-role cycle is completed once again as it is perpetuated from generation to generation.

SOCIETAL FACTORS AFFECTING
THE SEX-ROLE CYCLE

Such patterns of learning sex roles are also affected by other factors in our society. Depending on our social class, ethnic group, and to some extent geographical region of the country, our sex-role expectations may be enforced or modified in various ways. For example, although women are not expected to achieve or provide, women in the lower-class black culture may expect to earn most of the money for their families, since often they do not regard their husbands as dependable providers. Women in the upper-middle class, where husbands generally provide rather well, may still be encouraged to explore their achievement needs more so than lower-middle- and working-class women. Similarly, although men are generally encouraged not to be expressive, Mediterranean and Latin men may be more emotionally expressive than their Anglo-Saxon counterparts. But, nonetheless, despite these permutations resulting from class and cultural variations, men are expected to be the movers of the world—and women the supporting force.

The predominant pattern cited above receives immense support from another area of our society—the occupational sphere. Our world of work has traditionally been a world of men; even as women are entering this world in ever-increasing numbers they are finding that they must either do menial tasks or meet masculine expectations. Job descriptions and promotion criteria for the better jobs usually carry unconscious masculinized prescriptions for behavior. One expects, for example, that executives will be both tough and likeable, a combination that is generally not perceived in most women. On the contrary, women who are regarded as tough are usually not perceived as likeable, and therefore are often not seen as qualified by the men who might hire them. Consequently, women often fail to get these better jobs. Or, if they are hired, they earn less money than men holding comparable positions.

Thus, since men in this world earn most of the money, it is just one short leap to the conclusion that men are the best breadwinners—and possibly the natural breadwinners. Therefore, women, by default, must take care of the home. Our economic system, in a world in which economics is highly valued, gives out the message that men must work and women must tend the hearth. Any change is viewed as shaking the foundations of our world.

Yet today there are pressures to change our world—pressures

forcing us to come closer to the "vision" described in this book. Let us now examine some of the pressures that may bring us within reach of the androgynous alternative.

PRESSURES TOWARD CHANGE

If we allow ourselves to honestly survey our situation today in the mid-1970s, we will recognize that there are strong external pressures—technology, social movements, and intellectual reassessment—as well as internal pressures urging all of us to adopt a process-oriented, androgynous mode of being. Without doing so, in fact, our society may not survive.

Technological Pressures We have come to the point in our civilization where we now have the power to destroy each other—and may indeed do so unless we adopt a more cooperative value system that prizes the welfare of all humankind. Technology also has led us to a place where increased production of consumer goods may bring only disasters in its wake: We pollute the air and rape the environment; we fill our earth with disposable waste all the way from tin cans to cars; we teach people to buy more and more when long ago they had enough. The growth of technology has led to consequences that cry out for change in human values.

But, technology is forcing us to change our values in other ways. Through advances in transportation, communication, and production, technology has brought us closer together so that many of our traditional categories—including those of masculinity and femininity—are now sharply challenged by the need for flexibility, adaptability, and tolerance. We are today brought into contact with people of different cultures, different backgrounds, different life-styles—and in many cases must live elbow-to-elbow with them. Our traditional roles no longer fit these new circumstances. We can no longer maintain the rigidity of out-dated notions of the "way it is supposed to be." We can live together only if we can indeed accept, tolerate, and come to like the variety of human life and life-styles and the diversity of inclinations and talents. Such an acceptance is found only in process-oriented individuals who find their center within. In order to live in this world we must let go of our shells and come to find our centers from which we can delight in the diversity of humankind.

Ironically, technology is also facilitating such changes. Because of technology and the advance of medicine, we now live nearly twice as long as our ancestors did a century ago. Technology has also provided us with effective means of birth control so that we no longer need to be subject to the vagaries of the reproductive cycle or to the economic burdens of feeding more and more mouths— unless we choose to do so. In addition, technology has increased the productive capacity of each individual (although often through the repetition of monotonous tasks) and has brought to the forefront the possibility of a shorter work week. Thus, with our longer life-span, and the possibility of our smaller families and increased leisure time, many of us are now free to explore avenues previously closed to us. Many men now can explore child care and many women now can explore the world of work.*

Pressures by Recent Social Movements The necessity for a more realistic—and more process-oriented—view of life has also been recognized by numerous subgroups in our population. Since the early 1960s these subcultures have spawned political and social movements, which have brought the necessity of a more realistic world view to the attention of the general public.

In the 1960s a large minority of our educated youth made themselves highly noticeable by their protests against "establishment policy" both in the universities and in state and national governments. They argued, in general, that our policies (political, economic, and social) were hypocritical and served the needs of only part of our population—the well-to-do minority. The 1960s also gave rise to the Civil Rights movement, long a more subdued undercurrent that finally came into its own as people of different ethnic groups— especially our large black population—demanded that they be treated with respect, dignity, and equality. Once again their protest served to point up the inequities of the American system and indeed forced changes upon that system.

These two movements led to still another movement. The fight

---

*The choice by women to go to work may actually be brought about by necessity. Pressed by the rising cost of just about everything, many women enter the job market to maintain their standard of income. At any rate, the concept of the woman at home is indeed becoming a thing of the past.

for equality among the races led to the fight for equality between the sexes. Even as men and women worked together to rectify inequalities in our system, inequalities existed between them. In order to work against this inequity the Women's Liberation movement arose in the mid-1960s to fight for equal rights for women. Following in the wake of this movement we find an increased sensitivity in our culture to the rights of women—and an increase in legal injunctions against unequal opportunities for men and women. Just as the youths and the blacks raised an outcry against the workings of the American system, so too the women came to demand that they be given respect, dignity, and equal opportunities.

There have been many changes in the Women's Liberation movement since its inception, and these changes reflect changes in our culture. Much of the rhetoric of the 1960s that addressed itself to the fight of women *against* men (since men were seen as the oppressors) has been replaced. Instead of a movement of women against men, in the 1970s we have a movement of women *with* men, each sex struggling to become more fully human. In the midst of this change, the term androgyny has come to symbolize the vision of a new individual and a new world.

Other changes of the 1970s may be grouped under the title of the Human Potential movement, which espouses a philosophy that emphasizes the importance of individuals "getting their heads together." This decade has seen an enormous number of people join encounter groups, sensitivity training sessions, meditation groups, and other activities that promise to facilitate personal growth and understanding. As one commentator suggests, although we may no longer be fighting in the streets, individuals are certainly waging a battle within their own heads. In the 1970s we have turned inward.

Yet whether individuals wage battles on the streets or in their heads, much of the philosophy of the social movements of the 1960s and 1970s has certain values in common. All argue for equality, liberty, cooperation, diversity—and the respect and dignity of the individual. All the movements espouse a philosophy that argues against old distinctions and old categories, and that takes a stand in favor of seeing ourselves and others as we are—potentially fully human individuals.

Intellectual Pressures On another level, intellectuals have also been suggesting that we reexamine our values and the assumptions and actions that have followed from such values. Since the late

1950s social critics have argued strongly for changes in our belief system—pointing out the alienation of modern individuals that has been created by our technological culture. We have allowed our categorical distinctions not only to separate us from the environment, but also from each other. The final distinction is a separation from our sense of self. In pursuing our dreams we have lost ourselves. Surely it is time for a new integration.

Many scholars are searching for a basis for this new integration by reassessing the conclusions that we have drawn from research and by examining the values that underlay these conclusions. In doing so, social scientists have been restructuring our views of human nature as they reassess past views of human life. New researchers, many of them women, have gone back to old data on prehistoric people and have shown that early human beings were cooperative and gentle people, not killers as we previously believed. Our drive toward an aggressive competition with our world and each other is not an extension of our prehistoric roots but rather a travesty that denies these roots.

Moreover, recent assessments of past data do not show that men were always regarded as superior creatures while women assumed the inferior role. Although men's work was generally more physical and adventuresome and women's work often took them less far afield, there are suggestions that men and women in early times existed in a cooperative and sharing partnership of equals. It was only when work became separated from the home that such a distinction in power between the sexes resulted.

But now with the help of technology it is possible for us to return to what appears to have been a more equal world—a world of shared companionship and cooperation between all individuals. Such a concept of equality between the sexes does not run contrary to any known set of facts. Researchers have documented, time and time again, that there are no basic sex differences that can be traced to our anatomy. Contrary to all past and much present thinking, boys and girls and men and women are pretty much alike. The full flowering of their abilities might in fact lead to an androgynous diversity that could rekindle the spark of hope and faith in the potential of humankind.

All these changes in our society, noticed both in social movements as well as in research and theory, urge us to reevaluate our beliefs, attitudes, and patterns of living. With this in mind we turn to an examination of the process of individual change.

THE PROCESS OF INDIVIDUAL CHANGE

Individual change and growth are born of conflict, of an awareness that our lives as they now stand are not all that they should be, that the world as perceived is somehow insufficient. From this perception we begin an inner struggle to achieve a new integration—or to bring together the way we perceive the world and the way we believe the world could be. In other words, we attempt to bring closer together the reality and the vision.

Psychologist Carl Rogers tells us that all personal growth is accompanied by a sense of initial disorganization. It is not comfortable to acknowledge other alternative views of ourselves and our world, nor is it easy to accept facets of ourselves previously unnoticed. Such new awarenesses are, of necessity, accompanied by feelings of uncertainty and turmoil and are the preliminary steps toward a new integration. In the process of change we first come to perceive that we are, indeed, in conflict.

The resolution of such conflict will not follow easily—nor will our heightened awareness erase all doubts. As Rogers also stated, we always make important decisions on the basis of incomplete information. We never know enough, if we are honest with ourselves, to be really sure of the outcome of any new decision. In the course of our journey we thus will encounter moments of disorganization and perhaps seeming chaos—but in the end we will achieve a greater satisfaction than we have known before.

In addition to the conflict born of heightened awareness, conflict also occurs when we are faced with giving up our past. Although we must first be able to set ourselves apart from our origins in order to grow, to the same extent that we choose to create ourselves, we also risk losing what we have: the known self, the known place, and the known environmental supports. As a sage once remarked, creative individuals in our society are the survivors of a difficult struggle. They have chosen themselves and have emerged victorious.

Many of my students have come to realize that indeed they have no alternative but to begin a process-oriented journey in which the vision of their lives is fully in consonance with their reality. In undertaking such a journey they are willing to experience the conflict between the promise of the future and the fear of leaving the past. They struggle with their own limitations and those imposed by the outer world, and from their struggle they wrest new meanings from their lives. They allow themselves to let go, to experiment, to take risks, to become disorganized and chaotic in their perception of the world, as they await their own inner creation of a new synthesis.

In the 1970s more women than men seem to be making this journey. Many women have become disillusioned with their societal role or have found it unfulfilling, and are coming to grips with the conflict inherent in this realization. They are choosing for themselves who they want to be, having found insufficient the identity that was handed to them by men. Some women have been prodded to change by a death or a divorce; others have listened to slow rumblings from within that indicated their current situation was not fully satisfactory. Yet for most the journey has not been easy.

Janet, an older woman, struggled with her new self-awareness, faced the conflict, and then retreated. At the time the following paragraph was written, she chose to bury herself in the past to avoid both the pain and satisfaction of process-oriented change:

> *This course has caused much soul searching, arguing, and hostility. At the same time that I say I want to be liberated from my feminine role, I find that when my husband offers to take over a chore for me, I feel guilty about it. I have tried to live with this feeling and rationalize why I should accept it, but emotionally it just does not work. Emotionally I am a traditionalist. I do not want major changes in my life.*

However, Janet's later story emphasizes that change is ongoing and that any resolution is bound to lead to a new conflict. It is three years since she wrote the above paragraph; since then she has divorced her husband and applied to enter graduate school and now has career plans for working with disturbed adolescents. Despite these moves, though, she is not yet comfortable with the changes she is undergoing.

Another young woman, Lorraine, who earlier appeared in Chapter 9, finds herself in the grip of the same dilemma: She finds she must either be liberated or not liberated. The gray process-oriented in-between is dropped from view. Although she is not comfortable with her current situation, she has not yet accepted her own complexity and ambivalence, which is part of process-oriented living. She is struggling instead to find an easier solution to resolve this dilemma:

> *Where am I today? Oh, I call myself Ms., refer to the world as he or she, not just he. I buy feminist stickers, bracelets, nonsexist*

books, read MS. *magazine, speak up when I hear sex-role stereo-typing from people, try to assert myself when I feel I am being suppressed because I am a woman. But under all of that I don't think I am really much further ahead or liberated than I was five years ago. I have made strides in many obvious and not so obvious ways, but I still curl my hair, wear makeup sometimes, think about appropriate female behavior, watch myself in front of men, and am generally pretty hung up on sex roles, I think.*

So?

I feel a constant conflict between being aggressive and being passive. I don't want to be argumentative, but feel I have something of worth to contribute to conversations. Speaking up with opposing views creates anxiety for me, but keeping quiet is sometimes worse. I want to treat people as people, but I am conscious that I see them as men and women first. Most of all, this constant berating of myself I have always thought of as part of my personality—could it be that it is sex-role conditioning? What do I feel about things? What do I want to do? I am not sure, I have done a lot for myself on my own, but I have also done a great deal because it was expected of me as a woman. My goal for the future is to sort all of this out.

Has she sorted it out? Some of it has been sorted out, no doubt, but there are still new conflicts and problems that confront her as she slowly moves toward a process-oriented view of life.

Although change is apparent in more women than men, some men also are taking advantage of the new permissiveness to be open and "to be oneself." There are some men like Joe, who in mid-career has decided to leave the business world to seek a new and more satisfactory vocation. Another young man, a draftsman at a large automobile company, has also quit his job after ten years of service to seek new opportunities for himself. A single father, too, is back in the classroom, creating alternatives to his former management position. All these men are allowing their ongoing process to create new forms that fit their needs more satisfactorily than the old ones.*

A man in his 20s illustrates changes in his personal life that

---

*All these examples show men leaving the business world to find new careers in the social sciences. This is neither a reflection of the opportunities in the business world nor a negative judgment of the business world. Rather, these examples are a reflection of the interest students in my classes have in the behavioral and social sciences. Other examples could be given indicating choices in other careers: One of my long-term friends, for example, has given up teaching psychology and found his dreams fulfilled as an engineer in a well-known national company. He made this decision after the age of 30. It is not the occupation that matters per se but the question of choice.

occurred as he went through a new crisis of self-definition. He states that the previous five or six years had been spent working, drinking, and looking for women:

> *It was all a game. I was looking for a pretty face and a fantastic body. I expected some kind of a payoff when I met someone. My friends and I all thrived on each other's insecurities while at the same time telling fractured fairy tales about our exploits. . . .*
>
> *One day I told myself that this had to stop. I knew there was something wrong with my life but didn't know what. I stopped running into bars and I was fortunate to get an out-of-state job which got me away from my friends. This made the transition easier. I begin to look at things I had wanted to do, such as needlework and macrame. I wanted to do these things because I enjoyed the process and the end results but I found it hard to do them without feeling guilty or abnormal. I was really sold on the idea that such things were feminine. I struggled with this for a long time and finally decided to try it. . . .*

He listened to himself, faced the conflict, and created a new and more sustaining approach to his life. In allowing himself to be who he was, he came a long way toward the resolution of the dilemma: "Either be masculine or feminine." He found he could comfortably be both.

RESOLUTION OF CONFLICT: BECOMING OURSELVES

The resolution of conflict comes with the full acceptance of the complexity of self, accompanied by the realization that the self is constantly in process. Thus today's resolution may be one side of tomorrow's conflict. But in the process of growth we anticipate and accept the continual need for reevaluation, resolution, and recommitment. We learn to accept the "diffusion and integration" and the "disorganization and reorganization" that are part of the process of creative self-realization. We are flexible and fluid creatures and only through our own illusions do we seem rigid or solid. Living this fluidity and flexibility is exciting and satisfying, disturbing and painful, and the end result is a more profound satisfaction with ourselves and with others.

This acceptance of ourselves in all of our facets is indeed the process-oriented solution. We do not need to be something that we are not or struggle to become better than we are; we simply need to be *who we are* as we experience ourselves anew in each moment. Such a solution transcends all dichotomies: It acknowledges limits but allows for growth; it integrates in the present both the learning of the past and the hope of the future; it encompasses both the vision of what-we-can-be and the reality of what-we-are. In such a way we come to tolerate and accept the ambiguity of living, being fully in the moment, without precise knowledge of where that will take us tomorrow but with the satisfaction of fully experiencing the present.

This is, of course, a process that requires strength and inner security. We need strength to risk, to love, to care, and to accept the consequences of our actions. We need strength to break from societal molds and be who we are. We need strength to realize within our own lives the full vision of human potential.

This view is summed up by a young mother who has come, in the last few months, to a new realization of herself. She states:

> *I am choosing, making decisions, being in control. I love and I hate and that's O.K. There is conflict at times but that's O.K. too. I am finally learning who I am and accepting it. My son once said to me, "What are you going to be when you grow up?" Well, at last I'm growing up and we'll see.*

As long as we are all growing up and not grown up, we can leave ourselves open to the possibilities of change. As long as we are *en route* and have not arrived, we can experience the continuity and novelty of the journey without shaping ourselves to the demands of the expected destination. We can best realize the vision of process-oriented living, not by striving for a future goal or by holding fast to what has gone before, but by most fully being who we are. In allowing themselves to be in process, both men and women will be more fully human, androgynous individuals who can stand alone and stand together, who can work and play alone and together, and who can reach out toward each other with greater compassion, understanding, and love.

GLOSSARY

achieved status A status that has to be earned and depends to some extent on the abilities of the individual. See *ascribed status.*

allocentric An analytical cognitive style in which one detaches oneself from the problem under consideration. This facilitates abstract, goal-oriented thinking. See *autocentric.*

androgens A group of hormones (possessed by both sexes) that is responsible for maintaining masculine sex characteristics. See *estrogen; testosterone.*

androgyny A term describing attitudes and behavior that are neither strongly masculine nor strongly feminine but which are *both* masculine and feminine.

ascribed status A status assigned to individuals without reference to unique differences or abilities. See *achieved status.*

autocentric A personalized cognitive style in which the individual remains centrally immersed in the problem. This leads to personal, emotional problem-solving rather than to an analytic mode of thought. See *allocentric.*

Bem Sex-Role Inventory (BSRI) A scale for measuring androgyny that requires an individual to be *high* on *both* masculine and feminine characteristics in order to be androgynous. In addition to measuring androgyny it classifies individuals as masculine, near-masculine, feminine, near-feminine, or undifferentiated.

chromosomes (X and Y chromosomes) The rod-shaped bodies contained in the cell nucleus that transmit our genetic heritage. One pair of chromosomes determines our genetic sex—a pair of X chromosomes determines female sex, and an X and a Y chromosome determine male sex.

cognitive theorists Those theorists, generally psychologists, who think behavior is influenced primarily by the conceptual framework that we have adopted rather than by external or emotional factors.

conditioning The process by which individual behavior is shaped by the external environment. See *reinforcement; social learning theorists.*

conjugal role relationship See *joint conjugal role relationship; segregated conjugated role relationship.*

coordinate marriage A marriage in which the differentiation of roles is more dependent on the particular personal characteristics of the partners than on those prescribed by societal expectations. This results in an integration of family and work emphases for both husband and wife.

deviance Behavior and attitudes that differ from those we commonly expect; in other words, behavior that differs from the norm.

discrimination The process, whether overt or covert, by which we deny a person equal opportunity on the basis of certain characteristics such as race, sex, age, or creed.

dual-career family A husband and wife, usually having at least one child, who both pursue careers.

dysfunctional Behavior or attitudes that hinder the achievement of group goals or upset the equilibrium of the group. See *functionalism.*

egalitarian family A family in which no duty or function is assigned to either spouse on the basis of sex.

estrogen A hormone (possessed by both sexes) that causes development of the reproductive system and secondary sex characteristics in females. See *androgens; progesterone.*

ethnic groups Broad classifications of individuals on the basis of race and/or national heritage.

expressive The cluster of traits associated with the feminine sex role including traits labeled receptive, nurturing, submissive. See *instrumental.*

femininity The cluster of behaviors, attitudes, and values that reflect dependence, emotionality, subjectivity, submission, warmth, and nurturance. See *masculinity; sex role.*

forms Conceptions of universal, societal, and individual "truths" that are accepted by consensual groups as determining the "way the world is"; categories and structures that are accepted as true outside of one's own experience. They include conceptions of masculinity and femininity.

functionalism The school of sociology that evaluates behavior in terms of whether or not it is beneficial to society as a whole, i.e., whether or not such behavior is *functional.*

gender The maleness or femaleness of individuals. Gender is determined by genital and reproductive anatomy.

hermaphrodites Those individuals who possess genitals that appear to belong to the sex other than that of their chromosomal make-up. Also, those individuals having genitals similar to those of both sexes. In general terms, those individuals who do not have a clearly defined anatomical sex or gender.

humanistic theorists Those theorists, primarily psychologists, who believe that humans develop behavior, attitudes, and values from an interplay of cognitive, emotional, and external factors. They believe in human potential and view humans as trustworthy beings.

identification The process by which children learn behaviors, attitudes, and values by seeing themselves as *like* another person. They thereby incorporate in themselves the characteristics of this other person.

industrial society A society in which increasing the quantity of production is one of the most important values, thereby emphasizing economic, materialistic, and competitive efficiency.

inexpressiveness The inability to display emotions; generally associated with the masculine sex role.

instrumental The cluster of traits associated with the masculine sex role including traits such as independence, self-reliance, competence. See *expressive.*

interactional pattern A pattern of marital interaction in which both partners are involved in the relationship and emphasize the importance of companionship, understanding, and mutual responsiveness. See *parallel pattern.*

interrole conflict The conflict that is generated by assuming two or more dissimilar roles with incompatible expectations. See *intrarole conflict.*

intrarole conflict The conflict that is generated by opposing expectations within a single role.

joint conjugal role relationship A structure in the husband-wife relationship that involves the sharing of tasks and interests. See *segregated conjugal role relationship.*

kibbutz A communal living and working arrangement, found in Israel, that involves many individuals.

masculinity The cluster of behaviors, attitudes, and values that reflect aggression, independence, rationality, dominance, and competence. See *femininity; sex role.*

"maternal instinct" A biological predisposition in women that supposedly leads them to want to have and to rear children.

monolithic code A widely accepted American belief, supported by legal and religious sanctions, which states that marriage and family responsibilities are the chief preoccupations of men and women.

Within the context of life-long marriage and parental responsibilities one man and one woman *ought* to satisfy each other's needs.

norms The generally accepted standards of behavior and/or performance; specifically refers to the *average* behavior or performance of any group in a given situation.

occupational mobility The tendency of Americans to change jobs. Improved socioeconomic status often results.

"openness to experience" A willingness to be aware of all external and internal happenings; to be in touch with what is going on both in the world and within oneself.

parallel pattern A pattern of marital interaction in which spouses tend to live their own lives in sex-segregated worlds and to share little with each other in the way of companionship. See *interactional pattern.*

peer relationship A partnership, built on the premise of ongoing dialogue, whose purpose is to permit and promote the growth of each partner and of the partnership itself.

platonic relationship A relationship with another person, usually of the opposite sex, that generally involves a sense of intimacy, sharing, and companionship but in which there is no direct expression of sexuality.

postindustrial society A society that has progressed to the point where quantity of production is no longer the most important criterion of what is good for the system. In such societies competition yields to cooperation, quantity to quality, and economic values to human and ecological values.

power-to-be The inner strength derived from a sense of competence and security in the world. It allows the individual to stand alone without the need for external supports.

primary relationship A relationship with another person that is more important than all other relationships. Primary relationships do not necessarily exclude other relationships, sexual or otherwise.

process The inner flow of one's own experience.

process-oriented Behavior (or individuals who display such behavior) that springs spontaneously from the ongoing content of experience. See *role-oriented.*

progesterone The hormone second in importance only to estrogen in female development. It is responsible for physiological changes during pregnancy. See *estrogen.*

psychoanalytic theorists Theorists, generally psychologists, who are advocates of Freudian theory. They believe that individuals are motivated primarily by internal conflicts between their own desires, rational capacities, and internal values based on cultural norms.

reinforcement A concept indicating the reward that an individual receives from the external environment by producing expected behavior. See *conditioning.*

role behavior Actions expected of an individual playing a specific part in society. Certain expected role behaviors accompany each status or position held in society.

role conflict Individual stress caused by simultaneously occupying two distinct and culturally incompatible statuses or conflict of expectations within a status. See *interrole conflict; intrarole conflict.*

role-oriented Behavior (or individuals who display such behavior) that is motivated by adaptation to external norms and the expectations of others.

role reversal The process of adopting the behavior belonging to a reciprocal status.

roles See *role behavior; role conflict; role reversal; social roles.*

secondary relationship A relationship with another person that assumes importance in a person's life but does not displace or compete with the primary relationship.

segregated conjugal role relationship A structure in the husband-wife relationship in which spouses pursue separate activities and interests, usually with relatively little communication about their separate pursuits.

self-actualization The realization of most of one's potential in terms of work, love, play, etc. As a group, self-actualizing individuals tend to display openness, honesty, commitment, compassion, and concern for the welfare of others.

sequential pattern An alternation of career and family interests currently demonstrated in the lives of many women who go to work prior to having children, then stay home in order to raise their children, and finally return to work when the children are older.

sex roles The set of expectations about attitudes and behavior that are culturally assigned according to one's gender.

social change The change in the institutions, customs, and values of society as a whole.

social classes Broad categories into which individuals are classified according to their economic standing, their social interaction with similar individuals, and their value orientation.

GLOSSARY

socialization The process by which individuals incorporate within themselves the behaviors, attitudes, and values of their culture.

social learning theorists Those theorists, primarily psychologists, who believe that the environment and other people's behavior are the primary influences on one's development. See *conditioning; reinforcement.*

social roles The rights, obligations, and behavior patterns accompanying specific statuses in society.

statuses Positions held in society that carry with them expectations of certain attitudes and behaviors. See *achieved status; ascribed status.*

status quo The existing state of affairs.

stereotype A generalized expectation, without regard to individual differences, that a specific group of people will behave in a particular way.

structural-functionalists Sociologists adhering to the school of thought known as functionalism or structural-functionalism. See *functionalism.*

testosterone A hormone (possessed by both sexes) that affects genital development and development of secondary sex characteristics in males. See *androgens.*

transsexuals Individuals who psychologically feel that they are members of the sex opposite the one of their chromosomal and anatomical sex.

zero-sum game A situation in which it is not possible for both parties to benefit, or win, since all scores must add up to zero; that is, whatever one party wins, the other must lose.

NAME INDEX

NAME INDEX

NAME INDEX

SUBJECT INDEX